# The American Occupation of Germany

## Politics and the Military, 1945-1949

# John Gimbel

*Stanford University Press*
*Stanford, California   1968*

Stanford University Press
Stanford, California
© 1968 by the Board of Trustees of the
Leland Stanford Junior University
Printed in the United States of America
L.C. 68–26778

*For*
Gisela, John H., Karen, and Monika

# Acknowledgments

I had much help in the preparation of this book. Although I cannot list them all, a few sources of that help are particularly noteworthy. A Rockefeller Foundation research grant enabled me to do research in Germany for a year and in Washington, D.C., for three summers. An American Council of Learned Societies fellowship helped me to return to Germany and to Washington, D.C., for an additional year. The Army and military government records that were opened to me so freely were absolutely essential. Mr. Wilbur Nigh and Mr. Henry Williamson in the World War II Records Branch, Alexandria, Virginia, made the records available to me and gave me many helpful suggestions. German sources were also indispensable. The Hessian state government's decision to give me access to records in its possession opened materials previously untouched by researchers. The Bundesarchiv in Koblenz, the Staatsarchiv in Wiesbaden, and the Bundestag library in Bonn made additional materials available on a generous basis. The Institut für Zeitgeschichte, in Munich, and the Humboldt State College library gave me much help when I needed it. Elinor Stillman began as my editor and became my friend.

The conclusions and judgments expressed in this study are my own. They are not to be identified with the agencies, archives, and repositories that so generously made records available to me.

Preparing this book was a family venture. My wife and children left home, friends, and classmates (but not the dog) each time my research plans uprooted them. They carried on famously without me when research took me away on my own, and they took as a matter of course the apparent absentmindedness and inattention to them that concentration on research and writing causes me to display. They fully deserve the dedication of this book.

J.G.

# Contents

# Introduction

This book is a study of the implementation of American policies during the postwar occupation of Germany, and of their impact on Germans at the time. It is also a study of policy-making, because implementation usually entails interpreting and defining policy, and sometimes results in policy formulation as well. Certainly a description of what was actually done provides a basis for analyzing the policies governing those actions. The result of making administrative practice a main focus of my research is an interpretation of the American occupation that differs significantly from what has been written about it up to now.

The prevailing interpretation of the occupation is that policy was not clear; that the planners had not prepared for unconditional surrender; that Henry Morgenthau's intervention caused confusion and difficulties that policy planners did not overcome completely until 1947; and that conflicts between the State Department, which was responsible for developing policy, and the War/Army Department, which was responsible for carrying it out, often resulted in a policy vacuum. In any event, Lucius D. Clay, in writing his *Decision in Germany*, implied that such a vacuum existed. At least two writers, Manuel Gottlieb and Hans-Peter Schwarz, have described the policy that emerged from the confused postwar situation as a "policy of ambivalence." Others have simply assumed that the United States had no policy worth mentioning before 1947. The main flaw in all of these versions of the prevailing interpretation is that they focus mainly on the effects of shifts in American priorities, and regard these shifts as evidence of changes in fundamental interests adding up to a "policy of ambivalence." This makes conscious, landmark decisions out of what were in fact manifestations of the conflict between various departments in Washington over which interests should be given top priority, of the struggle between Congress and the administration for control of German policy, and of the continuing interplay of action and response between Americans and their Allies on the one hand, and Americans and Germans on the other.

At least two other men who have written on the occupation period —John D. Montgomery and Caspar Schrenck-Notzing—have departed from the prevailing interpretation by describing the American occupation as an attempt to promote directed political, social, economic, and ideological change. Montgomery's sympathetic study concludes that Americans promoted an artificial revolution on behalf of democracy, that they tried to force Germans to be free. Caspar Schrenck-Notzing's hostile interpretation insists that Americans applied socio-psychological principles in an attempt to transform the German character, to "character-wash" a people. Both views are based on the assumption that "reorientation" (a term used virtually interchangeably with "democratization" and "reeducation" by people working in the programs) was the chief American objective. Montgomery does acknowledge other aims, but he argues that negative programs such as denazification, demilitarization, and decartelization were simply means to an end. They were meant to be ways in which old institutions could be transformed or destroyed to make way for the new, in which the old Establishment might be replaced by new leadership, and so on. Thus, in Montgomery's view, the negative programs provided the coercive forces necessary to the achievement of the beneficent revolution he describes. It is true that the emphasis given by both these writers to reorientation can be seen in statements made at the time, for these objectives were repeated with regularity in directives and public pronouncements, and their importance was never denied, even by implication. But they competed with other American interests for priority, and, as I shall show, interests that were *not* stated in the directives often assumed a greater importance than the ones most talked about. Thus both of these directed-change hypotheses, which assume a consistently high priority for reorientation, suffer from over-selectivity. In fact, Montgomery's book appears to be a construction of a model for possible future policy use. Schrenck-Notzing's is a tract more helpful in explaining current conditions in West Germany than in contributing to an understanding of the occupation period.

My study of military government operations has revealed that American actions and policy in Germany were governed by a broad range of interests. Some of these interests were given high priority only during certain limited periods; others appear to have been followed with sufficient persistence to give occupation policy and practice a fundamental unity and continuity. Besides wanting to denazify, demilitarize, decartelize, democratize, and reorient Germans and Germany, Americans were also interested in seeing to their own continued security, bringing about the economic rehabilitation of Germany and Europe, and guaranteeing the continuance of free enterprise. They wanted to frustrate socialism, to forestall Communism, to spare American taxpayers' money, to counteract French plans to dismember Germany, and to contain the Soviet Union in Central Europe. All of these interests—some of which were stated in directives and some of which were not—assumed a vital place in American policy and practice in Germany. As mentioned above, the unstated interests often equaled in importance or took precedence over the negative purge programs provided for in the directives and the positive reorientation objectives stated in the directives and implanted in the hearts of American crusaders and idealists who found their way into the occupation forces.

In addition to suggesting a continuity in American interests underlying the course of the U.S. occupation, this study provides new insights into the role of France in postwar Germany and especially into the impact of French policy on American policy and practice. My findings on the nature of this impact in turn raise the question of the need for a reinterpretation of the role of the Soviet Union and of the influence of the cold war on the American approach. This study also casts new light on the origins of the Marshall Plan, the Bonn government, and the Berlin blockade. Similarly, the nature and evolution of American policy in Germany is shown in a new perspective by reinterpretations of the evolution of the American-zone Länderrat and the bizonal agencies, Clay's dismantling and reparations halt in May

1946, the evolution of American denazification policy, Byrnes's Stuttgart speech in September 1946, the German minister-presidents' conference in Munich in June 1947, and other events and developments of the period.

The limitations of the study are unfortunate and unavoidable. The book is based on extensive War/Army Department and military government records and on equally rich German materials. It reflects the materials from which it was drawn, and it concentrates only on that period to 1949 for which primary sources are available. It suffers from lack of access to State Department policy papers, to records of bipartite origin, to Allied Control Council papers, and to other materials of bi- or multipartite origin. Particularly unfortunate is the fact that no other government—Britain, France, or Russia—has seen fit to permit scholars to examine the occupation records in its possession. The result is that there is no truly adequate study of the operations— or the policies for that matter—of the other occupation powers. Scholars are thus able to fully examine, analyze, and judge American practice and policy, but cannot compare their findings with anything similar for the other occupation zones or powers. Though this does not fully justify, it at least accounts for, what at times may seem to be a myopic approach in this study. The limitations may be salutary in the long run, however. If this book prompts other agencies and other governments to open their records to scholars, it will have accomplished something it was not designed specifically to do.

# The American Occupation
of Germany

Occupied Germany, 1945–49

# 1 | American Plans and German Realities, 1945

Looking back in 1950 to his first few days as Deputy Military Governor for Germany in April 1945, General Lucius D. Clay wrote that the people in Washington who had prepared policies did not anticipate the conditions he observed in Europe. He and Lewis Douglas, whom James Byrnes had helped Clay secure as financial adviser, were shocked after studying the Joint Chiefs of Staff (JCS) directive 1067. He says they were shocked not by its punitive provisions, but by its failure to foresee the economic and financial conditions that prevailed.[1] Robert Murphy, Clay's political adviser, who had preceded him to the European theater, recalled a similar reaction. He, Clay, Douglas, and William Draper, Clay's economics adviser, had studied JCS 1067 about ten days before V-E Day, and had concluded that it made little sense. According to Murphy, Douglas said the directive was "assembled by economic idiots" who would "forbid the most skilled workers in Europe from producing as much as they can for a continent which is desperately short of everything."[2]

## An Apparent Discrepancy

The three American officials (Clay, Murphy, and Draper) in positions to influence the occupation most directly thus seem to have questioned from the outset the directives that governed their actions. It would appear that, for at least two years, a major discrepancy existed between official policy and the views of those who admin-

[1] Superscript numbers refer to Notes (pp. 265–322), primarily source references. Footnotes are designated by asterisks, daggers, etc. A list of abbreviations used in the text and the notes is supplied at the head of the Notes section.

istered it, for JCS 1067 was not formally revoked until July 1947, when it was replaced by JCS directive 1779. This assumption that the administrators were working under policies they found wanting from the beginning is basic to the prevailing interpretation of the occupation. The current view is that Secretary of State James Byrnes's Stuttgart speech on September 6, 1946, modified the tone of the directives, but that JCS 1067 remained basic policy until mid-1947.[3] A number of factors contribute to this interpretation.

On the whole, the military government followed the guidelines of JCS 1067 remarkably well for an organization being formed at the same time that it administered an area that had virtually disintegrated politically, socially, and economically. A United States Forces, European Theater (USFET) directive of July 7, 1945, translated the policy directive into administrative rules. It stressed denazification, demilitarization, disarmament, restrictions on political activity, and the necessity for military control at all levels of government.[4] Subsequent additions to the July 7 directive, issued in August and September, made denazification even more comprehensive. Allowing for deviations due to disagreements, inexperience, lack of interest, the confusion and chaos of rapid demobilization, and downright incompetence, one might conclude from the performance of the United States military government that it administered JCS 1067 religiously, even though its top administrators later recalled having had objections to it. Clay himself cabled the War Department as late as December 2, 1945, stating: "JCS 1067 as modified by Potsdam has proved workable. Much of 1067 has been enacted into Allied Control Authority laws and directives. . . . I don't know how we could have effectively set up our military government without JCS 1067."[5] The key point is Clay's reference to the modification by Potsdam, about which more will be said later.

Clay and Murphy have contributed to the belief that JCS 1067 remained intact despite their objections. Both describe their initial shock and concern, then shift to Lewis Douglas's unsuccessful mission to Washington to secure changes in the directive. Douglas's return with only minimal concessions on financial policies, his increasing disillusionment, and his early resignation all reinforce the belief that JCS 1067 was fixed and unchangeable until it was modified in emphasis by Byrnes's speech and replaced finally in July 1947.

Douglas's return to the scene in March 1947, as Ambassador to Great Britain, to play an active and effective role in German policy determination in 1947 and 1948 suggests, indirectly, that it took some two years for policy to return to his hopes of 1945.

Washington also contributed to the current interpretation. It avoided action or statements in 1945 and 1946 that suggested basic policy changes. There were myriad reasons for such scruple. The intense public interest in the United States over the way in which military government had functioned in Aachen late in 1944 was apparently enough to give pause to anyone who might suggest modification of the "hard policy" agreed on after many, many months of dispute in Washington. But Aachen was little more than a prelude to the furor over the remarks made by General George S. Patton on denazification and over the political composition of the Bavarian government installed under Patton's command and headed by Fritz Schäffer.[6]

In addition to the public attention on a national, and even international, scale that was generated by such dramatic and specific incidents, the military government was subjected to a constant stream of criticism for going "soft," when the directives clearly demanded a "hard" peace. Former Secretary of the Treasury Henry Morgenthau put personal pressure on the War Department,[7] spoke out regularly in public, and published his *Germany is Our Problem* in December 1945, to stimulate wide public discussion on the issues of "hard" vs. "soft" peace. Among Morgenthau's many followers and supporters, Bernard Bernstein was especially outspoken; he had been critical while serving in Germany, and he continued his campaign within the administration when he returned to Washington. Russell Nixon's accusations before the Kilgore Committee were treated by the press with considerable sensationalism. In the meantime, individuals and groups, such as the Society for the Prevention of World War III, kept the pot boiling.*

Clay revealed the impact of the public discussion even in internal, personal correspondence with John J. McCloy. On April 26, 1945, after talking about the need to revise thinking in Washington, he said:

---

* An example is the story that came out of Germany in the late summer of 1945 that Max Schmeling had applied for a publisher's license to reeducate German youth. See the *New York Times*, Sept. 6, 1945, p. 11; Sept. 7, 1945, p. 6. The War Department, Civil Affairs Division, subsequently received a thick file of protest letters, many of which were similar enough to suggest an organized writing campaign.

"I hope you won't think . . . I am getting soft. I realize the necessity for stern and spartan treatment. However, retribution now is far greater than realized at home. . . . " On June 29 he wrote that "any moves now to create even a minimum economy which requires some industrial activity are misunderstood and treated by those who write as steps to a soft peace."[8] Later in 1945, McCloy summarized what was probably the prevailing mood in Washington. Commenting to Clay on Byron Price's report to the President, which recommended policy revision, he said: "With recollections of the difficulties we encountered in getting Governmental agreement on JCS 1067, none of us has any illusions about the magnitude of the job of agreeing [on] a new comprehensive Directive."[9] A cable from the War Department to Clay on January 3, 1946, said essentially the same thing, but added that Clay's freedom of action was not limited by JCS 1067. It said that formal policy change would result in unfavorable comment in the press to the effect that the United States had abandoned its firm stand on the treatment of Germany.[10] Even as late as 1947, after Byrnes's speech and when there was much public discussion about the need to rebuild Germany and Europe together, some of this same caution and reluctance to be labeled "soft" remained. Assistant Secretary of War Howard C. Petersen, in giving the House Appropriations Committee a list of reasons for feeding Germans and Japanese, obviously felt the need to assure the committee that none of his reasons was humanitarian.[11]

Apparently influenced by all these pressures to hold to the original "hard" line, American officials gave out "explanations of policy" and "restatements of policy," and generally interpreted their own actions to the public and their allies as fulfillment of, rather than deviations from, the directives and the Potsdam agreement. Secretary of State Byrnes, on December 12, 1945, issued a "statement" on American economic policy toward Germany. His Stuttgart speech on September 6, 1946, was released as a "Restatement of U.S. Policy on Germany."[12] His July 11, 1946, invitation to the other occupation powers to unite their zones with the American zone was, he said, an invitation to expedite implementation of the Potsdam agreement.[13] Subsequent British-American negotiations in Berlin in August and September of 1946 deliberately left room for French and/or Soviet

participation in zonal union and for continued four-power cooperation. American and British representatives carefully avoided any
posture that might prejudice the political future of Germany or go
beyond the provisions of the Potsdam agreement politically.[14]

Only in 1947, after the failure of the Moscow Council of Foreign
Ministers meeting to achieve effective four-power German settle-
ments, did the emphasis change markedly. Secretary of State George
C. Marshall, who said on April 28, 1947, that "the patient is sinking
while the doctors deliberate," instructed the Office of Military Government for Germany, United States (OMGUS) to push ahead
to make Germany self-sufficient, develop a new level-of-industry
plan, and revise the reparations list. The July 15, 1947, directive
(JCS 1779) was part of this change.

## American Administrative Adjustments

As noted earlier, it has been generally believed that a discrepancy
existed between official policy and the views of those who carried
it out. However, Clay's and Murphy's accounts, when they are read
in the light of the documents of the time, show that the discrepancy
was insignificant. In the first place, the objection in early 1945 was
primarily—almost exclusively—to economic, financial, and fiscal
provisions of JCS 1067. Clay's statement that "JCS 1067 as modified
by Potsdam has proved workable" is crucial, because it suggests that
Potsdam eliminated the cause of his earlier concern. The records
show that Potsdam did, indeed, provide an escape from the economic
restrictions of JCS 1067. Even more important, it verified a basic
understanding that had developed before Potsdam, between Washington and the United States Group, Control Council (US Group CC),
regarding the meaning of JCS 1067.

In one of his earliest recorded observations of the scene over
which he would bear primary responsibility as Deputy Military
Governor and then Military Governor, Clay reported that "retribution . . . is far greater than realized at home. . . . Our planes and artil-
lery have . . . carried war direct to the homes of the German people."[15]
Clay's sober reaction to the destruction of total war and total defeat
was by no means an isolated one. Military men, reporters, statesmen,

and private citizens who set foot on German soil for the first time responded similarly. President Truman has described his own sense of depression as he drove among ruined buildings in Berlin and past the "long, never-ending procession of old men, women, and children wandering aimlessly . . . carrying, pushing, or pulling what was left of their belongings."[16] The Hessian military governor, whose observations could be supported by endless citations from military situation reports, described how Americans "came into towns and cities that were deathly quiet, that smelled of death and destruction. They came into villages where white flags were draped outside every door, where faces could be felt, not seen, behind barricaded windows."[17] The response of trained observers and reporters is perhaps characterized by Walter Millis's remark on arriving in Berlin: "This is more like the face of the moon than any city I had ever imagined." The shock at the unbelievable destruction may be inferred from Joseph Barnes's question to Russell Hill: "Why didn't any of you people tell us about this?"[18]

Clay, who had to carry on his shoulders the responsibility for much that would occur in Germany, had to give sustained attention to the problems that produced the shocked statements of reporters and official tourists who were only passing through. He told Assistant Secretary of War McCloy, in a letter describing his initial activities and his organizational plans, that "Washington must revise its thinking relative to destruction of Germany's war potential. . . . The progress of the war has accomplished that end . . . [for] the industry which remains, with few exceptions, even when restored will suffice barely for a very low minimum living standard in Germany." To provide a minimum living standard, Clay continued, "we must have freedom here to bring industries back into production. . . . " Production controls will be needed, he said, and hasty reparations removals could "make it impossible to bring order back into Germany."[19]

Lewis Douglas, who had been up front on a fact-finding mission when Clay wrote the foregoing, returned to OMGUS headquarters with a dismal report that reinforced Clay's estimate and supported Draper and Murphy who had argued similar views against Bernard

Bernstein and others in US Group CC staff meetings before and after Clay's arrival in the theater.[20] Douglas returned convinced that Germany faced a serious food crisis for the next eighteen months; that wartime destruction required attention to production rather than to further destruction; and that in the long run Germany's natural resources, production facilities, and manpower skills would be needed to produce for the welfare of all Europe. Douglas's findings, which also reached McCloy indirectly in a letter from Goldthwaite Dorr— who had seen and talked with Douglas several times during his fact-finding mission—were the basis for his "economic idiots" statement reported by Robert Murphy.[21]

By May 7, 1945, Clay had become even more convinced of the need for revision. In a report to General John H. Hilldring of the Civil Affairs Division (CAD), War Department, he said the plans for the German occupation were obviously made without reference to the actual situation the military government would face. The planners, he said, had led a "cloistered and academic life," and none had got out into the "mud." The file of existing plans was already so large that no one man could comprehend them all. The plans exhibited great mental activity, but they contained so many unrealistic assumptions that their value was negligible.[22] Revealing his own belief that existing policy was either inadequate or temporary, Clay said he hoped his directives could be "flexible and general rather than specific until we have been able to develop the information which will enable you at home to develop sound policy."

In part to provide material for Lewis Douglas's mission to Washington, and in part to gather factual data for US Group CC operations as directed by JCS 1067, military government teams prepared a series of detailed studies of the German situation in 1945. Teams in the field studied labor, public health, industry, transportation, finances, and government.[23] A particularly detailed study of this type was prepared for the Economics Division by a team under the direction of Calvin Hoover, the Duke University economist. It described the chaotic condition of the German economy and the "nearly complete paralysis of industry" caused by lack of coal and transportation. It predicted a crisis in food and agriculture caused by lack of transportation and by the loss of the agricultural surplus-production areas in the East.[24] In general, the studies show a rather widespread belief at the second administrative levels in the field that, given the destruction and dislocations ensuing from the war, "an affirmative program with respect to Germany should be developed as promptly as possible."[25]

There is evidence that Washington reacted positively to factual analyses that predicted or threatened failure in Germany under existing conditions and policies. On April 28, 1945, just after the draft of JCS 1067 had been sent to General Eisenhower, Brehon G. Somervell, Commanding General of the Army Service Forces, wrote to Hilldring that unless Germany produced magnesium, aluminum, and synthetic rubber and oil, it would be forced to import them, presumably at the expense of the United States government. The Joint Chiefs of Staff thereupon asked that the draft directive be changed to permit the American-zone commander to allow such production without prior approval of the Joint Chiefs of Staff. Though Morgenthau protested, the change remained in the directive approved finally by President Truman on May 11, 1945.[26]

Hilldring encouraged Clay to present his case in a similar manner, at the same time that he forecast the failure of Douglas's mission to secure a change in the directive. No directive that could be written now, he said, would provide more latitude in Germany for the present. Long-range United States policy toward Germany would have to "bubble up out of the facts you uncover in Germany." In the meantime, it would be advantageous for Clay to work with JCS 1067 rather than assume personal responsibility for making new policy. According to Hilldring, both he and McCloy believed JCS 1067 provided room for Clay to realize his objectives (with which they agreed), and he said that "the idea has the acceptance of the agencies across the river."[27] Less than a month later, Clay wrote that "like all general directives, JCS 1067 can be interpreted in many ways." Though he foresaw much cold and hunger in Germany during the coming winter, he said he could see a ray of hope.[28]

Thus, on the eve of the Potsdam Conference, the War Department and US Group CC had apparently reached an understanding that JCS 1067 was a more flexible document than current opinion would have us believe. In the meantime, however, problems of a more ominous nature came to the fore.*

## New Problems

In June 1945, President Truman became convinced that all of northwestern Europe faced a coal emergency.[29] Truman had had a personal report on Europe's immediate postwar prospects and needs from Judge Samuel Rosenman on April 15. On June 14, 1945, Harold Ickes, who apparently had seen the Potter-Hyndley report of June 7, reported a drastic deterioration of the European coal situation. He gave detailed current statistics on production and needs in France, Belgium, the Netherlands, Denmark, Norway, the United Kingdom, and Germany. Truman's response was twofold. Through the Joint Chiefs of Staff, he directed Eisenhower to make available for export from Germany to northwestern Europe ten million tons of coal prior to January 1, 1946, and another fifteen million tons by April 30, 1946. Although he says in his memoirs that he sent the coal directive to Churchill in June and to Stalin in July, it is clear that the decision was unilateral, and that the directive went out before Stalin saw it, "to avoid delay," Truman says he told him. Secondly, through Secretary of War Henry L. Stimson, he alerted the War Department to the pressure on Germany to increase coal production and export.[30]

Stimson, who had previously written to Truman on May 16 to argue for a more constructive policy on Germany,[31] wrote again on July 4, 1945, to outline the consequences of the coal directive for Germany. He said a program to increase coal production would require mining supplies and food, clothing, and housing for miners and their families; it would require management incentives and

* See Harold Zink, *The United States in Germany, 1945–1955* (Princeton, 1957), p. 95, for the statement that "General Clay could do more or less as he pleased in Germany, so long as he observed the formalities and accepted JCS 1067 as the general guide. What happened was that the American military government increasingly followed the middle-of-the-road course anticipated by the planners in the German Country Unit, in the U.S. Group, Control Council for Germany, and in Washintgon."

worker incentives in the form of consumer goods; and it would require restoration of the disrupted transportation system. Stimson argued that the program depended on occupation-sponsored imports and that "action on the coal front must accompany rehabilitation efforts on the entire economic front. . . ."[32] His concern that time was "of the essence" was related to an additional factor agitating the War Department at the moment.

In keeping with tradition, the War Deparment was reluctant to assume responsibility for exports from Germany unless the exports served some direct military purpose. The issue arose during initial War and State Department discussions on the coal directive. Assistant Secretary of State William Clayton assumed that the May 11, 1945, version of JCS 1067, approved by the President, had in fact charged military authorities in Germany with procuring and financing necessary initial imports to supply the occupation forces and displaced persons, to prevent disease and unrest, and also to "serve the purposes of the United States government in Germany."[33]

Though the Army recognized Eisenhower's dual military-political function in Europe as Commanding General of the U.S. Forces, on the one hand, and as U.S. representative on the Allied Control Council, on the other, it expressed concern about the amount of imports it would have to finance and about the source of funds for such imports.[34] Foreseeable imports included those needed to help maintain and protect American troops and to implement U.S. political policies in the American zone of Germany. Foreseeable, also, were imports into other zones, either from abroad or from the American zone, to maintain and protect troops of other occupying powers and to accomplish the political objectives of the United States in all of Germany. But the Army wanted to know whether it might have to import to produce reparations or offset reparations, to supply British and Soviet military needs, to provide relief, or to achieve other purposes not yet obvious. The questions were particularly vital because the Army's period of military supply responsibility for northwestern Europe was to end with the dissolution, on July 14, of the Supreme Headquarters of the Allied Expeditionary Force (SHAEF), and its budget allocations for civilian supply imports would be exhausted by October 1, 1945.

President Truman finally settled the question of responsibility on July 29, 1945, during the Potsdam conference.[35] He directed the Army to assume responsibility for financing import and export programs. The War Department had no funds available for the purpose, however, and inquiries showed no other government agency to have funds available for that purpose either. The upshot was that the War Department, which had been reluctant to assume the responsibility in the first place, would have to go to Congress to ask for additional appropriations that would be used to accomplish broad political objectives in Germany and Europe. McCloy wrote on July 30, 1945, that testimony before Congress indicated that funds made available to the War Department could be used to maintain other zones only during a brief turnover period, and not at all beyond the current calendar year. War Department funds, he said, were restricted to use in preventing disease and starvation.[36] There was an alternative, however, and the military government and the Army pushed hard during 1945 for its acceptance as a prime objective of American economic policy.*

JCS 1067 said the Control Council should "make available any foreign exchange proceeds of exports for payment of imports ... and authorize no other outlay of foreign exchange assets except for purposes approved by the Control Council or other appropriate authority."[37] It further provided that, pending Control Council agreement, the commander in the American zone should implement the directive there. During the interdepartmental negotiations on the coal directive, the foregoing provision of JCS 1067 was clearly interpreted to mean that the Army could carry the import costs as a first charge against exports of current German production, facilities, or stocks on hand in the United States zone or from Germany as a whole.[38] The basis was thus laid for a determined Army effort to encourage German production for export so as to cut its own budgetary requests before Congress, and to be relieved of defending publicly and before Congress a political program it had assumed reluctantly and only after presidential intervention.

The difficulty of implementing a program to balance imports and exports was already obvious from early observations and studies

* The alternative of having the State Department assume responsibility for the occupation was apparently premature at this time.

made by US Group CC. But the uncertainties attending four-power occupation and control added an imponderable factor. In fact, during the drawn-out negotiations for troop withdrawals and quadripartite occupation of Berlin, Eisenhower sounded out Washington on the possibility of negotiating tripartite agreements if four-power plans fell through.[39] Clay's response was that he hoped "a final decision with reference to tripartite government in Western Germany may never be necessary, in that we will make quadripartite government function."[40] In reality, the prospects were not encouraging. The determination of the French to have a voice in German affairs became increasingly clear as they insisted on a zone of occupation and refused to evacuate certain areas designated as American zone—particularly Stuttgart—until a firm decision was made. But the Soviet Union's unilateral decisions were even more ominous. It had been known for some time that the Soviets had assigned a portion of their German zone of occupation to Poland, and in May the United States sent a note of protest.[41] In July, during the negotiations on four-power occupation of Berlin, Marshal Zhukov revealed that he had instructions from his government to the effect that the resources east of the Oder-Neisse line were not available to provide food and coal for Berlin. He said there had been much fighting in Pomerania and Prussia, that fields were damaged and crops destroyed, and that, because Silesia had been assigned to Poland, the Soviet Union had no further control over resources there. Clay and Murphy, the American negotiators, protested on the spot, as did their British counterpart. On referring the issue back to Washington, they were instructed not to accept the Oder-Neisse boundary as fixed, and not to approve the unilateral assignment of a portion of the Soviet zone to Poland. Nevertheless, Clay and Murphy were advised that information in Germany not available in Washington might justify accepting responsibility for supplying food and coal to Berlin. Given such leeway, the United States accepted the responsibility for supplying the western zones of Berlin with 20,000 tons of food per month. The British agreed to do likewise and to send 2,400 tons of coal per day as soon as circumstances permitted.[42] The decision created an additional supply burden for the Western Allies. The incident foreshadowed the many difficulties that administrators who were attempting to promote economic uniformity would face so long as any occupation power could, in its zone, make unilateral commitments that affected the other zones also.

## Potsdam Promises Solutions

By the time the Potsdam conference opened, experience, observations, and studies on the scene had led American practitioners in Germany to a number of conclusions that were shared by some of their superiors in Washington. They were convinced that destruction in Germany had been far greater than policy planners had anticipated in making their restrictive and negative policies. Moreover, they were sure that the United States zone could not become economically self-sufficient. (This was the basis for the oft-repeated statement that other zones got something worthwhile and the United States got the scenery.) Knowing this, Americans concluded that the United States would have to finance imports to feed the Germans both in the U.S. zone and in Berlin, and to prime German industry—something they were not permitted by policy to do—so that it could eventually produce exports to offset import payments. The alternative to such steps was some form of interzonal economic balance that would link the agricultural and industrial sections of prewar Germany, preferably by treating the whole of Germany as an economic unit. This alternative, however, presumed that the prewar boundaries (1937 was the date most frequently cited) would remain, and that no territories would be lost to the united German economy. Self-sufficiency would be difficult to achieve even under those conditions, despite the minimum living standard that JCS 1067 envisaged for Germany. Further, Americans were convinced that reparations from current production, or excessive and uncoordinated capital equipment removals from the various zones, particularly in the face of the widespread destruction, could create economic havoc for the U.S. zone, which by its nature required "imports" from the other zones. Lastly, during the discussions in the summer on the impending coal crisis, it was concluded that substantial German coal production was essential to European recovery, and that both depended on the rehabilitation of industry, transport, housing, food production, and of the German economy and society in general.

Clay has stated that he and Murphy feared the Potsdam conference would impose financial and economic restrictions on Germany to the detriment of a "healthy Europe"; that it might impose reparations on Germany from current production with the effect that the United States would end up sending goods to feed Germans while other powers removed reparations; and that it might set premature minimum industrial production levels for Germany and thus reduce the flexibility of the Allied Control Council.[43] James V. Forrestal's diary mentions a July 29, 1945, meeting in Clay's Berlin guest house, during which Forrestal, Averell Harriman, Edwin Pauley, and Charles Bohlen expressed their concern over Russian negotiations on reparations, particularly because the Russian demands would strip every area and, obviously, leave an even greater vacuum to be filled by imports.[44]

Despite Clay's and Murphy's fears and despite the differences that developed later regarding the meaning of the Potsdam agreement, it nevertheless promised to solve many of the problems that had vexed American administrators before the conference. For those it did not solve immediately, it permitted a period of grace during which the problems might be solved. Most writers who deal with the subject admit heavy United States influence on the Potsdam agreement. They recognize the similarity between it and JCS 1067, and some even point up the similar phraseology.[45] Apparently, however, no one has noted how much Potsdam increased the American administrators' latitude in economic matters over that granted them by JCS 1067.

Potsdam's recognition of Germany as an economic unit gave hope for a solution to the problem of a U.S. zone that could not exist without imports. The principle of economic unity and the creation of central agencies to administer common economic policies seemed to assure an interzonal trade balance that would reduce or eliminate imports to feed Germans and to prime German industry. Eventually it would produce enough to meet Germany's proposed minimum standard of living. The requirement that imports be a first charge against German exports was a further guarantee against an excessive financial drain on any of the occupying powers, the United States in particular. Reparations from current production, though not prohibited, were not authorized either. Final determination of the amount available for reparations was delayed for six months to permit calculation of the capital equipment in Germany in excess of that needed to provide for the occupation forces, displaced persons, and an average living standard not exceeding that of European countries (excluding the USSR and Great Britain). In effect, the latter provision took into account the extent of wartime destruction, which Americans had commented on earlier but which no one had yet been able to calculate satisfactorily. The Byrnes compromise on reparations avoided setting a specific reparations amount, and, since reparations were linked to the study and calculation of excess capital equipment, the compromise seemed to forestall an imbalance within the German economy as a whole. It provided that the Soviet Union's and Poland's reparations were to be met from the Soviet zone and from German foreign assets in eastern Europe, and by transfer to the Soviet Union and Poland of 25 per cent of the capital equipment declared to be surplus in the other three zones. Ten per cent was to be delivered without payment or exchange and 15 per cent in exchange for food, coal, potash, zinc, petroleum, clay products, and other things.

From a purely economic point of view, the Potsdam agreement to regard the Oder and Neisse Rivers as the temporary boundary between Poland and the Soviet zone was an improvement over the uncertainty that had preceded the conference. Though the loss in productive capacity and agricultural surpluses was great, and though any line further east would have been economically more desirable, the decision at least provided a certain base upon which to calculate the German industrial capacity that would remain to provide the minimum needs described elsewhere in the agreement.

In addition to the flexibility in economic matters that Potsdam afforded American administrators over JCS 1067, it encouraged political activity, permitted trade union development, and looked ahead— though vaguely—to the restoration of a German government. Apparently basing his conclusions on American studies made in Berlin in August 1945, Clay wrote that the Potsdam agreement contained "a policy change of major import which influenced our administration of Germany almost from the start." He explained that Potsdam negated the financial and economic provisions of JCS 1067 in at least four ways: by treating Germany as a single economic unit, by ensuring an equitable distribution of essential commodities through central administrations, by establishing central administrations and common policies to replace the regional autonomy of JCS 1067, and by linking reparations to the requirement that Germany be permitted sufficient resources to subsist without external assistance.[46] What the Potsdam conferees did essentially was to write into an official policy agreement the understandings worked out by US Group CC and Washington between Clay's arrival in the theater and the Potsdam conference. It was indeed a policy change in this sense.*

There is no need to review here the extensive literature on the political and humanitarian facets of the Potsdam agreement.[47] A document of such scope that has been negotiated under the pressure of time, previous commitments, and power politics of the first order, and that has dealt with the most intricate and complex political and economic issues, obviously leaves much to be desired in precision. It was quite clear, however, that post-Potsdam Germany would differ from prewar Germany in many ways. For example, the loss of prewar territory to Poland and Russia and the temporary assignment of the areas east of the Oder-Neisse line to Polish administration required economic patterns in the remainder of Germany unlike those existing prior to the war. The population transfers—which were already under way—produced a major economic variable for the time being. There is also no question that the political decision to destroy war industries and emphasize "agricultural and peaceful domestic industries" required a basic readjustment of prewar German economic and export-import relations as well as of the resulting social patterns.

## France Frustrates the Promise of Potsdam

Events soon showed that the Potsdam agreement, though strong in promise for Americans, was weak in results. Many reasons have been advanced to explain this failure: the loss of the eastern territories; the

* For the press release accompanying publication of JCS 1067 and the statement that, where JCS 1067 and Potsdam differ, the latter is controlling, see U.S. Dept. of State, *Germany, 1947–1949: The Story in Documents*, Dept. of State Publication 3556, in European and British Commonwealth Series 9 (Washington, 1950), p. 21.

burden of feeding millions of refugees coming into Germany from the East; the unrealistic reparations compromise; the ambiguities of the agreement and the haste with which it was negotiated; Truman's desire not to go home empty-handed; the unpatriotic advice of leftist advisers; the remnants of the Morgenthau spirit; and the growing suspicion between the two great powers over affairs in Germany, atomic energy control, Iran, the Far East, and other world issues. The records show, however, that the most immediate reason was France's categorical refusal to accept key parts of the agreement unless certain other conditions were met. The conditions in turn would have upset the rest of the settlement. France's refusal had the effect of holding the entire settlement in abeyance. In the meantime, officials of the U.S. military government in the field, alarmed by conditions in Germany, feeling pressure from home, and hoping that a tactical maneuver might bring de facto French acceptance of the Potsdam economic solutions, moved beyond the Potsdam agreement and JCS 1067, thereby making both somewhat academic. The details will be developed in the following chapters.

France's response to Potsdam was immediate and firm. On August 7, 1945, Georges Bidault, the Foreign Minister of the French Provisional Government, addressed a series of similar notes to the ambassadors of the United States, the United Kingdom, and the Soviet Union. In them the French government expressed its regret that the Potsdam agreement had been made without French participation. France accepted much of the agreement, but it had specific reservations on the decisions to revive political parties and to establish central administrations for a Germany whose boundaries had not been fixed by all interested parties. France also noted that it foresaw difficulties arising out of the resettlement of people from Poland, Czechoslovakia, and Hungary, and indicated that it would have more to say later about the principles by which Germany was to be controlled economically.[48]

In September and October 1945, France took action that left little doubt that it intended to block the very economic features of the Potsdam agreement that Americans in Germany had greeted as welcome relief from the previous limitations of JCS 1067. On September 14, at the London Council of Foreign Ministers meeting, the French delegation presented a memorandum, making it unmistakably clear that France would not agree to central administrations that had authority over the Rhineland and the Ruhr area, and that France's representatives in the Allied Control Council would veto any decision that would prejudice the French demand for separation of those areas from Germany.[49] Two weeks later, on October 1, 1945, France's representative on the Allied Control Council insisted that discussion and debate on two draft proposals on central administrations be passed over. He said that, in view of his government's position as previously stated, he could only veto them as they existed.[50]

Faced with the situation described above, United States representatives in Germany followed various alternatives—at different times and with varying degrees of intensity and success to be sure—hoping somehow to break the impasse. They sought, as one alternative, to get French acceptance of the principle of economic unity and the establishment of central administrations. To accomplish this, they asked for government-level intervention from Washington. They sought clear definitions of policy that would allow them to act on their own authority in Berlin. They sought and got, in December 1945, a policy statement to replace at least the inadequate economic and financial portions of JCS 1067. They also moved ahead, under the authority they had in Germany, to create a Council of Minister-Presidents and to solve some of the economic problems of the United States zone. They tried to achieve ad hoc economic unification by interzonal negotiations in the field, and they came to believe that this approach might gain acceptance if the American-zone Council of Minister-Presidents did extensive preparatory and liaison work with their counterparts in the other zones. Each of these alternatives possessed a dynamic of its own, and it was apparently just as difficult for the administrators on the scene to keep up with the ups and downs of each and its relationship to the others as it is for the historian to describe them. For the historian, at least, the reward seems worth the effort.

# 2 | The Pressure for Reassessment and Clarification

Clay and Murphy have written that, after reporting to Byrnes at the London Council of Foreign Ministers meeting, they went to Washington late in October to secure revision of JCS 1067.[1] The State Department had a policy drafting committee, headed by James Riddleberger, and the State-War-Navy Coordinating Committee (SWNCC) took up the question of German policy in November.[2] The Informal Policy Committee on Germany had been dissolved at Potsdam on July 16, 1945.[3] Neither SWNCC nor State Department records for this period are open to private researchers, and the administrative machinery for policy revision at this time is not, therefore, exactly clear. It is thus easy to see why Clay's and Murphy's claim that they initiated a policy revision in 1945 and that it got a sympathetic hearing, but bore no fruit until July 1947, has been generally accepted— even by no less an authority than Paul Y. Hammond. Nevertheless, Clay's and Murphy's tremendous influence in Washington would seem to suggest that, had they tried hard enough for revision, they could have achieved more than they did. As a matter of fact, the available records of their visit to Washington show rather conclusively that policy revision as such was not their purpose. They sought clarification of existing policy as modified by Potsdam and verification of certain assumptions that underlay decisions on which OMGUS was acting or planning to act; and they asked for government-level pressure on France to implement the Potsdam agreement.

## Pressure for Policy Change

The pressure for policy change late in 1945 came from two main sources, both of which Clay tried to channel into support for his own position or to curb. The first source was the public clamor and congressional interest in the Calvin Hoover level-of-industry study of September 1945;[4] the second the White House attention to the recommendations of Byron Price, who sent his report to President Truman on November 9, 1945.[5]

*The Calvin Hoover Report.* The so-called Hoover report was actually the work of the German Standard of Living Board, created on August 10, 1945, in the American military government headquarters to prepare a study of the level of German peacetime economy under the Potsdam formula.[6] The Board, chaired by Calvin Hoover, completed its report on September 10, 1945, and submitted it to the Allied Control Council's Industry Committee on September 18.[7] The report is essentially a statistical compilation showing that the Potsdam standard of living for Germany would be about 74 per cent of the 1930–1938 average, or "roughly equivalent to that which actually existed in Germany in 1932, the worst year of the economic depression."[8] It showed that the combined effect of an industrial disarmament program and the loss of some 25 per cent of the prewar German food production to Poland and Russia would inevitably cause an annual export deficit of 818,000,000 marks ($81,800,000 at the prevailing ratio of 10 marks to the dollar). It said that the cost of occupation would raise that deficit to 3,555,000,000 marks per year ($355,500,000). The report suggested that the deficits might be reduced by "mining" German timber resources, by permitting production of ball bearings, and by other means. But its summary statement shows its generally dismal prediction: "The conclusion cannot be avoided that the conflict between an extreme degree of industrial disarmament spread over a number of key industries and the goal of maintaining a minimum German standard of living according to the assumed formula while providing for the costs of occupying forces seems insoluble under conditions such as those brought about by losses of territory."[9]

Hoover returned to the United States immediately after the study was done, and he apparently discussed his report with various officials in Washington. His findings made the rounds in private until the *New York Times* published a story in detail on October 8, 1945.[10] Once it was out in the open, the report received widespread public attention. Senators Wheeler, Eastland, Wherry, and Langer, among others, obviously seeing the report as an analysis of the economic consequences of the "harsh peace" and apparently sensing the political leverage it provided, revived the earlier arguments against the Morgenthau Plan and criticized the New Deal philosophy that had given birth to it.[11] Morgenthau, on the other hand, first demanded that Secretary of War Robert Patterson repudiate the report. Failing in this, he used the report's findings to heap criticism on the Army for abandoning the earlier harsh policy and JCS 1067.[12] Before all of this occurred, however, Clay had heard about Hoover's private discussions in Washington and warned the War Department that it should make clear to whomever necessary that the Hoover report reflected Hoover's personal abhorrence of destruction, that it was not official policy of OMGUS, and that it was only a preliminary study to be used as a basis for discussion within OMGUS and the Allied Control Authority.[13] What appears to be quite clear is that Clay and OMGUS did not send up the Hoover report as a trial balloon to stimulate policy revision, as Morgenthau and the critics were to charge. Clay's penciled note to Draper on an internal staff memorandum, which suggested possible escape avenues out of the dilemma described in the German Standard of Living Board's report, said that Potsdam would be adhered to 100 per cent until changed.[14] Such change—it should be noted—could not be achieved unilaterally in Washington, but would have to be accomplished by tripartite agreement.

*The Byron Price Report.* The strongest impetus for policy revision in 1945 came from the impact of the Byron Price report. Price, who had gone to Germany on a personal inspection tour for Truman, showed his preliminary report to Clay in mid-October and submitted it to Truman on November 9, 1945. The report was filled with gloom about the future of Germany. Price thought the American experience in postwar Germany and the conditions he saw there revealed certain basic problems that needed immediate solution. The primary problem was to develop exports that would make it possible for Germany to pay for indispensable food imports. The United States, he said, had to decide whether it wanted to withdraw from Germany or whether it wanted to supply the tools and funds needed to do a thorough job there. It had to decide whether it would permit starvation, epidemics, and disorders or whether it would ship in the food to prevent them. It should do something to increase the 1550-calorie food ration to at least 2,000 calories, and to alleviate the disorder and confusion caused by rapid denazification. It had to decide how far denazification and industrial destruction would go. Price recommended that the United States use its full diplomatic power to break the deadlock in the Allied Control Council; that it "decide whether obstructions raised by the French . . . are to be permitted to defeat the underlying purposes of Allied policy." He also recommended that supervision of the German press and radio be changed, that criminals be brought to justice rapidly, that American control in Germany be placed in civilian hands, and that high-level policy be revised.[15]

On November 23, 1945, McCloy wrote Clay that Byron Price had been pushing for a revised directive for the occupation.[16] Significantly, McCloy's letter went to Clay more than two weeks after the latter's Washington visit. Its contents suggest that no serious policy study looking toward revision had been initiated in the meantime. In fact, McCloy seemed discouraged by the prospect: "The task of tying together in one streamlined Directive all the relevant policies embodied in JCS 1067, the Berlin Protocol, and instructions transmitted by cable to my mind really poses a very complex problem of codification, editing, and renegotiation. With recollections of the difficulties we encountered in getting Governmental agreement on JCS 1067, none of us has any illusions about the magnitude of the job of agreeing [on] a new comprehensive Directive."[17] Nevertheless, the Civil Affairs Division, War Department, followed with a cable to Clay on December 1, saying that Byron Price's report suggested revision of the directives for Germany and that the President had circulated the report to the Secretaries of State, War, and Navy. The cable, apparently reflecting the force of Price's report in Washington, "imperatively requested" Clay's views on revision. Clay's answer, just one month after his return from Washington, where he supposedly sought policy revision, is instructive indeed: ". . . do not understand what Byron Price had in mind. On the whole, JCS 1067 as modified by Potsdam has proved workable. Much of 1067 has been enacted into Allied Control Authority laws and directives. Here any changes would be confusing except as we necessarily deviated from

JCS 1067 to obtain quadripartite agreement. It would be helpful probably to delete from JCS 1067 those matters covered by Potsdam and Allied Control Authority actions substituting [for] or referring to these actions. Some details require clarification or amplification, and a report covering these details will be furnished in about a week. I don't know how we could have effectively set up our military government without JCS 1067."[18] The War Department thereupon sought clarification and amplification that led eventually to the Department of State's December 12, 1945, statement, a move much more in keeping with Clay's and Murphy's purpose in coming to Washington late in October and early November.[19]

## The Clay-Murphy Visit to Washington

Clay and Murphy came to Washington seeking not policy revision, but clarification, agreement on OMGUS working assumptions, and government-level pressure on France. France's rejection of portions of the Potsdam agreement has been noted in the previous chapter. Her demand for decisions on the Saar, the Ruhr, and the Rhineland prior to the establishment of central agencies and economic unity under the Control Council had been made clear at the operating level in Berlin and at the diplomatic level in London. Her position restricted the economic latitude that Potsdam would have provided Americans in Germany and, in effect, returned United States military government officials to the economic directives of JCS 1067, which they had found wholly inadequate prior to the Potsdam conference and from which they thought Potsdam had relieved them.

*Field-Level Issues and Problems.* Clay has told the story of his field-level attempts to get Allied Control Council agreement on central agencies.[20] Beginning on August 10, 1945, and continuing well into 1946, French representatives at various levels of the Allied Control Authority blocked, delayed, or vetoed the several proposals for the establishment of central agencies called for in the Potsdam agreement. On September 22, for example, in a discussion on the creation of a central German transport department, General Louis M. Koeltz said he required a government-level decision before he could act. Clay tried to force the issue by stating that each zone commander could take the initiative in his own zone to negotiate with other zone commanders. He suggested that the lower levels of the Allied Control Authority be instructed to begin making plans for the centralized department despite the French minority position.[21] Two days later, anticipating further French refusals and delaying tactics, Clay cabled the War Department asking for authority to negotiate in the field with British and Russian representatives should France refuse to change her position.[22] On October 1, before Clay received a reply (which eventually came in the affirmative on October 21), General Pierre Koenig presented a formal statement on behalf of France to the Control Council. He referred to the French memorandum presented to the Council of Foreign Ministers in London on September 14, 1945, and said that, in the absence of a government-level decision, France would not agree to any decisions that might prejudice the future of the Ruhr and the Rhineland. Therefore, he could not agree to central agencies, and asked instead that the proposals for German transport and communications agencies be set aside.[23] Twelve days later, Clay proposed interzonal collaboration under the zone commanders' authority. He withdrew the proposal on October 16. His specific reason for doing so is not clear from available records, but it is clear that it was not done on instructions from Washington. On October 19 the working parties concerned with plans for the transport and communications agencies suspended further action.[24] In the meantime, progress on a central finance agency seemed doomed to a similar fate when France sent only an observer to the working session on October 9.[25] The impasse that resulted explains in part the immediate basis for Clay's and Murphy's visit to Washington in late October. But there were also other issues that needed clarification.

The German Standard of Living Board had finished its report, and lower-level Allied Control Authority negotiations on the level-of-industry plan had begun in September. The Foreign Economic Administration (FEA) had had a field mission in Germany from mid-August to early October 1945, to update and finish various FEA studies on German economics and industry.[26] The differing lines of investigation pursued by these groups shows that the Potsdam agreement permitted various interpretations among the Allies, within the American military government organization, and between the Allies and the FEA people.[27] As early as August 8, 1945, Draper's Industry Division interpreted Potsdam to mean that sufficient capacity must remain in each industry to supply German needs under the agreed standard of living, and "that enough additional productive plant must remain to provide sufficient exports to pay for required imports ... *because the economy cannot operate unless sufficient excess capacity over German requirements is retained to balance all required imports.*"[28] The disagreements that developed subsequently are revealed in a draft study by the OMGUS Industry Division late in September. The division interpreted the "intent of American policy to be to incite and encourage the German people to contribute to the welfare of Europe by holding out to them the promise that they will be permitted to raise their own standards indefinitely, so long as they help their neighbors up to the same level."[29]

The Industry Division study said its interpretation took into account the difficult German conditions: the destruction of transportation, housing, and other facilities; the economic dislocations caused by the war and the postwar division into zones; the loss of agricultural lands, forests, and coal in the east; the expulsion of people from the east and their migration to Germany; and the unknown but large capital equipment removals in the east. In effect, the study said in much detail what Clay, Douglas, and Murphy had said earlier in the spring: given the existing situation, a viable German standard of living—in this case the Potsdam formula, which the Hoover report had already questioned for its low 1932 level—could never be maintained without outside assistance, obviously from the United States. Cutting through the details, it may be observed that the basic issue was whether Potsdam had intended the standard-of-living figure to be a minimum (floor) or a maximum (ceiling). The Industry Division considered it to be a minimum, as did the Hoover report. The FEA studies assumed it was a maximum. Soviet negotiators in the Allied Control Authority, Industry Committee, reportedly saw it as a maximum and assumed that anything less was all right.[30] The entire question remained unresolved when Clay and Murphy came to Washington to seek clarification and guidance.

Several other problems confronted OMGUS administrators in the immediate post-Potsdam months. Clay told an FEA representative on September 1 that decisions on the level of industry in Germany and on the amount of reparations could not be made definite until the uncertainties arising from the Polish sessions, the Russian actions in their zone, and the French occupancy of the Saar were cleared up. The Polish, Russian, and French actions impinged on the Potsdam provision that Germany be permitted to subsist without external assistance. In addition, Clay observed that other European countries, particularly Norway and Sweden, had already shown some concern for their own economic life, should German industry be reduced to a low level permanently.[31] It might be noted how neatly the last point dovetailed with Douglas's views, expressed in May, with Stimson's views, expressed in July, and with the Industry Division's position that German recovery and European economic welfare were related in that they would improve simultaneously.[32] It might also be noted how early some of the basic tenets of the Marshall Plan were developed within the OMGUS organization.

*The Washington Discussions.* The Civil Affairs Division, War Department, prepared a record of Clay's and Murphy's discussions in Washington early in November.[33] There were internal discussions in the War Department on such topics as accounting procedures, civilian salaries, restrictions on travel by International Telephone and Telegraph people, the problem of evaluating manufacturing plants for restitutions and reparations accounting, and four-power control in Germany. In addition, Clay and Hilldring (the head of CAD) met with Murphy and State Department representatives including, among others, William Clayton, Freeman Matthews, and James Riddleberger. The record makes only cryptic reference to a SWNCC paper, but devotes great attention to other issues that seemed to have been most pressing. Clay wanted a statement of United States views on the French proposal to internationalize the Ruhr and the Rhineland. He said OMGUS and the Allied Control Authority were stymied because they could calculate neither the peacetime level of industry nor reparations without a clear decision on the Saar and the Ruhr-Rhineland area's future status. He was told that government discussions were under way and that a United States statement would have to await the results.

On the related question of central administrations under the Allied

Control Council, as provided by the Potsdam agreement, Clay reported that French representatives in the Control Council had government instructions to oppose central agencies pending a decision on their proposal for internationalization of the Ruhr and the Rhineland. He stated, further, that Soviet representatives believed that the United States and Britain tacitly supported French obstinacy and that he had tried to correct the Soviet error. Clay asked pointedly whether the State Department had applied diplomatic pressure on France to cooperate in the Allied Control Council. He was told they had not, whereupon Clay expressed his view that the Soviets would not agree to central agencies unless the United States took a position on the French demands on the Ruhr and the Rhineland.

Clay's obvious conclusion that France's policy frustrated the realization of Potsdam was countered by a suggestion that it was not clear that the Soviets intended to carry out the political and economic principles of the Berlin protocol. The inhumane and unplanned population transfers, the Soviet restrictions on interzonal travel and their failure to develop interzonal trade, their control of the press in the Soviet zone, their support of favored political parties, and their unilateral land reform and nationalization were cited as ominous indicators. Clay, apparently annoyed by the suggestion that Soviet intentions might be as obstructive as French actions, emphasized that until France accepted central agencies and until economic unity under Potsdam was a fact, the Soviet barriers on interzonal trade and travel had a rationale. He listed restrictions in the French zone that compared with some of the things mentioned about the Soviet zone and observed that, in the absence of central administrations, every zone commander could take unilateral action in his own zone, as the United States commander had also done.

On reparations and the level of industry to be permitted, Clay sought a number of clarifications. He wanted a firm decision on whether the Allied Control Council or the Allied Reparations Commission had primary responsibility for determining the amount of capital equipment not needed for the peacetime German economy and thus the amount available for reparations. Before Clay left Washington, the State Department agreed to rewrite the instructions for the United States representative on the Allied Reparations Commission, to the effect that he work closely with the United States members of the Allied Control Council. Clay said he needed a decision regarding the relationship of restitutions to reparations and that he needed instructions on how to deal with German external assets. There is no evidence that he asked whether the Potsdam level-of-industry figure was a floor or a ceiling. Subsequent correspondence and cables suggest, however, that he asked for it at some time, and it will be shown later that he got a clarification shortly.

Clay also requested operating instructions, clarifications, or agreement on a host of other matters. He reviewed the coal problem, and outlined the difficulty of meeting the President's coal directive, especially in the face of the related food and transport shortages.[34] He got Washington to drop the idea of ordering I. G. Farben officials to come to the United States to testify before the Kilgore Committee, and to agree that special interest groups who sought curtailment of German production to eliminate future competition should not be encouraged. Cotton textile producers, watch industry representatives, harmonica manufacturers, and optical instrument workers and management were mentioned as examples of interest groups that had already tried. Clay also got agreement that German industrial disarmament should be pressed, but the question of what to do with the German General Staff remained open after some discussion.

The nature of the discussions has been presented in some detail to show that policy revision as such was hardly a factor of major importance. The desire to bring France around to support the economic features of the Potsdam agreement seems to have been Clay's major concern, but he did not find enthusiastic support among the State Department representatives who would have borne the major responsibility for applying the pressure.

*Interpretations of the Washington Visit.* It can be seen, in retrospect, why Clay's and Murphy's explanations of their October-November mission have not been questioned. JCS 1067 was published for the first time on October 17, 1945, and—if revision was needed—this would seem to have been the logical time to press for it openly. Morgenthau concluded and the liberal press speculated that the Hoover report, which became public in October, was a trial balloon; that it expressed the old anti-Morgenthau, pro-German philosophy that had prevailed in the German Country Unit and the "pre-Morgenthau" planning groups. The pieces seemed to fit neatly into a picture in which OMGUS sought changes in policy right after the Hoover report and JCS 1067 became public knowledge. Furthermore, the Kilgore Committee hearings, especially the testimony of Russell Nixon, revealed details of a strong sector within OMGUS supposedly dedicated to German recovery instead of to reform, denazification, and industrial disarmament. Subsequent publications by disillusioned OMGUS officials, reformers, and idealists of one kind or another strengthened the contemporary belief that OMGUS officials—particularly William Draper, Larry Wilkinson, Rufus Wysor, Frederick Devereux, and Colonel Pillsbury—were out of sympathy with existing policy and therefore pushed Clay to seek changes.[35]

Why Clay and Murphy should have accepted their own critics' interpretation of their mission in October and November is indeed problematical. Perhaps the simplest explanation is the correct one. Events moved so rapidly in 1945, and the Byron Price report's impact came so soon after their own departure from Washington that the two events may have run together in their memories some years later. The fact that they had expressed dissatisfaction with policy before Potsdam and were to do so again in 1946, after the Paris Council of Foreign Ministers meeting, may have blurred their recollections of the fact that there was a brief period during which they had fought hard to give the Potsdam agreement a chance, essentially because they were convinced that it erased the economic anomalies of JCS 1067. In any event, the current interpretation is that there was a straight-line development from the early dissatisfaction with JCS 1067, to Douglas's attempted revision in the summer of 1945, to Clay's and Murphy's attempt in the fall, to Byrnes's efforts in Paris in 1946 followed by his Stuttgart speech in September, to Marshall's last attempt in Moscow in 1947 culminating in the first major policy revision in July 1947.[36]

The vital factor that gets lost in this straight-line interpretation is the double impact of France's unwillingness to accept what Americans in Germany thought to be absolutely essential, and the American response to the impasse that resulted. France, of course, did not participate in the Potsdam conference and therefore had sound legal reasons, in addition to political reasons, for disregarding its results. Her role at this point is crucial, however, because it—coupled with the American attempt to bring France around—reveals the basic error in the Soviet view at the time that the United States and Britain tacitly supported France's views. It shows, also, the weak foundation for Communist charges during the occupation and afterward that the Western Allies, particularly the United States, deliberately and conspiratorially broke the Potsdam agreement for their own purposes.[37] Further, it suggests that United States difficulties in Germany, though unquestionably influenced later by what had become the global compass of the cold war, were already manifest—for reasons hardly attributable to the cold war—before January 1946, when Truman said he was tired of "babying the Soviets." And perhaps they were a factor even as early as September 1945, when (as Byrnes later recalled on Dulles's prompting) our postwar policy of "no appeasement" was born.[38] Finally, it gives force to the repeated statements by Clay and other OMGUS representatives that their actions in Germany were not intended to subvert or ignore the Potsdam agreement, but to bring it to fruition. Their attempts to carry it out had a dynamic of their own, however, and it will be shown that by mid-1946 Clay was virtually demanding a new policy statement that would conform with what was already OMGUS practice in Germany.

## The Clay-Murphy Achievements

It has been previously noted that McCloy's assessment of the difficulties involved in agreeing on a new directive and Clay's belief that JCS 1067 as modified by Potsdam was adequate together dampened any enthusiasm for policy revision that Byron Price may have inspired. Hilldring wrote to Secretary of War Patterson on December 3, 1945, saying that Clay's answer to the suggestion for revision "indicates general satisfaction with the directives, suggests certain deletions, and states that some clarification is required."[39] The War Department had, in fact, already initiated separate actions to meet Clay's request for clarification and for pressure on France. On November 21, apparently fortified by Byron Price's recommendation that the United States use its full diplomatic power to break the dead-

lock in the Allied Control Council, Secretary of War Patterson formally asked the State Department to bring pressure on France to implement the Potsdam agreement on central agencies in Germany. He
also asked for a specific statement on what areas should be included
in Germany for purposes of peacetime level-of-industry planning in
Germany, thus raising Clay's request for a decision on the Saar, the
Ruhr, and the Rhineland.[40] Sometime after Clay's visit, though the
exact date is not clear from available records, the War Department
also asked the State Department a series of questions to clarify the
economic provisions of the Potsdam agreement. Hammond cites a
memorandum of November 11, but he also indicates that the questions went to SWNCC and then to the State Department, without making clear when they went from one agency to another.[41] In any case,
the War Department transmitted the State Department's answers to
OMGUS on December 8, 1945, and the State Department released
them in a statement on December 12, 1945.[42]

Clay's request for government-level intervention on the Ruhr-
Rhineland and on central agencies brought no effective results. A
unilateral statement seemed undesirable while the discussions at the
diplomatic level were still under way. It also seemed rather fruitless.
On November 30, Secretary of State Byrnes informed the War Department that, for purposes of peacetime economic planning, Germany's boundaries should be those defined at Potsdam (the Old
Reich less territories east of the Oder and Neisse Rivers). However,
a subsequent report received by the War Department from Dean
Acheson on December 13 indicated that boundaries and French support for central agencies were subjects of continuing talks.[43] Finally,
on January 12, 1946, Acheson reaffirmed Byrnes's memorandum of
November 30, 1945, on the boundaries, until such time as the agreements might be changed. He stated further that the United States position in favor of central agencies had been made clear to the public, to
the Allied Control Council in Berlin, and to Couve de Murville during the latter's visit to Washington from November 13–20, 1945. The
unanimity principle in the Allied Control Council, which the War
Department and the Joint Chiefs of Staff had supported during the
European Advisory Commission negotiations that set up the Allied
Control Council was, in Acheson's view, the real barrier to an im-

mediate favorable solution. He noted that, although the Control Council agreement provided for joint authority, each zone commander was free to act individually in his own zone. Under the latter provision it might be possible to set up central agencies for the British, Soviet, and the United States zones, as provided by the Berlin Protocol, which had been signed by the three powers in question. But Clay had already tried that without success, as has been shown previously.[44]

The War Department's request for clarification of the economic provisions of the Potsdam agreement proved much more successful. As summarized in Hilldring's cable to OMGUS on December 8, 1945, and in the statement released three days later by the State Department, the position agreed on was approximately as follows:

The level-of-industry plan due on February 2, 1946, will eliminate German war potential and determine the amount of reparations available. The United States does not propose to limit the German economy permanently, and the February 2, 1946, level of industry will be subject to constant review. Ultimately, the United States, in cooperation with its Allies, intends to permit the German people —under a democratic German government—to develop a higher standard of living, subject to restrictions on production and armaments.* The United States interprets the Berlin Protocol to mean that the German standard of living will not be reduced below a certain point because of German reparations payments, i.e., that the figure is a minimum (floor) and not a maximum (ceiling). Germany should be left sufficient resources to exist eventually without external assistance, and it must be permitted sufficient capital to produce exports to pay for needed imports. The United States does not propose to eliminate Germany's peaceful industries that would compete for world trade simply to protect American markets or to gain other selfish advantages. In calculating a standard-of-living figure, adjustments will be required to provide for population changes, to rebuild destroyed buildings, to rehabilitate transport within five years, and to overcome the housing shortage in twenty years. The boundaries of Germany, for purposes of calculating the

---

* Of the two sources used for this summary, the December 8 cable is in some places considerably more precise and direct. Regarding the restrictions on production, the cable not only suggests permissiveness, but talks about "furthering" a higher standard of living.

level of industry, are assumed to be the Old Reich less the territories
east of the Oder and Neisse Rivers. All of the foregoing interpretations are conditioned by United States acceptance of the Berlin
Protocol's provisions to weaken war industry, to provide material
assistance to United Nations countries that suffered under the
Nazis, to ensure that German recovery does not precede that of the
Allies who suffered under German aggression, and to destroy the
war potential that cannot be removed.[45]

B. U. Ratchford, who was close enough to the situation in Berlin
to have known, wrote in 1947 that the December 12, 1945, statement
did much to clarify the United States position for the other powers.
However, he continued, "it was not in any sense a change of American
policy but rather a formal statement and confirmation of the policy
already being followed. In fact, we in Berlin could easily recognize
many ideas and some of the phrases as those which had first appeared
in the Hoover Report and other U.S. papers presented in Berlin."[46]
The obvious relationship between the statement and the economic
questions raised by Clay and Murphy in November seems to be clear
enough. There is external evidence also that the War Department,
Civil Affairs Division, not only posed the questions but drafted the
answers.[47] The importance of this merits emphasis.

The statement, by focusing on the Potsdam agreement, recognized
publicly the OMGUS and War Department interpretation that the
economic restrictions of JCS 1067 had been superseded by the Potsdam agreement. It referred to the "disease and unrest" formula of
JCS 1067 as a short-term supply measure. It implied that the "disease
and unrest" formula had been needed because of wartime destruction
and the inability of Germans to resume production up to the limits of
industrial capacity owing to shortages of food and raw materials and
to the political and economic disorganization resulting from defeat.
For the long run, it envisioned Allied imports as a stimulant to production for exports in sufficient quantity to pay for current, and possibly past, import outlays. By defining the Potsdam standard-of-living
formula as a floor—though not necessarily a guaranteed floor during
the occupation period—it set no limitation on the increase in the
standard of living, provided that such an increase did not exceed the
European average. It thus linked the German economic future with

European economic development in a positive way. In effect, the standard-of-living formula and the level of German industry were tied not only to the reparations demands of the victors but to several extremely important variables: (1) the amount of exports sufficient to allow Germany to pay for imports, (2) the cost of rebuilding housing and transport, (3) the requirements of an increased population in the reduced area of Germany, (4) the rate of economic growth needed to enable Germany to exist without external assistance, and (5) the curve of the standard-of-living index in the remainder of Europe. Since no one considered limiting the increase in the standard of living for the remainder of Europe, the last of these variables provided the latitude—whereas the others provided the necessity—for a positive economic effort that JCS 1067 had neither foreseen nor permitted. By 1947, when it became clear that the latitude was not great enough to relieve the necessity—which had cost the American taxpayer heavily—the Marshall Plan came to the rescue. Long before, however, a number of military government actions in the field had produced a dialectic, the nature and significance of which merits attention.

# 3 | The Zonal Initiative

Late in 1945 American representatives in Germany sought policy reassessment and clarification. They asked for government-level intervention to break the deadlock in the Allied Control Council, and they initiated action in their zone of occupation to solve the economic problems they foresaw. From Clay downward, the people responsible for Germany's future feared the consequences of excessive hunger, cold, and unemployment, and they predicted that the cost of preventing disease and unrest would be high.[1] Reports from the field strengthened these fears and confirmed these predictions. The reports described the chaotic conditions caused by military defeat and accentuated by the collapse of German government, transportation, communications, and internal trade. German statistical agencies either no longer functioned, or were reduced to a limited area. Flour mills, bakeries, dairies, and other consumer industries operated from inventories, but the early depletion of existing stocks and the lack of coal and transport presaged trouble. There was little prospect that coal would be available for heating homes in the coming winter. Food reserves were at a low level; the uneven distribution of current agricultural production, coupled with the loss of agricultural-surplus areas and the influx of refugees, aggravated a condition already fraught with danger. Some areas reported urban consumer rations to be as low as 700 calories per day, a ration "decidedly below the minimum necessary to health and muscular activity essential to productive labor."[2] In summary, the field reports described the political, economic, and social disorganization that prevailed, and forecast a long period of shortages, hunger, cold, and unemployment, accompanied by general discontent and possible agitation. One such report probably summarized the prevailing views: "While a large measure of such economic distress probably cannot be avoided, delay or uncertainty as to our policies should certainly not be permitted to contribute to it unnecessarily."[3]

## The Council of Minister-Presidents—Länderrat

By mid-October, a keen observer of the American military government in Germany, who had talked at length with Clay, wrote that there was "apparent interim need for independent U.S. action in the U.S. Zone, in the absence of quadripartite agreement."[4] By that time, Americans had already begun to act on their own. On September 29, 1945, six days after Clay had told General Koeltz that he had no recourse except to take zonal action and five days after Clay had cabled the War Department asking for authorization to negotiate in the field with British and Soviet representatives on central agencies,[5] Clay reported to his staff that he had initiated a study of military government supervision at the lower levels. He said he planned to establish a coordinating agency for the U.S. zone in Stuttgart. The Council, as he called it, would be made up of the chief German officers of each of the three Länder (states) of the American zone. It would have no executive function, but would meet monthly to coordinate activities of the three Länder. Clay said that he was going to move fast and that anyone who did not like it that way should see him personally.[6]

Clay's staff study, directed by General Clarence Adcock and Hayden N. Smith, the Director and Deputy Director of USFET, was completed on October 1, 1945. It proposed a directive calling upon USFET to bring the minister-presidents of the American zone together to exchange ideas and experiences, to discuss plans for strengthening their respective governments and supervising the Sonderverwaltungen (former national postal and railway administrations), and to prepare a plan for a joint coordinating staff for all Länder governments and former national administrations. The staff study and the resulting directives leave no doubt that the failure to establish central agencies was the primary incentive to action. Until such agencies are created, the directive said, Länder governments would have to supervise the former national administrative services and to have a joint coordinating agency.[7]

Americans first arranged a series of lower-echelon meetings to explain the proposed plan.[8] Clay then met in Stuttgart with the minister-presidents of the American zone, Wilhelm Högner (Bavaria), Karl Geiler (Hesse), Reinhold Maier (Württemberg-Baden), and Senate President Wilhelm Kaisen of Bremen. Maier remembered that Clay brought a considerable military entourage. He estimated forty Americans in attendance and recalled the extraordinary military character of the meeting and his own impression that Clay knew precisely what he wanted.[9] Clay's chief advisers on the occasion were Robert Murphy; James K. Pollock, the future American liaison officer with the Council; Walter Dorn, a former Office of Strategic Services (OSS) member who would later become Clay's adviser on denazification but who was at that time on the USFET staff; Roger Wells, the future head of the Governmental Structures Branch of OMGUS; and Colonel William Dawson, the Military Governor of Württemberg-Baden, whose headquarters were in Stuttgart.[10]

Clay said that he was in Stuttgart as General Eisenhower's representative, and that the minister-presidents were there as German representatives. He summarized American policies and plans for Germany and said that the United States was determined to demilitarize, disarm, decartelize, and denazify Germany. Americans were arresting people now, but they would eventually ask Germans for proposals on denazification. Clay said he planned to have German local elections in January even though some of the minister-presidents objected to such an early date, and he planned to strengthen Länder governments even though the military government regarded Germany as a single entity. Central agencies for finance, postal services, industry, transport, and foreign trade—agencies provided for in Allied agreements in Berlin, to which Americans would add agriculture—had not been established. In the meantime, Clay continued, Americans wanted the minister-presidents to establish a coordinating agency in Stuttgart, and they wanted it done immediately. The minister-presidents were to begin discussions that day and were to strive for progress rather than perfection. Improvements could come later. In a subsequent working session with Pollock, Dorn, and Wells, the minister-presidents adopted the appropriate resolutions calling for creation of a General Secretariat, to which each *Land* would send a permanent representative. They agreed to meet and organize formally on November 6, 1945. Before the day was over, Clay accepted the proposals, took note of the tremendous step forward that had just been taken, and indicated that acceptance and distribution of refugees was perhaps the most pressing task in need of coordination.[11] The next day Clay told a meeting of Army commanders that central agencies had not been established because of French objections and that "the Länder President conferences will serve as an ad hoc arrangement for obtaining coordination between the zones."[12] It is not clear from the context whether he meant coordination between the districts of the American zone or whether he meant coordination between the zones of occupation. The former conforms with what he told Germans the day before, the latter with his concern for central agencies and with later developments.

The goal of spurring German economic recovery and of advancing other American interests as well was apparent in the origins of the Länderrat, and became even more obvious during its early activities. The agenda that Americans wrote for the first Länderrat meeting included items on food and agriculture; population distribution and refugees; electricity; exports and imports; industrial production for the U.S. zone and for export; prices and subsidies; statistics; food collections, rations, and distribution; and finances.[13] The minister-presidents' organizational plan adopted on November 6, 1945, provided for standing committees on legal coordination, industry and currency, taxes and finance, former national industries, food and refugees, and labor and welfare. It also provided that Land transport ministers coordinate policies on postal and railway services; but on December 7, 1945, USFET ordered the Länderrat to establish a zonal Directorate of Transportation as a permanent agency.[14] The first extant report by the American liaison office for the Länderrat, the Regional Government Coordinating Office (RGCO), lists sixteen committee meetings that occurred within a ten-day period in December. Only one meeting, that of the ministers of justice, was not devoted to economic problems, and the meetings scheduled for the future were no different in emphasis.[15]

On November 6, 1945, the minister-presidents named their organization the Länderrat des amerikanischen Besatzungsgebiets. They planned regular monthly meetings, to which the minister-president of each Land might bring one additional representative. The chair would rotate among the minister-presidents at three-month intervals. All decisions had to be unanimous and were to be made by the minister-presidents personally. The permanent staff included a general secretary, one representative from each Land, a corps of experts, and technical and clerical personnel. The functions of the general secretary were to be limited to preparing agenda in cooperation with military government, drafting and transmitting resolutions, helping to implement resolutions, and preparing reports as required by the military government. Each minister-president agreed to create a special office or to designate a special minister to serve as liaison officer between the secretariat and the Land government. The costs were to be borne by the three Länder equally.[16]

In the meantime, on November 1, 1945, OMGUS established the RGCO as a permanent liaison agency for the Länderrat. Its primary purpose was to promote uniformity of administration in the U.S. zone by coordinating the activities of the regional governments of Bavaria, Hesse, and Württemberg-Baden. The Director, James K. Pollock, a political scientist on leave from the University of Michigan, was to work under the direct command of the Deputy Military Governor. His office was described as a separate agency of OMGUS.[17]

## Länderrat Expansion

The rapid evolution of the Länderrat's organization and functions after November 1945 is extremely significant. The minister-presidents named Erich Rossmann permanent General Secretary on December 4, 1945. Rossmann was a Social Democrat who had come up through the ranks to become a Reichstag deputy for Württemberg from 1924 to 1933, only to suffer the eclipse so common to his type under the Nazi regime. Rossmann completed an organizational plan for his office on December 19, 1945. He proposed a staff of some thirty officials (Beamte) and sufficient secretarial and clerical assistants.[18] The Bavarian government protested immediately, insisting that the proposed staff was too large, that Americans wanted only a small coordinating office, and that it was a technical secretariat rather than a zonal authority.[19] A report from the Office of Military Government for Bavaria (OMG, Bavaria), early in January 1946, said there was "considerable unrest in Bavaria regarding the Länderrat." Bavarians thought that it assumed too much authority, that it operated as a zonal government, that it required Land officials to devote excessive time to meetings and committees, that it was expensive, and that Rossmann was building up a permanent staff.[20]

But Americans had their own plans for the Länderrat and the RGCO. By December 20, 1945, they described the RGCO as the main channel through which the U.S. zone would be administered. The schedule of committee meetings it fostered has already been noted. In December the Länderrat began an extensive study that eventually led to enactment of a zonal denazification law. On December 7, 1945, USFET ordered it to establish a directorate of transportation. During a conference of food ministers in Stuttgart on December 15–16, Colonel Hugh Hester, the OMGUS Director of Food and Agriculture, proposed specific powers for the Länderrat Food and Agriculture Committee; and on January 16, 1946, he asked that it be made responsible for implementing directives. The result was the creation of a Länderrat working party to draft proposals, a development soon duplicated by the creation of a similar working party for economics. In January, OMGUS representatives asked Germans to plan for an export control agency that would license private export firms. Also in January, Pollock asked the Länderrat for its reactions to the organization and powers of the central agencies foreseen at Potsdam; for recommendations on qualified personnel to fill the agencies; and for a study of the relationship between the Länder of the American zone, the Länderrat, and the proposed central agencies. In February, the RGCO ordered the Länderrat to work out plans to establish a zonal weather service requested by the U.S. Air Force and OMGUS.[21] The foregoing activities and projects that military government assigned to the Länderrat are by no means a complete list. Nevertheless, they suggest rather clearly that Rossmann's organizational plan of December 19, 1945, which Bavaria and Hesse had criticized, was indeed too modest to achieve the goals set by OMGUS.

Toward the end of March, the Länderrat's expansionist and restrictive currents clashed to produce a minor crisis. On March 27, 1946, Reinhold Maier, who was personally close to Pollock and probably best informed on American intentions and plans for the Länderrat, spoke in the Württemberg-Baden Vorparlament on the need for a stronger Länderrat. Two days later, Erich Rossmann presented to a special Länderrat meeting a memorandum describing the development of his agency during the preceding three months. He referred to his December 19, 1945, organizational plan, reviewed the criticism it received in January, then added that developments since December had made the recommendations obsolete. The demands on the office had required employment of staff far beyond his original estimates. The military government had put pressure on for more experts, committees, translators, and staff. It had demanded work that went far beyond coordination, particularly in the fields of food and agriculture and of economics, and had seen to it that committees and experts were assigned to Stuttgart.[22]

Rossmann offered his memorandum after a special Länderrat meeting with Clay on food problems. He wanted it to be a basis for an internal discussion among the minister-presidents on the need for more personnel in the secretariat and on the general question of the Länderrat's authority and competence. The importance of the issue and the source of Rossmann's initiative are both suggested by the fact that Pollock sent a special messenger to the minister-presidents' meeting to inquire whether any progress had been made. Rossmann had to tell him that Högner and the Bavarian special delegate left immediately after the formal meeting with Clay. All present agreed that it was undoubtedly a Bavarian protest against the planned increase in Länderrat personnel, power, and authority.[23] But the issue was not left to die.

In executive session on April 2, 1946, Reinhold Maier explained the intent of his March 27 remarks to Högner's satisfaction, but he repeated his conviction that the General Secretary needed more power to perform the functions demanded of him. He said that if the minister-presidents failed to strengthen the Länderrat it would be an insult to the Americans who had placed the instrument in their hands. He moved a detailed resolution that, among other things, would have assigned executive authority to the General Secretary, for a period of six months, over transport, postal services, food, power, trade, economics, and weather services. It would also have created a *Direktorium*, consisting of the department heads in each of the fields named in the resolution, responsible to the General Secretary and empowered to issue directives to the Länder ministers. After much discussion, the minister-presidents agreed to only one item of the resolution, and this was a point on which Clay had demanded action a week earlier. They agreed to a special grant of authority to Rossmann until August 31, 1946, to appoint a commissioner (*Sonderbevollmächtigten*) for food. This official would be responsible to the General Secretary and would chair the Food and Agriculture Committee, but he would not have power to issue orders to the Land ministers.[24]

During the discussion of Maier's motion on April 2, Rossmann remarked that Germans were applying brakes while Americans were demanding greater speed.[25] On May 7, after a speech by Clay, Länderrat reorganization again assumed a major share of the minister-presidents' attention in executive session. Rossmann, obviously responding to pressure upon him, asked for more power. Karl Geiler of Hesse agreed that the Länderrat had to be strengthened, but said that he feared its tendency to assume full governmental functions in the zone. Reinhold Maier read the handwriting on the wall clearly, however. Württemberg-Baden had had much experience with Americans, Maier said, and had learned something about American intentions. Germans didn't want Württemberg and Baden thrown together, he said, but Americans forced it anyway. In the same way, they were going to force some kind of centralization under the General Secretary of the Länderrat, and Germans had better prepare recommendations to salvage as many of their own ideas as they could. According to Maier, Clay's remarks in open meeting showed that he wanted a unified food administration, a unified transport administration, and perhaps others as well. The upshot was an agreement to call a special meeting for about May 16, 1946, to work out a new statute for the Länderrat and its committees.[26]

The May 15–17 meeting of Land representatives to the Länderrat (*Länderbevollmächtigten*) at Birkenstein, Bavaria, provided a few improvements. But they fell far short of Pollock's interpretation of Clay's demands before the Länderrat on May 7. Pollock, who wrote to Rossmann on May 16, while the Birkenstein meeting was in progress, said he was disappointed that Clay's remarks had not brought more action. He reminded Rossmann that Clay had asked the Länderrat to improve its organization as early as January. Pollock said the minister-presidents should change their organization so it might deal directly with the administrators of public agencies, such as railroads and communications. They should assume control of interzonal relationships and present only major issues to the military government.[27]

Pollock's response to the results of the Birkenstein meeting was reportedly not in character with his previous actions and attitude. He seemed unusually cold and appeared to be under heavy pressure from Berlin.* He argued that the problem had become critical, that the Länderrat was acting too slowly. Either the minister-presidents would have to meet more often, or they would have to appoint standing representatives to Stuttgart and give them power to act as a directorate (*Direktorium*) for the minister-presidents. Gebhard Seelos, the Bavarian delegate, suggested that his government would be happy to reconstitute the Länderrat if OMGUS issued an order to that effect. Pollock became extremely angry. On the same day he had asked Clay to send Murphy to Bavaria for a few days to straighten out certain Bavarian attitudes on cooperation in the Länderrat. His response to Seelos was that OMGUS did not want to issue an order, but expected the Germans to go ahead anyway.[28]

Within a week, the Americans got what they wanted. In executive session with the minister-presidents, Pollock reviewed in detail the inadequacies of current German proposals and emphasized the need for assigning more power to the General Secretary. He said that Americans desired economic unity for all of Germany, but that the decision was not solely an American one. What the Americans needed now was a stronger zonal administration, and they could establish

---

* The Hessian Economics Ministry representative at OMGUS reported home as early as March 1946 that Clay had decided to push zonal government if he failed to get central agencies established. "I am sick of doing all the work for the Germans," Clay reportedly said. Cf. Staatsministerium Gross-Hessen, Der Minister für Wirtschaft und Verkehr, Vertretung Berlin, Economics Div., OMGUS, "Bericht Nr. 2 vom 6.2—10.3" [1946], copy in Geiler Papers, Staatsarchiv, Wiesbaden.

one without consulting the other occupation powers. However, they did not want to do this without German cooperation, and Pollock believed a German failure to respond would block the most hopeful possibility Americans saw for establishing interzonal German unity. After Pollock's remarks there was much debate, during which Reinhold Maier said: "We in Stuttgart feel the pressure exerted by the Military Government most directly. I beseech you to take a decisive step in this matter."[29] The end result was a proposal to adopt a new statute for the Länderrat, giving the General Secretary increased powers and—most critically—creating a standing Direktorium that had power to act in the name of the minister-presidents.[30] The minister-presidents approved the new statute on June 4, 1946, but only after further debate and after Rossmann reported on discussions with the RGCO in which he learned that Clay was angry about the failure to get agreement on economic unity and had decided to concentrate on zonal improvement in all areas ("die Zone auf allen Gebieten auf höchste Touren zu bringen"). The Direktorium met for the first time on June 21, 1946.[31]

## Interpreting the Länderrat's Early Role and Context

The foregoing account of the origins and early development of the Länderrat is significant because it shows the economic priority of Americans in 1945 and 1946. It shows the American interest in using the Länderrat as a stepping stone to broader economic unity. It shows that the American interest in economic problems assumed precedence over the grass-roots political interests expressed by Germans and Americans alike. The account also reveals the intense concentration of OMGUS on solving the problems caused by France's failure to accept central administrations. Accordingly, it serves to correct certain distortions that have crept into the current interpretations of the nature and the contribution of the Länderrat.

The official history of the Länderrat and publications of former participants in its work have portrayed it as a landmark of political reconstruction that contributed—by example and experience—to the establishment of the federal principle in postwar German politics.[32] The case is effectively presented, but it rests mainly on theory

and structural considerations, and on selected evidence that mini-
mizes the extent to which the Americans intervened to make the
Länderrat, and therefore the Länder, conform to the larger objectives
of the United States in Germany. Clay's own assessment of the Länderrat is noteworthy. He said that its most effective work was done in
1946 and early 1947. "By then, financial and economic matters were
handled by the bizonal administration and there was little left for
the Laenderrat."[33] More will be said later about the process by which
the bizonal agencies eclipsed the Länderrat, but in the meantime some
consideration of other factors that led to the Länderrat's foundation
may be in order.

*Keeping Pace with Other Zones.* Americans were impelled toward
zonal coordination by the fact that other occupation powers were
moving in that direction. Carl J. Friedrich has written that the
Länderrat was established "because American policy needed to
secure an equivalent to the unified German setup in the Soviet
Zone."[34] The Soviet Military Administration established central administrations (*Deutsche Zentralverwaltungen*) in the Soviet zone in
July 1945.* A US Group CC internal memorandum of August 15
described the Soviet-zone administrations and said they were likely
to "attain sufficient prestige to constitute a threat . . . by being a de
facto functioning national government and the only one."[35] The
British military government also established central economic agencies that functioned directly under military government supervision.[36]
Although there is no evidence that Americans viewed the British-zone
central offices as an immediate threat, they became concerned later
that the highly active British-zone administrations would supply the
key personnel for the national central agencies proposed at Potsdam.

*The Drive for Administrative Efficiency.* The formation of the
Länderrat resulted also from Clay's determination to have an effective, efficient, and smooth-running organization. He was convinced
that demobilization would undermine the American administration
in Germany, and he believed American public opinion would not

---

* Doernberg, *Die Geburt eines neuen Deutschlands, 1945–1949*, pp. 86–87; Krautkrämer, *Deutsche Geschichte nach dem zweiten Weltkrieg*, p. 57; Deuerlein, *Die
Einheit Deutschlands*, pp. 171–72. Deuerlein notes that the Soviet-zone agencies were
first announced publicly on September 11, about two weeks before Clay told his staff
conference about his plans to form the Länderrat.

support a long, costly occupation.* He was beset by organizational problems in the initial post-hostilities period. German government had collapsed nationally and locally. Policy plans did not provide for the kind of occupation that unconditional surrender required. The public debate on the Morgenthau Plan and the criticism of the military government in Aachen late in 1944 introduced uncertainties about the future. The problem of adjusting the military command structure of a combat army to the tasks of political, social, and economic occupation was made all the more difficult by redeployment, demobilization, and the dissolution of SHAEF, which necessitated organizational realignments; as a result of all this, local detachments were often left to their own devices to solve problems as they saw fit. Not to be forgotten, in this respect, is the United States commitment to a decentralized political structure, and the pragmatic political philosophy espoused by many military government officers. Also pertinent is the grass-roots, federalist political tradition out of which so many military government officers came.[37]

The initial phases of military government were characterized by the uncoordinated pragmatic efforts of local detachments to restore a semblance of order and security to community life. At the same time they attempted to arrest former Nazis and round up former military personnel; denazify the public service; confiscate Nazi and German army property and establish property control administrations; provide for displaced persons; enforce nonfraternization regulations; curb the activities of anti-fascist committees; provide accommodations and billets for American troops, and eventually for their dependents; adjust to the continuing personnel changes caused by redeployment, demobilization, and the variety of reasons that military men had for either entering or leaving the military government; and attend to a myriad of special tasks peculiar to their locality.[38]

Given the chaotic administrative situation in which the Deputy Military Governor for Germany found himself, and given his personality, temperament, and background, it now appears to have been

* In an interview on December 8, 1966, Clay told me that he had been influenced in his conclusion by Stimson, who visited Clay on the eve of the Potsdam conference and compared American policy and practice in the Philippines with what was likely to occur in Germany.

natural that fundamental changes in organization, command structure, and administration would occur early in the occupation. Lucius
D. Clay brought to the military government the experience of an
Army engineer and administrator who had had brilliant success in
a variety of projects requiring skill in organization and control. His
performance as Deputy Director in the Office of War Mobilization
and Reconversion under James F. Byrnes almost certainly got him
the appointment as Deputy Military Governor under Eisenhower.
His work under Byrnes and his earlier experiences as an Army engineer on construction projects in Texas, with MacArthur's headquarters in the Philippines, and with the Civil Aeronautics Administration
—not to mention his relief of the bottleneck in the port of Cherbourg
in 1944—showed him to be a man of great resourcefulness. He had
displayed an amazing capacity for long, hard work and a rather
intense impatience with anyone who did not match his powers of concentration or his own capacity for self-discipline. Clay gave the appearance of a determined, self-motivated man—prone to reject the
views of others if he listened to them at all, somewhat ruthless in
crisis, and generally autocratic.

Those privileged to read Clay's correspondence and cables for the
period from 1945 to 1949 will, however, discover in him a sensitive
and humanitarian quality that apparently escaped those who observed
him during these years. His humane qualities never emerged, in part
because Clay appears to have been personally close to few people and
because he led an extremely busy and lonely existence while in Germany. It is certainly not true, as Hans-Peter Schwarz suggests, that it
took the Berlin blockade of 1948 to change Clay's attitude toward
Germans.[39]

*Germans Must Replace Americans.* Whatever his true motives were
in 1945, Clay's letters to McCloy during the summer and fall of 1945
are filled with discussions of reorganization, of staff reassignments,
and of the need for administrative efficiency. He expressed concern
about the high cost of maintaining a large, permanent field force of
Americans in Germany, and he saw that redeployment and demobilization would eventually deplete the military government of its best
people, leaving the tasks in the field to the inexperienced, the oppor-
tunists, and the people who had "found a home" in Germany. Mind-

ful of the American federalist tradition, which he proclaimed regularly, imbued with an abiding faith in elections, and supported by the
Potsdam provision to restore democratic principles through elective
councils, Clay expressed his concerns in a positive program resting
on the basic grass-roots political approach so dear to Americans.
Writing to McCloy in September, he noted that the Potsdam agreement called for restoration of democratic self-government through
elective councils. "If the Germans are to learn democratic methods,
I think the best way is to start them off quickly at the lower levels."
Many officers will be returning to the United States in the coming
months, he continued, and "we will certainly not be able to staff a
large number of the local detachments with qualified men, even by a
vigorous recruiting program." The democratization program at the
lower levels, he wrote, "will help us reduce substantially the personnel
required for military government. . . . We can hardly withdraw the
local detachments until the officials appointed by us have been replaced by others selected by the Germans."[40]

Clay initiated a planned personnel reduction program, the speed
and thoroughness of which frightened the War Department's Civil
Affairs Division, for a time.[41] To replace the American personnel,
Clay pushed for German administrative and political reconstruction
and elections at the local level, again with sufficient speed and thoroughness to give pause to his own advisers and to bring protests from
the Germans.

*Local Elections.* Clay has told about his decision to hold community elections in January 1946, and of his advisers' reluctance. He
recalls teasing James K. Pollock, "a liberal professor of political science trying to restrain a hard-boiled soldier running a military occupation from promptly restoring the ballot to a people who had been
deprived of their right to vote." He only alludes to the fact that Pollock reflected what were apparently the views of the OMGUS Civil
Administration Division, and he seems to dismiss the issue by recall-
ing his remark to Pollock that "to learn to swim you have to get in
the water."[42]

But Pollock's reluctance was shared by the German minister-presidents and by lesser officials whom Americans had appointed. Though
many of them preferred to forget it later,[43] some Germans made a

determined effort to head Clay off. In November, the Hessian minister-president, Karl Geiler, reported to his cabinet that Hessian military government officials had told him they had a strict order from Berlin to hold elections in January 1946. He said he had tried to get a postponement, but the best he could get was a two-week delay. There is evidence that Hessian political party leaders supported Geiler's request for postponement, and there is further evidence that similar views prevailed in Bavaria and Württemberg-Baden. In fact, on December 4, 1945, the Länderrat petitioned OMGUS formally, asking for postponement of local elections and pleading both that rapid denazification was impossible and that there was insufficient time for parties to organize, to assemble candidate lists, and to campaign. The effort proved fruitless, however; Clay denied the petition. *Gemeinde* (village) elections were held in January. They were followed by elections in the *Landkreise* and *Stadtkreise* (roughly equivalent to rural counties and urban counties), then constituent assembly elections, and finally elections of representatives to the *Landtage* (state legislatures), all according to a schedule released by the military government in February 1946.[44]

At the same time it demanded elections, OMGUS reorganized its own administrative structure and that of the German civil administration in the American zone.* After much ground work had been done by James Pollock, Walter Dorn, and other Americans and Germans, General Eisenhower issued Proclamation #2 on September 19, 1945, creating the three Länder of the American zone.[45] At the same time, US Group CC underwent a major reorganization intended to facilitate coordination of military government activities with central German administrative departments and to prepare for the ultimate transfer of military government powers to civilian agencies separate from military forces. On October 1, 1945, US Group CC became the Office of Military Government for Germany (OMGUS); G–5, USFET, be-

---

* Lutz Niethammer, "Die amerikanische Besatzungsmacht zwischen Verwaltungs-tradition und politischen Parteien in Bayern 1945," *Vierteljahrshefte für Zeitgeschichte* (Heft 2, 1967), pp. 153–210, shows how the military government reorganization had widespread ramifications in Bavaria, and how it influenced even such important matters as denazification policy, the dismissal of Fritz Schäffer as minister-president, and the relief of General George S. Patton as commanding general of the Eastern Military District.

came OMGUS (USZone), and the Land detachments became Offices of Military Government for Bavaria, Hesse, and Württemberg-Baden. For military government purposes, the chain of command was thus effectively separated from normal military command channels.[46]

Four days later USFET released a schedule according to which Landkreis detachments would be relieved of their functional responsibilities by November 15 and district government (*Regierungsbezirk*) detachments by December 15, 1945. It promised that details would be issued later on the new civilian channels and on elections. These details went out through the new OMGUS channel of command on November 21, 1945, and were issued as directives to the Länder at various times before they became effective on January 1, 1946.[47] The objective was to transfer full responsibility and authority for state government to Germans, subject only "to such control as must be exercised by Military Government to accomplish the purposes of the occupation, and except as the exercise thereof would be in conflict with actions heretofore or hereafter taken by the Control Council of Germany or any central authority established by it."[48] Under these limitations, which are remarkable for their elasticity, each state received full legislative, executive, and judicial powers under the military government. The first two powers were to be exercised by the minister-presidents, the third by the ministers of justice. The directive issued by OMG, Hesse, summarized the details cogently: "Effective 1 January 1946, no orders or instruction concerning Military Government, with the exception of those necessary for the performance of the functions of [property control, Military Government courts, political activities, and certain details on denazification] ... will be issued by Regierungsbezirk or Kreis Detachments to officials at any level of civil government unless an emergency arises requiring immediate action."[49] The OMGUS instruction and the Land military government directives all described the role of the new Länderrat and emphasized that its coordinating function would be mainly in the "field of economics, transportation, communication, etc."[50]

Several observations may be pertinent at this point. Considering the factors of time and sequence alone, there is reason to doubt that OMGUS ever intended the Länderrat to be a capstone to a political program of German self-government starting from the grass roots in the Gemeinde and rising to the Kreise, to the Länder, and then to the entire zone. As a matter of fact, the local self-government program and the grass-roots elections were influenced heavily by the necessity arising out of redeployment and demobilization and by Clay's conviction that the United States would not support a long, expensive administration in Germany. Furthermore, the Länderrat came into being prior to local self-government and prior to elections of any kind, and it functioned as an administrative coordinating agency, principally for economic affairs. It drew heavy pressure from the military government whenever political interests—Bavarian states' rights, for example—came into play. We shall see later that the pressures applied by the military government in 1945–1946 were mild compared with those applied in 1947 and 1948. Though his is perhaps too cynical an interpretation, Harold Zink at least hinted at a basic fact when he wrote: "Perhaps the frustrations in the economic field led to a concentration on constitution-drafting and elections so that some progress could be reported by the Military Governor at an early date."[51]

Leaving aside theory and speculation altogether, we might take note of three important points: the people who created the Länderrat said they did so because efforts to establish central economic administrations had failed; Americans demanded more power for the Länderrat at least in part to lay the basis for full economic unity; and finally, Clay believed there was little left for the Länderrat to do once bizonal agencies assumed financial and economic authority. Herein may be seen the economic priority that led to the creation of the Länderrat at the same time that the military government granted political and administrative powers to German agencies at the state and local level.

# 4 | The May Crisis and a Field-Level Experiment

Clay has written that he and Murphy were still optimistic about future quadripartite government in the fall of 1945, but "by the spring of 1946 much of this optimism had gone."[1] The intensity with which Americans concentrated on strengthening the Länderrat in the spring of 1946 suggests more than simple pessimism as a moving force. Much additional evidence permits the conclusion that the multiplicity of unresolved problems confronting OMGUS and the vigor with which France pursued her objectives in Germany, coupled with Clay's impatience with the half-loaf solutions that normal diplomacy usually produces, created a crisis atmosphere in OMGUS.

## Central Administrations and Economic Unity Delayed

Overriding all other issues, and affecting most of them at least indirectly, was the failure of OMGUS to get the central economic administrations and to achieve the economic unity so vital to its zone, which was not self-sufficient. Clay's attempt in November 1945 to bring government-level pressure on France did not result in effective action. Acheson's letter of January 12, 1946, showed the matter to be in abeyance. He merely suggested the alternative of negotiations in the field, which Clay had already tried without success.[2] In February, Byrnes appealed personally to Georges Bidault to lift the French veto, but on March 5, 1946, the French cabinet voted unanimously to continue its firm position on the Ruhr, the Rhineland, and the Saar.[3] United States–French negotiations resumed on March 8, 1946, but more than a month later a War Department report to OMGUS on the discussions revealed little positive progress. In fact, the War Department reaffirmed Clay's authorization to go ahead and establish central agencies in cooperation with the Russians and the British, even though the State and War Departments knew that Clay had tried doing this before.[4]

Clay's initial proposal, on October 12, 1945, for UK/USSR/US field-level agreement on central agencies and its withdrawal on October 16 have been noted previously. Having received specific authority on October 21 to proceed in this way, Clay wrote to Sir Brian Robertson, his British counterpart, on November 13, suggesting that they invite their Soviet colleague to join with them in discussions.[5] There is no available evidence of British or Russian interest at the time. On December 21, at a meeting of the Allied Control Council Coordinating Committee, France rejected another proposal for a German central administration (communications and postal services), and Clay formally proposed its establishment on a tripartite basis. The British and Soviet representatives agreed, however, that Clay's proposal should be postponed.[6]

Other problems added to the crisis atmosphere. Since the end of the war, and despite Potsdam, rumors had persisted that France was encouraging certain Germans to work toward dismembering Germany permanently. Partial verification of the rumors reached OMGUS in April, when Pollock reported that French officials had approached Reinhold Maier—the American-appointed minister-president of Württemberg-Baden—seeking his collaboration on various schemes to separate parts of Germany.[7] On a less sensational level, but perhaps a more serious one, some Germans seemed to be gradually working out arrangements that recognized or at least took into account the zonal division. An example is a trade agreement of January 1946 between Hesse in the American zone and Thuringia in the Soviet zone. The two states had kept an informal liaison in 1945, made possible by personal visits and friendships among individuals in each of the two governments as well as by geographical proximity. In December 1945, the two states began formal discussion on a possible trade agreement. In January they agreed on the exchange of auto tires, dyes, medicines, pharmaceuticals, cellulose, and other products from Hesse for seeds, vegetables, agricultural tools, glass, artificial silk, optical glass, and other commodities from Thuringia.[8] When the treaty came to OMGUS, the latter approved it, but as an exception only. Berlin reportedly wanted to reject it at first, but OMG, Hesse, had committed itself so far that annulment would have proved embarrassing. In approving the agreement, OMGUS instructed OMG, Hesse, to permit no such treaties in the future. The head of the OMGUS Industry Division, Trade and Commerce Branch, explained to German liaison representatives in Berlin that OMGUS believed such trade agreements worked against its overriding purpose of forming an economic unit of Germany, that someday the Soviets would insist that trade between the zones was going fine, and that the need for central administrations would be thereby reduced.[9]

## The Problem of Food and Unity

The prospect of maintaining adequate German food rations seemed to be hopeless in March and April of 1946. In November 1945, Clay had promised the American-zone minister-presidents that the United States would maintain a 1550-calorie normal ration in the U.S. zone, even at the expense of U.S. imports. The army had been releasing supplies in Europe for German use since August 1945, and in January 1946, direct imports for German use began.[10] Nevertheless, on March 29, 1946, Clay told the Länderrat, with obvious regret, that the 1550-calorie ration could not be maintained. He said it would have to be reduced to 1275 calories, despite the U.S. commitment to ship 50,000 tons of grain to the American zone in each of the months of April, May, and June. That amount would support only a 1275-calorie ration, and the world food crisis—on which Clay commented in detail—made it impossible to predict what would happen beyond June 30. He asked Germans to improve their collection and distribution of food, and promised U.S. transport assistance. He suggested that the Länderrat appoint a food commissioner to serve during the crisis and that Germans reduce their livestock population to conserve food.[11]

The seriousness of the food crisis is illustrated in other ways. At Clay's request, Herbert Hoover's team, which was investigating the European food situation for President Truman, spent considerable time in Berlin and the American zone.[12] The record of Hoover's discussions with Germans in April, as well as much other evidence generally available, emphasizes the reality of the food crisis in Germany. In addition to supplying much detail on production, population, and economic bottlenecks, Germans reported to Hoover that of every thousand children born in Germany three hundred died during their first year of life.[13] To help publicize the Army's problems in Germany, Secretary of War Robert Patterson arranged a War Department–sponsored tour of Germany in March and April of 1946 for thirteen leading editors and newspapermen. The new director of the Civil Affairs Division, General O. P. Echols, who had returned from serving as Clay's chief of staff to assume the position, wrote to Clay that "the people back here seem to have a keen appreciation of our problems. . . . I think this group of newspapermen will do us a lot of good."[14]

General Echols also publicized OMGUS problems most actively in his new assignment. On April 6 he wrote Clay that he had had conferences at the War and State Departments to discuss the vital need for central agencies, and that he had met members of the press individually to try to show them that the level-of-industry plan could not work unless central agencies were established and that without central agencies the American zone would "become a large WPA project for the United States."[15] He had said essentially the same thing before a Senate committee on April 5, where he stressed the OMGUS position that it was France's policy on the Saar, the Ruhr, and central agencies that had led to the current difficulty. On April 17 Echols sent Clay a copy of a speech in which he had argued that establishing democracy on a 1275-calorie diet was impossible, that France had held up progress in Germany, and that the entire occupation was in jeopardy unless Germany was treated as an economic unit. He told Clay to note that "I am taking every opportunity to stress the importance of economic unity to Germany." "Keep up the good fight," Clay answered. "We can already feel its effects on American public opinion."[16]

General Echols's campaign is significant because it shows the impact of the food crisis, and points up the continuing OMGUS focus on economic unity and central administrations as the solutions. It also identifies French policy as the impediment. Although the OMGUS focus had not changed markedly since Potsdam, there were signs of a change in approach. A German assigned to the Economics Division of OMGUS, apparently to provide easy liaison in the event central administrations were set up, reported to his home base early in March 1946 that Americans in Berlin wanted to shift the discussion of central administrations from the Allied Control Council to government level. If they failed in the attempt, or if the discussions proved fruitless, OMGUS planned at least two moves: first, they would proceed to set up an independent government in their own zone and give it power to act (Clay reportedly said in this connection, "I am sick of doing all the work for the Germans"); and second, if the shift to government-level discussions proved fruitless, Americans planned to call a halt to dismantling.[17] The OMGUS pressure to convert the Länderrat into an effective economic administration was the application of the first alternative. Before turning to the second, it might be appropriate to review Clay's published assessment of the German situation in May.*

## Clay's May 26, 1946, Report

Clay's May 26 cable to the War Department is actually three different things: a report, a series of recommendations for action and policy change, and an effort to shift certain problems to government-level discussion. He reported that after a year of occupation the zones were almost airtight territories: four small economic units, of which only the British and Soviet zones could eventually become self-sufficient. Economic integration was becoming less each day; inflation was threatening; in the absence of economic unity "further dismantling would result in disaster"; the uncertainty regarding boundaries was a problem and, he continued, "the political or economic

* Clay, *Decision in Germany*, pp. 73–78, reproduces his cable of May 26, 1946, "almost in full." I have compared it with the original (OMGUS to AGWAR, May 26, 1946, WWIIRC 177–3/3) and found the deletions to be insignificant. It might be noted also that on May 22 the Hessian Minister of Economics and Transport, after intimate discussions with OMGUS officials in the Länderrat's Main Committee, reported to his cabinet colleagues on the German crisis, concluding that it was clear that a development approaching catastrophe threatened Germans if the current Control Council system continued. "Wir sind uns völlig klar," he wrote, "dass eine nahezu katastrophale Entwicklung bevorsteht, wenn das bisherige Kontrollratssystem weitergeht." Rudolf Müller, Memorandum, "Länderrat Stuttgart–Deutsche Krise," May 22, 1946, Staatskanzlei, Wiesbaden 1d20–30/lf.

separation of the Ruhr-Rhineland [from Germany] would be a world disaster.... We face a deteriorating German economy.... The next winter will be critical under any circumstances and a failure to obtain economic unity before next winter sets in will make it almost unbearable."

Clay recommended that the concept of economic unity, which had been agreed on at Potsdam, be quite firmly defined. De-industrialization and reparations policies assumed economic unity, he said, and "central administrative agencies are essential" to the latter. Common policies on foreign trade, finance, transportation, communications, industry, and food and agriculture had to be agreed upon and implemented nationally. Drastic fiscal reforms to reduce currency and monetary claims were needed, but could not be obtained on a zonal basis. Immediate decisions were needed on boundaries, especially on the Ruhr and Rhineland, which might be internationalized but, Clay felt, should not be separated from Germany.

Clay said that the time had come to establish a provisional government. He recommended that it be modeled on the Council of Minister-Presidents of the American zone, and suggested that if four-power agreement was not possible, the United States and Britain should merge their zones of occupation and make it clear that the other two zones might participate at any time. Clay believed that the British would accept his proposal for merger, and that the Russians would find it acceptable because it was in accord with Potsdam, "although in detail many difficulties will arise with Russian representatives." He expected strong French resistance, however. Thus, Clay made his original recommendation for bizonal merger under the assumption that France was the principal roadblock to unity. Furthermore, almost a month after his dismantling stop he still expected Russian cooperation in general, and believed France to be the nation on whom government-level pressure was needed to solve problems in Germany.

## The Dismantling Halt

Much has been written about Clay's decision to halt dismantling operations in the American zone on May 3, 1946. Two views in particular merit comment. The liberal and leftist critics of the occupation have seen in Clay's action another example of the influence of the anti-Morgenthau, soft-peace tendency of those who made and administered occupation policy after 1945. They see the halt in dismantling as a reflection of the decision to rebuild German industry by de facto rejection of the March 1946 level-of-industry plan and by circumvention of the Potsdam reparations agreement. According to their view, the event is an outgrowth of Clay's, Draper's, and Douglas's dissatisfaction with policy, of Calvin Hoover's and Byron Price's criticism of the effects of U.S. policy on the German future, and of the U.S. capitalist-industrialist impulse to reconstruct Germany and to be freed of the frustrations of the Potsdam agreement. There is, however, little to support this interpretation. In the first place, Clay's satisfaction with Potsdam and his determined efforts to translate the agreement into reality are hardly disputable. Second, his performance, especially on steel capacity determination, during the level-of-industry plan negotiations does not support the thesis that he sought to subvert rather than to fulfill Potsdam. Third, and more important, is the fact that German production in May 1946 was at such a low level that a stop in dismantling was not needed in order to retain plant capacity for increasing production. An OMGUS press release on May 4, 1946, reported that U.S. zone industries were operating at only about 20 per cent of capacity, or at about one-third of the capacity that would be left in 1948 after all reparations had been removed under the March 1946 level-of-industry plan. Thus, it may be noted, production in the U.S. zone could have increased by two-thirds without any change in the level-of-industry plan or any disruption of the dismantling program. Furthermore, the 20 per cent production figure had been achieved, in part, because firms were drawing resources from existing stocks of basic chemicals, metals, components, and half-assembled equipment rather than from current output. Current output was so disrupted, and the economy in such imbalance, that OMGUS doubted German ability to maintain even the 20 per cent figure.[18] Almost two years later, when Clay tried desperately to fight off congressional attempts to reduce or stop dismantling provided for in a revised bizonal level-of-industry and reparations plan—which Clay wanted to implement—he argued that shortages of fuel, materials, electric power, and manpower still prevented full use of permitted capacity for about three or four years more.[19]

The other major interpretation of Clay's dismantling stop is based upon hindsight rather than upon analysis of the context out of which it came. According to this view—which is widely held—Clay's action was the first sign of the open rift between United States and Soviet policies and thus the first manifestation of the cold war in Germany. The current descriptions of the immediate events leading to the suspension of dismantling seem to follow Clay's account, although Manuel Gottlieb does quote Coordinating Committee minutes, which Clay used but which are not open to private researchers at this time.[20] It is true that Clay announced his decision immediately after an exchange with General Mikhail I. Dratvin on import-export policies and their relationship to reparations. It is also true that the United States had been concerned about Soviet unilateral reparations removals from the beginning of the occupation,[21] and that the issue had reached a serious point on April 20, 1946, when OMGUS protested Russian dismantlement of the Deutsche Maizena-Werke, a food processing plant owned in part by Corn Products Refining Company in the United States. Clay insisted that neither the Potsdam agreement nor the level-of-industry plan called for removal of agricultural processing plants as reparations, and pointed out that such removals would make it impossible to establish an import-export balance. He wrote that "if this is to be the practice, I feel that reparations deliveries must be stopped until our program as a whole can be reviewed."[22]

Clay's account of the events leading to the dismantling stop shows that it was he who opened the discussion on April 8, by bringing up in the Coordinating Committee an item that was actually being considered at the lower Economics Directorate level. Apparently, however, his readers have overlooked the significant explanation he gave for doing so. He objected, he says, to financing reparations to the Soviet zone and to stripping the American zone of its already insufficient capacity "without getting the benefits which would come from amalgamation of all zones," thus implying clearly that he had no objection to reparations *per se*. At the next Coordinating Committee meeting he focused more clearly by asserting that "reparations was only one of the bricks that built the house" and that piecemeal solutions were impossible without general agreements. He quoted from the Potsdam agreement those sections calling for administration of Germany as a single economic unit, for a balanced economy, and for creation of central administrations. It seems apparent that he wanted to link the export-import question to reparations and thus to get at the larger questions that had troubled him since at least October 1945. Significantly, Clay states in his account that, while Dratvin remained silent after he had quoted these terms of the Potsdam agreement, Koeltz reiterated that France had reserved these matters for discussions on the foreign ministers' level. On May 3, after another attempt at agreement, Clay announced suspension of further reparations in the American zone, except for the 24 plants scheduled for immediate dismantling and delivery as reparations, some of which were already being loaded and shipped.[23]

Clay explained his dismantling stop in a press conference on May 27, 1946. A reporter asked about the halt in dismantling for reparations going to Russia, but Clay said the stop applied to everybody. "We simply announced, insofar as the U.S. Zone is concerned we are not going to dismantle any further plants except the ones that have already been allocated and committed as advance deliveries, until the economic unity on which reparations is based has been attained." Clay said the decision was urgent at this time because OMGUS was ready to declare another list of plants available for reparations. He had decided, however, that in the absence of economic unity and in view of the United States subsidy of about $200 million per year to Germany he would not dismantle any more at this time. If economic unity is not achieved, he said, the governments will have to decide what to do next.[24]

If the foregoing does not show adequately that the dismantling stop was an attempt to force a government-level agreement on the general economic features of the Potsdam decisions—a wedge designed to force economic unity and central administrations rather than a basically anti-Soviet measure—then a few other considerations might be in order. First, the American zone had comparatively little industry. An OMGUS report of 1947 states that the American zone (including Bremen) contained only about 19 per cent of the total German manufacturing capacity for domestic production and industrial exports.[25] Considering the Potsdam provision that only 25 per cent of excess capacity in the western zones was to go to Russia and Poland (and only 10 per cent without reciprocal payments), one must conclude that if this was a threat to the Soviets, it was indeed a weak one. As a matter of fact, it might be argued that, because the Inter-Allied Reparations Authority (IARA) got 75 per cent of the excess plants from the American zone and because France alone was allotted 22.8 per cent of such equipment by the IARA, the threat was considerably more serious to France than it was to the Soviet Union. Thus, if one continues to insist that the dismantling stop was a move against Russia, one must do so on the basis that Clay assumed Russia to be more desperate than France or that he did it unthinkingly. The first cannot be substantiated, and the second is so out of character that it appears ridiculous.

Clay's dismantling stop, viewed as an attempt to force a decision on economic unity, a balanced economy, and central administrations, is consistent with his previous actions and aspirations. It conforms with his earlier attempts to get such a decision beginning in October and November of 1945 and continuing into 1946. It conforms with his apparent decision, made after he failed to make headway in the Allied Control Council, to force the discussions upon the governments themselves. His statement that it affected everybody and the fact that it would hit France harder than it did the Soviets leave intact the view that Clay had been eager for the fulfillment of Potsdam and that he was convinced France was the chief obstacle. Lastly, his belief, expressed in the May 26 cable to the War Department, that the Soviets would support his recommendations (though they might quibble on details), and that France would resist them strongly, continues to make sense if the dismantling stop of May 3 is interpreted as it has been here.

## A Field-Level Experiment in Interzonal Unity

At the same time that OMGUS was working to improve the administrative structure of the Länderrat and Clay was trying to force government-level discussions on economics, OMGUS pushed a field-level experiment through the Länderrat in Stuttgart. The experiment, which began in December 1945, is not unrelated to the pressure OMGUS was applying to expand and strengthen the Länderrat. The fruits of the expansion were important to the experiment.

James K. Pollock, who was serving as the director of the RGCO, seems to have initiated the field experiment in mid-December.[26] He wrote to Robert Murphy that "the American-developed idea of getting the three Laender within the American zone together for conference and cooperation, might well be extended to other zones. It might be desirable from various angles for the American-zone Laenderrat to have a meeting for instance with the German heads of the administrative subdivisions of the British zone to talk over problems affecting both zones. Such a conference would provide an opportunity to demonstrate the advances made in our zone, and would be progressing one stage further toward the reestablishment of a government for the whole of Germany. If all the heads of all the Laender or similar administrative units within all the zones could come together, the four powers would then have a national council of states with which they could deal until an elected constitutional assembly existed. This would be promoting a federal and decentralized Germany which is in accordance with stated American policy. A meeting with the British or French counterparts could be staged in Stuttgart; one with the Russians in Berlin."[27]

*Stuttgart, February 6, 1946.* Pollock's proposal seemed to provide a glimmer of hope for ad hoc cooperation between the zones in the absence of central agencies, and it held forth the guarantee of the federalist development that was so basic to American political objectives. At any rate, on January 8, 1946, Clay told the fourth meeting of the Länderrat that a British- and American-zone minister-presidents' meeting to discuss mutual problems was being planned. There is evidence that much informal discussion occurred in January and that there was disagreement about whether the meeting should take place in Berlin, where at least some Americans wanted it held, or in Stuttgart, where the American-zone minister-presidents—and apparently Pollock—wanted it.[28] The difficulty arose, in part, because Americans wanted the meeting but asked the minister-presidents to take the initiative and extend the invitations.[29] Reportedly, everything was still in flux when Pollock informed Rossmann on February 1, 1946, that the Länderrat would be visited by two British-zone Oberpräsidents, Hinrich Kopf of Hanover and Robert Lehr of Düsseldorf, who would be accompanied by two British military government officers.[30] Pollock asked that the meeting receive no advance publicity, but told Rossmann he could report it later in his usual press conference. The confusion, the speed, and Pollock's advice all seem to be explained by the fact that the OMGUS Economics Division and the economics ministers of the U.S. and U.K. zones had been pressing hard for a bizonal economics ministers' meeting. OMGUS insisted that no such meeting could occur until the American-zone minister-presidents and the British-zone Länder chiefs had held an initial liaison meeting, and there is evidence that Clay and Robertson had personally arranged for the Stuttgart meeting on short notice.[31]

The meeting took place on February 6, 1946. Though no formal minutes were kept, there are sufficient personal notes, memoranda, and reports available to describe its nature.[32] Geiler, of Hesse, the major speaker for the American-zone minister-presidents, described policies and developments in the American zone. He said Americans wanted to build from the bottom up. First they established the Länder, then they joined them in a Länderrat, and "now they dangle before us the combination of the zones. Coordination between the British and American zones is the purpose of our meeting." He called upon Germans to dedicate themselves to German unity and suggested that the conference take a position on the future of Prussia. The two British-zone representatives followed Geiler, describing policies and developments in their zone and commenting on the future of Prussia.[33] The political nature of the opening remarks brought objections from the finance minister of Hesse, Wilhelm Mattes. He wanted to shelve political questions as premature and discuss economics. Minister-President Högner of Bavaria agreed, saying that he thought the military government looked with disfavor on a discussion of Prussia and other political questions.[34] Högner's Bavarian particularism may have influenced him more than fear of the military government's objections. In any case, he found it convenient to focus on economics rather than on politics, and he too advised silence on the latter and emphasis on the former. It is interesting that the British-zone representatives, who had received less political authority in their zone than their American-zone counterparts, were the most aggressive about political questions. Lehr reportedly said that the military governments had allowed them to meet and that it would be too bad if they missed their chance. Even on the matter of economic cooperation, he saw a chance for political action: "We have to search for temporary solutions in this area and proceed, step by step, to gain more ground."[35]

Despite the political speeches, the only specific recommendation to come out of the meeting was a resolution to call a meeting of bizonal economics ministers, an outcome that was in part influenced by the military government representatives in attendance. During the course of one of the sessions that was attended only by Germans, Pollock's letter of February 4, 1946, calling for a meeting devoted to economic questions, was introduced. The discussion had already moved into the realm of economics at that point, and a resolution to hold such a conference in Frankfurt, on February 19–20, passed easily.[36] The Germans also offered a joint resolution calling for uniformity of German government in the two zones, but opposition from the British military government representatives caused it to be watered down to a decision that Germans could present their personal views to the military governments of their respective zones.[37] The British reportedly did not want to take any action that might induce others to accuse them of venturing outside the established four-power structure.

Three additional bizonal meetings followed the Stuttgart meeting of February 6 in rapid succession: the conference of German food, agriculture, and economics officials in Frankfurt on February 26–27; the conference of American-zone minister-presidents and their British-zone counterparts in Bremen on February 28–March 1; and a similar conference, including British-zone political party leaders, in Stuttgart on April 3, 1946.

*Frankfurt and Bremen, February 26–March 1, 1946.* The Frankfurt meeting was the fruit of the OMGUS Economics Division effort. It had been delayed by the decision to establish political liaison first. Draper addressed the conference twice. He outlined some of the problems that needed solution and said that the main purpose of the meeting was to promote interzonal trade and link the economies of the two

zones more closely. He asserted that the American government regarded itself as the agent for the realization of German economic
unity as agreed upon at Potsdam.[38] Major E. H. Clay, a nephew of
the Deputy Military Governor assigned to Draper's division, seems
to have grasped most clearly the difficulties of the game being played.
He said that the planned interzonal economic cooperation must in no
way threaten the economic unity of Germany.[39] OMGUS apparently
wanted no piecemeal, ad hoc trade agreements similar to the Hesse-
Thuringian deal of January 1946 to come out of this meeting. They
hoped instead to enlist Germans in their program to realize the economic unity, balanced economy, and central administrations agreed
on at Potsdam. The conference passed a series of resolutions asking
for uniform price controls, production quotas, and transport regulations, and uniform policies on coal and steel production; for freedom
from travel restrictions that would hamper trade; and for an exchange
of permanent liaison representatives between the Länderrat and the
German Economic Council (Wirtschaftsrat) in Minden, British zone.
The food and agriculture subcommittee agreed to exchange information on agricultural production, to hold monthly experts' conferences
to agree on common actions, and to exchange liaison representatives
between the zones.[40]

The Bremen chiefs-of-state meeting on February 28–March 1, 1946,
concentrated more on political cooperation between the two zones
and was thus more in keeping with Pollock's original suggestion to
Murphy in December to expand the Länderrat idea to the other
zones.[41] Bavaria's refusal to send an official delegation is, perhaps,
adequate testimony of the meeting's political objectives, but it also
foreshadowed the difficulties Pollock's project would encounter. Reinhold Maier—by reporting the aside of a British general officer that
Germans were dreaming when they spoke of expanding the Länderrat idea to the British zone—leaves the impression that Britain
blocked progress at Bremen.* But the Germans in attendance also
disagreed among themselves.

Lehr and Kopf reported on their Stuttgart visit on February 6,

---

* Maier, *Ein Grundstein Wird Gelegt*, pp. 214–17. In his account of this meeting,
he says also that Clay gave his own plane and pilot for transportation, and he reports
Bavaria's lack of interest. He has the date of the meeting confused, however.

1946, and Lehr repeated a previous written suggestion he had made for expansion of the Länderrat. Maier made a strong plea for bizonal union, describing the Länderrat as a forerunner of a rump Reich government ("der Vorbote einer Rumpfreichsregierung") and calling for a form of super-Länderrat for the two zones.[42] The response proved to be divisive, however. British-zone representatives said they had not discussed the Länderrat thoroughly; one warned against making the area between the Rhine and the Elbe a political unit, and speculated that the Rhine and the Oder might be more viable boundaries; he also advised that they do nothing to exclude the Soviet zone. Lehr took this to be a criticism of his Stuttgart visit and defended himself vigorously, saying they had written off nothing at Stuttgart even though they had discussed political questions. Leaving aside further details, it is obvious that a significant number of British-zone participants wanted to move slowly, in part because the British military government had agreed to form a Zonal Advisory Council (Zonenbeirat) on February 15 and they wanted to await its establishment.* Wilhelm Kaisen, of Bremen, probably summarized the significance of this when he said that the Zonenbeirat had to be established in order that a larger unit might develop from it. Rossmann's report to the Länderrat, which said that the conference showed the need for a close union ("enge Verbindung") between the two zones as a forerunner of German economic unity, reveals more hope than information. Pollock, who attended the meeting, seems to have been encouraged enough to ask Clay to "invite the Russians and French to Stuttgart on a similar basis to that followed in the case of the British."[43]

*Stuttgart Again, April 3, 1946.* The Zonenbeirat having been in operation since early March, the April 3 Stuttgart conference of the Länderrat and Zonenbeirat officials followed logically from the results of the Bremen meeting. It is important because it shows the self-momentum of some of the German groups that were being asked to promote what was essentially an American-inspired plan. The Zonenbeirat had political party leaders as members, and Kurt Schumacher of the Social Democratic Party (SPD) and Konrad Adenauer of the Christian Democratic Union (CDU) used the gathering as an occa-

---

* Dorendorf, *Der Zonenbeirat*, esp. pp. 23–28. The Zonenbeirat met for the first time on March 6, 1946.

sion to promote party business.[44] The conference itself heard a full schedule of speeches and reports. It adopted resolutions stating that immediate economic unity was mandatory, that economic unity without political unity was not feasible in the long run, that Germany could contribute most to European recovery if it was united, that the German people wanted to contribute to European recovery, that Germany needed the support of the United Nations and the occupying powers, and that uniformity in Länderrat-Zonenbeirat structure was especially desirable. According to Rossmann the highlight of the meeting was the common desire for economic and political unity. Pollock's report to Clay listed two additional highlights: the desire of British-zone Germans to have an organization similar to the Länderrat, and the discussion of the critical raw material situation and its implications for interzonal trade.[45]

*Other Attempts.* Pollock's report outlined for Clay certain policy alternatives that presented themselves after the meeting. He stated that the Länderrat was a most flexible organization and that it could be adjusted in any of several ways. As one option, it could be reduced in function or eliminated. In that case it would have contributed three strong Länder to a German federation and could supply many excellently trained people with experience in democratic cooperation to the central agencies. A second option would be to have the Länderrat discontinue operations in one or more fields as central agencies were formed and to have it continue in other areas. Lastly, it could become a zonal government immediately instead of a central administrative and coordinating agency. For the time being, Pollock said he would approve no more top-level meetings until better liaison had been established between the Länderrat and the British-zone organizations —in any case not before June.[46] His decision permits at least four interpretations: (1) he wanted time for consolidation of gains; (2) he preferred his second option; (3) he was apprehensive that repeated top-level meetings might develop an even stronger German self-momentum and thus be harder to keep within the bounds of the American experiment; (4) he preferred for the time being to concentrate on similar exploratory meetings between American-zone representatives and their Russian- and French-zone counterparts. The first three are supported by evidence already presented, the fourth by a speech Clay made before the Länderrat on May 7, 1946, in which he said that Americans put special value on meetings between officials of their zone and others. He stated that he looked forward "to an increasing exchange of visits, correspondence and information," provided the Länderrat be kept informed so that it could keep the meetings under close control and report any results coming out of them to OMGUS.*

The available evidence suggests that the attempt to bring American-zone Germans together with Russian- and French-zone Germans bore little fruit. Dr. Rudolf Paul, of Thuringia, visited the Länderrat on June 4, 1946, fulfilling a promise of continued cooperation that he and Geiler had exchanged in April.[47] There was an American/Soviet zone conference on interzonal trade in Berlin on June 13–14, 1946, and a British/American zone food conference, attended by the two military governors, in Hamburg at the same time.[48] Sufficient activity was under way, nevertheless, to encourage imaginative and hopeful Germans to attempt a four-zonal minister-presidents' conference in Bremen in the fall, an event we shall return to in another context.

## A Summary and a Preview

The various alternatives that Clay, OMGUS, and the War Department had promoted with vigor in the spring and summer of 1946 did produce a measure of success. Elections were either under way or scheduled, as was the program for having the Germans write state constitutions. The Länderrat was a going concern, and it had been strengthened to cope with some of the economic problems of the American zone. The experiment in interzonal cooperation showed sufficient progress, especially with the British, to provide hope for its continued value. Clay's dismantling stop, though badly misinterpreted, did have the effect of publicizing widely the export-import deficit and the problems associated with reparations and restitutions. Even though Clay's May 26 cable brought no immediate restatement of policy, he continued to have a sympathetic listener in Secretary of State Byrnes, his former superior in the Office of War Mobilization and Reconversion. Supported by an American press that had

---

* Speech by Clay to Länderrat, May 7, 1946 (copy in Staatskanzlei, Wiesbaden, 1g06/01). This is the speech in which Clay also pressed the minister-presidents to strengthen the Länderrat and to give the General Secretary more power.

begun to describe some of the OMGUS problems, in contrast to its earlier inclination to emphasize mistakes, laxity, and denazification faults, and frustrated by developments in the Council of Foreign Ministers, Byrnes began to apply government-level efforts to the solution of the problems facing OMGUS.

Paradoxical as it may seem, the successes proved to be somewhat of an embarrassment. Unquestionably, the primary objective of OMGUS after the Potsdam conference had been to achieve the economic improvements that the conference had forecast: central administrations, a balanced economy, economic unity, and the assignment of necessary import costs as a first charge against export proceeds. It has been shown that these economic priorities of OMGUS were based on a number of factors: the need to be relieved of the economic restrictions of JCS 1067, the insufficiency of the zone it had been assigned to administer, the desire to reduce subsidies to Germany and thus to cut congressional appropriations, and in general the conviction that agreements such as Potsdam are made to be implemented until changed.

In working to achieve its primary aim, OMGUS tried a number of alternatives—at various times, with varying degrees of intensity, and with varying hopes of success, to be sure. Given the OMGUS focus— it appears to have been almost a fixation—the alternatives seemed to be consistent with each other and thus to constitute a coherent policy. However, once they were under way, some of these alternatives could and did gain a momentum of their own; and the results often diverged from the original aim. Consequently Americans often found themselves confronted with crosscurrents of activity that sometimes plagued them, sometimes embarrassed them, and sometimes forced them to exercise their power to keep the focus on their original main goal.[49]

Before turning to details, a preview might be in order. Clay's push for local and Länder elections and for self-government under constitutions encouraged particularism and states' rights interest groups that resisted his intention to promote economic unity and centralized economic decisions first at the Länderrat and then at the bizonal level. His creation of the Länderrat and the assignment of considerable power to it created a zonal particularism—almost a zonal political ethnocentrism—that became difficult to overcome in favor of bizonal cooperation and economic uniformity. It might be noted in passing that some of the particularism remained throughout the occupation, in no small measure because American theory and propaganda in favor of federalism supported it, even while American actions denied it. Clay's search for government-level intervention to solve economic problems and to break French resistance was a factor that influenced Byrnes to call for a formal merger of the zones, a move that reportedly threatened previous political developments in the American zone.[50] The experiment in interzonal cooperation, exchanges, and minister-presidents' conferences facilitated the development of German political forces and coalitions with interests of their own, some of which were quite foreign to the interests of OMGUS.

# 5 | Byrnes, Bizonia, and the Question of Policy

## The Paris Council of Foreign Ministers

The first session of the Paris Council of Foreign Ministers in April and May of 1946 saw the German question raised in two ways, even though Germany was not on the agenda. First, Byrnes formally presented the United States proposal for a four-power treaty that would guarantee a demilitarized Germany for 25 years. Second, Bidault formally presented the French position regarding the Saar, the Ruhr, and the Rhineland.[1] Since both had circulated before, the significance of the two proposals was not in their novelty but in their formal presentation, apparently for discussion and compromise. Vandenberg almost sighed into his diary: "At long last, we got around to Germany (the core of the whole European problem). . . ."[2] Byrnes, who hoped his own proposal "would quiet the fears of Germany's neighbors," seemed agreeable to negotiation, and proposed that deputies be appointed immediately to prepare material before the Council's planned second session in June.* Nevertheless, Molotov refused to accept Byrnes's proposal, and the first session adjourned on May 16. There has been much speculation on Russia's reasons for refusing. The cold-war scholars, such as Fleming,[3] see it as indicative of the deepening cleavage, aggravated especially by Churchill's "iron curtain" speech in March and by a host of other things. Clay, on the other hand, believed that the Soviets had no "definite, long-range plan in mind,"

* Clay, *Decision in Germany*, pp. 125–26. Clay lists the matters Byrnes wanted the commission to study. They are all related to France's demands and to central agencies.

and he implies that they were simply not ready for a full-scale German discussion.[4] In any case, the prospect of further discussions in June stimulated considerable activity in Washington and Berlin.

Clay's May 26 cable[5] was in fact a response to a War Department request for information. On May 23 the Department had cabled that German discussions would probably continue at the Council of Foreign Ministers meeting in June, and that it was working on plans (eventually to be submitted to SWNCC) regarding German policy in the short and long run.* It asked OMGUS for recommendations and comments on the German settlement and specifically on reparations, political structure, economic unity, and the disposition of the Ruhr and Rhineland. In replying, Clay commented at length on the German situation and recommended a bizonal merger, should other efforts fail.[6]

## Clay's Attempt to Reveal the May 26 Report

As the second session of the Council of Foreign Ministers meeting approached in June, Clay—having apparently received no response to his recommendations—proposed a press conference in Berlin to discuss some of the major items in the May 26 cable.[7] It is not clear just how much Clay wanted to discuss, but he intimated that the British military governor, Sir Brian Robertson, would probably make a press statement soon about British plans for a German government.

---

* AGWAR to USFET, May 23, 1946, WWIIRC 9–35/16. I have found no evidence of unusual activity, however, until this came along, and I suspect that Byrnes's need for material at the June conference spurred the decision to revive the whole question of policy. As a matter of fact, after the attempt at revision inspired by the Byron Price report and after the discouragement of it by Clay in December, the War Department seems to have abandoned its efforts to secure basic policy change early in 1946. It favored, instead, a series of limited statements that it would draw from the Department of State, as it had done in the case of economics and reparations on December 12, 1945. This approach is clearly stated by J. H. Hilldring in CAD, Memorandum for Assistant Secretary of War, Subj: Statement of U.S. Political Policies in Germany, Feb. 13, 1946, WWIIRC, WDSCA O14 Germany. Hilldring proposed to ask State for position statements on central government, political parties, the Ruhr and Rhineland, denazification, and the length of the occupation. This approach did not prove fruitful, however, in part because Assistant Secretary of War Howard C. Petersen asked for a War Department staff study which, when completed in April, tried to pass the buck to SWNCC. It was then held up and abandoned in June because State was involved in negotiations in Paris and, one suspects, because Hilldring had moved over to the State Department by then.

The cynic might see pure pressure politics in Clay's reference to British intentions, but there is evidence that Murphy reported to Clay early in May—after talks in London—that the British were prepared to continue to work for economic unity, but that they were also determined not to let the western zones deteriorate in the meantime.* Whatever Clay's motives may have been, Washington advised him not to hold a press conference on the subject. The War Department said that Byrnes planned to use the material in the May 26 cable at the coming Paris meeting, and that it believed Clay's prior release would reduce its effect. Besides, it advised, policy questions of such importance should perhaps not be released in a press conference. Clay might state, if he wished, that he had recommended to his government that the successful political program of the United States zone be urged for adoption in the other zones.[8]

## Paris Again

When the Council of Foreign Ministers returned to the German question in July, Molotov presented a prepared paper that went into detail on the German question.[9] He said, among other things, that the 25-year treaty should be for 40 years, that current programs for security against German resurgence were inadequate, that the Allies had reneged on Potsdam, and that Russia held firm to its demand for $10 billion in reparations from Germany. On the following day he talked about German recovery, the future of Germany and the Ruhr, the need to increase steel production, and the need to make peace with Germany.[10]

Byrnes's response to Molotov was limited and cautious, despite the apparent passion of his remarks. He responded to the first Molotov speech by defending current security measures, agreeing to a 40-year treaty, and arguing that reparations were linked to the import-

* This is probably also the source of Clay's confidence that the British would go along with his proposals on bizonal union. Cf. RGCO, Meeting with Liaison Officials, June 20, 1946, WWIIRC 39-2/11, which contains the following statement, apparently by Pollock: "Unless all four powers can agree to give effect to the Potsdam Agreement for treating Germany as an economic unit, there has to be some combination of zones—obviously between the U.S. and British Zones—for the British are now willing to put the two zones together, possibly before the end of the year."

export balance of payments in Germany. His response to the second speech was to invite all the other occupying powers to combine their zones in economic unity with the American zone. Although the invitation turned out to be a major step later, and although it is generally interpreted as an example of American initiative and determination, it was nevertheless a cautious response in its context. It was a far cry from the recommendations Clay had made in May, and it was a repetition—at one step higher in the government hierarchy to be sure— of proposals Clay had made repeatedly in the Allied Control Council since October 1945. It failed to touch on the proposals for a German provisional government, which Clay had wanted to announce publicly in mid-June, and it was, in Byrnes's own words, "brief because I wanted to keep attention focused on the immediate objectives of appointing deputies and putting them to work. I intended to withhold a detailed statement of our German policy until the Council of Foreign Ministers was prepared to act on the German question."[11] Molotov had, however, raised a whole spectrum of issues, on many of which Clay had made recommendations. It appears from this that Washington's primary aim at Paris had been to use the Byrnes 25-year treaty proposal as a wedge to open serious negotiations with France on the issues that had brought a stalemate to Potsdam. Byrnes's limited and cautious response to Molotov suggests that Washington was unprepared to go beyond that.

## Clay's Policy Statement of July 19, 1946

*Background.* Clay's subsequent action and Washington's response support the conclusion just stated. Clay had hardly arrived back in Berlin from Paris when he sent a detailed summary of U.S. policy to Washington, explaining that he had dictated it for release, but wanted to clear it first.[12] Clay's irritation with the way his earlier recommendations had been treated may be inferred from his decision to send the statement for clearance rather than as a recommendation. He was apparently also piqued by Molotov's appeal to public opinion.[13] Besides, Clay was convinced that the spring food crisis foreshadowed even more serious ones later unless something was done immediately. He had said in May that the "next winter will be critical

... and a failure to obtain economic unity before next winter sets in will make it almost unbearable."[14] However, probably the strongest influences on Clay at this point were the results of the field-level experiment. The momentum achieved in the Länderrat and in the interzonal conferences and exchanges was sufficient to warrant a U.S. statement that would, in fact, give American personnel and German officials under their jurisdiction a program with which they could appeal to Germans in the other zones.[15] In short, developments in the zone had gone so far that recommendations of the type Clay had sought in November 1945 were no longer sufficient. He had moved beyond asking for mere central administrations to the idea that a provisional German government modeled on the Länderrat was needed. Therein lies the deep significance of the zonal initiative of 1945 and the field-level experiment of 1945–46.

The point at which Clay decided that central agencies alone were not sufficient can be fixed rather clearly. On January 30, 1946, Pollock had asked the Länderrat to study central agencies and related matters.[16] The Hessian minister-president, Karl Geiler, responded with a detailed recommendation for a Länderrat-type structure in each of the four zones and a super-Länderrat made up of representatives of each of the zonal Länderräte and answerable to the Allied Control Council. The super-Länderrat could establish central administrations and appropriate subcommittees. Pollock sent the proposal to OMGUS, and Clay asked for a staff study on the proposal.[17] The Economics Division objected to Geiler's plan to establish a super-Länderrat as an intermediate body between the proposed central agencies and the Allied Control Council, but the Internal Affairs and Communications Division thought Geiler's plan had tremendous strategic value. It might make French acceptance easier in that it sought central agencies by voluntary association rather than by Allied Control Council decree. Clay did not concur. On March 15, 1946, he wrote on the study that "We must either have central machinery and then central government or go it alone. No hybrid creation will work —of that I am sure."[18]

Clay did accept the staff study's recommendation to establish an Interdivisional Committee on German Governmental Structures. He charged it with the task of preparing plans for central agencies and for the ultimate structure of German federal agencies. The committee completed a report on central agencies on April 29, 1946, and Clay approved it on May 1.[19] However, in almost complete reversal of his March 15 position, he added the following comment to his approval: "Actually, in view of the delay which has already taken place in establishing this machinery, I would prefer and recommend a direct move towards creation of a German government with administrative agencies reporting direct thereto and only the overall German government taking orders directly from ACC." One month later the committee had complied. It submitted another report, which stated that "the time has come to establish a central German government," and recommended a transitional stage modeled on the American-zone Länderrat.[20]

*Summary.* Clay's July 19, 1946, summary of United States policy is interesting because of the context in which he prepared it and because it is a convenient summary of Clay's interpretation of policy and practice a year after Potsdam and a year before the July 1947 directive was issued. It began with a general statement of U.S. objectives: the destruction of war potential, the reeducation of Germans to a liberal philosophy of life and government, the reestablishment of self-government under democratic procedures, and the eventual acceptance of Germany into the United Nations. The remainder dealt with specifics, which may be condensed as follows:

> The United States believes the Potsdam agreement must be implemented as a whole and not in part. The United States agrees to demilitarize, to denazify, and to remove equipment for heavy industrial production, using it as partial payment of reparations. Germany must be treated as an economic unit; indigenous resources must be used first to meet essential German requirements and second to produce exports that can finance essential imports.
>
> Under Potsdam, the United States proposes early German self-government based on elections and uniform democratic procedures. It favors a decentralized government with a large measure of responsibility left to subordinate units. It proposes reeducation of the population by Germans under Allied control, a vigorous trade union program, and freedom of press and radio at an early date. United States policy contemplates early establishment of a

provisional government to function until a constitution can be drafted by convention and ratified by the people.

On reparations, the United States adheres to the Potsdam agreement. Plants in excess of those needed for the level of industry are to be removed and made available to the Soviet Union, Poland, and the Inter-Allied Reparations Authority for further allocation. However, the United States accepted the level of industry as a minimum, and it will not agree to other forms of reparation that would be a further tax on the German economy. It cannot agree to reparations from current production unless there is a surplus not required to maintain the minimum standard of living agreed on or to finance essential imports. The United States has agreed to the level of industry on the condition that Germany be treated as an economic unit, and it is prepared to proceed toward the full accomplishment of the reparations program as soon as that condition is met.

The United States believes a common financial policy is essential to rehabilitate Germany and to prevent runaway inflation. It supports drastic fiscal reform to reduce currency and monetary claims, to revise the debt structure, and to provide a sound financial base.

The United States is convinced that transportation, communications, and postal services should be uniform, that maximum agricultural production and equitable food distribution require a central German administrative agency, and that similar agencies are essential for industry and foreign trade.

On political structure, the United States has consistently supported the Potsdam provision for central agencies. "However, it is convinced that the delay in establishing these agencies now makes it desirable to establish concurrently a provisional government to which these agencies would report." The United States favors a decentralized government, composed of a small number of states joined together in a confederation or a federal type of government, which would have sufficient power to achieve economic unity. The United States proposes to establish a provisional government, consisting of a Council of Minister-Presidents under the supervision of the Allied Control Council. The Council of Minister-Presidents would coordinate the work of central administrations and prepare a preliminary draft constitution for review by the Allied Control Council, for presentation to an elected convention for final drafting, and for submission to the German people for ratification. The constitution must contain certain minimum essentials of democracy, such as the principles of popular sovereignty and the rule of law, the requirement of frequent elections between at least two competing parties that are democratic in character, the guarantee of basic individual rights, and the limitation of central government powers to those agreed on by the several states.

The United States accepts the Potsdam agreement on the eastern boundaries of Germany. It will support the separation of the Saar and its economic integration with France, subject to adjustments in reparations to France and from Germany. The United States supports no other reduction in German territory because the German economy needs the Ruhr and the Rhineland and because the separation of these areas would promise difficulty in the future. The United States will, however, consider any rational plan for international control of the coal and steel industries in the Ruhr and the Rhineland.

The United States does not ignore the danger of a fully revived Germany. It supports the limitation on heavy industries—though not on peaceful light industries—until the United Nations are convinced that Germany is no longer a threat to peace. It is not interested in vengeance, and wants to conclude as quickly as possible the trial and punishment of war criminals and the leaders of the National Socialist party who led the Germans into a ruthless war of aggression. It recognizes the need for an occupation until Allied objectives have been accomplished, and it has agreed to a 40-year treaty of guarantee to ensure against a future German threat to peace.[21]

*Response in Washington.* Washington responded to Clay's summary, saying that it was good and clear, but that its implications were broad, and that the State Department was studying German problems for Byrnes's use at future foreign ministers' meetings.[22] One gets the impression that Washington did not want Clay to release the statement, but preferred not to say so directly. Clay apparently had the same impression: he said he did not want a policy study, just a concise summary based on OMGUS operations, and that unless instructed otherwise he would publish it within a week. On August 12, 1946, Washington clearly instructed Clay not to publish the summary because it contained statements on the early establishment of a provisional government and on eventual admission of Germany to the United Nations, neither of which was firm and definite U.S. policy. Furthermore, U.S. policy was under study for possible revision in the areas of heavy-industry removals, financial planning, frontiers and boundaries, and internationalization of the Ruhr and the Rhineland.[23]

In confirming the instruction, Clay wrote that it would leave the military government at sea. He had argued, at various times during the episode, that the summary was based on OMGUS operations, "on original directives as modified by the passage of events," and on basic policy "now being clarified by interpretation."[24] In short, Clay's interpretation of policy as required by administration, the accumulated instructions Clay had received by cable, by letter, and during personal visits in the course of a year of occupation, and the flow of events in Germany had led OMGUS to move in certain areas well beyond what Washington assumed policy to be.

Confronted suddenly with Clay's plan to publish a concise summary of American policy and practice in Germany, Washington responded in what was in many respects a most logical way. It remained sensitive to the possible effect upon United States public opinion of a policy summary that obviously went beyond JCS 1067, which was still the official policy directive for the occupation and was not yet under the heavy attack it was to receive in 1947 and later. Washington remained sensitive also to the possible effect on relations with other occupation powers of a summary that went beyond the Potsdam agreement in some respects. Clay could argue, of course, that French vetoes and Soviet actions had stripped Potsdam of some of its most vital and crucial features while the United States poured money into its zone and still faced the prospect of utter chaos. In the meantime, OMGUS had moved to counter French and Soviet actions, to bring them to accept the Potsdam agreement, and to prevent hunger and chaos in its zone while Potsdam was in abeyance. In effect, Clay's argument was an admission that neither JCS 1067 nor Potsdam applied fully to the activities of OMGUS from at least the spring of 1946 on, if not somewhat earlier.

Washington would not agree to publication, nor would it agree to partial publication, since omission of certain items and problems would be a tip-off that United States policy was not definite or was under revision on those particular issues. It proposed instead that an existing State Department study committee be charged with a complete review of German policy; its report would be based on Clay's statement, on consultations in Berlin and the theater, and on other materials and studies the committee would develop. Four days later, after having objected to this committee approach, Clay wrote that "I have, of course, thrown it [the July 19 summary] in the waste basket in view of my instructions."[25]

## Byrnes's Invitation to Unite Zones

In the meantime, the invitation that Byrnes extended to the Allies on July 11, 1946, to merge their zones with the U.S. zone brought about an even more rapid flow of events in the theater. It also placed OMGUS in the rather awkward position of having to choose between two alternatives it had pushed earlier with vigor and élan. Clay's instructions, which he received from Washington on July 18, called for economic merger of the zones and stated that the proposal was intended not to divide Germany but to speed economic unity. The decision to avoid concurrent political union is implied throughout the instructions, but it comes out sharply in the statement that the United States government had approved the May 1, 1946, OMGUS plan for central German agencies and in the omission of any reference to the June 1, 1946, OMGUS plan for a German government. It will be recalled that OMGUS had, on Clay's urging, prepared the latter as a substitute for the earlier plan.[26] OMGUS officials, who understood the instructions as well as the significance of the omission, began immediately to worry about the political program under way in the United States zone and about the plan to expand the Länderrat idea to other zones.

Even before Britain formally accepted Byrnes's invitation on July 30, 1946, Clay wrote to his British counterpart that "Somehow in the picture I do have to preserve the political structure in our zone and protect the delegated policy [sic] which we have given German officials. This may offer some problem in perfecting administrative detail but I am sure that it is one we shall be able to settle." At about the same time, Pollock warned Clay of future trouble.[27] He said the

British zone administration was far behind the American zone. The British had released little power to Germans, and had established their own central administrations. Union, he continued, would be a drag on United States zone efficiency, and, because of administrative problems, he foresaw little economic benefit from merger. He did not expect the French to come in, and he did not want to dig "deeper the ditch which separates the eastern zone from the western zones." It is apparent that Pollock had also tried to solicit Walter Lippmann's help in Washington, because Lippmann wrote him on July 29, saying he had found little sympathy in Washington for Pollock's hope to establish a good "regional underpinning" before the establishment of central agencies. According to Lippmann, the White House, the War Department, and the State Department were concentrating on economics and administrative unity. Neither Clay nor Murphy had been able to convince Byrnes that there is a "vital connection between what has been done at Stuttgart and what is to be done with Germany as a whole."[28]

OMGUS had helped to bring on the problem it now faced. The OMGUS effort to bring government-level pressure to bear on the problems of economic unity and so on, though slow in producing results, was now bearing fruit. The publicity given to the spring food crisis, the Hoover visit and its gloomy predictions, the press visits, the efforts of General Echols and others, all began to affect German policy. No doubt, a host of other factors was influential also, including the increasing cold-war suspicion of Russia after Churchill's Fulton speech, the speeches and resolutions in Congress on hunger and starvation in Germany, and similar publicity by church groups and others.[29]

Given the kind of backing that economic merger received from official Washington and from the public, the economic fusion of the American and British zones moved rapidly. In August and September of 1946, officials of the two zones negotiated agreements creating bizonal agencies in the fields of economics, food and agriculture, transport, finance, and communications. A government-level financial agreement between the U.S. and Britain, arising from bizonal cooperation in the field, produced the Bevin-Byrnes Bizonal Fusion Agreement of December 2, 1946, effective January 1, 1947.

## Bizonal Fusion

The agreements establishing the five bizonal administrations, signed separately as contracts between German officials during September and October of 1946, were negotiated under strong pressure from the military government to impel the Germans to move rapidly, but to avoid political union. Wolfgang Friedmann, who participated in the negotiations on the British side, wrote later that "Americans, in pursuit of their general policy of presenting at least the appearance of a revival of German self-government, persuaded their British colleagues to have the agreement signed by the German representatives . . . ."[30] But the OMGUS plan was more complex than that.

Clay advised OMGUS negotiators to "*feel* our way to final agreement—always remembering our desire to preserve political structure in [the] U.S. Zone; to avoid political union; and to permit Germans to do the work."[31] The desire to avoid political union caused problems with Germans later, and it soon became clear that the Americans wanted to do nothing that would prejudice four-power unity in the future.[32] Clay and Draper both stated the American position quite clearly to the Germans. Clay told the Länderrat on October 8, 1946, that political unity was not opportune because it would make future unification difficult.[33] Draper, speaking at the third session of the Bizonal Executive Committee for Economics in Minden on October 11, 1946, said the United States wanted economic and political unity for all of Germany, "but if we try to move too fast and join politically as well as economically we are likely to destroy the entire effort. We want, if possible, to have the Soviet and French Zones join in economic unity and then a provisional government given [sic] for all of Germany. If a provisional government for these two Zones on a political basis were set up at this time it might later retard or make impossible the major objective."[34]

Despite the American insistence that Germans themselves draw up and sign the agreements, the minister-presidents of the American zone received only a brief comment on the project from Clay on August 6, 1946. General C. L. Adcock, who was the Assistant Deputy Military Governor, and Draper presented the details to the Länderrat

Direktorium in Stuttgart on August 12, just three days after British and American agreement had been reached in Berlin. Adcock and Draper brought American functional experts to the briefing session and asked the Germans to begin discussions immediately after presentation of the plan. Adcock said the contract for food and agriculture should be ready for submission to Berlin in two weeks, for transport in three weeks, and for the other agencies with comparable dispatch.[35]

Draper, in outlining details, said that the bizonal administrations should have executive officers empowered to take day-by-day action "to carry out decisions for both zones," without benefit of legislative control. There was no bizonal legislature, and the military government expressly prohibited creation of one under its policy to avoid political union. However, it should be noted that German voters in the American zone had elected constitutional assemblies on June 30, 1946. According to an American schedule released early in 1946— again contrary to the more cautious advice from Germans and some advisers alike—the constitutional assemblies were to have Länder constitutions drafted for OMGUS review by September 15, so that ratification and elections could be completed no later than November 3, 1946.[36] Though extremely important to the present discussion, it hardly needs to be said that the election-constitution schedule of OMGUS went forward amidst much propaganda about the tremendous progress American-zone Germans were making toward self-government and local responsibility.

The contract establishing the Bizonal Economics Administration (Verwaltungsrat für Wirtschaft), signed in Frankfurt on September 11, 1946, translated General Draper's ideas into administrative and institutional reality.[37] The agency, to be located in Minden (North Rhine–Westphalia), was empowered to issue directives to all participating Länder and existing administrative agencies in the U.S. and British zones. It was allowed to issue directives on foreign trade, production, distribution, internal trade, price controls, industrial standardization, statistics, and more—the only apparent limitation being existing and future quadripartite agreements. Especially noteworthy is the contractual provision that the Länder were obliged to carry out the decisions of the Executive Committee for Economics and that the latter was empowered to control the execution of its decisions and regulations through its own administrative agency.

Heinrich Köhler, the Württemberg-Baden Economics Minister and Deputy Minister-President, later described the intentions of the contract's negotiators. He said he was surprised to learn that some Germans later questioned the committee's mandate to legislate by directive.[38] Having participated in the negotiations, he recalled that they had never even discussed the idea that the committee might not have power to legislate. On the contrary, Köhler had formed the opinion at the time that the military government would grant special legislative authority to the bizonal agencies, and he was continually strengthened in this view by representatives of the military government. The negotiators were of the opinion that directives ("Gesetze") agreed on by the Executive Committee for Economics would have to be promulgated ("veröffentlicht") by the Länder.[39]

During the negotiations, several Germans and at least one American (Colonel William Dawson, the acting head of the RGCO after Pollock's departure from the theater), raised the question of the relationship of the bizonal agencies to the scheduled American-zone constitutions and governments in the Länder. General Draper was asked the question by the Bavarian representative on August 12, but he referred it back to the Germans. Dawson heard the same question from a German delegation immediately after the meeting with Draper and Adcock on August 12, 1946. Two days later the Württemberg-Baden cabinet affirmed the Länderrat's superior legislative power, declared the minister-presidents to be responsible under military government mandate for administration in the Länder, and stated that ultimate, exclusive legislative power would be lodged in the parliaments being created in the American zone. Reinhold Maier explained the background of his cabinet's position to Dawson. Many German officials, he said, "have the impression that the functional officers in Berlin are suspicious of and are shocked by parliamentary procedure." Germans also believed that the plans for executive agencies conflicted with American plans to build democracy from the bottom up.[40] On August 14, 1946, Dawson reported the German concerns to Adcock and raised similar questions on his own accord.

Adcock answered with a long letter, explaining that the Länderrat would still play an important role, but he also referred to its temporary character.[41] Adcock's answer and a host of other attempts at clarification did not satisfy the minister-presidents and the German politicians in the American zone, for they had been led to believe that they were on the way toward responsible government, at least on the Länder level.[42] The lines were drawn, and OMGUS gradually found itself pushed into the position of having to choose between its zonal democratization program and its bizonal economic interests. Before this occurred, however, certain other political developments came to the fore.

## Byrnes's Stuttgart Speech, September 6, 1946

Byrnes has said that he had not intended to make a detailed statement on German policy until the Council of Foreign Ministers was prepared to act, but he changed his mind. Encouraged by Clay, he went to Stuttgart on September 6, 1946, and made a speech that has since been heralded—not without the assistance of Washington's instructions to the Information Control Division of OMGUS on how to interpret it[43]—as a landmark or watershed of American policy formulation for the occupation period. The forces behind Byrnes's change of mind are complex and significant.[44]

Although Clay says he did not write Byrnes's Stuttgart speech,[45] a careful comparison of it and Clay's July 19 policy summary shows that the speech was almost certainly drafted from the letter, with the following exceptions: Byrnes added some points concerning the bizonal developments; his reference to the United Nations was more general than Clay's; he talked about security and control of the Ruhr and the Rhineland, and did not mention internationalization of the coal and steel industries as Clay had (although Byrnes did not rule out internationalization); and he made certain additions and deletions to meet the needs of the occasion and the form of presentation. The similarity between Clay's letter and Byrnes's speech was so close, however, that the letter supplied the exact phraseology in certain places.

The temptation is great to say that what Clay could not get through official channels in July and August, he obtained through personal contact with Byrnes in September; or to speculate on Clay's natural drive to realize his objectives when frustrated, the way he had been in August. Leaving all speculation aside, however, there is sufficient evidence to indicate the pressures on Byrnes. Molotov's Paris speeches certainly left a void that Byrnes had been unprepared to fill at Paris, partly because Washington was concentrating on the 25-year treaty and its impact on France. Clay's repeated requests and recommendations for policy clarification (in view of Potsdam's being held in abeyance) dating back to October and November of 1945, and certainly to May 1946, plus the impact of the July 19 letter itself, were certainly in the background of Byrnes's speech. The difficulties Americans were experiencing with their German counterparts in bizonal negotiations most certainly influenced Clay to appeal to Byrnes in Paris for some kind of statement on Germany's political future, its economic prospects, and its general situation as seen from the American point of view. Likewise, the American experiment in interzonal exchange at the minister-president and Länderrat level required a political statement to renew the vitality it had had early in 1946 and, perhaps, to permit American-zone Germans to present it more effectively to their counterparts in the Soviet and French zones.

Byrnes's decision to deliver the address in Stuttgart, therefore, had a special significance. USFET and American-zone military government headquarters were in Frankfurt; OMGUS headquarters were in Berlin. But on Clay's advice, Byrnes chose Stuttgart, the seat of the Länderrat. From Stuttgart, American-zone Germans worked to expand the Länderrat idea. From there they tried also to limit the rapid establishment of bizonal economic agencies by insisting on their own executive and pseudo-legislative authority. In a sense, Byrnes's speech was meant for German ears. It asked them to look at the American program and put their faith in American actions, even though some of the actions might appear regressive to an outsider. In another sense, the speech was for Clay and OMGUS. It verified publicly the decisions and interpretations Berlin had made or received since the beginning of the occupation, and it put an official stamp of approval on OMGUS actions that had been taken with reference to reparations,

German self-government, economic rehabilitation, and so on. In this context, Clay's own words are revealing. In discussing the U.S. Group Control Council's manual for the military government, which had been suppressed in Washington during the Morgenthau intervention in German policy, he wrote that reading the manual "now will show that it deviated little from American policy *which was to develop for Germany and to be proclaimed first by Secretary of State Byrnes in in his Stuttgart speech.*"[46] B. U. Ratchford said essentially the same thing: "It [the speech] crystallized and made official the policies which the U.S. Military Government officers had been hammering out, slowly and painfully, in Berlin during the previous year."[47]

The American-zone minister-presidents, whose close contacts with the Regional Government Coordinating Office had given them an insight into OMGUS plans and operations before the Byrnes speech, were probably more impressed by the physical presence of Byrnes, by his entourage, and by the ceremonial pomp of the occasion than by the specific details of the speech. They were naturally exhilarated that American policy had been proclaimed publicly before them, and they issued a statement thanking Byrnes and the American people for whom he spoke, and emphasizing some of Byrnes's points that they thought gave Germans new encouragement and hope.[48] They also grasped the opportunity Byrnes had thrust upon them.

## The Field-Level Experiment Again: Bremen, October 4–5, 1946

Ever since the initial American zone/British zone conferences of February, March, and April 1946, the program seemed to have stalled, even though Clay had encouraged it on May 7, and Geiler had suggested a four-zonal minister-presidents' conference on June 4.[49] According to Thilo Vogelsang, the British-zone Länder chiefs resolved to work for such a conference on August 11, and there is evidence that Geiler and Rudolf Paul, of Thuringia in the Soviet zone, were making similar plans about the same time.[50] The available sources do not record adequately the reasons, but they do show that there were difficulties. Högner and Maier had enough reservations in June to dissuade Geiler. Apparently some Social Democrats in the British zone opposed a meeting, even though Wilhelm Kaisen, a leading Social Democrat, took soundings in other zones. Vogelsang also shows Hinrich Kopf, a Social Democrat, to have been interested. The difficulties are obvious, however, from the records of an executive session of the Länderrat on the day Byrnes spoke in Stuttgart. In fact, the RGCO asked the minister-presidents to decide definitely whether they wanted a meeting, and whether the military government should call Bremen to ask Kaisen to withdraw his plans. The minister-presidents said they wanted a meeting, preferably somewhere in the American zone; and in order to encourage the French to accept, they asked that it not be held in any government seat. They did not want to undertake anything against Bremen, however.[51]

Four days later, Adcock and Dawson told the minister-presidents that all misunderstandings were cleared up, that Bremen would issue the invitations, and that the military government would like to see the agenda. They said OMGUS did not feel instructions were necessary, because the meeting would probably deal with a number of general topics. Dawson said he believed the minister-presidents could handle the situation. Immediately thereafter, the minister-presidents agreed in executive session that the meeting place would be Bremen, that the date would be October 4 and 5, and that the agenda would include reports of Länder chiefs on administration in their zones, exchange of information regarding coordination, and discussion of general interzonal questions.[52] Kaisen, who said later that the Byrnes speech gave the Bremen meeting its agenda, issued the invitations on September 16.[53] He reported that the time was probably not ripe for definite accomplishments ("greifbare Ergebnisse") and that he had therefore decided to keep the agenda brief, informal, and somewhat unstructured. The three items he mentioned were the same ones the American-zone minister-presidents had agreed to on September 10, 1946.[54]

Although the proposed meeting bore the marks of a German initiative, and although Clay reportedly presented it as such to the Allied Control Council Coordinating Committee, Americans worked hard behind the scenes to bring it off. They used their facilities to speed communications; they provided Kaisen with air transportation to make personal visits; and they offered air transportation for the delegates themselves.[55] Nevertheless—perhaps as a result—the conference remained a rump; neither the French-zone nor the Soviet-zone representatives came. The Soviets, who had originally shown interest, changed their minds at the last moment. The French-zone Germans were denied permission to attend by their military government. They arranged to send an observer anyway, and Carlo Schmid asked Geiler to send him an informal report after the meeting on those things that would not appear in the record. The conference reportedly left two chairs vacant to symbolize the open invitation to the other two zones to participate at any time.[56]

The Bremen conference of October 4–5, 1946, is interesting for a number of other reasons. First, it passed resolutions that were sent to the military government for presentation to the Allied Control Council; second, the discussions revealed certain disagreements among the Germans; and third, it stimulated activity for political union of the bizonal agencies, which Americans and British wanted to avoid.[57]

The conference adopted resolutions calling for a four-zonal liaison office, for politically chosen administrative committees for the bizonal agencies, for Allied Control Council action to form a German Länderrat (representative body of the states) and Volksrat (popular representative body), for implementation of a ten-point program of four-zonal economic cooperation, for Allied Control Council action on currency reform, for the appointment of a denazification study committee, and for a German court that would try Nazi criminals under German law.*

The conference disagreed on denazification and on the nature and the method of promoting political union. Geiler had prepared a *Denkschrift* on August 4, 1946, based on a redraft of the original plan he had sent to the military government in February. The redraft was actually the work of Walter Strauss, who later believed his handi-

---

* This last point came into the meeting unexpectedly, because the Allies had just released Schacht, von Papen, and Fritzsche (see *Süddeutsche Zeitung*, special edition, Oct. 1, 1946, p. 1 for details), and there was debate on what, if anything, ought to be done with them. There was a rather sarcastic exchange between several delegates on whether the three should be tried in German courts, and if so, which ones. The speakers were obviously needling each other about previous public statements they had made regarding war crimes trials. The details are unclear, but the discussion was certainly spirited.

work had exerted considerable influence on future political developments in Germany.[58] In a major address to the conference, Geiler
presented the gist of the paper and proposed a four-zonal liaison
office to exchange information on laws, draft legislation, and so on;
a four-zonal legal committee; and a four-zonal cultural committee.
Some delegates objected to the detail of the proposal, while others
remarked on the failure to specify the need for liaison on land reform,
agriculture, and other economic matters. The American-zone minister-
presidents' concern for bizonal political coordination kept creeping
into the discussion, and Maier perhaps stated the problem most
clearly. He said that some Allies wanted immediate economic unity,
but that he and his colleagues were convinced that economic unity
without political unity was a fiction ("Wir [sind] uns klar . . . dass
es eine wirtschaftliche Einheit ohne die politische Einheit nicht
gibt.")[59] The upshot was three resolutions: the vague one on a four-
zonal liaison office, the one asking for politically chosen bizonal administrative committees, and the one asking the Allied Control Council to form a German Länderrat and Volksrat. The request that the
Control Council set up the representative bodies perhaps reveals the
disagreement among Germans as well as anything else.

The exchange on denazification shows additional disagreement.
The Hessian Minister for Political Liberation, Gottlob Binder, gave
a report and made a plea for uniformity, especially since bizonal
agencies were being established and staffed. Landespräsident Drake
of Lippe in the British zone, said they were finished with denazification and did not want to begin again. Maier admitted that denazification had been a problem, but he argued that it was a prerequisite
for American concessions, especially those included in the Byrnes
speech.* The discussion deteriorated rapidly into a series of accusations and counteraccusations. To his credit, Kaisen had the presence
of mind to close further discussion and to continue to cut off (some-

---

* Maier's exact words: "Erst nachdem der Amerikaner gesehen hat, dass wir
die Gesetze nicht nur beschliessen, sondern durchführen, und zwar in sehr gründ-
licher Weise durchführen, war die Byrnes-Rede in Stuttgart überhaupt möglich." He
was in for a rude awakening a month later, when Clay gave his famous denazification speech to the Länderrat and in fact threatened to take the program back under
the military government if he saw no clear evidence of improvement within 60 days.
RGCO, Speech of . . . Clay, Delivered at the Fourteenth Meeting of the Länderrat,
Stuttgart, 5. Nov. 1946, Bundesarchiv, Koblenz, Z1/65.

what abruptly at times) further vilification of this nature throughout the entire conference. His action, which came on the first day, probably saved the conference from becoming a complete failure.

The conference action that had the most immediate impact was the decision to demand political control over the bizonal administrations. Though the issue was to come up again and again in the future, its immediate effect was to increase the American problem of trying to stave off political union while it pressed hard for economic union. It has been noted in another context that just three days after the close of the Bremen conference, Clay told the Länderrat that political union of the two zones was not opportune, and that Draper elaborated more fully on the reasons on October 11, 1946.[60] But these remarks were only a prelude to the full debate that developed soon thereafter.

# 6 | Democracy or Necessity: An OMGUS Dilemma

## Elections and Constitutions

By the end of 1946, Clay's program to establish a degree of local and state self-government based on elections, constitutions, and the principle of political responsibility had progressed significantly. Village elections had been held in January, Landkreis and Stadtkreis elections in April and May, Land constitutional assembly elections in June, and combined constitutional referenda and Landtag elections in November and December.[1] The new state legislatures met in Munich, Wiesbaden, and Stuttgart in December 1946 to organize and to elect minister-presidents.

By January 1947, the American-zone Länder had been urged and guided by a benign military government to establish the institutional framework of a democratic government. Lest there be doubts about the military government's benignity at this point, an exchange of cables between Clay and the War Department in October 1946 should be sufficient to dispel them. Washington objected to portions of the draft Länder constitutions, especially to Bavaria's. Clay defended the constitutions, saying they were drafted with OMGUS advice and consultation, that existing drafts were the best that the military government could get and still expect successful ratification, and that the state constitutions could be reviewed again when a federal constitution was written. Should the War and State Departments still object, Clay—through Assistant Secretary of War Howard C. Petersen, who was in Germany—asked that the issue be taken to the President.[2] The military government's assurances against abuse of these institutions by nondemocratic elements took various forms: denazification and its attendant disabilities and disenfranchisements; the military government's review and supervision at every stage in the development itself; and its continued observation and control under the broad powers of the occupation. These powers were specified in an OMGUS directive of September 30, 1946, and in Clay's letters to the presidents of the constituent assemblies, approving the constitutions for submission to the people for ratification.[3]

The September 30 directive and Clay's letters of approval reveal the immense gap between the form and the essence of German self-government in 1946. Among other things, they listed the restrictions that would continue upon civil governments, or—what amounted to the same thing—the powers reserved to the occupation despite the constitutions. All matters regarding Germany that were the subject of current and future international agreements were beyond German reach. Likewise, German constitutions were limited by current and future four-power policy decisions, laws and regulations, and by basic policy decisions of the US/UK Bipartite Board affecting central agencies. The constitutions did not affect the rights of the occupation forces to remain, to preserve peace and order, and to resume full occupation powers in the event that the purposes of the occupation were jeopardized. From the U.S. viewpoint, these purposes included establishment of an independent judiciary, a decentralized government, economic unity, and such elements of democracy as elections, democratic competition between parties, and protection of the basic rights of the individual. The occupation forces also reserved all powers contained in "such proclamations, laws, enactments, orders, and instructions of U.S. occupation authorities as continue in force or shall hereafter be promulgated."

The military government's reserved powers on all matters subject to international, bipartite, or unilateral decisions in the future are especially important to the present discussion. Less than a month after the September 30, 1946, directive, and before the constitutions were ratified, OMGUS issued two letter directives defining the relationships of the new bizonal agencies and the projected Länder governments.[4] In essence, the directives foresaw no change in the existing political and legal structure, but they provided bizonal agencies with "sufficient power to permit the prompt and efficacious conduct of their affairs." They thereby reduced the potential power of the Länder.

It may be noted, in summary form, that at least three major developments in Germany—all of which OMGUS had urged and promoted at various times—were converging rather sharply as 1946 came to a close. On the one hand, the American-zone Länder had constitutionally anchored legislatures and minister-presidents who were moved by conviction, supported by electoral mandates, and inspired by American propaganda to represent the will of their constituents. On the other hand, bizonal agencies had been created and empowered by contractual agreements to solve certain interzonal problems uniformly by executive and administrative action under grants of authority from the military government, rather than from their constituents. Lastly, the minister-presidents of the American and British zones had established an ad hoc conference which, among other things, proposed to promote German political control of some sort over the bizonal agencies.

## Bizonal Agencies and Land Constitutions

OMGUS was clearly concerned by this course of events and by the cleavages that had manifested themselves late in 1946, which Edward Litchfield—the former head of OMGUS, Civil Administration Division—described as "not only puzzling but also politically embarrassing." Clay thus took the occasion of his regular visit to the Länderrat on January 8, 1947, to explain in detail the relationship of the bizonal administrations and the new American-zone political institutions as OMGUS interpreted them.[5] In briefest summary, the issue boiled down to two questions with numerous ramifications:

(1) Could the minister-presidents, who were duly elected and constitutionally responsible to their Landtage, legislate by decree, under the special authority that the military government granted them as members of the Länderrat in those areas that required zonal and/or bizonal legislative uniformity, without at the same time causing irreparable damage to the constitution?

(2) Could a Land cabinet minister (e.g., the minister of economics), as a member of a bizonal agency, use the special authority granted him by the military government to issue directives and regulations that his own minister-president would be obliged to implement and enforce, with or without Landtag sanction?

Clay's explanation, which is a very interesting discussion of the questions raised by American policies, proved no more satisfying to Germans than had numerous previous attempts by lesser officials. The minister-presidents, with various assistants and consultants, sought clarification in a closed session of the Länderrat immediately after Clay's formal presentation. But the meeting ended in general confusion, which a German source (apparently Rossmann) diplomatically attributed to a probable "poor translation" of Clay's speech.[6] That it was more than a problem of language is evident from what followed: the minister-presidents took up the issue with their cabinets and Landtag factions; it was a central issue in closed Länderrat and Direktorium meetings on January 22 and February 2, 11, and 13; and it was the predominant theme of an American zone/British zone minister-presidents' conference held in Düsseldorf on January 25, and another held in Wiesbaden on February 16–17, 1947. In addition, it was the subject of much disagreement and discussion within OMGUS itself.[7]

## Bizonal Political Coordination

*The Minister-Presidents at Minden and Düsseldorf.* The Bremen minister-presidents' conference of October 4–5, 1946, had resolved to promote political coordination over the bizonal central agencies. On January 8, 1947, during the Länderrat meeting held after Clay's speech, Wilhelm Kaisen suggested this bizonal approach as a way to solve the problem of jurisdiction in the American zone.[8] The minister-presidents had not been idle after October 4–5. Nevertheless, their main effort came after Clay's speech, and it intensified after they were provoked by the results of a meeting in Minden late in January. Once the minister-presidents' conference took up the issue in earnest, they broadened and clouded the American-zone controversy considerably.

Late in January the American and British military governments arranged a meeting to announce specific programs arising out of the Bevin-Byrnes Agreement and to work out plans for increasing coal production. The meeting shifted from Minden to Düsseldorf and then to Essen for its sessions. It was attended by the military governors and functional experts on the Allied side, and by the minister-presidents of the two zones, their economics ministers, and their labor ministers on the German side. There were meetings with trade union representatives, management representatives, and others. Clay and Robertson announced government programs that would support increased coal production. The various sessions developed plans to increase miners' pay, restore pensions, establish housing priorities, provide increased food rations and special coal rations, increase consumer goods in general, and institute the inevitable public information program to gain public support.[9]

The conference program included a special meeting of the Bizonal Executive Committee for Economics, at which Draper and others spoke. Draper explained the Bevin-Byrnes Fusion Agreement of December 2, 1946, and emphasized the long-range importance of the Committee. He said that it was the primary agency for economic reconstruction in the two zones, and that it would serve as an example and a magnet for the rest of Germany. Perhaps, he speculated, its success would induce the other two zones to merge with Bizonia. Draper was, in fact, suggesting that the bizonal economics program might foster cooperation among the four zones, even though the minister-presidents had tried unsuccessfully to do this at the political level in Bremen. But there was more. Draper obviously had not altered his views of August 1946 on the authority of the bizonal agencies, and he stated that the decisions of the Executive Committee for Economics must be carried out by the Land ministries and the minister-presidents. Responding to a question from Minister-President Kopf of Lower Saxony, Draper's British counterpart observed that the economics ministers had greater power as members of the Executive Committee for Economics than they did as Land ministers. Draper, in turn, emphasized that they represented not only their Länder, but also 40 million Germans; they represented their constituents *and* the general interest.*

---

* "Bericht über die Sondersitzung des Verwaltungsrats für Wirtschaft in Minden am 25. Januar 1947," Staatskanzlei, Wiesbaden, 1d06/01. It might be noted here that the Executive Committee for Economics concluded at its next meeting that it had the power to issue regulations with the force of law ("Rechtsverordnungen mit Gesetzeskraft") for the two zones. It agreed not to try to force the issue on principle, but to proceed by individual cases. See "Bericht über die 8. Sitzung des Verwaltungsrats für Wirtschaft ... 31.1.1947," *ibid.*

The minister-presidents met in Düsseldorf for a conference of their own. They agreed to establish a bizonal office to study questions related to the peace (the "Friedensbüro"); they agreed—contrary to the views of the military government—that Länder representatives on bizonal committees would have to be instructed by the Länder; and they agreed that coordination of bizonal agencies should be the responsibility of the minister-presidents.[10] They apparently planned to meet again soon, preferably before the British-zone plans for a structural change in the Zonenbeirat could be completed.[11] Rossmann tried to arrange a conference in Garmisch for February 13, but the attempt failed. The minister-presidents finally met in Wiesbaden on February 16 and 17, and they were greeted by Minister-President Stock with the statement that they were actually continuing their Düsseldorf-Minden-Essen meetings of January.[12]

*Continuation in Wiesbaden.* The first resolution of the Wiesbaden conference was a request that the military government authorize the minister-presidents and the chairmen of the bizonal administrations to meet in Stuttgart on February 28, 1947. Though not stated in the resolution, there is considerable evidence that the minister-presidents sought means to undergird and coordinate the bizonal administrative agencies with a legislative council, and there is some evidence that they hoped to work out an ad hoc arrangement for political control if the former failed. Secretary Rossmann's letter of February 19, enclosing the Wiesbaden resolution and requesting approval for the meeting, is in the OMGUS papers. Attached to it is a memorandum of a telephone conversation between Clay and Colonel Charles D. Winning, the acting director of the RGCO, showing that Clay said "No," and that he wanted to talk with the American-zone minister-presidents.[13]

*Clay's Veto.* The meeting between Clay and the American-zone minister-presidents was held in Berlin on Sunday, February 23, 1947.[14] A number of topics were touched on, but the question of political coordination and relationships between the Länder and the bizonal agencies overshadowed all others. It was not clear whether the minister-presidents had power to issue laws, decrees, and directives without consulting their parliaments; whether the Landtage had the power to reject decisions of the bizonal administrations or of the minister-presidents acting in the Länderrat as agents of the military government; or whether the Land governments were required to implement bizonal decisions. Reinhold Maier, the Minister-President of Württemberg-Baden, speaking in the course of the conference, summed up the sentiment of the minister-presidents by reporting a sense of confusion that threatened to halt the entire legislative process in the Länder.[15]

Clay, obviously determined to achieve a settlement, outlined American attempts to get central administrations and economic unity. He said frustrations motivated OMGUS to form states in the American zone and to push for bizonal fusion. In effect vetoing the Wiesbaden resolution, Clay said that the minister-presidents' plan to achieve political coordination over the bizonal agencies, though desirable in itself, would have to be set aside. He alluded to the impending Council of Foreign Ministers meeting in Moscow and insisted that the economic agencies would have to be made to work, for the time being, without a political apparatus.* He emphasized, however, that they *had* to be made to work, and thus shifted over to the question of relationships between the Landtage in the American zone and the bizonal agencies. He asserted that he had a heavy responsibility to the American taxpayer: the United States had already committed 40 million dollars to further German industrial development, and OMGUS had asked the U.S. Congress to appropriate another 300 million dollars for bizonal food purchases. In return, OMGUS had to show Congress that it was developing industrial capacity in Germany, and Clay said that such a demonstration depended upon effective economic union of the two zones. "We ... cannot ... , after having determined something is essential to the economic revival of Germany ... , submit the question to a State Parliament. We would be in the impossible position of either having to disapprove the action of a State Parliament or else having desirable uniform laws not passed because one Parliament

---

* In 1949 Litchfield told an interviewer in the OMGUS Historical Division that "we had to say that it was not a political organization, it was only an economic organization.... Clay insisted on that right to the end, even to people close to him on it. He knew, he must have to himself recognized [sic], that this was really a political organization and not an economic organization." See Hubert G. Schmidt, *U.S. Military Government in Germany: Policy and Functioning in Industry* (Karlsruhe, 1950), p. 114.

refuses them. . . ." Returning to the same topic later in the meeting, Clay continued: "We cannot permit a proposal to be defeated by one parliament which is absolutely essential to the success of our economic program, and I certainly don't want to be in the position to have to disapprove a parliamentary act. I am sure it is more democratic never to submit that act to parliament." Let it be said that Clay realized immediately how far the rapid exchange and the tension had carried him. He suggested that perhaps the topic had been exhausted, unless someone else wanted to add something. Thereupon, the discussion turned to less controversial items.

At an RGCO liaison officers' meeting on February 27, 1947, the American officer from Bavaria commented that the Germans who came back from Berlin were confused. Nevertheless, Christian Stock, the Minister-President of Hesse, seems to have grasped the meeting's significance. Reporting to his cabinet on February 26, he said that final disposition of the problem of bizonal political coordination would have to await the results of the Moscow conference. In the meantime, he continued, the Länder governments should not hinder the bizonal agencies. Germans would have to work for harmony among the Länder, the bizonal agencies, and the military government. The meeting requested by the Wiesbaden minister-presidents' conference would not be held, and all preliminary arrangements were being cancelled.[16]

On March 1, 1947, a revision of military government regulations stated: "At every level of government, legislative power is subject to the superior authority of Military Government, the Control Council, the Bizonal Agencies, and any other authority which may later be established by the Control Council or by Military Government." OMGUS Proclamation No. 4, issued the same day, listed international agreements, quadripartite legislation, and "powers reserved to Military Government in order to effectuate basic policies of the occupation" as limitations upon the constitutional governments of the Länder, thus repeating by proclamation the restrictions of the September 30, 1946, directive and those contained in Clay's letters to the presidents of the constituent assemblies in the American zone late in 1946. The proclamation stated further that legislation in the reserved fields, when approved by OMGUS and promulgated by the minister-presidents, had the force of law as it had had prior to the establishment of constitutionally elected Landtage and minister-presidents.* On March 12, 1947, the chairman of the Bipartite Economic Control Group notified the chairman of the Bizonal Executive Committee for Economics that "no authority exists in German Civil Government which can issue a law binding on both Zones" and that the bizonal agencies could only recommend legislation to the two military governments. The latter would promulgate the appropriate legislation, each in its own way.[17]

In sum, economic necessity had prevailed over democratic idealism. In the interests of bizonal economic cooperation and the more rapid economic rehabilitation it promised, the constitutionally elected governments in the American zone had to accept virtually unlimited restrictions on their authority and freedom of action; the field-level experiment to achieve cooperation among the four zones and coordination at the Länderrat–minister-presidents' level was being held in abeyance on orders of the military government; and the military government had restated its own determination either to legislate in the reserved fields (which were open-ended), or to relegate such power to the minister-presidents, as they had done prior to the establishment of constitutionally elected legislatures and executives. The military government also denied that bizonal agencies had legislative power, which at least some thought they had by contract. The only apparent consolation to Germans was the repeated assurance that everything was only being held in abeyance until after the Moscow conference.[18]

The way in which and the degree to which the military government continued its control over German developments, despite the forms of constitutional government, varied from issue to issue and problem to problem, depending upon such circumstances as availability of personnel, the personal inclinations of the people involved, the degree of pressure from the United States, the intensity of public interest at home, and the priority of competing interests. The struggle over denazification may serve as an additional model.

---

* OMGUS, Subj: Revision of MGR Title 5, Section B, "German Legislation" AG010.6 (LD), March 1, 1947, WWIIRC 32–1/11; U.S. Dept. of State, *Germany, 1947–1949*, pp. 157–58. The similarity to Article 48 of the Weimar Constitution did not escape German attention.

## The Politics of Denazification

*Early Policies and Studies.* Denazification began as a program to seek out, purge, and punish the evil forces that gave rise to Hitler's *Reich.* But other OMGUS programs soon began to affect it. First, the plan to establish responsible and democratic German governments inevitably brought Germans into the picture. Second, the plans to reduce American personnel made administration of the program by Americans impossible, especially after it was expanded in August and September of 1945. In the search for a more thorough cleansing, successive early military government denazification directives attempted to close more and more loopholes, and thus the program became broader in scope and more difficult to administer. The SHAEF directive of November 9, 1944, essentially required removal of all persons from public office who had joined the Nazi party before Hitler became Chancellor in January 1933. The July 7, 1945, USFET directive listed 136 mandatory removal and exclusion categories and stipulated that membership in the Nazi party prior to May 1, 1937, or holding office in certain of its affiliated organizations was cause for mandatory removal or exclusion from "positions of importance in quasi-public and private enterprises," commercial, agricultural, and financial institutions, and from positions of "more than minor importance" in public affairs. The August 15, 1945, USFET directive expanded and clarified the program by defining persons in "positions of importance in quasi-public and private enterprises" to include those in private business, the professions, and those of "wealth and importance" who were unemployed. The September 26, 1945, Military Government Law #8 extended denazification over the entire German economy except agriculture, and made Germans themselves criminally liable for failure to remove Nazis from positions other than ordinary labor, except when expressly authorized to desist by the military government.[19]

Implementation of the denazification directives proved to be most difficult. In part, this was due to the directives themselves. At least two of them were drafted under great pressure for speed and thus contained many vagaries in addition to features that needed constant revision by regulation.* The immense scope of denazification, the lack of sympathy with which individual Americans and Germans approached the program, the attempt to apply categories as objective criteria for judging human action, the conflict in the field between desires for efficiency and the need for removing some who could make operations more efficient if they stayed—all these and a host of other factors added to the difficulties. Clay, perhaps, covered them all when he reported to Hilldring in Washington that even if the War Department were to send him 10,000 Americans for the purpose, he could not denazify the U.S. zone and keep it denazified. The War Department seems to have agreed, for it had in fact already admitted publicly that redeployment required gradual assignment of denazification functions to German screening boards.[20]

The military government undertook a systematic study of denazification for the first time in November 1945. At the time, the Land governments in the American zone were all working up denazification laws of their own.[21] But the impetus for the study apparently came from OMGUS, Legal Division, which objected to the variety of approaches to denazification used by OMGUS divisions and suggested formation of a planning agency. Clay thereupon approved the establishment of a Denazification Policy Board, saying it should "formulate a complete overall program for denazification in the U.S. Zone with as much responsibility as possible placed on German officials for the long range."[22]

The Board which appears to have been important enough to include OMGUS division heads and general officers only, was directed to formulate the program and submit its report by December 31, 1945. In the meantime, no division or office was to issue directives to

* Griffith, "The Denazification Program," p. 82, says the August 15 directive was known in the military government as the "Butcher of Augsburg Directive," because Clay ordered it drafted after visiting Augsburg and hearing that a butcher there favored Nazis in meat distribution. Russell Hill, *Struggle for Germany,* p. 71, says Law #8 came as an aftermath of the Patton affair. He said it had been considered before, but it was drafted and published hurriedly "in order to appease public opinion in the States, indignant at the reports from Bavaria." Hilldring to Adcock, Nov. 15, 1945, and Adcock to Hilldring, Dec. 7, 1945, WWIIRC, WDSCA 014 Germany, analyze the difficulties of interpreting Law #8; and a list of the law's weaknesses is contained in OMGUS, Public Safety, Staff Study draft, Feb. 1946, Subj: Strengthening Enforcement of Law No. 8 and Proposed Amendment of Regulation No. 1 Thereunder, *ibid.,* 120–2/15.

the field and no four-power agreements were to be made without the Board's concurrence.[23] The Board's report, which was not finished until January 15, 1946, reviewed in detail the basic weaknesses of the existing denazification program, making five major criticisms: it resulted in arbitrary effects in certain cases; it failed to reach certain active Nazis; it lacked German participation; it lacked long-range projection; and it lacked integration with other OMGUS programs. As a basis for its recommendations, the Board defined the relationship of denazification to the broader objectives of the occupation. The basic objective, it said, was to reduce Germany as a threat. Disarmament and demilitarization did this in part, but the military government had also to eliminate the fundamental conditions that made the German menace possible. The best way to assure a peaceful Germany, the report said, was to create "a free democratic society in which political and economic power rests upon a broad popular base, undominated by fascist or militaristic elements." Basic German attitudes had to be changed and "political and economic power [had to] be shifted from the ruling groups in German society during the Nazi regime to other groups in whom we may justifiably have greater confidence." Denazification could assist in the shift, and "the accomplishment of this aim [would involve], in essence, a political and social revolution." The report said that Germans had to participate in the program, in part to avoid creation of a group of martyrs and social outcasts who would be fair game for agitators, and in part to give Germans themselves a stake in the program and its political objectives. It also said that the punishment of wrongdoers was a secondary aim of denazification.[24]

The effort to secure German participation in a program to meet such revolutionary American objectives produced a number of confrontations on denazification that were matched only by the showdown between bizonal power and states' rights described above. As in the latter case, the issue was extremely complex, especially because OMGUS was insisting on elections and responsible German governments at the local and state level at the same time that it was trying to bring Germans into line with a basic American objective.[25]

*The Law for Liberation from National Socialism and Militarism.* While Americans were studying their program, the American-zone

ministers of justice completed a draft denazification law for the zone
on December 22, 1945. The Länderrat accepted it on January 8,
1946, and transmitted it to the military government. On January 30
Pollock wrote Rossmann that the draft was at OMGUS headquarters,
that OMGUS had a committee of its own, and that the Länderrat
draft required changes to meet the objectives of OMGUS.[26] Pollock
said that Charles Fahy, chairman of the Denazification Policy Board,
wanted to meet with the justice ministers and their experts in Stuttgart. Thus began the series of negotiations that produced the March 5,
1946, Law for Liberation from National Socialism and Militarism.

The meeting requested by Fahy took place on February 11–13,
1946. Fahy told Germans that their law must include the list of presumptive guilt categories contained in Allied Control Council Law
#24, released on January 12, 1946.* He argued that the categories
would make administration of the law easier. He said they assured that
all Nazis would go through the tribunals, because if a person fell within any of the listed categories he was presumed to be guilty until he
proved his innocence.[27] In short, Americans insisted that denazification be based on presumptive guilt, and that people be removed
from office until the presumption had been rebutted in individual
hearings. OMGUS negotiators elaborated their views in detail. They
said that Law #24 reflected the Potsdam agreement, that affected individuals were to be removed until they could prove clearly and con-
vincingly that they did not fall within the presumptive guilt categories of the law, and that OMGUS was determined to remove the
leadership group from German cultural, political, and economic positions of importance and to install a new leadership group in its stead.
("Es handelt sich um eine Art Umwälzung, die Ablösung der bisheri-
gen Schicht, die am Steuer sass, durch eine neue Schicht.") If Germans failed to accept the basic provisions regarding removals, lists,
and so on, Robert Bowie threatened, the military government would
continue to denazify on its own, though reluctantly and perhaps less
successfully and fairly, he said. With the threat went a warning: de-

---

* It is interesting that the December 20, 1945, preliminary report of the Board
criticized the presumptive guilt categories of the July 7, 1945, directive rather
severely. It appears obvious that the Allied Control Council law affected the position
of the Board later, but I have been unable to determine just when, why, or how.

nazification was a mandatory precondition to German reconstruction. ("Die vollständige Bereinigung Deutschlands sei eine unerlässliche Voraussetzung für den Wiederaufbau.")[28]

Following the February 11–13, 1946, meetings, Germans engaged in intense discussions at various levels. The Hessian cabinet members, for example, disagreed among themselves on the use of a catalog of guilt categories, on the law's automatic features, and on many of the technicalities of implementation. They voted first to refer the matter back to the Länderrat for further study, but finally accepted the American demands in hopes that German administration of denazification would be more equitable than that of the Americans.[29] According to the RGCO director, the long, strained discussions almost crumbled the foundations of cabinet government in Hesse and Württemberg–Baden, but "the Bavarian Lion stood firm."* Walter Dorn later wrote that Geiler "never ceased to emphasize the extreme reluctance with which he had signed the Law, and Dr. Meier [sic] ... made no secret of his intellectual dissent."[30] Although some features of the German draft were incorporated into the final law, the available evidence shows sufficient disagreement among Germans to indicate that it could not have passed as it did without American guidance and/or pressure.[31]

On March 5, 1946, the minister-presidents and Clay joined in an impressive ceremony in the Munich Rathaus to sign the Law for Liberation from National Socialism and Militarism. Thereafter, all Germans over eighteen years of age had to fill out questionnaires (*Meldebogen*) and German tribunals (*Spruchkammern*) tried the denazification cases. The German and the Allied press gave much attention to the early cases. There was much criticism and speculation on the ultimate success of the program. Denazification remained a burning issue among the Germans who applied the law as well as among those who were affected by it. Walter Dorn wrote later that "the monthly meetings of the Laenderrat Committee of the Ministers of Liberation became a veritable tug-of-war between the German Ministers who sought to reduce the scope and whittle down the sever-

* Pollock to Clay, Feb. 23, 1946, WWIIRC 3–2/1. On Pollock's recommendation, the law was promulgated and signed in Munich to recognize Bavaria's great contribution and also to bring it out in the place where Nazism got its start.

ity of the Law and the representatives of Military Government who insisted on the application of the Law in its undiminished rigor."[32] But with the exceptions of the tremendous field-level activity to discover delinquencies and errors, of the specific incidents and cases that came to the military government's attention, and of the declaration of a youth amnesty in July 1946, denazification did not receive the kind of concentrated OMGUS attention at the policy level that it had in early 1946 and that it was to receive again in the fall.

*Clay's Länderrat Denazification Speech.* On November 5, 1946, Clay took the occasion of his regular visit to the Länderrat—which was celebrating the anniversary of its first meeting—to reprimand, lecture, and threaten Germans regarding denazification. He said that "we are sorely disappointed with the results and we have yet to find the political will and determination to punish those who deserve to be punished. . . . I do not see," Clay continued, "how you can demonstrate your ability for self-government nor your will for democracy if you are going to evade or shirk the first unpleasant and difficult task that falls upon you." He said he had examined 575 cases that public prosecutors had placed in Class I (major offenders), only to find that the tribunals had exonerated 49 and found 355 to be followers. Declaring denazification to be imperative, Clay said he was issuing orders that no one whom the military government had removed previously could be reinstated as a result of a tribunal decision without prior military government approval. Although he asserted that he had never theatened the Länderrat and was not doing so now, he did say he would review the work of the tribunals for 60 days, and that unless there was real and rapid improvement, he would assume that the Germans did not want to do the job.[33]

Clay's speech and its timing have been the subject of much comment and speculation. It has been called, at one extreme, a big bluff that was intended to confuse Americans rather than frighten Germans.[34] On the other hand, it has been described as a philippic that struck the Germans like a bolt of lightning out of the blue.[35] It has been viewed as a natural culmination of the growing conviction among OMGUS officials that the German tribunals were being too lenient; it has been seen as a manifestation of the old Morgenthau spirit of revenge (particularly by those Germans who believe Clay changed from a policy of retribution to one of recovery only slowly and not really until the Berlin crisis of 1948); and it has been explained as a response to increasing public criticism of German denazification in the U.S. press and on U.S. radio broadcasts. Though many of these interpretations touch on reality, none seems to have captured its essence.

There is much evidence to show that Americans were not pleased with the way German denazification tribunals performed in 1946. Delinquency and error reports from field detachments showed that tribunals were exonerating people whom the military government had removed earlier, that they were reducing classifications from the higher guilt categories to the lower ones, and that they were arriving at judgments which many Americans and Germans—for a variety of reasons—found to be unacceptable. The military government reports and press reports repeated almost endless examples of denazification faults, and of individuals who were somehow escaping the effects of the purge.

Clay perhaps provided the best summary of his own position on denazification almost a year later, on August 5, 1947. At that time he told the American minister-presidents that a political purge was sometimes necessary in the history of a nation, and he made the following points about the denazification program: that it was a precondition to German recovery and rehabilitation; that it was necessary before Germans could develop a sound democracy; that its laws and procedures would not be relaxed until Germans showed some willingness to assume responsibility for thorough denazification; and that the military government would do the job if the Germans did not want to.[36]

Despite Clay's firm conviction that denazification was necessary—both morally and politically—and despite the dissatisfaction of Americans and some Germans with the way German tribunals were doing the job, there is no evidence available to show that either Clay or OMGUS as a whole was building up a reserve of hostility toward the performance of German denazification tribunals immediately preceding Clay's November 5, 1946, speech to the Länderrat. As a matter of fact, the evidence seems to show more clearly that the military government continued to hope that negotiation, pressure, and proper supervision might prod the Germans into improving their effort and eliminating the imperfections that almost everyone recognized. Particularly noteworthy in this respect are Clay's remarks to the Länderrat on October 8, 1946. He asked the minister-presidents to review the activities of the tribunals, and said that more determination and a stricter application of the laws were needed. His remarks were friendly in tone, however, and they came during a speech in which he also recalled the Länderrat's formation a year earlier, and commented with obvious sincerity on its important service and accomplishments.[37] As a further example of the hopeful attitude of OMGUS officials, it might be noted that bizonal discussions on denazification had been initiated late in October. It is clear from the record of those discussions that Americans hoped U.S. zone denazification laws and procedures would become a model for the British zone—a hope that hardly suggests growing hostility toward the program.[38]

Two things are very clearly in the immediate background of Clay's speech, and one seems to have been of such overriding significance that it permits a suggestion as to Clay's intentions and motivations. First, an OMGUS division completed a staff study on denazification on November 1, 1946. The study included information gathered up to the end of August from the military government special branch offices in the field. It provided statistics showing, among other things, that large numbers of people in the category of mandatory removals had been found to be followers or less by German denazification tribunals. There is evidence that Clay saw this staff study before his Stuttgart speech, and it no doubt influenced his thinking; but the second factor in the immediate background seems to have been more important.[39]

On November 1 and 2, Clay had informal meetings in Berlin with George S. Meader, the chief counsel for the U.S. Senate Special Committee Investigating the National Defense Program. Meader met with various OMGUS denazification staff members on the first, but his only scheduled activity on November 2 was the conference with Clay. The published "Meader Committee" report shows that Meader focused sharply on denazification, that he talked with military government field officers who "were in almost universal agreement that the Germans are whitewashing Nazis and that high officials are escaping with practically no punishment," and that Meader believed denazification deserved full study by the Senate committee. The report shows, further, that Meader had a field study from Bavaria showing that of 575 most ardent Nazis, the tribunals had determined "almost 400" to be followers and "only 25" to be major offenders. A comparison of the OMGUS staff study statistics with those quoted by Meader suggests that Clay took the latter as the basis for his Länderrat speech; the 575 figure almost certainly was Meader's, because it does not appear in the staff study.[40]

Clay held a press conference in Berlin on November 4, 1946, before he went to Stuttgart for his regular meeting with the Länderrat. He said that he was dissatisfied with denazification, especially with the results in Bavaria, and that he would make denazification the theme of his remarks in Stuttgart. He also reported that he and Murphy had been called to Washington by Byrnes.[41] One might argue that Clay's announcement of his visit to Washington was routine and that his decision to deal with denazification was merely an effort to take some of the sting out of the Meader report before it was released. There appears, however, to be a more positive connection between the two announcements.

Clay and Murphy were going to Washington to participate in financial discussions that were eventually to lead to the Bevin-Byrnes Bizonal Fusion Agreement of December 2, 1946. Quite clearly bizonal self-sufficiency could be accomplished only by priming German industry and by supplying basic necessities in the meantime. The money would have to come from U.S. appropriations because it was becoming clear that Britain's ability to contribute was ebbing. President Truman's unpopularity at the time, and the congressional election campaign just concluding (the elections were held on November 5), suggested that the Republican Party would almost certainly control the new Congress and that the Republicans would be in the mood to look closely at administration policies with a view to gathering ammunition for the presidential election two years hence. Meader's recommendation that his committee study denazification, plus his general criticism of the occupation and the international agreements under which it was conducted, could hardly be taken lightly, for it raised the specter of rather direct congressional intervention into the administrative province of OMGUS. Such intervention would have been most objectionable to one with Clay's temperament, independence, and self-reliance; but, more seriously, it might have affected all OMGUS requests for appropriations, some of which were in the works. In effect, Meader's report threatened to set back, if not jeopardize, the entire bizonal economic program and the American-zone political program involving constitutions, legislatures, and responsible minister-presidents who were being encouraged to promote interzonal cooperation at the time.

Given all these possible consequences, Clay's remarks about Germans demonstrating their ability for self-government and democracy are instructive, as are those about Germans evading and shirking the first difficult task that came to them. Even more revealing are his comments in a Berlin press conference on December 13, 1946, just after his return from the Washington and New York consultations. He reported that the American public was much more interested in Germany than it had been a year before, and that it paid special attention to denazification, better nourishment, reconstruction, economic unity, and German self-sufficiency.[42] Since he failed to mention currency and financial reform, decartelization, dismantlement, reparations, restitutions, school reform, civil service reform, land reform, or democratization—all of which were well-known features of American policy—the conclusion almost springs forth that Clay came back fresh from discussions at which it was agreed that economic rehabilitation and adequate denazification must be interdependent, perhaps to hedge against the kind of investigation that seemed to be in the offing when the new Republican-controlled Congress convened. Economic rehabilitation was also a German interest, but denazification on American terms was not. Success in this case lay with those who had the money, and denazification on American terms was the price Germans had to pay for economic recovery—at least until Americans changed their minds.

# 7 | Bizonia as Necessity and Economic Magnet

The priorities and operations of the military government shifted discernibly as 1946 ended and 1947 began. The military government had established the institutions of local and state self-government, but it hedged them in by limitations and then stripped them of authority in favor of the bizonal economic program. The earlier field-level experiment to spread the Länderrat idea to other zones had shown limited success, but the military government curbed its momentum in favor of the bizonal agencies and in anticipation of the Moscow conference of the Council of Foreign Ministers. Clay told the Länderrat on February 4, 1947, that for "understandable reasons" he wanted no informal minister-presidents' discussions in the next months. When the minister-presidents decided to meet "unofficially," the RGCO director wrote to Rossmann that the military government had no objection provided it was understood that an unofficial meeting could not act or make agreements to alter existing bizonal relationships. The minister-presidents finally met in Wiesbaden, but as we have seen, Clay refused to react to their resolution to meet with the heads of the bizonal agencies. Clay called the American-zone minister-presidents to Berlin on February 23 and told them that an overall coordinating agency for both zones was undesirable. He said it would prejudice the Moscow conference, and he did not "want to give anyone the right to charge the American and British zones with having made a 'fait accompli' in establishing a political organization in the two zones." One minister-president explained that the Germans had been discussing bizonal coordination, not a government, but Clay replied that "A rose by any other name smells just as sweet." On February 24, 1947, the RGCO director informed Rossmann that his request to call a meeting of minister-presidents and bizonal heads for February 28 was disapproved. He said further that Clay did not want any more such meetings until after the Moscow conference.[1]

## The Priority of Bizonia

Clay's reaction to the minister-presidents' meeting and the developments in denazification suggest that OMGUS and Washington had decided that the bizonal experiment should have top priority. Americans became convinced that Bizonia promised eventual relief from congressional appropriations and that successful bizonal economic unity would serve as a magnet to draw all four zones together. Bizonia thus became the key to the achievement of full unity, economic balance, and central administrations—in short, to the fulfillment of the promise of Potsdam. This conviction underlay the repeated American assertions that they were fulfilling Potsdam, not destroying it.

Draper seems to have been one of the earliest public advocates of the economic magnet thesis.[2] He had declared, in March 1946, that the American government regarded itself as the agent for the realization of the unity agreed upon at Potsdam.[3] Speaking before the Bizonal Executive Committee for Economics on October 11, 1946, Draper said—in cautioning the Germans against premature political experimentation—that the United States wanted full economic and political unity of the zones and that it had decided on bizonal merger as a means to full economic unity, which would be followed by a provisional government. He repeated the idea often thereafter.[4] The War Department seems to have accepted Draper's thesis fully. Secretary of War Patterson, writing to a friendly newspaperman on November 18, 1946, said: "We hope that France and Russia will be so impressed by the success [of bizonal economic merger] that they will fall into line and join us."* A month later, after talking at length with Draper in Washington, Patterson seemed more firm in his conviction. He

* Patterson to Clayton Fritchey, *New Orleans Item*, Nov. 18, 1946, WWIIRC, OSW 091 Germany. Interestingly, Patterson wrote to compliment Fritchey on his recommendation for caution in congressional investigations of the military government in Germany, saying that an investigation might show that Americans have little confidence in their military government and thus hamper the success of Bizonia.

wrote to Palmer Hoyt, editor of the *Denver Post*, that Draper's "program offers the real solution in the most vexing problems we have in occupation Germany; I mean taking the cost of occupation off the books of American taxpayers. We have hopes that it will lead to complete economic unity of all Germany, and that it will pave the way also for creation of a political entity in Germany."[5] Similarly, Hilldring testified before the House Appropriations Committee in February 1947 that "we think economic vigor and political independence in our part of Germany will have the same result it has had in Austria. . . . If we succeed in the program we have instituted now in western Germany, it will require all our partners in Germany, including the Soviets, to carry out their agreement arrived at at Potsdam."[6]

## Frustrations in the Field

*A Slow Start for Bizonal Fusion.* The military government's first task under the economic magnet thesis was to make bizonal fusion work. The picture was not bright. The Bevin-Byrnes agreement was in fact a three-year economic plan to make Bizonia self-sufficient by the end of 1949. It provided for imports, at United States and British costs according to an agreed formula, to prevent disease and unrest (Category A) and to aid economic recovery (Category B). It set up the Joint Export-Import Agency with authority to plan a program of exports to pay for needed imports. While the agreement was being negotiated, in November 1946, Clay reportedly said that there would be no need to disturb the four-power level-of-industry plan, because production in the two zones was only at about 60 per cent of capacity.[7] Nevertheless, pressure for revision built up. In January the British government announced that it had plans to increase the 5.8 million ton steel production agreed to in March, 1946, to 11 million tons. American functional experts in Berlin also questioned the ability of Bizonia to become self-sufficient by 1949, and they said that the level of industry must be increased.[8] However, with production currently at 60 per cent of agreed capacity, such conclusions were obviously based on projections well into the three-year plan. We will never know whether the British and American functional experts were correct, because the level of industry was changed in 1947, long before the three-year plan had a chance to prove itself. Thus, the bizonal problems early in 1947 lay in current operations, rather than in projections into the future.

At the operational level the early bizonal experiment seemed from the beginning inadequate to the task of achieving the two purposes of its advocates: to make the two zones self-sufficient and to attract the other two zones into a union. Far from attracting the Soviet and French zones, the program's new vigor after the Bevin-Byrnes agreement, which became effective on January 1, 1947, caused France to protest that Germany's heavy industry would be revived. It aroused heated political debate in France over Germany's future power. It also caused the Soviets to charge Britain and America with violating the Potsdam agreement, and they publicized the charges widely in Germany. General Vassily Sokolovsky brought the accusations before the Allied Control Council on February 25, 1947, and the Soviet-licensed press published detailed accounts of his speech.[9] Operational-level problems seemed to show also that the bizonal experiment would not produce self-sufficiency in the near future.

The situation in Bizonia during the first months of 1947 was, in fact, characterized by frequent disagreements, long delays, false starts, and general confusion.[10] The five agencies, which had been established hastily in 1946, were located in five different cities. Except through the requirement that each secure military government approval for consequential action, the five had no effective means for coordinating their programs or for securing the concurrences so necessary to an administrative apparatus. Staffing the agencies with adequate personnel proved to be extremely difficult. Officials had to be moved, and housing was virtually nonexistent. Many German officials preferred to stay put in the Länder rather than join a bizonal agency that was proclaimed as a provisional, transitory phenomenon.* Denazification caused problems also: the two zones approached the task quite differently, and the two military governments had an agree-

---

* "Speech of . . . Clay, Delivered at the Seventeenth Meeting of the Länderrat . . . 4 February 1947," WWIIRC 28–1/11. The statement that under existing agreements "an executive that was jealous of his reputation would be a fool to accept the chairmanship of the Bizonal Executive Committee" appears in OMGUS, Food and Agriculture Branch, Subj.: The Need for Strengthened Bizonal Food and Agriculture Administration, April 7, 1947, *ibid.*, 126–1/1.

ment that they would not challenge each other's clearances. American-zone Germans complained that bizonal agencies employed people who were mandatory removals under American denazification laws, but it is hard to separate those who wanted more stringent denazification from those who sought a wedge to prompt American relaxation.[11] Regional governments resisted the consequences of merger. A Munich newspaper speculated that a reduction in Bavarian food rations to provide more equal rations throughout Bizonia would encourage Bavarian separatism. The Bavarian Food and Agriculture Minister submitted his resignation, reportedly because in agriculture the military government "used threats, blandishments and . . . gestures," while in coal mining "radios, schnapps, clothing, food," and other incentives were "dangled before the producers." He remained, however, and he reportedly told General Walter J. Muller, the Military Governor of Bavaria, that he would go jail rather than obey Muller's order to deliver more Bavarian fats. The Länderrat refused to take positions on draft legislation prepared by bizonal agencies until the military government had reviewed them first. Allied functional experts complained that bizonal agencies lacked drive, initiative, and power; one report went so far as to criticize the German chairman for being a moderator rather than an executive who issued orders, for not establishing control machinery in the field, and for not establishing closer contact and liaison with other bizonal agencies.[12] It mattered little, apparently, that the things the chairman should have done were all prohibited, either by the contracts establishing the agencies or by the military government.

Three fundamental and interrelated factors seem to have contributed to Bizonia's difficulties, which were threatening to create an impasse. The first was the imminence of the Moscow Council of Foreign Ministers meeting. The prevailing hope—stronger in some than in others to be sure—that the Moscow conference might produce agreements on Germany certainly caused the Americans and the British to hesitate rather than move to a point of no return just before the conference. The hope definitely kept bizonal political coordination in abeyance, as has been shown. The second factor was the cumbersome administrative apparatus available to implement the bizonal programs; it was not being streamlined because of the hopes for the

Moscow conference. It was cumbersome because the two powers had been so intent on attracting the other two zones in 1946 that they had separated the five agencies to avoid the appearance of political union. They had separated them also to avoid the appearance of domination by either of the two zones. The third factor also influenced the second: the military governments did not want to release essential power and authority to the Germans, and they—especially the Americans—simply lacked sufficient personnel to do the detailed economic planning that was required. Initially, the decision to withhold economic power from Germans was a political one: four-zonal unity should be encouraged, and possible four-power agreement, especially at Moscow, should not be prejudiced. However, since neither France nor Russia gave any sign that they might reconsider their original rejections of Byrnes's invitation in 1946, and especially once they began openly to criticize and attack the bizonal program, the political reason for denying Germans effective power hung only upon the fading hope of a breakthrough at Moscow. Thus, the implication is strong that there were other reasons, and the indicators are that they were economic.

Obviously, since Britain and the United States were paying the bills for German rehabilitation in the form of Category A and B imports, no one expected them to release full control. But American reluctance—and certainly Clay's—to become a partner to a planned economy that would encourage socialism or nationalization in Germany was, perhaps, even more important. Although the records open to the researcher do not permit certainty, many things suggest that British and American discussions in November and December of 1946 already assumed that French and Russian agreement to merger was remote. Therefore, the top priority, though not to the exclusion of the other, was to make Bizonia less of a financial burden as rapidly as possible.* But given the destruction caused by war and the resulting

---

* See U.S. Dept. of State, *Germany, 1947–1949*, p. 451, esp. par. 5 of the agreement. It is also interesting that when Britain announced its plan for a new level of industry in January 1947, it also said the March 1946 plan had assumed economic unity. There seems to be an unstated assumption that unity would not occur. Patterson's letter to Palmer Hoyt about Draper's plan for "taking the cost of occupation off the books of American taxpayers" is also pertinent.

shortages of transport, coal, electricity, food, manpower, and most of the factors necessary to production in the modern world, a program to make Bizonia self-sufficient rapidly invited—if it did not demand— a thoroughly planned economy. A planned economy would encourage and strengthen German socialists, and therein lay a problem.

*The Challenge of Socialism.* Wolfgang Friedmann, who had observed Americans in bipartite negotiations, wrote that officially the United States said socialization was up to the Länder, "but the bias of the U.S. authorities is as anti-socialist as is compatible with this theory, or perhaps even greater than that."[13] Clay's response in 1946 to Article 41 (on socialization of industry) of the Hessian constitution is instructive in this context. He permitted its inclusion only after insisting that it be successfully passed in a separate referendum during the constitution's ratification. Clay's decision to have a separate vote is in itself interesting. It seems to suggest distrust of the voter's ability to weigh the entire constitution on its merits, or it reveals a hope—vain as it turned out—that the voters would reject socialization if that were the only issue they needed to vote on. At any rate, even after some 71 per cent of the Hessian voters approved it, "Clay decided, while it would remain in the constitution, its operation would be suspended for the time being." Clay subsequently refused to approve all Hessian attempts to implement the article.[14]

Clay's opposition to socialization is reflected also in other ways. He fought in 1946 against the views of his advisers—especially of Draper—for an effective decartelization law, and he told his staff that his main reason was that effective decartelization would deter socialization.[15] When Washington overruled Clay on decartelization— during the discussion on bizonal merger late in 1946—he asked for a policy statement on socialization.[16] Washington's statement said, in effect, that the United States had no objection if the German people decided on it in proper democratic fashion. Almost immediately, OMGUS asked for reconsideration, because the Berlin city council had drafted a broad socialization bill for four-power approval in the Kommandatura. OMGUS objected specifically to the Berlin bill's failure to provide fair compensation and to several other features. OMGUS also reported its fear that approval of the bill would commit the United States to a policy of socialization "probably without [the] US public or Congress realizing such a basic issue had been decided."[17] After much delay, caused by differences in Washington, Clay finally got a tentative policy statement in May 1947. In the meantime, the Berlin bill had died, essentially on its own merits. British and French representatives supported American opposition at the lower levels of the Kommandatura. Nevertheless, bizonal developments in January 1947 are illuminated considerably by what we know of U.S. opposition to socialization.

On January 16, 1947, the Executive Committee for Economics, the key agency for bizonal rehabilitation, unseated its chairman and elected Victor Agartz, Kurt Schumacher's "right hand man."[18] The Committee membership had changed after German governments in the American zone were elected under the new constitutions, and its members were all Social Democrats (SPD).[19] It is general knowledge now that the SPD had carefully sought to control the Executive Committee for Economics in the interests of their program for socialization, and the *New York Times* saw the election of Agartz as a triumph for socialism in Germany.[20] The SPD action to gain control of the key bizonal agency for its party program not only violated Clay's determination to keep the military government politically neutral, but it also threatened Clay's and Washington's purpose of making the road to a socialist Germany difficult if not impossible. Agartz's election thus influenced Americans to continue the policy of assigning as little power as possible to Germans, even after the political reasons for doing so were fading—except, of course, for the hope that Moscow might bring a breakthrough.

Representatives of the military government, noting that the Committee's membership had changed, warned as early as January 13, 1947, that no hindrances would be permitted in bizonal development, the clear inference being to leave party politics out of Committee affairs. Agartz's election, three days later, seemed to fly in the face of this warning, and it was not long before the committee agreed that it had power to issue regulations with the force of law ("Rechtsverordnungen mit Gesetzeskraft"), although it preferred not to force the issue on principle, but to proceed rather by cases.[21] The American military government moved in several directions, seemingly to counteract the effects of the SPD's control of the Committee. The approach was indirect, however, because OMGUS wanted to avoid an open clash on socialization. Such a conflict would clearly have violated the OMGUS posture of political neutrality, and it would undoubtedly have stirred up further disagreements in Washington. OMGUS also wanted to avoid open disagreement with British policy, which favored socialization. Clay expressed chagrin to the Länderrat at their having failed to put capable American-zone administrators on the bizonal committees. The RCGO wanted a definite term of office established for the agencies, and it is clear that it wanted to forestall further "political-type" reorganizations. There is also evidence that OMGUS objected to the minister-presidents' attempt at political coordination of the bizonal offices, out of fear that the Social Democrats of the British zone would combine with their party colleagues in the American zone to do at that level what they had done in the Executive Committee for Economics in Minden. At least one German observer believed that Clay's February 23, 1947, meeting with the American-zone minister-presidents was arranged out of concern over developments in the Executive Committee for Economics.[22]

This explanation of the meeting illuminates the otherwise curious fact that while the military government made clear the Länderrat's restricted mandate on bizonal matters, it also decided that the bizonal agencies had no legislative powers either. Clay's handwritten memorandum summarizing the policy on February 19, 1947, merits full reproduction. "My position is: Bizonal German agencies may recommend but may not enact or require enactment of legislation. Within existing law, they make decisions which must be carried out in the Laender. There is no provision for uniform legislation for British and U.S. Zones, and such legislation must be enacted unilaterally. If decisions of bizonal agencies require legislation, the proposed legislation should come as a recommendation to Gen. Robertson and myself. If we accept it, then each Military Government would proceed according to its methods to secure promulgation. If this is not clear or you do not agree, please see me. Otherwise, please implement as U.S. position."[23] The March 1, 1947, revision of military government regulations, Proclamation #4, and the March 12, 1947, letter of instructions to the Executive Committee for Economics, previously noted, all translated the memorandum into official policy.[24]

## The Moscow Conference

When the Council of Foreign Ministers opened its session in Moscow in March 1947, Bizonia was in stalemate. The military government lacked the personnel to administer the program directly and, perhaps, even to review adequately and in detail each stage of its development.* Bizonal agencies lacked legislative power without military government review and approval. The Länder lacked bizonal legislative power without military government approval. The Länder resisted implementation of directives, especially in food and agriculture, partly because they disagreed with bizonal and military government production estimates and delivery quotas. Functional officers could only recommend more power for bizonal agencies. Perhaps a breakthrough at Moscow was not only a hope, but also a necessity.

*Marshall's Report.* The Moscow conference failed to bring four-power agreement on basic German issues, and Marshall's report—seen in the context of events previously described—is most interesting. Along with a summary of basic issues, agreements, and disagreements, he made several statements that appear in the present context to assume a new meaning: First, he announced that Britain and the United States "cannot continue to pour out hundreds of millions of dollars for Germany because current measures were not being taken to terminate expeditiously the necessity for such appropriations." Second, he said that "the rehabilitation of Germany to the point where she is self-supporting demands immediate decision," and that after "long and futile" efforts to secure the unity of action necessary to rehabilitation, the British and the Americans had combined their zones because "certainly some progress towards economic unity in Germany

---

* See, for example, the assertion that the import-export program began well but that "unless major limitations and weaknesses are corrected it may be expected to break down within a few months when its size passes the capacity of Military Government personnel to deal with it." (OMG, Bavaria, Deputy Director, to OMG, Bavaria, Director, Subj: Problems of Policy in Effectuating the Import and Export Program, April 2, 1947, WWIIRC 99–3/15.)

is better than none." Third, he said that "we cannot ignore the factor of time involved here. The recovery of Europe has been far slower than had been expected. Disintegrating forces are becoming evident. The patient is sinking while the doctors deliberate. . . . action cannot await compromise through exhaustion. New issues arise daily. Whatever action is possible to meet these pressing problems must be taken without delay." Finally, Marshall referred to the bitter Soviet charges that bizonal merger broke the Potsdam agreement, replying that the Soviets ignored "the plain fact that their refusal to carry out that agreement was the sole cause of the merger."[25]

These brief excerpts from a speech that merits rereading indicate that, amidst the disagreements on central German agencies, a provisional German government, the nature of democracy, reparations, coal, the level of the German economy, and many other things, Marshall had made at least one definite decision in Moscow; and he seemed to be tending toward another. The definite decision was to push toward bizonal economic self-sufficiency no matter what the political and economic costs might be. The decision to which he was tending was to concentrate on Russian obstruction as the primary cause for the German problem, and to ignore prior French recalcitrance in the hope of winning France over to the cause. Clay, OMGUS, the War Department, and the current stalemate in Germany certainly influenced the first decision. In the second one, the influence of John Foster Dulles is unmistakable, though one is led from available materials to suspect—in the absence of access to sources that might reveal the contrary—that second-level State Department officials preferred some form of accommodation to France. The tug-of-war between the Clay–OMGUS–War Department position and the Dulles–State Department position is what led to the flurry of rumors and reports during the Moscow meeting and thereafter that there was a serious Clay-Dulles and later a Clay-Marshall dispute.[26]

*Dulles at Moscow and After.* Dulles's January 17, 1947, speech, "Europe Must Federate or Perish," given before the National Publishers Association in New York, is the key to his Moscow advice. In the speech he described the Soviet challenge of social revolution and nationalist expansion; he said that Soviet expansion had been halted in Iran, Turkey, and Greece in 1946. He went on to identify several existing danger spots, and then he focused on the Moscow conference. The conference, he said, should think less about the Potsdam dictum of Germany as a single economic unit and more in terms of European unity. But Dulles's Europe was obviously western Europe, for he said, in elaborating, that the Rhine basin could supply the economic vitality for a prosperous "western Europe," and that if western Germany's industrial potential could not be safely integrated into "western Europe," Germany ought not to use it alone. Britain and the United States had decisive power in western Germany, he continued, and they could give Europeans "precious assistance" in a constructive plan.[27]

Dulles's influence in Moscow is discernible in things other than Marshall's kind words about him on April 28. Marshall's tendency to emphasize the Soviet and ignore the French causes for the American economic problems in Germany fits Dulles's January 17 theme precisely. Furthermore, according to Dulles's own account, *his* memorandum served as the basis for Marshall's policy conference in Berlin on the way to Moscow. The memorandum emphasized the danger of a Soviet-controlled Germany on the one hand, and of an independent Germany on the other. He said "Marshall . . . had an immediate grasp of the total strategy," which was, of course, to turn Germany westward.[28] There is more. When the American delegation returned from Moscow, Marshall's report to the nation seemed full of gloom, and it ended on a note of near desperation: "The patient is sinking while the doctors deliberate. . . . Whatever action is possible to meet the pressing problems must be taken without delay."[29] A James Reston article shows that Marshall was not alone: "Washington is in a black and cynical mood," he wrote. "On Capitol Hill . . . there is nothing tonight but pessimistic resignation to an endless procession of relief and military appropriations."[30] In contrast, Dulles's report seemed almost optimistic. He listed failures and commented on them, to be sure, but he said "We did not come home empty-handed. Neither did we come home discouraged. . . . Moscow was a splendid testing ground for the development of concrete policies." He referred in very general terms to improved Franco-American relations as a result of discussions at Moscow, but he could write later that at Moscow the United States brought France much closer to the United States position. It had done so, he said, by agreeing to support French claims in the Saar at the peace treaty negotiations, by agreeing to deliver more German coal to France as German production increased, by agreeing that some form of control over the Ruhr would be established, and by generally supporting France's proposals on Germany.*

## Bizonia Reorganized and Strengthened

Besides moving tentatively toward a policy that would link Germany to western Europe and satisfy French interests, Marshall decided at Moscow that Bizonia should be made self-sufficient without delay. In mid-April Clay, who was back in Germany from Moscow before the conference ended, began to talk about bizonal reorganization, and his staff initiated an urgent study of power distribution and a possible bizonal government.[31] On April 25, 1947, Marshall stopped in Berlin for a two-hour luncheon at Tempelhof Airport with Clay, Murphy, Cohen, Bohlen, and Dulles. Clay says that he received instructions there to change and strengthen bizonal agencies and to revise the level of industry upward.[32] Clay's staff had a draft proposal ready for submission to the British military government on April 26, but it was held up to await further discussions in Washington.[33] Nevertheless, Clay and Robertson began informal talks, and on May 6, 1947, Clay told the Länderrat that bizonal agencies would be gathered together in Frankfurt and that an economic council would be created; but, he added, the details were still not clear.[34] A day later Clay received instructions from Washington (to be discussed later), and the two military governments hammered out an agreement between them by May 29, 1947.

The negotiations on bizonal revision in 1947 differed markedly from those that produced the original agencies in 1946. Whereas in 1946 Germans had actually negotiated the contracts and established the agencies, in 1947 the two military governments prepared

---

* Dulles's summary, found in *War or Peace*, pp. 103–5, is not completely accurate. France had already annexed the Saar economically late in 1946. It did so unilaterally, but the U.S. and Britain made no formal protests. See *Europa-Archiv*, 9. J. (20 July 1954), p. 6755, for the French declaration to the New York Council of Foreign Ministers meeting on December 9, 1946. The U.S. finally agreed to separation of the Saar late in 1947. The Moscow Sliding Scale (coal agreement) was worked out as Dulles says. (See *Die Neue Zeitung*, April 25, 1947, p. 1, for details.) The agreement on control over the Ruhr was not worked out until late in 1948, and only after serious difficulties with France at the time.

the full proposal with no apparent German discussions or consultations. Once they were in nearly final form, the military governments sent a number of officials and advisers on the circuit to present the plans and secure individual German reactions and comments.[35] The two military governments then established a new bizonal structure by proclamation, each in its own zone. Having done that, Americans went out again to explain its meaning, its functions, and its operations.

*New Bizonal Institutions.* The significance of the procedure would be unclear without a description of the new bizonal organization. OMGUS Proclamation #5, and the appended Agreement for Reorganization of Bizonal Economic Agencies, established three new bizonal institutions: an Economic Council (*Wirtschaftsrat*), an Executive Committee (*Exekutivausschuss*), and Executive Directors (*Direktorium*).[36] The Economic Council, to be made up of 54 members (later reduced to 52), was to be chosen by the Land legislatures on a principle of political proportionality. The Executive Committee would have one representative from each Land, appointed by the Land government. The Executive Directors would manage administrative departments, and were to be nominated by the Executive Committee and appointed and removed by the Economic Council.

The Economic Council received powers "to direct permissible economic reconstruction," subject to the approval of an Allied Bipartite Board. It could adopt and promulgate ordinances on communications, postal services, and similar administrations; on matters of general policy affecting more than one Land regarding production, allocation, and distribution of factors of production; on foreign and internal trade; on prices; on production, importation, collection, allocation, and distribution of food; on public finance and related matters; on civil service management for bizonal agencies; and on "such other functions as may from time to time be determined by the Bipartite Board." The Council could adopt and promulgate implementing regulations, or could delegate such power to the Executive Committee or Executive Directors. All of the foregoing were subject to specific Allied Bipartite Board review and approval by endorsement. In addition, the Council could delegate certain powers to the Executive Committee, but not the power to adopt and promulgate ordinances. It could appoint and remove the Executive Directors. It could consider and pass annual estimates of revenue and expenditures of the Council and its departments.

The Executive Committee could recommend ordinances to the Economic Council, issue implementing regulations under powers delegated by the Council, and coordinate and supervise the executive functions of the Executive Directors. The Directors were to administer their respective departments, to serve as accounting officers of their departments, and to issue implementing directives under authority delegated by the Council.

On June 3, 1947, Clay devoted a portion of his closed discussions with the Länderrat to the new bizonal organization. He told them that the Economic Council would be another proving ground for German capacity to govern. It gave the two zones a political basis, even though it could not be presented and described as such. Clay hinted, confidentially, that the Executive Committee might eventually develop into an authentic upper chamber and that it and the Economic Council might then serve as a model for a future German government.[37] The minister-presidents' questions to Clay indicated certain problems they saw and reservations they had, but these emerged more fully in Edward Litchfield's meeting with British and American-zone minister-presidents and other officials, held in Wiesbaden on June 15–16, 1947.[38]

The military government called the Wiesbaden meeting to discuss the implementation of Proclamation #5 and its accompanying agreement, and to work out the physical arrangements needed to transfer the bizonal agencies to Frankfurt. During the discussions Germans expressed considerable disappointment in not having had a hand in the planning, particularly after having negotiated the contracts in 1946. Some participants believed, apparently correctly, that British and American differences had led to a compromise that they did not want disturbed by additional German discussion and participation. Amidst much other discussion to clarify details and arrangements, one issue seemed to dominate the entire meeting: the Germans were not clear on the competencies of the Länder representatives to the Executive Committee, nor were they clear on the responsibilities of Länder representatives to their home governments and to their minister-presidents. Perhaps they understood this well enough but simply did not like it. At any rate, Litchfield's attempt at explanation brought an interjection on the floor from Hermann Lüdemann, the Social Democratic minister-president of Schleswig-Holstein, who accused Litchfield of giving a typical double-tongued answer; Litchfield declared that this had been his intention. At least some minister-presidents wanted to represent themselves at Frankfurt, but Litchfield said it was prohibited, as Clay had said earlier. Both asserted that it was a full-time job. The issue was a basic one, however: could the minister-presidents fit themselves or their designated Land representatives into the bizonal structure in such a way that the Länder would have effective power over bizonal decisions and legislation? If they could do that, the SPD would be in a position—through its five (of eight) minister-presidents—to exercise a vital influence at Frankfurt. The discussion shifted from details to fundamentals and back to details again, and when it was all over, Minister-President Ehard of Bavaria probably summed matters up (or warned?) as well as is possible: "It is doubtful that the expert who appeared today has been able to give the last authentic word on this matter."[39]

*Centralism vs. Federalism vs. Socialism.* Clay's instructions from Washington shed much light on the procedures and the results of bizonal reorganization in May and June of 1947, as well as on the reasons for the German response. Washington said that it shared Clay's fears of a highly centralized, controlled economy and of socialism, which would reinforce centralization. It advised Clay to reduce the danger by using care in structuring the organization, in defining and limiting the powers of the bizonal council, and in retaining the power of the military governors to give or withhold approval, particularly over Economic Council legislation. The instruction said that there should be central determination of production, of export-import levels, and of fuel and materials allocations to industries, but that these determinations should be accompanied by military government inspections to ensure compliance by Germans at all levels. Central powers should be defined to preclude socialization at the bizonal level, and the Länder should administer central decisions as much as possible. Clay's reserved power of approval over Council legislation, his instructions said, would give him control over excessive centralization and over all critical decisions by making them subject to the agreement of the military governors and the Allied Bipartite Board. If these men disagreed, the issues were to be referred to the government level for decision, and the inference was clear that Washington would back Clay and OMGUS in the event of difficulty with the British.[40]

On the surface, there is a striking contrast between Clay's instructions on centralization and the way OMGUS applied them. If centralization was to be avoided, one would naturally assume that Länder power would be enhanced at Frankfurt as a balance against the numerous powers assigned to the Economic Council. Nevertheless, Länder power was precisely what OMGUS resisted most doggedly. Perhaps economic necessity, rather than principle, dictated the action. Bizonia had certainly reached an impasse, and the decision after Moscow was that it had to be made a going concern. According to the best observers, the German food situation hit a new low in March and April of 1947.[41] Hoover's mission in February—arranged by the War Department apparently at Clay's request—publicized this fact, and predicted dire consequences for Germany and Europe in the absence of rapid and measurable improvements.* Faced with crisis, Germans and Allies began to blame each other publicly for lack of progress, and in April German miners in the Ruhr went on a strike to protest inadequate food rations.[42] Food imports totaling 1.5 million tons, using 170 "victory ships" and 100,000 railways cars, and costing United States and British taxpayers 163 million dollars (from January through April of 1947), seemed inadequate to meet the needs of the situation. The food ration remained at 1550 calories, but many consumers were unable to purchase even those meager allotments.[43] Unquestionably, the situation demanded vigorous and unified action, and the Allies assigned considerable power to the Economic Council to make it possible.

But, since the military government retained the power of ultimate

---

* Hoover's report to Truman is in the *New York Times*, March 24, 1947, p. 4. The Hoover mission is a good example of the War Department's use of private observers and missions to get publicity for its aims and objectives in Germany. Although Hoover was sent on a fact-finding mission, he told reporters before he left that his objective was to find ways to save taxpayers' money. The *New York Times*, January 23, 1947, p. 1, reported: "Increased exports and foreign exchange for food purchases, indefinite deferment of reparations withdrawals, and adjustment of the 'level-of-industry' plan were mentioned among items Mr. Hoover would explore." These sound more like commitments than the usual questions of a fact-finding mission.

decision by insisting on review, approval, and endorsement of Economic Council legislation, they could still have permitted a strong Länder function at Frankfurt in the interests of federalism. Particularly, one would expect Americans to push for Länder power in the interest of encouraging the development of an essentially federal governmental structure once the current emergency had passed and once the military government gave up its review and approval function. Clay, it will be recalled, forecast such a development for the American-zone minister-presidents on June 3, 1947. However, giving the Länder more power would have brought in the eight minister-presidents, of whom five were Social Democrats and one an old Centrist with socialist-labor leanings. Whether because of economic necessity or fear of socialism, or both, Americans resisted Länder influence at Frankfurt with finesse and determination. They would not let the minister-presidents serve on the Executive Committee themselves, because—according to Clay and Litchfield—it was a full-time job that required twelve to fourteen hours a day.[44] In addition, they refused to define the exact relationship between the Länder representatives who would serve and their minister-presidents and home governments. The first ruling, in effect, removed the leading party professionals from the inner councils of Bizonia, and the second permitted only tenuous—at best undefined—connections between party professionals and those who would serve on the councils. But the containment of Social Democrats and socialism continued to preoccupy Americans, as we shall see later, in part because their British partners supported the cause and the party quite openly.

## The Länderrat Eclipsed

If the earlier bizonal developments had threatened the Länderrat idea and curbed the minister-presidents' conference, bizonal reorganization in May and June of 1947 virtually put them both into limbo so far as the military government was concerned. The military government had not consulted these groups formally, nor had it incorporated them into the new framework. Americans in particular resisted the minister-presidents' attempt to incorporate a bizonal Länderrat idea into the Bizonal Executive Committee, though—it should be said—they had considerable support from some Germans, such as Hans Ehard of Bavaria. The result was that field officials close to the Länderrat began to speculate about its future. Litchfield reported this to Clay on May 28, saying: "Since it is not your desire to immediately liquidate the Laenderrat, I tried to soft pedal this discussion especially in the presence of German officials."[45] Nevertheless, the speculations persisted. Delbert Clark, a *New York Times* reporter, seems to have had some inkling of what was happening, although his story on the subject was not directly to the point.[46] Rossmann told the RGCO director on June 4, 1947, that certain German circles were being especially kind to the Länderrat because one should not speak evil of the dead.[47] In July Clay admitted that "we have been too tough and . . . it is destroying our Laenderrat . . . which I don't want to do just yet."[48] On August 5 he spoke encouragingly to the Länderrat. It is somewhat doubtful whether he knew that Rossmann had, on the day before, described its future role as essentially political rather than economic.[49] The Länderrat had to become, Rossmann said, the representative of the United States zonal interest; it could be the point of political contact with the military government in the American zone, because in Frankfurt Americans would have to do everything in cooperation with the British, while in Stuttgart they could go it alone. The Länderrat, he continued, would most likely be the point at which the Americans would consult with American-zone Germans as they implemented their new policy directive permitting the formation of a future German government. Besides, the Länderrat should continue to function in those areas of competence not assigned to the Bizonal Economic Council: justice, labor, refugees, education, and statistics.

Rossmann's belief that the Länderrat had a political role suggests that despite the bizonal developments in the first half of 1947, German institutions, hopes, and plans—many of which the military government had fostered earlier—had maintained sufficient momentum to endure into 1947 in a very real way. That momentum merits description and analysis.

# 8 | The German Momentum Continues

At Moscow, Britain and the United States decided to make their two zones of occupation self-sufficient and to restructure German bizonal economic and political institutions. But the Germans, who had to live with the results of the change, who had political and economic interests of their own, and who had been encouraged earlier to press at the field level for zonal strength and interzonal cooperation, were not easily turned about to suit the rapidly changing approach of the occupation authorities. In fact, the Germans continued to push in several directions to maintain, reinvigorate, and revise the political programs that the military government had fostered earlier in the hope of influencing or forcing a field-level acceptance of economic unity, central agencies, a balanced economy, and the like. The attempt of the minister-presidents to secure for themselves a definite place in the bizonal structure has already been discussed. Rossmann's desire to convert the Länderrat into a political agency in the American zone in mid-1947 has been noted. In addition, the American-zone minister-presidents established an institute that at least some hoped would help to gain them greater public acceptance, and thus more political leverage.[1] Two other developments merit special attention: the attempt at reinvigoration of the Minister-Presidents' Conference on a four-zonal basis, and the attempt to conduct German foreign affairs in the interim through the German Office for Peace Questions (Deutsches Büro für Friedensfragen, commonly known as the "Friedensbüro").

## The Munich Minister-Presidents' Conference

The Bremen meeting of bizonal minister-presidents on October 4–5, 1946, resolved to promote four-zonal liaison. But the energies of the Minister-Presidents' Conference were initially directed toward political coordination of the bizonal agencies. The meetings in Düsseldorf in January and Wiesbaden in February are examples of the effort. The military government's resistance, for reasons already described, frustrated these efforts, and bizonal reorganization without effective minister-president consultations finally spelled out their failure. Shortly after the Moscow conference ended, and before the nature of bizonal reorganization was completely clear, Minister-President Ehard revived the Bremen approach to four-zonal coordination and gave it a Bavarian accent. On May 7, 1947, he invited the German minister-presidents of all the zones of occupation to a conference in Munich.

*Bavaria's Invitation.* Despite Ehard's previous record as a champion of states' rights, his initiative is not altogether incongruous. The military government had repeatedly denied approval of further minister-presidents' meetings in February, explaining that nothing should prejudice the Moscow conference. Ehard's attempt, after the Moscow conference, thus seems most natural. Nevertheless, Ehard's supposed plans, purposes, motives, and timing have been subject to so much discussion, commentary, and analysis that it has become difficult to keep in focus the context in which he sent out the invitations. Hans-Peter Schwarz suggests that Ehard was motivated by the desire to wrest the idea of a "national representation" out of the hands of the political parties and place it in the hands of the "Länderchefs" (the minister-presidents and their counterparts). According to Schwarz, Ehard envisioned the solution of numerous problems: federalism vs. centralism; the cleavage between Berlin and West German party leaders, especially in the CDU, the SPD, and the Liberal Democratic Party (LDP); the cleavage within parties between "Länderchefs" and party headquarters; and primarily the differences between pro-Western and pro-Soviet advocates in Germany. Schwarz's account, though highly suggestive, is somewhat limited in that it accepts as Ehard's motives the sum of the judgments of Ehard's most violent critics. Kurt Schumacher and the SPD, Wilhelm Külz and Jakob Kaiser (the Soviet-zone LDP and CDU political leaders respectively), and the Soviet-zone Socialist Unity Party (SED) all discerned similar motives in Ehard's plans at the time, and they criticized him unmercifully.[2] Wilhelm Högner's statement that Ehard probably wanted to prove Bavarian loyalty to the Reich seems to avoid, rather than clarify the issue. Hans Georg Wieck's suggestion that the Ellwangen Kreis* initiated the idea is based on a letter dated September 20, 1953, which should be taken at discount value because it came six years after the fact and because individuals in and friends of the Ellwangen Kreis have gone out of their way to credit the group with legion service in the creation of a federal republic in Germany. Ehard's own argument, made immediately after the conference and reiterated fifteen years later, that he had no large objectives in mind, and that he merely wanted a discussion on how Germans could get through the next winter was—in 1947—less than candid, and—in 1962—an apparent attempt to influence the historical interpretation of the event.[3]

Ehard's invitations to a four-zonal minister-presidents' meeting went out on May 7, 1947. Invitations did not go to the Saar or to Berlin. He invited the Saar later, reportedly out of fear that failure to do so would be tacit recognition of French claims. He eventually invited Berlin also, explaining that the omission had been unintentional. Overlooking Berlin and the Saar may have been simply the result of human error, but it also suggests a hasty decision and hasty preparation. Ehard reportedly cleared the idea with Clay in an informal conversation during the regular Länderrat meeting in Stuttgart on May 6, and he says now that the standing Bavarian representative in Stuttgart had taken earlier "soundings."[4] There is no evidence of a Clay-Ehard conversation in the available records of the May 6 meeting, but this lacuna does not negate the possibility of an informal exchange. Moreover, material does exist that may shed

* The Ellwangen Kreis was a political group made up of CDU and CSU people in South Germany who wanted to counteract the centralist tendencies of the CDU in the British zone.

light on Ehard's immediate concern, his motivation, and his opening for an approach to Clay.

Clay and the minister-presidents touched on the usual range of topics in their May 6, 1947, closed meeting. They discussed food deliveries and production quotas, denazification, and export-import problems. Clay reported on current plans for bizonal reorganization, saying that the five agencies would be centralized in Frankfurt and that a representative council with authority over economic questions would be created. The minister-presidents asked about supervision and budgetary control over the former national administrations, and Clay replied: "What you need is a government, and I know as well as you what the lack of such a government means."[5] Clay's remark was, perhaps, Ehard's opening for an informal approach to Clay. Clay's report on bizonal centralization was undoubtedly the reason for Ehard's immediate concern, and a report the minister-presidents had just received on developments in the British zone is also particularly pertinent to Ehard's response to Clay's remarks.

The minister-presidents, in their own closed meeting on May 5, had heard a formal report on Rossmann's visit to the British zone late in April. Rossmann said that the British military government had originally agreed to the British-zone minister-presidents' attempt to establish a Länderrat alongside the political council in the Zonenbeirat, but that on February 21, 1947, Robertson had declared everything to be in abeyance.[6] Beginning in February, directors of the bizonal agencies had been attending Zonenbeirat meetings and answering informally to that political body. On April 30 Robertson spoke to the Zonenbeirat, saying that the latter might request bizonal directors to attend its meetings and supply information and answer questions. In essence, informal practice was on the verge of institutionalization, and Rossmann concluded that British-zone developments indicated lack of sympathy with the federal principle.

Given Ehard's federalist views, in addition to Clay's plans for a bizonal representative central council and Rossmann's report on British-zone developments that seemed to correspond with what Clay had in mind, Ehard's attempt to revive the spirit of Bremen does not appear to be out of place. In any case, Litchfield reported later in May that Ehard feared bizonal reorganization would abolish states' rights and subordinate the Länder to the Economic Council completely.*

Ehard's telegram of May 7 reported the German people to be physically and spiritually unable to face another winter of cold and hunger amidst the poor housing of destroyed cities, economic deterioration, and political hopelessness. He proposed the meeting to prepare the way for cooperation of all German Länder in the interests of economic unity and future political unification.† In a press conference on May 10, Ehard explained that his government decided to call the meeting because of disappointment over the failure of the Moscow conference to achieve economic unity or to agree on a political superstructure ("politischen Oberbau").[7] The minister-presidents, he continued, will discuss "how the German people can be brought through the winter. Included in the discussion should be provisions for food, clothing, heat, homes, transportation, and political coordination, so far as possible, in order to ensure a better economic organization."[8]

*Criticism and Change.* Almost immediately Ehard's invitation received heavy criticism. The SPD questioned Ehard's assumption that minister-presidents were the true spokesmen for the German people. The SPD believed political party leaders performed that function better. An SED spokesman in Thuringia reportedly said he felt the same way. SPD headquarters in Hanover predicted Ehard's Munich meeting would fail in the same way Kaisen's Bremen meeting had.[9] By May 18 the SPD had crystallized its position. Schumacher, in a speech at Kassel, said the SPD applied the same conditions to the Munich meeting as to the idea of "national representation"‡ spon-

---

* OMGUS, CAD, to Military Governor, Subj: Discussions with Ministers-President Regarding Bizonal Reorganization, May 28, 1947, WWIIRC 166-3/3. Interestingly, Litchfield also reported Kaisen of Bremen to be enthusiastic, Stock of Hesse to be pleased, and Minister of Interior Ulrich of Württemberg-Baden—in the absence of Maier—to be in agreement. All three were Social Democrats.

† The text of Ehard's telegram is in Württemberg-Baden, Landtag, Verhandlungen, 19. Sitzung, May 9, 1947, pp. 414–15. Vogelsang, *Hinrich Wilhelm Kopf*, p. 95, notes, correctly, the political promise of Ehard's invitation. But cf. Ehard, "Vom ersten Versuch die Einheit wiederzugewinnen," *Bayerische Staatszeitung*, Nr. 23 (June 8, 1962), p. 1, in which he says that the Allies prohibited political discussion from the beginning, and that he had to negotiate for a long time before he could even send the telegram.

‡ The essential aim of "national representation," an idea that originated in the Soviet zone, was to construct some form of German agency, conference, or institu-

sored by Jakob Kaiser and others: no SPD minister-president could negotiate at the same table with SED representatives so long as the SPD was not recognized as a political party in the Soviet zone.[10]

Faced with much criticism and public comment on his political motives and apparently only then becoming aware of the deep SPD-SED dispute his invitation brought to the surface, Ehard began to soft-pedal the political promise of his invitation and to emphasize the practical, economic benefits that could be achieved. He defended himself before the Bavarian Landtag on May 28, saying he had not intended to divide Germany further, that no outside source had suggested the meeting, and that he had not intended to eclipse the advocates of national representation.[11] On the same day, however, the Soviet-zone minister-presidents forced Ehard's hand. They wired, asking that the meeting consider both political and economic matters, especially German unity; that political party and trade union representatives be invited; and that the meeting be moved to Berlin, the old capital and the seat of four-power government.[12] Ehard answered that plans were too far along to move to Berlin, that the meeting was only a first step, that the broader political issues would come up eventually, and that the issues raised by the Soviet-zone minister-presidents could be discussed at the scheduled June 4 meeting, when the agenda would be prepared, and again at the June 5 minister-presidents' meeting, when the agenda would be firmly set.[13]

Ehard was obviously caught in an SPD-SED political dispute that was not of his making. Had he decided to reject out of hand the SED's request for political discussions, the Soviet-zone minister-presidents would undoubtedly have refused to attend (as Rudolf Paul verified in December 1947), and Ehard would have had to face the SED charge that he had widened the German split, thus doing in Germany what the United States and Britain had done at the Allied level in Moscow. On the other hand, had he agreed to the SED's re-

---

tion that could represent Germans and Germany to the occupation powers and to the rest of the world (in the absence of a German government as such). Some people thought it should be constructed by or made up of the minister-presidents of the various Länder. Others thought it should be constructed by or made up of the political party leaders. Still others favored a combination of these. There were numerous variations of the idea, though no single one ever predominated. The ideas eventually merged to become the Volkskongress movement in the Soviet zone.

quest, the success of the meeting would undoubtedly have been doomed because of the SPD position. Vogelsang has stated that the British-zone minister-presidents agreed on May 30 that under no conditions would they permit political themes to be discussed at Munich. At about the same time Schumacher told an SPD conference in Frankfurt that the Munich conference had no authority to discuss a future German constitution or the relationship of the Länder to the whole of Germany. Nor did it have the right to "commit the Social Democrats to a policy regarding other parties" (i.e., the SED).[14] Ehard's reply was clearly an attempt to save the meeting, and he hedged considerably on its political nature to do so. At this point France announced a decision that saved the meeting for Ehard.

*France to the Rescue.* On May 30, the French foreign office announced that it had approved the attendance of the French-zone minister-presidents (except for the Saar) on the condition that the meeting not go beyond Ehard's announced purpose of dealing with economic necessities and that it not discuss political reconstruction in Germany. It warned that France would review its decision at any moment if centralization was brought up. The foreign office also took the occasion to say that it had not changed its mind on the Ruhr or on the separation of the Rhineland from Germany. France, in effect, answered the Soviet-zone minister-presidents' telegram for Ehard. Whether the French intended this is open to speculation, but the selective way in which they read Ehard's announced purpose is fairly obvious. In any event, the Bavarian government immediately released a list of topics that could not be discussed: political questions regarding the nature of future German reconstruction, financial equalization, German frontiers, and reparations.[15]

Since that time an effort has been made—apparently a successful one—to shift the blame for the restriction on political discussions to the Allies, and—most curiously—to shift it back all the way to May 6 and onto the shoulders of Lucius D. Clay. At least three important German studies state unequivocally that Ehard had to clear the agenda with Clay before he could send out the invitations on May 7, and other authors seem to have gone along with this.[16] Shifting the blame to Clay may satisfy the desire of some not to stir up West German Social Democrats. It may satisfy the desire of certain German particularists not to offend their best ally, France, any more than necessary. It may satisfy a West German desire to blame the Soviet-zone minister-presidents for first trying to change the original purpose of the meeting (if Clay said "no politics" on May 6, that restriction would be part of the original purpose) and for then exploding the conference when their attempt failed. It may simply illustrate the ease with which Germans have shifted the responsibility for various unpleasant things to Clay. In any event, it does not satisfy the facts of the case.

There is no evidence in the OMGUS records or in any available German sources to show that Clay talked with Ehard about the agenda on May 6. The earliest agenda information in the OMGUS records is a memorandum of June 4 from Litchfield to Clay, listing eleven items that Litchfield said he got "from Munich."[17] Ehard's invitation, his May 10 press conference, and his May 14 radio address all contained references to possible political discussions, and thus conflict with any restrictions on this topic he may have received from Clay on May 6. Furthermore, the scheduled June 4 meeting to prepare an agenda, and the June 5 minister-presidents' session at which the agenda was to be fixed definitely, belie the assertion that the agenda had been prepared and cleared before May 6. Immediate postconference reports and statements suggest the same conclusion.[18]

Bavaria's attempt to tone down the emphasis on political topics, even before France announced its conditions, indicates that German internal differences were pushing Ehard to make a decision and that France simply provided the leverage he needed to restrict the meeting's controversial topics and reduce the chances of an SPD-SED showdown. That the condition posed by the French was not a crucial difficulty but was rather a convenient assist comes out in the postmortems, of which a few examples must suffice. Carlo Schmid reported to his Landtag that Germans did not want to talk politics, because they did not want the first meeting to make all future meetings impossible. Had the Soviet-zone minister-presidents succeeded in placing their item on the agenda, the conference would have collapsed for domestic political reasons (that is, it would have raised the issue of the minister-presidents' mandate to speak for the German people), and for foreign political reasons on which Schmid preferred not to comment. Another minister-president, Hermann Lüdemann, told his

Landtag that acceptance of the Soviet-zone agenda item would have resulted in a political demonstration that western-zone minister-presidents wanted to avoid "at all costs." Besides, he said, French-zone representatives were restricted by their military government.[19] Wilhelm Boden, the man who reportedly said French restrictions required him to leave the June 5 session if the Soviet agenda item was accepted, told his Landtag later that all western minister-presidents objected to the item, and he failed to mention the French condition.*

*The Rupture and the Results.* The main conference took place on June 6–7, 1947, but after the night of June 5 all else seemed anticlimax. After having left doubts about their appearance until the last moment, four Soviet-zone minister-presidents appeared without experts and advisers for the June 5 meeting. They wanted to add an item to the agenda, which had been tentatively prepared at a meeting on June 4. It read: "Formation of a German central administration by agreement of the democratic German parties and labor unions in order to create a German centralistic state," and they wanted it to be item number one.[20] Much debate followed, during which Wilhelm Boden of Rhineland-Pfalz, French zone, reportedly said he would have to leave if the item were accepted. The Soviet-zone minister-presidents withdrew for a caucus, during which they talked with Ehard and were joined by their fifth colleague, who had arrived late. According to Rudolf Paul, Ehard refused to budge: he refused to permit them to submit a written declaration, and he would not permit Paul to make a formal speech to the conference on behalf of the Soviet-zone representatives. The Soviet-zone minister-presidents then left the meeting, but not to leave Munich in the early morning hours as is usually maintained. At least two attempts were made during the

---

* Högner, *Der Schwierige Aussenseiter,* p. 292; Rheinland-Pfalz, Landtag Stenographischer Bericht, June 13, 1947, pp. 15–19. It is interesting and curious that the Bavarian government's official publication on the conference, which was reprinted in 1965, failed to include anything about the fateful June 5 meeting at which the Soviet-zone minister-presidents decided for a second time not to participate, and walked out. In response to a direct question, I was told by one source that Bavaria had published the report that way to avoid embarrassing France. But this hardly seems congruous, since it was general knowledge what the French conditions were, and since Hermann Lüdemann told reporters on June 7 that French conditions caused the difficulty. (See *Frankfurter Rundschau,* June 7, 1947, p. 1.) Until the materials on the June 5 meeting are made available, one can assume that the reasons for the curious omission are perhaps more complex than the ones now given.

night to mediate—one by Ferdinand Friedensburg of Berlin and another by Friedensburg and Kaisen of Bremen.[21] At least one minister-president (Maier) believed that compromise would have been possible, and Rossmann reported that the withdrawal might have been avoided except for "the action of the Minister Presidents from the North, the SPD and Dr. Schmidt [*sic*] (Tübingen in the French Zone)."[22]

The conference heard opening and closing addresses by Ehard, speeches and reports on German prisoners of war, on food, on Berlin's food and health problems, on the state of the economy, on refugees, and on a proposal for an occupation statute. It passed resolutions on all of these matters and on denazification. In addition, it issued a call to Germans who had fled abroad during the Nazi regime to return home, and to all Germans throughout the world to see for themselves that their compatriots in Germany wanted peace and to use their influence to help rehabilitate Germany. Ehard sent the resolutions to the Allied Control Council and requested an audience for a delegation of minister-presidents. The Soviet-zone minister-presidents also asked to be heard, and after much discussion at various levels of the Allied Control Council, the matter was removed from the agenda without action on July 30, 1947.

The long-range value of the discussions and exchange of information that Munich permitted is indisputable, though not subject to measurement. The closer cooperation established in June between Germans from the U.S. and British zones and those in the French zone is noteworthy in light of the fact that the United States, Britain, and France had already established a closer liaison at the government level during the Moscow conference in March and April of 1947. Germans also initiated at Munich their drive for an occupation statute —that is, for a legal basis for the occupation. Perhaps more significant, however, was Munich's clear demonstration of the split that had developed during the two years of zonal division, of the deep-seated cleavage between the SPD and the SED, of the disagreement between the political party leaders and the minister-presidents on who was the best representative of German interests, and of the lack of consensus among Germans themselves as to the nature of their problems and the proper solution for them.[23] Equally noteworthy is the evident abandonment by Americans of their experiment to spread the Län-derrat idea to other zones. Clay, in fact, had given OMGUS specific instructions to keep "hands off," an order certainly in keeping with the change of approach that bizonal reorganization had signified.[24] Munich, therefore, came too late to reap the kind of benefit the Bremen meeting got from American encouragement, support, and intervention with other Allies. It came too late in the sense that the domestic split was so great, especially between the revolutionary East and the West, that a public meeting of the kind Ehard planned could only develop into an exchange of accusations and counteraccusations. Ehard's kind of meeting was, perhaps, ordained to failure so long as the East continued its revolutionary course and the West focused on rehabilitation and restoration, each sustained and encouraged by the occupation forces in its own area.

## Deutsches Büro für Friedensfragen

*Origins.* The minister-presidents of the American and British zones first agreed to form an office for peace questions at their Düsseldorf-Minden meeting on January 25, 1947. Its purpose was to collect and prepare materials that might be used in future peace negotiations. They disagreed on whether Germany's chief spokesmen at possible peace discussions should be political parties or should be the min-ister-presidents, and they said the office would not be empowered to decide on how the material was to be used. At Wiesbaden, on February 17, 1947, the minister-presidents resolved to establish the office near Frankfurt. They appointed an administrative committee and instructed it to begin work immediately.[25]

A number of factors influenced the minister-presidents' decision. Perhaps most important was the knowledge that the Council of For-eign Ministers meeting in Moscow would begin to discuss the German peace treaty, and the hope and speculation that Germans might be consulted in some way. But the minister-presidents also wanted to coordinate the various agencies, private groups, and individuals who were working on foreign policy. Many former foreign office people, presently unemployed or assigned to other duties, continued to dabble in foreign policy and some were publishing articles and gaining considerable attention.[26] Land governments had established offices to collect materials relating to the peace, and they were often duplicating each other's efforts. Bremen, for example, had been collecting materials on reparations; Bavaria and Hesse had designated certain offices as collection centers; Lower Saxony was developing materials on Germany's eastern boundaries; and there was a fairly active agency—the Forschungsgemeinschaft für ernährungswirtschaftliche Fragen—headquartered in Hanover.[27]

The American-zone Länderrat became concerned about the lack of coordination on peace questions late in December 1946. In keeping with their hope for extension of the Länderrat idea, the American-zone minister-presidents considered themselves the legitimate spokesmen for the future of Germany, and as such they wanted some control over developments in foreign affairs. On December 19, 1946, the Länderrat Direktorium asked Rossmann to prepare a report and recommendations. On January 7, 1947, he asked the Länderrat to create an agency to prepare for a future German government and to prepare position papers for peace treaty discussions, both for submission to the Allies and for possible use by a German peace delegation. Rossmann believed the Moscow conference provided the minister-presidents with an historic opportunity, and he suggested an urgent priority for his recommendations. A day later the minister-presidents brought the issue to Clay in closed meeting. Clay and Murphy, who accompanied Clay, seemed interested but were noncommittal. Clay wanted to see what developed in Moscow first. Clay's speech on Länderrat, Länder, and bizonal relationships caused so much confusion during the minister-presidents' follow-up session, however, that the proposal for an agency to deal with peace questions never came up again.[28] The American-zone minister-presidents then brought the matter before their British-zone colleagues in Düsseldorf-Minden, and the result was the agreement of January 25 and the Wiesbaden action of February 17, 1947.

The administrative committee appointed at Wiesbaden met in Düsseldorf on February 27, 1947. It chose the name of the office, selected Fritz Eberhard (a Social Democrat in the Württemberg-Baden government) to head the Friedensbüro, agreed on tentative working rules, and disagreed—as the minister-presidents had—on who would use the materials that would be collected. The committee suggested three possible alternatives, but before these could be debated or resolved, the military government intervened.

*Military Governors Prevent Bizonal Approach.* Clay vetoed the plan for a bizonal Friedensbüro on March 11, 1947, apparently in keeping with his earlier decision to avoid bizonal political activity and in keeping also with an understanding between him and his British counterpart. Clay said he had no objection to a zonal office under the Länderrat, provided it was a research organization, but he preferred that it not be publicized. It might establish liaison with a similar British-zone office. American-zone representatives thereupon drafted a proposal for a zonal Friedensbüro to be located in Stuttgart.[29] It recommended only a loose connection with the Länderrat, to avoid any appearance of a zonal government and to make multizonal development easier. The hope for early success of attempts to get multizonal plans started is clearly indicated in the provision that no agreements and commitments should be made for more than two or three months. The Länderrat considered and approved the proposal on April 15, 1947. Among other things, the Länderrat provided that all agreements and decisions would be in force for three months and be automatically renewable for additional three-month periods unless the minister-presidents decided otherwise. It stated, further, that the minister-presidents would issue all directives to the Friedensbüro, that they would make all political decisions for the office, and that they would decide on how the materials would be used.[30]

With interzonal coordination frustrated, the various groups continued to pursue their diverse ideas, under the stimulation of efforts to form the zonal office and of the Moscow conference. The German municipal league passed a resolution on a German peace treaty at an interzonal meeting in Wiesbaden held March 14–15, 1947. There were exchanges within the military government and among individual Germans, especially on whether Germans should sign a peace treaty. Friedensbüro personnel in the American zone began drafting and debating proposals for a future German constitution, in part to keep abreast of the SED, which had a draft in circulation. The Bizonal Executive Committee for Economics set up an office to handle

reparations information related to the peace treaty, and there was
action in the British zone to set up an office for peace questions.[31]

The American-zone Friedensbüro in Stuttgart organized itself into
five branches to prepare materials on legal questions, territorial questions, economics, demilitarization, and general matters. It decided
the branches should prepare materials that would be usable directly
and immediately in negotiations. Long and detailed "Denkschriften"
were to be avoided in favor of clear, concise, and pregnant briefs
accompanied by statistical and visual presentations where possible.
Briefs were to be meticulously accurate in factual content, carefully
drafted to avoid bias, and coordinated with other briefs to guard
against internal contradictions and inconsistencies.[32]

An early Friedensbüro draft of a contract to form a German confederation of states is particularly interesting for the present discussion.[33] It provided for contractual confederation in the areas of
economics and trade, food and agriculture, transportation, postal
services and communications, public finance, and labor. The confederation would establish a *Volksrat* (representing the Landtage) and a
*Staatenrat* (representing the governments), which in turn would create the central agencies and offices. The confederation would represent Germans before the Allied Control Council. Especially noteworthy in the proposal is the continuation of the ideas put forth at
the Bremen minister-presidents' meeting of October 1946 and the
attempt to reinvigorate the German efforts at unity, which had stalled
before the Moscow conference. Also noteworthy, however, is the
fact that it had hardly been prepared when it was eclipsed by the
May 29, 1947, British-American agreement on bizonal reorganization.

Americans, in fact, worried about the functions and the size of
the Friedensbüro, which was organized on a zonal basis and had a
budget more than half the size of the Länderrat's. At least one major
OMGUS adviser concluded that "we must surely follow what they
are doing."[34] In addition to working on a draft constitution and on a
contract for a confederation of German states, the Friedensbüro prepared papers on the results of the Moscow conference and on the
occupation of Japan; it began studies on the port of Kehl and on the
Saar; and it sought connections in Switzerland, where it hoped to

secure foreign exchange to buy newspapers, journals, and books. It sent its materials into the British zone, and in July the minister-presidents there decided to push forward again for a bizonal Friedensbüro in Frankfurt.[35] The upshot was a two-day conference in Ruit, near Stuttgart, between American-zone and British-zone representatives, and the revival of the German dispute regarding use of Friedensbüro materials.

*Bizonal Discussion and Disagreement.* The Ruit conference was in two parts: a specialists' discussion of techniques and work loads, and a government representatives' discussion of bizonal cooperation, direction, channels, and use of materials. The first is interesting for the type of argument and brief Germans thought to be most effective. Briefs on international law, they believed, would appeal to British and American peace negotiators, as would those that emphasized European security. Economic arguments that focused on the Marshall Plan would be most effective with Americans, and would appeal also to Europeans interested in German consumers and producers as a basis for trade. An effective paper might be a map showing the imports needed to replace the production in each former German *Kreis* lost to Russia and Poland or under Polish administration.[36]

The second part of the conference was crucial. The British-zone minister-presidents had decided on July 4, 1947, that political party representatives should participate in decisions on the use of materials. Schleswig-Holstein and Lower Saxony insisted on a politically selected controlling body for a bizonal office. American-zone representatives seemed unwilling to move to Frankfurt under those conditions, and the discussions went round and round. The Bavarian representative compared the Friedensbüro's purposes with those of the Munich minister-presidents' conference in that both tried to bridge the division of Germany, and both worked for the combined interests of Germans, even though not actually representing each area specifically.[37] He might have added that the attempt at bizonal union was floundering on one of the same issues—representation—that had caused the difficulty in Munich. The conference failed to produce an agreement.

Although the Friedensbüro in Stuttgart continued to work most actively on various projects, no agreement could be reached on bizonal unification. Another attempt in August failed to get off the ground, in part because the agency in Stuttgart was working well, and perhaps mainly because American-zone Germans believed bizonal agreement would bring in the British-zone political parties. In October the Friedensbüro recommended that the minister-presidents state policy positions on specific issues, such as on dismantling and on the Saar. It believed this tactic to be necessary because the victors were obviously going to solve problems piecemeal without a peace treaty and because German interzonal cooperation was as remote as ever.[38]

The Friedensbüro made its last concerted effort to achieve interzonal cooperation just before the Council of Foreign Ministers meeting in London during December 1947. Early in November it prepared a detailed recommendation that the minister-presidents join in declaring to the Allied foreign ministers their willingness to work together for a peace treaty. It said that the minister-presidents should report that they had factual reports, studies, and experts available on the major questions relating to a German peace treaty. Further, they should declare that interpreters were available so that Germans could participate in mixed commissions on short notice. In addition to a list of specific positions the minister-presidents might take, the recommendation stated that, until a unified German state existed, the minister-presidents possessed the legitimate right to represent German interests in foreign affairs.[39] At this point, the work of the Friedensbüro and the idea of the Minister-Presidents' Conference meshed, but it brought forth in the Friedensbüro the same fundamental disagreements among Germans that had caused the Munich conference to fail.

*The Social Democratic Veto.* On November 4, 1947, the American-zone minister-presidents accepted the Friedensbüro recommendations and authorized it to arrange a minister-presidents' meeting. Friedensbüro delegates who had gone to the French zone reported interest among the minister-presidents and in the French military government headquarters, although they got no positive commitments. But negotiations with the British-zone minister-presidents broke down completely. The British-zone minister-presidents were skeptical at first because they feared a display of disunity reminiscent of Munich and of the October 1947 minister-presidents' meeting on dismantling. On further consideration, Lower Saxony, Hamburg, and Schleswig-Holstein declined to participate, and recommended instead that each minister-president communicate with his respective military governor. If the Friedensbüro wished, it might prepare a resolution that could be submitted to the minister-presidents by mail.[40] The basis for the action was an SPD decision to oppose further use of minister-presidents' meetings. The reason for the SPD decision is revealed in another incident.

Erich Rossmann, who was actively supporting the Friedensbüro plan, made a major speech in the Parliamentary Advisory Committee of the Länderrat on November 18, 1947. He outlined in detail the German situation following the capitulation, and compared it with the Holy Roman Empire. He said the time had come for action; he believed that German governments, parliaments, and political parties should demand representation in London. He repeated the Friedensbüro position that the minister-presidents possessed a democratic legitimation to speak for Germany in the absence of a single government. The speech brought a formal motion of censure from the SPD for Rossmann's individual approach, and especially for his declaration that the Länder and the minister-presidents had legitimate powers to deal in foreign affairs for the German people.[41]

The Friedensbüro continued to function in Stuttgart until it was taken over by the Bonn government in December 1949. It performed important service on the Occupation Statute and during the discussions leading to the formation of the West German government. During 1947, however, it represented the continuation of a German initiative that had been frustrated by the military government in anticipation of the Moscow conference and then abandoned by the military government in favor of the economic solutions that bizonal reorganization promised. It also brought forth some of the basic political disagreements among Germans that persisted even within the bizonal framework—political disagreements that in part influenced Americans to go it alone in the economic field rather than to try to solve German political problems along the way.

# 9 | The Washington Focus

Clay observed in December 1946 that the United States public was more interested in Germany than it had been a year earlier. Whether because of interest aroused by the news of the coming Moscow conference, a natural response to news coming out of Germany and Europe, the success of the Republicans in the November congressional elections, or the natural tendency to take stock at the end of one year and the beginning of another, American public opinion certainly focused sharply and critically on Germany and Europe early in 1947. In Germany the developments in Bizonia and in denazification were affected by this attention, but they hardly reveal the intensity of the interest, or the persistence of the German problem as a news item in America.

## United States Interest in the German Problem

*The Spectrum of Opinion.* Organized groups took up the German problem. For example, in November 1946 the National Planning Association released a report replete with recommendations on the treatment of Germany as an economic unit. The Council on Foreign Relations polled community leaders in 22 cities of the United States, and reportedly found agreement that a "prosperous Germany is essential to economic stability in Europe." The Association for a Democratic Germany heard Reinhold Niebuhr speak on four-power control, its inadequacies and deficiencies. Newspapers, Congress, government agencies, and individuals joined in. John Foster Dulles's speech of January 17, 1947, has already been noted, as has the War

Department's sponsorship of the Hoover mission. A House Military Affairs Committee report criticized OMGUS for being too cautious and for avoiding dollar diplomacy: "We have never swung an economic club to accomplish those political and economic principles for which we stand." The *New York Times* editorialized on Germany, "The Great Issue of 1947," to launch what appears from space allocation and coverage to have been a determined effort to expose the American public to the economic problems in Germany and Europe.[1]

Indicative, perhaps, of the effect of the new interest in Germany is the negative response to it that sprang up. In Britain an international committee on Germany, which included Lord Vansittart among its members, released a report condemning the tendency to restore Germany and ignore denazification. In the United States, Eleanor Roosevelt and Ansel Mowrer invited some five hundred people (including Henry Morgenthau) to a "National Conference on the German Problem." It met in New York City on March 6, 1947, and protested against the apparent interest in German revival, against Dulles as an adviser at Moscow, and against the abandonment of the Yalta and Potsdam agreements. Senator Claude Pepper publicly charged Dulles, Vandenberg, Taft, and Dewey with wanting to increase rather than eliminate "Germany's ability to build for new aggressions." The public debate went on and on.[2]

*Germany as the Key to European Stability.* A predominant theme of much of the discussion early in 1947 was the idea that German rehabilitation was the key to European stability and economic progress.[3] The reverse side of this theme was that stability and economic development in Europe were essential to German self-sufficiency, and were thus a precondition for relieving the United States from the financial drain that the German occupation had been and promised to remain, especially after the Moscow conference. No one, apparently, saw the reverse side of the argument more clearly than Clay.

When Marshall and Bevin decided in Moscow to push for German self-sufficiency, and when Marshall ordered OMGUS to proceed in Berlin, Clay warned him of certain financial difficulties that stood in the way. Marshall asked Clay to summarize his ideas in writing and Clay did so on May 2, 1947.[4] Germany, he said, had lost all her foreign balances, her external assets, and her gold reserves during the war and as reparations. Disease-and-unrest appropriations had kept her from starvation, but those funds were restricted and were thus not available for other purposes. Foreign loans and grants were unavailable to Germany because she was a poor credit risk. Only self-liquidating inventory advances had been available, such as a $7.5 million Reconstruction Finance Corporation advance, which was used mainly for purchase of raw cotton to produce textiles. Nevertheless, Germany needed money and foreign exchange to buy raw materials so it could produce for export, and it needed profitable foreign trade to produce its own foreign credits. Without credits Germany could not become self-sustaining; and there seemed to be no way to achieve them.

The US/UK bizonal export-import program, which was designed to produce foreign credits and help Germany pull itself up by its own bootstraps, did not promise rapid capital accumulation in the amounts needed. Germany's neighbors did not want to trade with Germany in any way that brought a net profit to Germany. This was understandable, but as Clay noted, "We must realize that any transaction which brings a loss ostensibly to the US/UK Zones of Germany today does, in fact, bring that loss to the US/UK Governments instead and jeopardizes the success of our efforts to balance the economy." As a matter of fact, Clay said, the American and British governments had been paying indirectly certain charges levied against Germany by her neighbors, because Germany was unable to finance them. He mentioned, as examples, the requirements that Germans use Antwerp and Rotterdam as ports of entry and exit and that they pay the costs in foreign exchange, even though they might use Hamburg and Bremen without foreign exchange outlay. He mentioned Czechoslovakia's use of German railroads and port facilities without returning foreign exchange to Germany, and the United Nations Relief and Rehabilitation Administration's one-million-dollar freight bill, which it wanted offset against the U.N. agency's much lower costs for administration of the displaced persons program in Germany. In both cases, Germany was performing services for which she would normally receive foreign exchange or credits in return. France had retained prisoners of war and recruited German workmen to stay in France. She paid them with captured German *Reichsmarks,* and thus received the "fruits of the labor" while Germany paid the costs. At the same time, Clay continued, France was demanding increased coal deliveries from Germany. Although he did not do so, Clay could have multiplied his examples with such things as the comparatively low export price the Allies had set for German coal ($10 per ton), which was costing the bizonal area some $50 million in foreign credits annually.* In summary, Clay cabled, "Germany is bankrupt"; she could not become self-sustaining, he argued, until her debts were reckoned and fixed, and until normal trade relations could be resumed "unhampered by the curse of her past political mistakes." In the meantime, American and British taxpayers paid the German penalties, from which they could be unburdened "only by returning Germany to a satisfactory trading position or by abandoning her to chaos."[5]

## The German Problem and the Origins of the Marshall Plan

Clay's summary of his Berlin discussion with Marshall puts the origins of the Marshall Plan in a new perspective. If Dulles was correct in saying that Marshall began to form the idea of the Marshall Plan on the plane trip home from Moscow, Clay's analysis of the German problem most certainly had a direct bearing upon the plan.[6] Marshall's report to the nation on the Moscow conference seems to support this conclusion. He referred to Germany and Austria as the "vital center"; he emphasized the importance of Germany's coal to the European economy; and he seemed clearly aware—in the way he discussed the reciprocity of German and European recovery—that Germany could not achieve self-sufficiency without considerable economic feedback from the remainder of Europe. His instructions to OMGUS in Berlin to put Bizonia on a self-sustaining basis and his instructions to George F. Kennan's policy planning committee in Washington to look at the entire European situation are thus more closely related to each other than any known publication has shown.[7]

---

* Clay to Petersen, July 15, 1947, WWIIRC, ASW 091 Germany. Cf. Balabkins, *Germany Under Direct Controls*, p. 124, who says the world price ranged from $25 to $30 per ton. He estimated the net loss to Germany in foreign exchange to have been about $200 million.

Available records provide no new insights into the intricate inter-relationships that gave rise to the Harvard speech in which Marshall set forth his European recovery program. Clayton's policy memo-randum of May 27, 1947, is apparently unpublished, as is the Kennan committee's report of May 23, and the State Department Committee on Foreign Aid paper that circulated in May and was finished in June, after the Harvard speech.[8] There is sufficient evidence, however, at least to suggest that a major thrust of Marshall's early planning was the search for a way to rapid German recovery that would make un-necessary the US/UK subsidies that were going to Germany directly and to other European countries indirectly, through Germany. Stated in other words, the question was how to gain American and European public acceptance for a German policy that raised the specter of a rehabilitated Germany, equipped with the manpower and the indus-trial, economic, and technological facilities that it had used so effec-tively in the past. The Marshall Plan's great contribution in this re-spect was its focus on general European recovery rather than on Germany per se. It made it possible for Washington to push for German rehabilitation by arguing for Europe and without having to defend each policy change so necessary to German recovery in terms of what was being done or had been done in Germany proper. If all of Europe was at stake, denazification, decartelization, democratiza-tion, German federalism, school reform, civil service reform, and the many other programs that Americans had wanted in Germany ap-peared in a new perspective. If all of Europe was at stake, specific issues in Germany naturally assumed a new location on the scale of American priorities. How vital this was to the story of the American occupation in Germany may be illustrated from available materials on selected OMGUS operations in the field.

## The New Level-of-Industry Plan

The instructions Marshall gave Clay in April 1947 to proceed with bizonal reorganization also asked Clay to plan a new level of industry for the two zones. Berlin working parties began immediately—appar-ently without detailed instructions—to calculate a tentative plan. They secured clearances as they went along. One of the major problems, according to OMGUS, was coal production, which in turn depended on increasing the 1550-calorie food ration, of which normal consumers were able to buy only about 1100 to 1200 calories daily.[9] Coal production was so vital to the program that it became the basis for a separate negotiation, to which we shall turn shortly.

On July 2, 1947, after the six-week deadline set at Moscow for completion of the new plan had passed, Washington asked Berlin to expedite agreement and sent some general instructions. Washington said steel and machine production should be increased, but it asked Clay to make sure that substantial reparations deliveries from the bizonal area would be available for IARA countries. The instructions stated that the United States was committed to deliver complete and usable German capital equipment to the countries devastated by Germany.*

Clay, it will be recalled, had already cabled Marshall in May that Germany was bankrupt and that her self-sufficiency depended on both a fixed German debt and resumption of normal trade "unhampered by the curse of [Germany's] past political mistakes." He responded to his instructions of July 2 by asking for clarification in such a way that he repeated even more clearly his conclusions of May 2, 1947. The instructions were contradictory, he said, because making Bizonia self-sufficient and providing reparations in the form of complete and usable German capital equipment for IARA nations "cannot be accomplished at the same time." The revised level of industry would leave excess steel plants, miscellaneous plants, and separate machinery, but little in the form of complete and usable German capital equipment. Besides, he said, IARA nations were interested in essentially the same kind of capital equipment that OMGUS needed to keep in Germany in order to promote exports and supply immediate European needs. In short, Clay wanted a decision on whether German self-sufficiency or IARA needs would govern the new level of industry. If the latter were to govern, Clay needed advice on the minimum needs of IARA, because these would have the effect in Germany of

* War Department to OMGUS, July 2, 1947, WWIIRC, ASW 091 Germany. The IARA nations were: Albania, Australia, Belgium, Canada, Denmark, Egypt, France, United Kingdom, Greece, India and Pakistan, Luxembourg, Norway, New Zealand, Netherlands, Czechoslovakia, Union of South Africa, United States, and Yugoslavia.

fixing the amount of industry left in the bizonal area.[10] Clay implied that the industry remaining would be less than enough to make Germany self-sustaining.

The exchange is extremely important because it shows clearly the box that OMGUS was in after the Moscow decision to make Germany self-sufficient. To do that, OMGUS would have to modify the reparations agreements of December 1945, and a change in those would upset the IARA nations. It reveals also the vital connection between German recovery and the Marshall Plan. In effect, the Marshall Plan substituted direct grants to IARA nations from the United States in place of reparations deliveries from Germany, which the United States would have paid for indirectly in any case, unless it wanted to abandon Germany to chaos, as Clay said in May.

On July 12, 1947, before Washington had responded to his request for clarification and decision,[11] Clay reported agreement in Berlin on a bizonal level of industry. Among other things, the plan proposed to permit sufficient capacity to produce 10.7 million tons of steel annually in the two zones, or 11.5 million tons for all of Germany if production in the other two zones were added. It allowed for production at about the 1936 level, whereas the March 1946 level had been about 70–75 per cent of the 1936 level, or 55 per cent of the 1938 level. Heavy machinery production would be at 80 per cent of 1936, precision optics at a level sufficient for domestic consumption and the 1936 level of exports, photo equipment at a level sufficient to export 150 per cent "of prewar" amounts, and so on.[12] Clay reported agreement with Robertson to send IARA a preview copy of the plan and to publish it by joint US/UK release in Berlin on July 16, 1947. As soon as possible thereafter, a list would be published indicating those plants available for reparations and those released from the reparations lists that were based on the March 1946 level-of-industry plan. Clay said there would be plants available for reparations, but not in quantities sufficient to satisfy IARA demands.

*Publication Delayed.* Three days later, the War Department responded to pressure from above, and ordered Clay not to publish the agreed plan, to give no further publicity to it, and to do his best to insure against information leaks.[13] At the same time, the War Department itself protested the decision to halt publication. It said that the decision was a sign of weakness, lack of leadership, and that it was contrary to the view "that German levels of industry must be set solely with regard to the needs of the German economy as that economy is to be revived to assist in the economic recovery of all Europe."[14] The War Department argued that French objections to revision were based on the realization that increased German steel production would impinge on French demands for more German coal. Nevertheless, the decision stood: Marshall informed Bidault that France would be consulted. Three-power talks were held in London on August 22–27, 1947, before the new level-of-industry plan was published on August 29, 1947.[15]

Before publication could occur, however, Marshall and Kenneth Royall (who had, during the controversy, replaced Patterson as Secretary of War) signed a formal agreement to confirm an understanding that no other country would have a vote, a veto, or power of decision over the bizonal level-of-industry plan, and that it would be published no later than September 1, 1947. They agreed also that no other country would participate in the scheduled American-British coal conference or have a vote, veto, or power of decision on the ownership, the management, or on other matters affecting the bizonal coal industry. Furthermore, they agreed that the export price of German coal was to be determined and announced by bizonal authorities (but if the latter wanted to raise the price immediately, the change would have to be confirmed by the coal conference).[16] Clay, who objected to the three-power discussions and reportedly was on the verge of resigning, got one concession and a visit from the new Secretary of the Army. The concession was a promise of Washington's support for an 1800-calorie daily food ration in October.[17]

*French and British Concerns.* We know from contemporary press reports and subsequent publications that "extraordinarily strong French objections caused first London and then Washington to instruct their Military Government chiefs ... to postpone publication of the new industrial level plan."[18] We can discern, from the published communiqué of the London tripartite talks of August 22–27, that France objected on security grounds and out of fear that Germany would be rehabilitated first. She objected specifically to the higher production capacity for machine tools and basic chemicals, and to the prospect of diminishing German coal and coke exports as German steel output increased.[19]

The British government's decision to support France's demand for consultation received much less attention than France's protests at the time, and it has since been passed over with the superficial explanation that Britain supported France out of fear that France would discontinue Marshall Plan discussions in Paris otherwise. This explanation seems hardly adequate to the seriousness of the decision to hold up plans previously accepted and already delayed much beyond the six-week deadline originally set. Nor does it account for the speed and determination with which Britain moved. Furthermore, Marshall Plan discussions gave France as good an opportunity as she might ever have to counteract plans that would make Germany recover too rapidly. There is thus room for doubt that France was prepared to explode the Marshall Plan talks. There is also room for the conclusion that the British government wanted government-level consultation itself because Britain was having serious difficulties with her bizonal partner on several other issues at about the same time. It is not clear from available sources whether Britain merely wanted to keep the discussions going and to centralize the diverse discussions that were under way, or whether she hoped to bring France in as a counterweight against the United States. It is beyond doubt, however, that the issues were coal, finances, and socialization of industry.

It will be recalled that the Minden-Düsseldorf-Essen coal conference in January 1947 had been the first major military government step to implement the Bevin-Byrnes agreement in the field. For various reasons coal production did not rise to the 300,000 ton daily average sought. It reportedly hit a high of 238,000 tons in March and went down again to 215,000 tons in June.[20] Various solutions to the problem were offered in public. Among these was a plan suggested by the International Bank of Reconstruction and Development, headed by John J. McCloy, to create a supreme coal authority, to put an American in charge, and to give him a production goal of 350,000 tons per day and considerable freedom to decide on how he would achieve it.[21] But OMGUS had worked up a plan of its own, and Draper presented it to his British counterparts in June. Essentially, Draper's plan called for a five-year trusteeship for German coal mines, during which time the mines would be managed by German trustees under a British-American supervisory board.[22] The plan differed sharply from what had been done in the past. The British military government had confiscated the mines in December 1945, and had operated them directly under coal control authorities it had established. Furthermore, the trusteeship plan would have held the question of ownership in abeyance for five years, and it thus departed radically from the well-publicized British intentions to permit Germans to socialize the mines at an early date. German plans were already under way. The newly elected Minister-President of Land North Rhine–Westphalia, Karl Arnold, had pledged on June 16, 1947, to work for a new economic order in the Ruhr and the Rhineland.*

Clay reported the OMGUS trusteeship proposal to the War Department on June 24, 1947, and commented on the British response. He said the British seemed to think he would agree to socialization on a Land basis, but he protested that he had never taken that position. His position was that he would accept socialization, provided it resulted from a "freely expressed desire of the German people."[23] But he believed conditions in Germany made free expression impossible, at least until a future government and central administrations had been set up. He objected particularly to socialization by North Rhine–Westphalia, because it would give that state a dominant position in the future German government. He feared, however, that Germans had gone so far under British control that the development would be difficult to stop. Therefore, he said, he needed an immediate and urgent decision from Washington on whether it was willing to accept socialization now, or whether it would have him make an effort to maintain a reasonable degree of free enterprise while the issue was deferred under the trusteeship plan.[24] Four days later, Clay reported that Robertson had accepted the coal mines trusteeship plan and was strongly recommending it to his government. Clay still believed the British government would find it difficult to go back on its announced plans for early socialization and ownership in North

* Nordrhein-Westfalen, Landtag, Stenographischer Bericht, 4. Sitzung, June 16, 1947, pp. 8–15. Arnold said: "The capitalist economic system has run itself into the ground under its own laws." ("Das kapitalistische Wirtschaftssystem hat sich an seinen eigenen Gesetzen totgelaufen.") He talked about "community production" ("Gemeinwirtschaft") and about dispossession with compensations.

Rhine–Westphalia, but he suggested that no discussions be initiated in Washington for the time being. He thought that Robertson's agreement was based on some knowledge of his government's intentions and that Britain would eventually approve and leave the details to the field.[25] But it was too late. Assistant Secretary of War Howard Petersen had already forced government-level action on the entire question.

Petersen had been in Germany early in June, where he had talked with Lord Pakenham, the newly appointed Minister for the British Zones of Germany and Austria. He returned so worried about food problems and socialization that he asked Secretary of War Patterson to bring these two matters to the President's attention. He said the 1550 daily calorie ration was not being met and the goal of 1800 calories in October required a decision, binding on all departments, to give German food shipments priority. Petersen said Lord Pakenham had told him candidly of the British interest in socialization of the mines, and Petersen was concerned that it would occur by default unless the United States government took a firm stand. He reviewed earlier attempts to provide Clay with a policy statement on socialism and said all Clay got was a "negative statement" in draft form which said that "anything goes (presumably even communism) as long as it is the result of the freely expressed will of the German people." Petersen believed production should come before economic and social reform and thought Forrestal would agree.[26] Negotiations were evidently completed when Clay's report on Draper's trusteeship plan arrived in Washington on June 24, because Petersen informed Clay by letter on June 25 that he had achieved one tangible result from his trip to Germany: agreement that Washington would ask the British to delay socialization for five years and would invite them to a coal conference in Washington to discuss increased production.[27] By the time Clay's subsequent cable of June 28, 1947, arrived, asking that no action be taken in Washington in the light of Robertson's agreement, Petersen could only report that the invitations for the coal conference had already gone out, that Clay would be advised of the results, and that Clayton—who was in London—had already talked with Bevin on the need to increase Ruhr coal output and had told him that this was no time for experimentation. Clay protested that negotiations on German internal affairs were being conducted at so many places and on so many levels that no single person or agency could comprehend them all, but it was too late to bring about any change in plans.[28]

Washington wanted the coal conference to begin on July 21, but it was delayed because Bevin was in Paris for Marshall Plan discussions. There was also a disagreement about the agenda and the purposes of the meeting. The United States wanted a British commitment to delay socialization for five years, and the British wanted to broaden the talks to finances for the bizonal area. Britain's foreign exchange problems were evident from the discussions on Greek and Turkish aid, and the decision to suspend convertibility was only a month away.

Unable to agree on broadening the talks, the two parties agreed to concentrate on increasing coal production when they finally met in August. Nevertheless, the United States trusteeship plan was accepted, and finances came up for additional discussions in October, after the British government had suspended convertibility.*

Britain's support for further discussions with France on the bizonal level-of-industry plan came in the foregoing context. It suggests that Britain was perhaps as concerned as Clay about the rapidity with which decisions on Germany were being made in Washington. Her decision to support French demands for discussions apparently reflected a growing fear in London, as well as in Paris, that Washington was so determined to solve the economic problems in its zone that it overlooked the legitimate interests of its allies. Washington certainly intervened directly, as it had not done before, and the progress of denazification in the United States zone serves to illustrate that fact even more firmly.

## Denazification

After Clay's November 5, 1946, denazification speech, the military government continued to apply pressure for a more thorough purge, and Germans continued to propose changes in the law and its ad-

---

* See *Süddeutsche Zeitung*, Sept. 20, 1947, p. 1 (editorial), for a story that the North Rhine–Westphalian Landtag had a coal socialization bill in the works when the coal conference killed it by order of the military government.

ministration. Clay's staff prepared a study in January 1947 for resumption of denazification by the military government, apparently so they would be prepared if Clay decided it was necessary to resume after the 60-day trial period, which had already expired. On February 4 Clay told the Länderrat that Germans needed more facilities and personnel for denazification, and suggested the Landtage pass laws to permit drafting people for the tribunals. Two days later he instructed field offices to follow up and to see to it that the minister-presidents and local officials drafted personnel and requisitioned buildings, equipment, and supplies to get the job completed.[29] A Hessian incident reveals the intensity of the OMGUS pressure.

Early in April James Newman, the Military Governor of Hesse, decided he had waited for German action as long as he could. In the absence of Minister-President Stock, he had Deputy Minister-President Werner Hilpert come in to receive two letter orders. One directed him to requisition services, space, equipment, and facilities; the other directed the Minister for Political Liberation to speed up his work, and gave details on how it was to be done. Among other things, Newman told Hilpert that the military government had a right to issue such orders, that Germans had been given a chance to work out their social and governmental problems democratically, and that "only when such democratic processes are used or misused . . . to avoid, hinder or defeat the requirements imposed on the German people . . . under occupation policies . . . [will] Military Government . . . exercise its reserved powers and issue direct orders." Newman said he was "not going to wait for action on the part of the Landtag." Hilpert doubted that "we can convince the Landtag that its sovereignty has not been attacked." Newman recalled that "Nero fiddled while Rome burned," and quoted himself at a recent press conference: "So long as the Greater Hesse government operates within the framework of its Constitution and does not violate or fail to carry out orders of American Military Government, they will have their own democracy." Newman also met the Hessian Landtag faction leaders, who protested that his orders would make the American-sponsored democratic and parliamentary governments look bad indeed. Newman reportedly told them the American public would not be informed of his orders.[30]

But Americans began to have doubts themselves. Walter Dorn,

Clay's denazification adviser, prepared a "Denkschrift," apparently early in April, summarizing German opinion and suggesting various alternatives that might be used to change the law and speed the purge.[31] He reported that "the monthly meetings of the Laenderrat Committee of the Ministers of Liberation became a veritable tug-of-war between the German Ministers who sought to reduce the scope and whittle down the severity of the Law and the representatives of Military Government who insisted on the application of the Law in its undiminished rigor." He observed also that German arguments against the ordinary labor provisions of the law had had "devastating" effects, especially when Germans talked with American business-men. Besides Dorn's, there were other suggestions for change within OMGUS. Some of them were based on fear that the Moscow conference resolution to speed denazification would cause the other occupation powers to wind up rapidly and leave the United States as the only power with an unfinished denazification purge.[32]

German legislatures, denazification ministries, and minister-presidents passed amendments to the law, recommended changes, petitioned for administrative alterations, and debated numerous proposals.[33] Nevertheless, Clay remained firm, apparently out of a conviction that denazification was necessary to democracy and that it was a precondition to large-scale United States economic aid to Germany. He had a long and bitter closed session on denazification with the minister-presidents in Stuttgart on August 5, 1947. The minister-presidents had brought up the July 18 Heidenheimer Resolutions of the denazification ministers and reported, among other things, that the political parties all supported changes in denazification. They said there were indications that some parties might withdraw their personnel from the tribunals if the law were not changed. Clay responded that if the parties did not want to do the job, the military government would. Germans had been given a youth amnesty and a Christmas amnesty, he continued, and they still had not sped up their work significantly during the past nine months. He insisted that the law would not be changed unless the Germans made a greater effort. He said German actions had, in fact, been predicted by his advisers, who had not wanted denazification turned over to Germans in the first place. Concluding that a political purge was sometimes necessary in the history of a people or a nation, Clay observed that Americans regarded denazification as a precondition to German recovery and rehabilitation. In this he erred, perhaps because he himself had not been able to keep pace with the rapid change of public opinion in the United States and especially of attitudes in Washington.

Kenneth Royall came to the theater in August 1947, shortly after he became Secretary of the Army. Among other things, he brought instructions to end denazification by April 1, 1948. His instructions preceded by about a month a State Department decision to send Clay a policy statement that would have sped conclusion of denazification. The Soviet announcement of rapid termination on August 16, 1947, obviously moved the State Department to do what Murphy's staff in Berlin had advised earlier, but it withheld its policy statement when the Army informed them that changes were already under way. Royall recalled for the Senate Appropriations Committee in December that he could have stopped denazification right away in August. But, he said, since Germans were doing it and since some people had already been tried and others not, Clay advised a time limit and a narrower compass. Royall agreed.[34]

On September 9, 1947, in his first meeting with the minister-presidents since his bitter session in August, Clay gave them an oral summary of concessions he would make on denazification.[35] The concessions are technical and detailed, but in general they permitted people in the "follower" class to resume employment while awaiting trial (it had been prohibited), except in public administration, education, and public information media. Public prosecutors could also reduce higher classifications to lower ones on the basis of their investigations rather than wait for the tribunal process, as had been the requirement. Clay's concessions prompted a full round of discussions between Germans and Americans, and led to changes that were accepted by Clay on October 3, 1947. It is interesting, and perhaps indicative of where the initiative originated, that the OMGUS denazification personnel who came to Stuttgart to negotiate with Germans on September 23 were unaware of Clay's September 9 memorandum of concessions until they got to the meeting.[36]

When it was all over, OMGUS reported that henceforth all members of the Nazi Party and affiliated organizations (except for the

SD, Gestapo, SS, and Leadership Corps of the party, which the Nuremberg tribunals had declared to be criminal organizations) were to be charged strictly in accord with the evidence, and that "followers" might resume their positions prior to trial. The Department of Army, Civil Affairs Division, said the changes would reduce the number of lengthy trials for followers, cut the completion time in half, and reduce the number of cases in the higher classifications from 750,000 to 250,000. The press talked about traffic-court denazification.[37]

Particularly noteworthy in the change is the discrimination between employment in the private sector (which was permitted for followers without trial) and in public administration, education, and information media (which was prohibited for such people). Its significance was not overlooked by Germans, one of whom said "the implementation of the Marshall Plan is responsible" ("dahinter stehe die Durchführung des Marshall-Planes").[38] How correct he was became clear very soon.

# 10 | Decision in Washington

The interest taken by the American public in Germany, and the periodic and specific Washington interventions in occupation affairs in early 1947 were but mild preludes to what happened late in 1947 and early in 1948, when Congress held hearings and debates on interim aid and the Marshall Plan. The full details of the United States debate on German and European policy in 1947 and 1948 are beyond the scope of this study, but a number of currents in that debate may be identified. The currents often ran together in the discussions—and perhaps also in people's minds—but there were nevertheless several distinct clusters of ideas.

First, there was the idea that the immediate crisis in France, Italy, and Europe bore affinities with the Greek-Turkish crisis of the spring, that the foundations of society and the political order were threatened in Western Europe, and that this threat contributed to the Soviet intention to spread its Communist ideology and its influence as world power into Western Europe. Truman expressed this view to Vandenberg on September 30, 1947, when he requested immediate congressional action on the interim aid bill. Marshall repeated it before the Senate Foreign Relations Committee on November 10, and Dulles went into great detail before the same committee on November 14.[1]

Second, there was the idea that general European recovery, accompanied by possible Western European federation, promised a multiplicity of desirable results: rapid and certain rehabilitation for the whole and its parts; frustration of Soviet intentions and leftist hopes; solutions for the convertibility problems of our European allies; eventual unification of Germany by drawing the Soviet zone into the West with the economic magnet of higher production, better living standards, and the like; possible attraction of Czechoslovakia and Poland by this same economic magnet; and an end to the drain on United States appropriations for emergency aid in unforeseeable amounts and for an indefinite time. These ideas were espoused in whole or in part by a host of people, including Marshall, Lewis Douglas, Kenneth Royall, Dulles, and the Harriman Committee.[2] They appealed also to older isolationist instincts, in that they promised a single-package aid program that would permit Europe to recover and develop a harmonious political-economic balance that would seemingly make further United States aid and intervention unnecessary. Marshall held forth this promise regularly, and one wonders whether Senator Vandenberg's great service in getting interim aid and the European Recovery Act passed was not in part stimulated by an unstated isolationist bias. Interestingly, these same ideas appealed to a modified Morgenthauism as well. Proponents of the Morgenthau view continued to fear German economic and military potential, but they realized that for larger economic and political reasons Germany could not be crushed and annihilated. She must therefore be submerged in larger European solutions, such as international control of the Ruhr, the Marshall Plan itself, or the European federation espoused by Dulles.

Third, there was the idea that economic aid to Germany was essential to European recovery—an idea that figured very prominently in the original impetus for the Marshall Plan and continued to hold a primary position in Washington circles. As early as June, when the Paris talks were just beginning, Washington asked OMGUS to prepare information on Germany's role and possible contributions to European recovery, and on Europe's possible contributions to German rehabilitation.[3] By July 10, 1947, Washington informed Clay of agreements that Germany would play a vital role in the Marshall Plan and the future of Europe, even though no initiative in proposing such a role should come from United States representatives. Washington had agreed that should European recovery threaten to delay German self-sufficiency, the United States would either increase its expenditures in Germany or compensate by providing sufficient relief monies to the countries benefiting from German trade to enable them to pay Germany. Adding force to the commitment, Washington advised Clay that any substantial proposals likely to delay a self-sustaining German economy were to be referred for government-level decision.[4]

Despite Washington's promise to OMGUS that the Marshall Plan and German self-sufficiency would be smoothly coordinated, the public appetite for discussion of the German problem had been whetted by the discussions early in 1947. The public mood seemed to favor an attack on previous policy and practice. The variety of approaches seems almost infinite, but a selection of examples may be illustrative. Allen Dulles wrote that Germany must be industrially prosperous. Congressman Frank B. Keefe of Wisconsin told Robert Patterson that Germans "cannot even fish as they should; they cannot carry on industry to produce the fertilizer they should; they cannot go into their heavy industry . . . ," and he said he was going to tell this to the American people. M. S. Szymczak, a member of the Board of Governors of the Federal Reserve System, reported to Truman the need for food, coal, currency reform, imports and exports, and better industrial management in Germany. American businessmen, editors, publishers, and others joined in force. One recommended more economic recovery and less democracy. Another was appalled at the time wasted on the Morgenthau Plan. He insisted that time was running out, and said he believed that the contest between restoring Germany and abandoning it to socialism and communism was already at hand. Still others saw trade unions and works councils as the chief deterrent to maximum production because they wanted co-management. Many thought denazification was a deterrent to recovery because it weakened management; and they were critical of decartelization because it destroyed employer associations. Reinhold Niebuhr urged Truman to permit Germany "to leave the relief rolls and become a full and self-respecting member of the society of nations." Herbert Hoover wrote John Taber, the Chairman of the House Appropriations Committee, calling for U.S. action to increase production and "bring these burdens upon our taxpayers to an end." Congressmen went to Germany in such numbers in the late summer of 1947 that Clay wired Washington that if he were needed for financial talks with the British, the talks should be delayed for a month so he could remain in Germany. Some congressmen revealed their commitments to German recovery on the spot. When Germans told the Case Committee that "economics have priority; solution of this problem is a prerequisite to everything else," Congressman Cox of Georgia said, "I like that." Other congressmen were less outspoken, but the consensus of Congress seems best summarized in the final report of the Case Committee. As a last example (from many, many more), the President's Committee on Foreign Aid showed how the American desire for German recovery and the economic needs of Europe dovetailed neatly, provided that political-military factors were ignored. It said that, in the main, other countries needed German metals, machinery, and chemicals, which Germany could produce and export in quantities adequate to attain self-sufficiency. If Germany concentrated on textiles, ceramics, and consumer goods, she would have to increase production to about 90 per cent above prewar figures. Since this goal seemed impractical, the committee recommended increased steel and machinery production in preference to consumer goods. At the same time, it urged the formation of a West German government, because "Delay is too costly. The start must be made in the West with what we have."[5]

During the Marshall Plan hearings, the importance of German recovery to the success of the plan was never left to be assumed. Vandenberg's first question to Marshall during the Senate hearings on January 8, 1948, concerned whether "there is a dependable hope for this program without a restabilization and integration of western Germany into the program." Marshall replied that "the inclusion, or integration, of western Germany . . . is essential. . . . Germany is a major source of coal." Vandenberg, who had said his question was too basic to leave to the Secretary of the Army, wanted more, however. He asked whether it was not just as important to have West Germany stabilized as to have a program for any of the rest of the countries, and, after some hedging by Marshall, he got the latter to admit a decision that the United States was going ahead in West Germany without four-power agreements.[6]

The case for German recovery had been made long before the public discussion stopped. This is indicated in part by the Marshall-Vandenberg exchange, in part by the July 10, 1947, War Department cable to OMGUS regarding agreements on Germany's role in European recovery, and in part by the favorable public reception of the

July 15, 1947, directive (JCS 1779), which was much more permissive than JCS 1067 or even the Byrnes speech had been.*

The continuing flood of commentary on and analysis of German policy and practice is important, however, because it apparently fixed firmly the idea that the United States had no policy for Germany before 1947, or that if it had one it was influenced heavily by revanchists, leftists, visionaries, and dupes, who consciously or inadvertently contributed to the Soviet intention to spread Communism to postwar Europe. This view encouraged reinterpretation of earlier events, leading to the conclusion that, since the Soviets now objected strongly and violently to bizonal reconstruction, to rehabilitation of the western zones without four-power agreement, and to the Marshall Plan, the Soviets were also the ones who had blocked the realization of Potsdam and economic unity from the very beginning. This interpretation, in turn, took France off the hook as the chief obstacle to the realization of Potsdam, and paved the way for interim aid to France, for concessions to France on coal, on the Saar, on international control of the Ruhr, and on various other things. All of this made the Marshall Plan, and eventually the West German government, acceptable to France.

George Marshall, John Foster Dulles, and George Kennan all contributed to this line of interpretation. Marshall, in his April 28, 1947, Moscow conference report to the nation, blamed the Soviets for the failure of the Allies to establish a balanced economy in the first place. Dulles contributed to it in his January 17, 1947, speech, analyzing Soviet expansion and calling for new ideas and for a Western approach. George Kennan, above all, did so in his "Sources of Soviet Conduct."[7] Perhaps none of these ideas would have germinated, had

* Assistant Secretary of War to OMGUS, July 10, 1947, WWIIRC, ASW 091 Germany; U.S. Dept. of State, *Germany, 1947–1949*, pp. 33–41. There was, however, a significant contradiction between the July 10 cable and the July 15 directive. The cable said the United States would either increase expenditures in Germany or compensate by giving aid to other countries so they could pay Germany if European recovery threatened German self-sufficiency. In part, European recovery still depended on reparations in the form of capital equipment from Germany. The directive said, however, that the United States would not "finance the payment of reparations by Germany to other [members of the] United Nations by increasing its financial outlay in Germany or by postponing the achievement of a self-sustaining German economy" Part V, par. 16, sec. c).

it not become obvious that Congress and the public responded more readily to threats of Communism's spread than to complicated economic data and intricate analyses of the situation in Europe. Joseph Jones has described a White House meeting with congressional leaders in February 1947, during which Marshall had difficulty explaining Greek and Turkish needs. Acheson helped out by describing how the Soviets were encircling Turkey and Germany, and he communicated immediately. Jones explained: "Acheson discovered that he had to pull out all stops and speak in the frankest, boldest, widest terms to attract their support for a matter which in parliamentary democracies without a tradition of isolationism would have been undertaken quietly and without fanfare." In another place, Jones revealed how SWNCC information officers, who drafted Truman's March 12, 1947, message to Congress, decided to emphasize anti-Communism because "the only way we can sell the public on our new policy is by emphasizing the necessity of holding the line: communism vs. democracy should be the major theme." In the weeks following Truman's speech the State Department's Office of Public Affairs studied the public's response to the Truman Doctrine and concluded that "most public support was based on the conviction that the security and well-being of the United States required resistance to Soviet or Communist expansion."[8] This not only illustrates the theory of self-justifying expectations, but it also says something about the fertile soil out of which anti-Communism grew in the United States.

Among those who probably did most to drive home the idea that the United States had no real German policy before 1947 were Lewis Brown, Gustav Stolper, and Freda Utley.[9] They catalogued faults, failures, and inadequacies, and they were read and cited widely. Brown saw his report as "an industrialist's attempt to analyze the problem of a bankrupt company and to determine the simple common-sense fundamentals necessary to get the wheels of production turning, and the company on a profitable basis as soon as possible."[10] Stolper reported the "realities" he had, in part, been prompted to see by Germans during his trip with Herbert Hoover in February and on another visit during the summer, when he met regularly with Germans while writing his book.[11] Freda Utley, a former Communist turned patriot, emphasized the influence of leftists and subversives on German policy and administration.

Neither Clay nor Murphy corrected the basic flaw in the interpretation of their administration in Germany that emerged out of this context. The flaw is that it asserted, on the one hand, that the United States adhered to Potsdam religiously and did all in its power to realize it, but insisted, on the other, that the U.S. had no effective policy until July 1947. Nor have subsequent scholarly works been any more successful. Manuel Gottlieb merely applied a scholar's term to a familiar idea and called the U.S. policy and administration in Germany a "policy of ambivalence." He has been imitated most recently by Hans-Peter Schwarz, who would also apply the term to the period after 1947.[12] Correction of the flaw would, of course, show that the United States had as its policy JCS 1067 "as modified by Potsdam" and by numerous other decisions, clarifications, and interpretations in the theater and in Washington. Clay's July 19, 1946, summary of policy, which formed the heart of the Byrnes speech— and which most writers recognize as the beginning of a "new" policy —appears to be adequate testimony to that. Given the existence of a policy, any attempt to correct the flaw in the interpretation inevitably points to France as the stumbling block in the realization of that policy; but this is to some an apparently unfathomable conclusion in the light of the U.S. liberation of France and the decision to give interim aid, Marshall Plan aid, and make other concessions to France after 1947. Traditional American concepts of national and international morality did not include the idea that nations responsible for blocking treaties should receive aid and support. Admission of the fact that we were giving aid and comfort to the nation that had frustrated our German policy would probably have been too great a shock to take. But the decision was made, and its consequences for the military government were substantial.

## Effects in the Field

The effects of the Washington decisions in the field cannot be judged from directives, because no comprehensive policy directive was ever issued. The July 15, 1947, directive applied to Germany, but it left much unsaid about the intricate international economic, financial, and political relationships arising out of the European Recovery Program. We must thus turn to administrative applications in Germany to assess the impact of the Washington decisions with some degree of precision. Bizonal administrative reorganization and the new level-of-industry plan were applications of this type, but there were many other things.

*Socialization.* Both the Secretary of the Army and the Secretary of Defense offered Clay support in his policy to prevent socialization of industry. Clay had been troubled by the lack of a policy statement earlier, and it has been shown that the United States got a five-year delay on socialization of the coal mines during the coal discussions in the summer of 1947. But coal was only one industry, the British appear to have been reluctant, and German socialists—who used the democratic institutions and procedures available to them in the Länder—were impatient and active. In October 1947, Royall and Forrestal asked Clay whether he needed any further directives on socialization. Clay said he needed none for the moment, because he had interpreted his instructions to mean that "there must be economic and political stability in Germany before the German people can be expected to freely express their views," and the British had tacitly accepted his interpretation. "Time is on our side," Clay continued. "If we can thus defer the issue while free enterprise continues to operate and economic improvement results, it may never become an issue before the German people."[13]

Clay had told the Länderrat essentially the same thing on September 9, 1947. The United States would not impose its economic structure on Germans against their will, he said. But the German will had to be expressed by the entire nation. If a Land wanted to socialize, it could, but not if it affected the rest of Germany.[14] OMGUS applied Clay's interpretation regularly, and it is most clearly seen in Hesse, where the government tried to implement Article 41 of the constitution by taking over I. G. Farben properties held in trusteeship by the state under military government property control laws. In November 1947, OMGUS informed the Hessian Minister of Economics, Harold Koch, that his plans for socialization conflicted with Allied Control Council laws and that the United States would not permit it in any case until a national German government existed.[15] One thing led to another until the Office of Military Government for Hesse issued an order on December 2, 1948, that "until further notice, no steps whatsoever will be taken by the Hessian Government, or for it by an officer, official or employee, to socialize any property in Hesse under the provisions of Articles 39 and 41 of the Constitution, or under any law in implementation of said constitutional provisions, unless the approval of Military Government is first had [sic] and obtained."[16] In effect, there would be no socialization at least until the West German government was established.

*Denazification.* Congressional visitors to Germany in the fall of 1947 joined in the chorus of criticisms of denazification, particularly for its effect on economic recovery. At least one member of the Case Committee told Germans that he had made up his mind that denazification was a failure.[17] The entire committee made clear its objections to continued denazification, and recommended in its preliminary and final reports that denazification, except for major offenders, be ended by May 8, 1948.[18] C. J. Friedrich, who was a consultant for the Case Committee, interpreted the committee's intentions by quoting from the final report. "It seems reasonably clear now that the American denazification policy went too far and tried to include too many. Its categorization was too broad and too rapidly applied . . . nevertheless it was something that had to be attempted and would at least demonstrate the sincerity of the Americans in wishing to provide conditions under which democracy would have a chance to grow. . . . In accordance with the approach adopted in the OMGUS directive on 30 September 1946, *it would now be wise to turn denazification really over to the Germans with freedom for them to develop such legislation as they see fit.* . . . The overall control of German governmental and other key personnel should be sufficient to prevent the appearance of 'Nazis' in 'positions of influence.' "[19]

Spurred by pressure he had received from Royall and by his uncanny sense for interpreting signs of coming trends, Clay had a study made on the economic effects of denazification. Teams of investigators went out between August 19 and September 13, 1947, to interview the principal officers of 60 companies and firms: 33 in Bavaria,

17 in Hesse, and 10 in Württemberg-Baden. The firms employed over ten thousand people at the time; they had had 4.4 per cent of their personnel removed as a result of denazification. They had 0.6 per cent of available positions unfilled as a result of denazification. The study concluded that of all the factors that deterred business resumption, denazification was a poor last. In some firms it had, in fact, been used to get rid of "superannuated, inefficient management." Only one firm gave denazification as a problem, and that one had general management difficulties. The most serious factors working against industrial recovery were shortages of raw materials, fuel, power, lack of manpower (not due to denazification), and wartime destruction. How Clay used the report is not clear from available records, but it is clear that pressure for termination continued.[20]

In March 1948, Royall brought up the issue in a teleconference with Clay, and OMGUS finally gave way to the demands from Washington. OMGUS weighed several alternatives, ranging from canceling out the program completely, to instituting a broad amnesty, to trying a less drastic liquidation of the program over the 60 days left to meet the Case Committee deadline.[21] The crash nature of the proposed liquidation is evident from the recommendation that military vehicles be used to return people to their communities for trial, that field offices set up production schedules for the tribunals, and that Land offices stop issuing "delinquency and error" reports. The 60-day liquidation became the option. Theo E. Hall, the Public Safety Director of OMGUS, went to Stuttgart to work out the details with Germans on March 19, 1948.

The March 19 meeting presents one of the most interesting role reversals in the entire history of the occupation. Denazification, which OMGUS had always pressed as a precondition to economic recovery, was now supposed to come to a speedy conclusion as a precondition to economic recovery. Hall began by observing that it should be clear to the denazification ministers that public opinion in the United States and in Germany no longer supported denazification after three years of occupation. He reviewed some statistics, said that a way had to be found to bring the program to a close rapidly, and asked the denazification ministers for suggestions, after first giving them to understand that the military government was prepared to accept them. The

Germans at the meeting, who had anticipated what was coming, hesitated. They did not want to end denazification so abruptly. The minor cases, which required less preparation, had naturally been tried first, and the cases left included some of the major ones which had been in preparation for some time.[22] But some of the Germans also worried about the political effects of rapid conclusion. One observed that Germans were first required to denazify and now they were being required to end it. It would thus be clear to all concerned that the existing governments had been the agents of the occupation on denazification all along. They would suffer a severe political setback at the hands of those who had criticized denazification for their own reasons. Essentially, such criticism had come from conservatives and rightists, but rapid termination would add radicals, leftists, and Communists to the list of the disillusioned. A long discussion ensued, but Hall wanted agreement, not discussion. He got one change by agreeing to lift the entire "delinquency and error" reporting system in return. He got other changes after lecturing Germans on the need for bizonal economic recovery, on an $800 million United States appropriation bill, and on the possibility that Congress would refuse to vote the money if denazification continued to hinder German economic recovery. He said that OMGUS was carrying out the wishes of the United States Congress no matter who liked or disliked it in Germany. He gave an example of the kind of change that might be instituted, and in doing so he said a great deal about the program's earlier injustice. He gave the hypothetical case of a young man who had been in an internment camp for two years. According to the law current then, he would have been put into Class I or Class II and tried. "Everybody knows that he was nothing more than a follower. Thus he should be charged as a follower, and we are rid of the business."

Three major changes in denazification came out of the new negotiations. Prosecutors got full discretion in filing charges, whereas Class I and II had still been mandatory by category list after the October 3, 1947, changes which Royall had pushed. Pretrial restrictions against Class II people were removed for those entering private industry and business, but still not for those entering public service. Tribunals could reduce sentences in consideration of pretrial confinement or employment restrictions. The Länderrat adopted the changes on

March 25, 1948. Two days later (on Saturday) OMGUS approved, thereby establishing a speed record for such review. On Monday morning the RGCO director delivered the approved documents to Rossmann's office. It was a German holiday, and the office was closed. On April 2, 1948, the RGCO director wrote a formal complaint to Rossmann about the delay in implementation. In the meantime, military government field offices had received instructions to make available to German denazification ministries and tribunals until May 1, their special branch personnel and office space and equipment if needed.[23]

As of May 1, 1948, OMGUS reported 28,065 hard-core cases still awaiting trial. Royall agreed that these should be tried in a phase-out program. There were, however, more than 100,000 cases left for which paper work had to be completed, and the ministries received about 50,000 new registrations each month. In August 19,370 cases were still left, and OMGUS became concerned that they would not be closed by January 1, 1949, and thus would embarrass not only the military government but also the new German government being formed. A year later, when certain proposals for change came over the OMGUS, Chief of Staff's desk, he wrote on them in pencil: "Leave to Germans to decide as they wish."[24]

*Dismantlement and Reparations.* When Marshall instructed OMGUS to prepare a new and higher bizonal level-of-industry plan in April 1947, this meant also that the list of plants to be dismantled and made available for reparations would have to be reduced. The interrelationship of these three factors was the result of the Potsdam reparations compromise, which linked dismantlement (except for war plants) and reparations directly to the standard-of-living and level-of-industry calculations of the Allied Control Council.

All of the occupation powers had removed reparations from Germany since 1945 without regard for the agreed Potsdam formula. None of these "extra" removals was ever accounted for accurately, and apparently none has been calculated as reparations payments to this day. The powers themselves did not want to share their information, and no one was ever able to come forth with a universally acceptable distinction between war booty and reparations as such.[25] Throughout the occupation numerous attempts were made, especially by the Soviet Union at the Moscow conference, to change the reparations agreement to permit taking reparations from current production of goods and services instead of only in capital equipment.[26] The United States, in particular, resisted such attempts because it wanted current production for interzonal exchange to reduce the need for imports into the United States zone and to provide exports to pay for needed imports. It all related to the basic economic insufficiency of the United States zone. One suspects, also, that some opposition to reparations from current production came because of the rapid establishment of state enterprises in the Soviet zone that would undoubtedly produce the goods there, and because of fear that heavy eastward traffic in trade would become a fixed pattern and thus turn a future German economy in that direction. Reparations from current production would also have required a level of industry in Germany much higher than anything contemplated before 1948–49. At any rate, Marshall expressed a consistent American position when he said at Moscow that "we will not follow Mr. Molotov in a retreat from Potsdam to Yalta."* Thus, when the new level-of-industry plan was developed for the bizonal area, the United States still adhered to the Potsdam formula on reparations and dismantling.

On July 12, 1947, when Clay reported his plans to release the new bizonal level-of-industry plan, he announced also that a new dismantling and reparations list would follow soon.[27] French and British government-level reaction delayed the plan. It was subsequently released on August 29, after the three-power talks in London on August 22–27, 1947. The so-called final dismantling list and reparations figures were delayed another six weeks, causing a six-month (rather than six-week) lapse of time between the Marshall decision and its implementation. The delay suggests difficulties. There were repeated Soviet protests against bizonal developments, which are too well known to require repetition. But there were other problems with France, the IARA nations, and within the United States government, where an increasingly assertive Congress was using its power of appropriation to try to take German policy out of the hands of the State and War Departments.

The London three-power talks of August 22–27, 1947, had not

* U.S. Dept. of State, *Germany, 1947–1949*, p. 372. It might also be noted that the London Council of Foreign Ministers adjourned just after a basic disagreement on reparations.

produced agreement, especially not on coal and coke for France. The French refused to withdraw their objections, and full agreement had to be postponed "pending a satisfactory outcome" of further coal talks in Berlin.[28] The Berlin talks continued into December. Their nature made dismantling calculations difficult, if not impossible. France continued to demand increased coal and coke, an adjustment in the Moscow sliding scale, and permanent separation of the Saar. Meeting the French demands would have made it necessary for Bizonia to retain plants that might otherwise have been dismantled for reparations, in order to offset the multiplier effect of a decrease in German coal consumption. This was particularly important, because coal was such a vital factor to the entire level-of-industry plan. Eventually agreements were worked out whereby France got the Saar and a revision of the Moscow sliding scale, which provided more coal and coke at higher levels of German production in return for Saar coal deliveries to Bizonia for a specified time and for certain downward reparations adjustments to offset Saar acquisitions.[29] By that time, as we shall see, the new dismantling lists had already been published.

The IARA also showed considerable impatience with the rate of reparations deliveries from Germany, not to mention the Soviet charges that the Western powers were going back on their earlier pledges. The IARA had complained as early as October 1946 about slow deliveries.[30] Clay's unwillingness to deliver advance copies of the delayed level-of-industry plan—even to the U.S. representative to the IARA—suggests caution lest he be charged with wanting to rebuild Germany at the cost of reduced reparations to former allies. Although the IARA sent another formal complaint to the London Council of Foreign Ministers meeting in November 1947, the available records are insufficient to tell the whole story of IARA concerns and pressures. There is sufficient scattered evidence, however, to indicate the broad lines of the problem.

The third major area of difficulty, the intervention of Congress, may be seen more clearly. The United States debate on German and European policies in 1947 brought to public attention many of the economic anomalies inherent in the immediate postwar reparations and dismantling programs, which had been designed to meet political and military objectives. The anomalies were not unknown to OMGUS in

Berlin. It has been shown that they were a subject of concern to Clay, Draper, Murphy, and Douglas before Potsdam. They remained a factor in plans for bizonal recovery, the level-of-industry plan, decartelization, and in almost everything the occupation did. They also had deep-seated social implications, for they were simply the outward manifestations of the attempt to force a conversion of German national economic patterns from emphasis on heavy industry, machine tools, steel, and chemicals to an emphasis on agriculture and light industries—textiles, ceramics, and consumer goods, in the words of the Harriman Committee. They became unbearable anomalies only when U.S. economic priorities forced the social, political, and military objectives so far into the background that Germany came to be regarded as the key to European recovery.

Criticism of dismantling became heavier and heavier in the United States as the debate on German policy continued in 1947. The criticisms, taken together with the emphasis on Germany as the key to European recovery, seem now to have been clear indicators—especially to someone with Clay's perception—that the dismantling program and reparations deliveries to the Soviet Union were up for review and reconsideration.[31] Nevertheless, OMGUS—which had held the line against complete abandonment of denazification—tried in this case to maintain some form of balance between the extremes of complete conversion and of complete restoration of German national economic patterns. The result was that Clay and his staff became villains to the reformers for abandoning previous policy and villains to the restorationists for not wanting to accept economic realities.

The British and American military governments released the new dismantling list in Berlin on October 17, 1947.[32] It named 682 plants to be removed. This figure included 251 plants previously allocated as war plants or as advanced deliveries, some of which were already dismantled or in the process. The list represented a considerable reduction from the 1,636 plants or parts of plants that reportedly would have been dismantled under the 1946 level-of-industry plan.[33] The official statement that accompanied the release, which was given out by Robertson because Clay was in Washington for financial discussions, said the list was final and that no major alterations would be made. Germans might recommend adjustments or substitutions during a two-week period, and plants with uncompleted orders could complete them. The statement said the removals would not restrict Germany's progress under the Marshall Plan, because the plants were surplus to the level-of-industry plan of August 1947, and would thus remain idle, fall into disrepair, and become obsolete if not removed. The removals would increase management efficiency and save fuel, power, and transport by concentrating production in fewer factories. The removals would, of course, cause temporary dislocations of labor and other factors of production, but this was one of the costs Germany would have to bear in justice to the countries that had borne the brunt of its aggression. Germans should, however, measure their costs against the fact that some of Germany's victims were keeping her supplied with food. In summary, the statement said that there would be temporary dislocations and difficulties, but that the removals would in no way "prejudice the future economic well-being of Germany."[34]

The angry reaction of Germans to the published list was not unexpected, but the response in the United States was such that Congress and the Germans virtually joined forces against the military government, the War Department, and the State Department to revise the dismantling list and thus also—in effect—the level-of-industry plan of August 1947. Germans, some of whom had protested in anticipation of the list,[35] protested widely after it appeared. Numerous individuals made formal statements. Political parties took up the matter, as did various Landtage. Some Landtage scheduled and held full-dress debates on dismantling. The Hessian government issued a formal statement, as did the Länderrat of the American zone. Trade union leaders met to consider action, and industrial groups prepared studies.[36] The two major concerted efforts were at the minister-presidents' level in Wiesbaden on October 22, 1947, and at the Bizonal Economic Council level on October 29, 1947.

The German arguments and statements on dismantling took various forms, but they tended to repeat the same general themes: industries would do more good for Europe if they were left in Germany to begin production immediately, because dismantling and transportation of factories would take much time and cause a loss in production. Thus dismantling of factories was a contradiction of Marshall Plan objectives. Furthermore, it would cause unemployment and economic dislocations, and thus would reduce the German ability and will to contribute to European recovery. It invaded private property rights and proposed to take reparations from individuals rather than from the state or the nation. The lists were drawn without German consultation, and the 14-day deadline for suggesting alterations was too short to allow changes that would affect the list materially. At least one spokesman said the list was politically, economically, morally, and psychologically indefensible.[37]

The minister-presidents of the British and American zones met with their labor and economics ministers and with representatives of the Frankfurt Bizonal Economic Council and Executive Committee in Wiesbaden on October 22, 1947. The meeting had been called hurriedly by Minister-President Karl Arnold, of North Rhine–Westphalia. It was poorly organized, and as a result there were apparently no minutes kept. There is not even an agenda among the few remaining records available. The meeting heard Johannes Semler, the Bizonal Director of Economics, as its major speaker. It then broke up into informal committees for discussion during the remainder of the day. The conference issued a very low-key press communiqué that touched the major bases of German protest. There was, however, violent disagreement at the meeting between those who wanted to issue a call for action—via demonstrations, protest meetings, and possible strikes—and those who wanted to make a more moderate approach to the military government. The latter course of action seemed more prudent, but it raised the serious question of who should take on the task. The Bizonal Economic Council was the logical agency in the light of the urgency resulting from the 14-day deadline. But that agency had already been told that the reparations question was one of the issues reserved to the military government, that it had no grant of authority to act on reparations, and that the military government would not receive or take cognizance of any documents prepared on the matter by the Economic Council.[38] In the absence of adequate records, one can only wonder how close the existence of this restriction came to making the views of the radical, activist group prevail at the conference. There is evidence that those minister-presidents who were oriented to states' rights were also among those who objected to Economic Council action. A compromise favoring moderation finally emerged: Semler, the Bizonal Director of Economics, would join with the economics and labor ministers of the Länder to study dismantling and then discuss it with the military government, but only after full coordination with and agreement from the bizonal Länder.[39]

Although some Germans took a long time to see the wisdom of moderation at Wiesbaden, its tactical success became obvious almost immediately. Styles Bridges, the chairman of the Senate Appropriations Committee, who happened to be in Germany just then, spoke to the U.S. Press Club in Frankfurt on October 22. He said that he opposed dismantling and that his committee would call for a delay until Congress could study the whole matter. There was no doubt about Bridges' intentions, for he said he preferred to leave the plants in Germany and have Germans pay reparations from current production.*

Semler's ad hoc dismantling committee met with military government representatives for the first time on October 28, 1947. Clarence Adcock, the American member of the Bipartite Control Office, told them that Germans had a right to make statements, but that it was a mistake for them to think that dismantling and the Marshall Plan were two separate entities. He warned that public protests and further objections to reparations would only damage German interests when Congress met for its special session in November. Britain and the United States were supplying money that was absolutely necessary for achieving a decent German standard of living, he continued, and it should be clear to all concerned that the will to continue to vote money would be reduced if Germans in responsible positions stirred up their people to protest against reparations. Responsible Germans would do their country a great service if they approached dismantling objectively and if they set an example of moderation in the future. One day later, the Economic Council passed a resolution stating that the military government had released the dismantling list after informing Germans that all decisions relative to reparations and the level of industry were reserved to the military government. The Coun-

* *Frankfurter Rundschau*, Oct. 25, 1947, p. 1. Senator C. Wayland Brooks told reporters he agreed with Bridges. When Clay was asked by reporters about Bridges' statement, he said it was an illustration of American freedom of expression. *Ibid.*, Oct. 30, 1947, p. 1.

cil hoped discussions in the Länder would successfully ameliorate losses to production in basic industries, losses to individual workers and communities, and losses due to cancelled orders. It directed Semler's office to try to equalize the burdens attending dismantlement, to prevent profiteering, and to ensure rational use of remaining plants, equipment, and power. Spokesmen told reporters that the meeting with Adcock had influenced the resolution measurably, and that the major parties had agreed to emphasize a positive rather than a negative approach.[40] Apparently, the military government had won the battle, but the Congress of the United States revived the issue.

When Congress met in special session to consider interim aid, Francis Case, the chairman of the subcommittee on Austria and Germany for the Herter Committee, introduced two resolutions on dismantling (House Resolutions 364 and 365). The first would have stopped dismantling and the shipping of plants from Germany. The second raised a number of specific questions on German policy. Vandenberg's intervention prevented the first from becoming an amendment to the interim aid bill, but when the Foreign Aid Assistance Act was passed in April 1948, it included section 115(f), which said that the Economic Cooperation Administration (ECA) head would request the Secretary of State to get approval from other countries to retain "such capital equipment as is scheduled for removal as reparations from the three western zones of Germany . . . if such retention will most effectively serve the purposes of the European recovery program."

In the meantime, Congress had been asking the State and Army Departments for explanations of German policy. The tone of the questions—especially those of House Resolution 365—was hostile and critical. On December 6, 1947, Clay defended the October 17 dismantling list by arguing that fuel, raw materials, electric power, manpower limitations, and the August 1947 level-of-industry plan would make the plants surplus for about three to four years. Royall and Draper testified accordingly before the Senate Appropriations Committee on December 10. The committee pushed its witnesses very hard on dismantling and reparations, however, and it got Draper to state that shipments to the East should stop if the London Council of Foreign Ministers conference failed.[41]

In this context, and perhaps because Harriman, the chairman of the President's Committee on Foreign Aid, was also ready to take a fresh look at dismantling and reparations, Royall and Marshall agreed to bring the matter to the President's cabinet in January. In February a special cabinet technical committee was appointed to study dismantling.[42] The cabinet committee sent a mission (the Collisson Mission) to Europe for six weeks in April and May, and it prepared a report in July calling for a cut in the dismantling list of more than 300 plants. Both Army and State Departments objected to the draft cabinet committee report, because the Collisson Mission had failed to consider political and security factors in gathering its data. Clay sent objections, saying that the additional plants recommended by the committee for retention in Germany were not needed for the next three to five years, because shortages in coal, power, transportation, and labor still held current production to only slightly more than 50 per cent of the level-of-industry permitted in Germany.*

But before the report went to the President formally, the House Foreign Affairs Committee intervened again. It called Army, Interior, State, and ECA representatives into executive session and told them that Congress interpreted section 115(f) of the Foreign Assistance Act to mean that *all* plants for retention and removal needed ECA approval. In effect, this meant that Congress felt the cabinet technical committee had unduly limited the scope of their recommendations. The Foreign Affairs Committee wanted a study not only of the remaining unallocated plants (which the Collisson Mission had done), but also of plants already allocated to IARA and of so-called war plants that had commercial value.[43] The new departure required another study.

In August 1948, ECA Administrator Paul Hoffman proposed to send a technical commission consisting of 40 engineers to Germany. The commission was to be headed by George Wolf of U.S. Steel Export Company, who had done a study for the Department of the Army

* Royall to Julius A. Krug, June 29, 1948, WWIIRC, CSCAD 387.6; CSCAD to OMGUS for Draper, June 30, 1948; Draper to Dept. of the Army, July 1, 1948; Clay to Dept. of the Army, July 1, 1948, WWIIRC, SAOUS 387.6 Germany. Available records also show that Army and State were concerned about timing. They feared that publicity on the cabinet committee (Collisson) recommendations might cause the French Chamber of Deputies to reject the London agreements (regarding a West German government, an occupation statute, a Ruhr agreement, and so on), which it was currently considering.

earlier in 1948, on the recommendation of Benjamin Fairless and Draper. Clay's objection to the commission of engineers summarized the Army-State-OMGUS position in the entire controversy very well. Examining individual plants, he said, would produce a variety of conclusions, because one could make a case for almost any one of them. At issue was the existence of past agreements, the maintenance of the agreed level of industry, and the economic fact of life that coal, power, transport, and labor resources did not exist in sufficient quantity to permit use of the plants on the October 1947 list for the next few years. Clay said that, speaking for himself, he felt his job would be a lot easier if no more plants were dismantled, but the United States was committed to the dismantling operation by past agreements and the demands of security. He believed that sending American engineers and inspectors into hundreds of plants at this time would revive Communist criticism of the United States stand on reparations, and would "burst into flame the smoldering fire of resentment against dismantling to include possible protracted labor disturbances and strikes." Further delay in the program might make additional removals impossible except by force. If force were necessary, Clay concluded, the United States would have failed to achieve its political objectives in Germany.[44]

Hoffman subsequently modified his plans for an engineers' mission. He created instead an ECA Industrial Advisory Committee, headed by George M. Humphrey and since known by his name. This committee sent George Wolf and a task force to Europe in October, November, and December of 1948. The Humphrey Committee went itself to London and Paris to secure concurrences from Britain and France on its recommendations. Of 381 plants referred to it for review, the committee recommended retention of 167 in Germany. The Humphrey Committee had instructed the Wolf task force to make a technical study, and to disregard political and security factors for its purposes. The full committee, in preparing its report and recommendations, said that it was aware of political and security problems, and that it was impressed by the danger of future German threats to the peace as a result not only of too much industrial power, but also of too low a standard of living in Germany.[45] Why the data collected by a task force that did not consider political and security factors was taken over intact by the full Humphrey Committee and converted into a report that supposedly considered those matters is a mystery not revealed by available sources.

While Washington studied, restudied, and delayed the dismantling and reparations program, Germans continued to try to save individual plants, to stop the program entirely, and to halt operations and deliveries that were the result of prior allocations and commitments. The Bizonal Economic Council asked for a new study in May 1948. The South-Baden and South-Württemberg governments in the French zone resigned in August 1948 to protest against French military government orders to begin dismantling plants that had been designated earlier. The minister-presidents of the three zones, on the initiative of the French-zone members, took up the issue at Rüdesheim on August 31, 1948.[46] They were subsequently told by the three military governors that dismantling was in the hands of their governments and that the military governors were no longer competent to discuss the matter. The minister-presidents asked the military governors for a meeting on September 11, 1948, but they were told there was no point in meeting. The minister-presidents persisted, however. They had reports prepared that they wanted to discuss with the military governors or to bring directly to the attention of the governments of France, Britain, and the United States. They had frequent opportunity to do the former because they were meeting regularly with the military governors on details for the formation of a West German government. They were encouraged to do the latter by press reports that U.S. congressmen (Senator Bridges was mentioned) were in basic agreement with German views.[47]

On October 1, 1948, the minister-presidents submitted a report on dismantling through the military governors to the three governments. On October 29 they inquired of the military governors whether Hoffman had seen the report and what his reactions had been. They denied any intention of applying political pressure. Karl Arnold of North Rhine–Westphalia said he was under considerable fire from trade unions at home.[48] Clay's reaction was a response to the obvious political pressure being applied, the denial of which made it only more obvious. Hans-Peter Schwarz's view that Clay's answer is an example of his everlasting unwillingness to speak with Germans on equal terms ("in partnerschaftlichem Geiste zu sprechen") covers up a basic political issue by referring to Clay's personal inclinations. One could argue, in fact, that Clay was angry because Germans had bypassed him and were talking on equal terms with the United States congressmen who had kept Clay from realizing a program he believed in and wanted to carry out according to agreements made by the U.S.

Clay said that the sixteen IARA nations were entitled to reparations as agreed. The loss to Germans should be measured against the $4 billion the Western Allies had poured into Germany, an amount roughly ten times the capital value of the plants scheduled for removal. Besides, Germany still had more industrial plants than it could use efficiently for some years. Clay said that the minister-presidents' continued agitation and submission of memoranda showed that they were considering only their own interests. He concluded, in obvious anger, by repeating the dated threat that German actions could only endanger their position and perhaps make United States aid more difficult to achieve.[49] The evidence already presented shows that it was a lame threat indeed, and the minister-presidents knew this full well.

Dismantling and reparations were reviewed again and were ended in 1951, after the Bonn government came into being. Available records throw no new light on that period. It is time now to return to the bizonal organizations created in 1947 and the momentum developed toward the creation of a West German government.

# 11 | Dissension in Germany

The Bizonal Economic Council created by the military government had opened on June 25, 1947, with formal "ceremonies befitting its possible future significance as a nucleus of a central German government."[1] The promise remained unfulfilled, because the occupation powers were not yet ready for a political solution. The military government wanted to emphasize economics and forestall further French suspicions and Soviet charges that Bizonia represented a rejection of Potsdam. Nevertheless, certain issues arising out of discussions and controversies among German political parties could not be put aside. These issues had come to the surface at the Munich minister-presidents' conference, in the American-zone Länderrat, in the discussions on the German Office for Peace Questions (the "Friedensbüro"), and elsewhere. The Economic Council, for the first time, provided a convenient forum for German bizonal political dialogue and maneuver, a function the military government had not intended it to fulfill.

## Politics in the Bizonal Economic Council

Germans had had serious reservations about the new bizonal structure from the beginning. They were concerned about the fundamental political issue of federalism vs. centralism. The Social Democrats feared loss of political power and advantage in the Economic Council. Even before the Council met in Frankfurt in June, the SPD objected to the "rightist tendency" evident in the proportionality of the seat distribution.* Nevertheless, the six SPD members on the Executive Committee controlled the eight-member Committee, and thus had the power to nominate the executive directors of the five bizonal departments.

The political battle was joined from the outset. The Executive Committee nominated a single list of director candidates for the Economic Council's election. They nominated Social Democrats for the all-important posts of Director of Economics and Director of Finance, and men from the Christian Democrat–Christian Socialist coalition (CDU/CSU) for the other three. The Economic Council responded first by asking for alternative nominees from whom to choose. The Executive Committee thereupon nominated one additional candidate for each post, but each of the alternates came from the same party as the original nominees. The CDU then objected to having a Social Democrat as Director of Economics, because the SPD already held all the Land economics ministries in the bizonal area. The Free Democrats (FDP) finally voted with the CDU/CSU to defeat the list. The SPD declared it would withdraw all its candidates and assume the role of opposition party in the Economic Council. The CDU/CSU and FDP coalition subsequently elected CDU/CSU members to all the directorships. The military government looked with disfavor on the intrusion of political interests in the Economic Council affairs, but the SPD remained in opposition throughout the Council's existence.[2]

German political disagreements slowed and stalled the work of the bizonal agencies, and made the military government act cautiously. The military government tried to keep the power relationship between the Economic Council (CDU/FDP-dominated) and the Executive Committee (SPD-dominated) in balance, and seemed unwilling to delegate authority that would permit a greater display of political activity within the bizonal structure. That caution had the effect of reducing the powers the Frankfurt agencies might have assumed, and thus slowed and stalled the work even more. A case in point was the

---

* *Frankfurter Rundschau,* June 24, 1947, p. 1. The SPD headquarters in Hanover noted that the CDU got one more seat than the SPD, even though there was only a 13,000 vote difference between the two parties in Bizonia. The Free Democrats (FDP) got 5 seats and the Communists (KPD) got 3, even though the latter had 13,000 votes more in Bizonia than the FDP.

Economic Council's Ordinance 4-20, passed on September 5, 1947. It proposed to give the Executive Committee and the departmental directors a special grant of authority to issue emergency directives (in the absence of Economic Council ordinances and implementing regulations) to the Länder in urgent matters relating to food, consumer goods, and transport. The ordinance was limited to a three-month period. It contained provisions for Economic Council review, amendment, and cancellation of directives. It would, however, have given the Executive Committee an administrative entry into policy formulation as well as execution; the military government refused to accept such a general delegation of authority and vetoed the ordinance.[3] Germans decided not to make an issue of it, but they asserted repeatedly that one of the major deficiencies in the organization was the inability of the central body to get adequate enforcement from the Länder. The only apparent alternatives open to the military government were to assign greater power to the Germans at Frankfurt or to issue direct and binding orders to the Länder. Neither alternative seemed attractive. The first was undesirable because the military government wanted to maintain sufficient control to protect its heavy financial stake in Germany. It wanted to maintain the fiction that Bizonia was an economic and not a political apparatus, and to prevent the SPD from gaining through administration what it had failed to gain politically. The second alternative was unattractive—according to the American representative in the Bipartite Control Office—because the immediate foreign political situation made police methods undesirable. Americans had just begun an active program of public information to criticize Soviet administration in Germany and "to do so on euphemistic terms" by attacking "methodology" rather than the Soviet Union or the Soviet Military Administration.[4] The military government preferred to use moral suasion, but this was of little avail, and the problems continued to mount.

## Bizonal Administration—Länder Conflicts

Frankfurt and the Länder fought a series of battles during the later months of 1947 and into 1948. The crises and incidents involving food deliveries and distribution were the most serious. The Bizonal Food and Agriculture Office petitioned the military government for a direct grant of emergency powers, but it was denied.[5] It organized a crew of 100 field inspectors to go out and make spot-checks on enforcement and deliveries, but the Bavarian Food and Agriculture Minister issued an order that no bizonal inspectors would be allowed in Bavaria unless they reported to him first to secure written authorization to visit food offices. In a radio address, he reportedly said that "should the inspectors from Frankfurt come to Bavaria without being authorized by me, every farmer has my permission to chase them out of the country."[6] The military government thereupon ordered the Länder to cooperate with the inspectors, and sent some five hundred American and British personnel out to make spot-checks of their own. The result was that Germans and the Allies developed different production estimates and delivery quotas. The military government insisted that its figures be used, and applied sanctions by reducing grain imports to those Länder that delivered less indigenous food than the military government production and delivery quotas called for. There were "potato wars" and "meat wars," in which various Land ministers, supported by their Landtage, defied the Frankfurt agencies and ignored their directives. The Bizonal Food and Agriculture Director, Hans Schlange-Schöningen, made personal visits to Bavaria and Schleswig-Holstein, and agreed to reduce quotas in return for a promise of better delivery. He wanted to do the same in Lower Saxony, but cancelled his visit when Minister-President Kopf made remarks in the Landtag that Schlange-Schöningen considered to be threatening. According to Balabkins, "the Länder continued, openly or secretly, to defy bizonal agencies. In the absence of sanctions, this conflict was never resolved in Frankfurt's favor," and it did not come to an end until after the currency reform in 1948.[7]

## Bizonia on Dead Center

At no time during the occupation was there so little initiative and experimentation or so much indecision regarding Germany's future as there was in the last half of 1947. Neither Germans nor Americans seemed able or willing to strike out pragmatically as they had before, or with a definite goal in mind as they were to do later. Instead they let their relationships deteriorate and engaged in a series of reciprocal criticisms until they faced each other down in January 1948 over the intemperate and substantially accurate remarks of the Executive Director for Economics in the bizonal organization. The bizonal organizations were admittedly not working; and moral suasion, a few structural changes,[8] and piecemeal—though frantic—efforts to solve the food delivery and distribution problem consumed energies that might otherwise have been directed toward changing the organizations. The minister-presidents' conference had proved a failure at Munich, and the attempt to revive it to focus on dismantling at Wiesbaden caused more disagreement and confusion; the American-zone Länderrat had lost its economic powers and seemed unable to assume the political functions its general secretary had outlined for it in August; the Friedensbüro floundered amidst disagreements on the competency of the minister-presidents to represent Germany; political parties were torn by an attraction to national representation and the idea of a peoples' congress (*Volkskongress*) on the one hand and a strong dislike of their Soviet-zone sponsors on the other.[9]

The Allies seem to have been as frustrated as Germans. Pollock had written early from the United States, expressing concern for the future of Germany. Clay had wanted to integrate the British and American staffs at all levels of the Allied bizonal organization, but his British counterpart wanted to await the results of the London meeting of foreign ministers in November. Adcock complained bitterly to OMGUS headquarters that the minister-presidents refused to give wholehearted and nonpartisan support to the bizonal agencies, and he compared the situation to Bavaria's early fears of the Länderrat.[10] Nevertheless, when OMGUS asked for details, Adcock could not produce a single example, and instead referred to "the general blatant tone of non-cooperation or active hostility to German Economic pronouncements from Frankfurt [that] appear almost daily in the newspaper News of Germany which you no doubt see."[11] American advisers told Germans that their actions on food deliveries and collections did not measure up to their reports thereof, and they eventually let them know that the military government had become disillusioned with German-style federalism.[12] The dispute regarding the dismantling list of October 17, which we have already described, is a further example of the deterioration of relations between Germans and occupation authorities. But the most dramatic example of the deterioration came early in January, when Johannes Semler, the Bizonal Executive Director of Economics, made a speech before a CSU political gathering in Erlangen, Bavaria.

*Semler Speaks Out.* Semler had experienced daily and at first hand the frustrations in the Frankfurt agencies in the face of Länder defiance. He had been the principal speaker at the Wiesbaden minister-presidents' meeting on dismantling in October 1947. He had borne the brunt of the military government pressure on the Economic Council to refrain from intervening in dismantling, and he was not yet aware that the failure of the London Council of Foreign Ministers had actually cleared the way for several new approaches in the western zones. Disillusioned by all of these frustrations and apparently stimulated by the reception of his remarks out in the hustings, Semler lashed out frankly, heatedly, and immoderately against what he thought to be the cause of the difficulties in Germany.[13]

Semler's analysis included many of the same items Clay had reported to Marshall in his "Germany is bankrupt" cable of May 2, 1947.[14] He said that Germany's loss of external assets and gold reserves had made her dependent upon Allied help for rehabilitation. Her failure to develop foreign credits under the bizonal administration was due in large part to the policies and practices of the occupation authorities. For example, France paid for German exports and services with confiscated Reichsmarks, and she failed to return German railway cars when Germany needed transportation desperately and was allocating scarce commodities to the construction of new cars. The occupation powers had set coal export prices lower than world market prices, and Germany suffered the loss in foreign credits. They had also set an arbitrarily low price for German scrap iron. The Allied Control Council had failed to agree on currency reform, which might have given Germany a better basis for trade. The occupation powers prohibited shipping and shipbuilding, fishing and whaling, and they restricted trade and economic activities of many kinds. The Germans, Semler said, were heading into the worst food crisis since the end of the war, and Allied policies made a basic solution impossible. Americans, he said, had sent much food and aid, but they expected German gratitude and cooperation in return. When the response was less positive than anticipated, Americans threatened to cut imports and raised the specter of congressional retribution. The dismantling list was a bitter pill that Germans had to take, despite their warnings that it was ill-conceived. The continued threats in the face of German failure to meet the military government food delivery quotas was another. Germans should stop saying thanks for Allied aid, said Semler, because (except for that sent by private charities) Americans considered their aid to be a first charge against German foreign exchange balances in the future, and they would eventually present the bill. Americans, he said, sent the Germans grain and "Hühnerfutter" (literally "chicken food," but in context and terms of reference "corn"), and expected them to pay dearly in dollars.* Semler's slip may have been unintentional, but his comment that American pressure on Germans to deliver more food was designed to save American taxpayers' money and earn a good name for Clay seems to have deserved the charge of maliciousness made in the letter dismissing him.

At least one analysis of Semler's speech concluded that "his statements on the basic economic problems and especially on specific procedures and transactions mentioned were substantially true." His polemics and his timing were the reasons for his fall. Another observer asserted that the effect on congressional committees of Semler's statements on "chicken feed" and American taxpayers' money, if publicized, needed no comment.[15] It can also be said that Semler apparently failed to realize that if he rocked the boat too much, he placed in jeopardy some of the basic changes that were already under way in Bizonia and in West Germany after the collapse of the London Council of Foreign Ministers meeting.

*Semler's Dismissal and After.* Clay and Robertson dismissed Semler as Bizonal Executive Director for Economics on January 27, 1948.

---

* "Hühnerfutter" got Semler into much trouble, in no small measure because the English-language press and OMGUS translated it as "chicken feed." See Memorandum, OMGUS, CAD to C/S, Subj: Speech made by Dr. Semmler [sic] at Erlangen, Jan. 16, 1948, WWIIRC 107-2/1. It might be noted that Germans had been unhappy about an earlier American decision—forced upon them by world supply and market conditions—to substitute corn imports for wheat imports. According to Lord Pakenham, the German distaste for corn bread was shared by Bevin (Francis Aungier Pakenham, *Born to Believe: An Autobiography* [London, 1953], p. 184).

They said that his statements on payments for food and coal were contrary to the facts, that his criticism showed "malicious opposition to the Occupying Powers," and that economic recovery could not be promoted by such an attitude. Though Germans had a right to express their opinions, such rights did not permit officials to make false statements or to continue in a public office that required cooperation with the occupying powers they criticized.[16]

The Semler incident has an interesting double epilogue. First, Semler compiled a massive commentary on his Erlangen speech and included in it much material on the operations and problems of the bizonal agencies. Second, the Bavarian Landtag elected Semler as the Bavarian representative to the newly reorganized Economic Council in Frankfurt on February 18, 1948. Although some warned that his election would be a provocation, others believed it would be a good test of whether Germany had a real democracy or a puppet democracy. If it was a test, the answer arrived before the sun set. The military government sent special messengers to the Landtag as soon as the election had taken place. They found Minister-President Ehard and told him Semler's election was unacceptable. Ehard went to the rostrum and read the "order" he had received, and the CSU asked for a recess to caucus.[17] On the same day, Clay had Ehard and Josef Müller, the head of the Bavarian CSU, flown to Berlin. OMGUS had already prepared a draft proclamation dissolving the Bavarian Landtag, and the Land Director of Military Government in Bavaria reported "the General told me I was apt to wind up as Land Director with no government if I did not get things straightened out." After Ehard and Müller returned to Munich, the Bavarian Landtag dropped the matter and elected a replacement.*

The fundamental problem within Germany late in 1947 seems to have been the political vacuum that resulted from the abandonment of earlier OMGUS and German programs at a time when the larger programs of the Marshall Plan and the Atlantic Community were

* "Diary: Semler Case," Feb. 18–24, 1948 [dictated by Murray van Wagoner], WWIIRC 102-2/15. See also Bayerischer Landtag, Verhandlungen, 55. Sitzung, Feb. 19, 1948, p. 886; Frankfurter Rundschau, Feb. 19, 1948, p. 1; Süddeutsche Zeitung, Feb. 21, 1948, p. 1; Feb. 28, 1948, p. 2. OMGUS subsequently made a thorough investigation of Semler's prewar and wartime activities, but the information it collected was apparently never used.

emerging, but had not yet been decided firmly. Uncertainty and doubt seemed to affect everything. The Army's most serious proposal that the State Department assume responsibility for the occupation received active attention starting in August 1947. The State Department's take-over was announced in January, but it was delayed by the President in March 1948.[18] The debate in Washington on German policy and the Marshall Plan left more unanswered questions than solutions, at least until early 1948. Congressional and public hostility left doubts about the future of denazification, dismantling, reparations, and decartelization. French objections created doubts about the level-of-industry plan, coal exports, and the Saar. Britain's financial crisis raised doubts about her ability to continue to contribute even a smaller portion of the costs of category A and B imports, and it raised the question of Britain's withdrawing from Germany in the near future.[19] Soviet-zone land reforms, nationalization, and active support for the Socialist Unity Party (SED) left doubt about the possible union of that zone with the rest of Germany, especially since the Soviet and American military governments had begun active propaganda campaigns against each other in Germany.[20] The prospect of another foreign ministers' meeting to consider the German question gave pause to many who might have experimented. There is evidence of considerable discussion on whether to wait or to go ahead with various plans, but caution carried the day.[21]

## The London Council of Foreign Ministers as Watershed

The meeting of the Council of Foreign Ministers in London was, in a sense, a watershed or a parting of the ways as Robertson had predicted in July. The failure to agree on any substantial questions and the decision to adjourn without making plans for a future meeting provided an incentive and a rationale for a tremendous push toward pragmatic solutions and toward new policy decisions, many of which had been delayed less out of hope than for reasons of polity. Marshall reported that "we cannot look forward to a unified Germany at this time. We must do the best we can in the area where our influence can be felt."[22] Clay wrote later that the London conference verified the

American view that the Soviets would not allow German freedom and security next to their satellites, and that "we were now engaged in a competitive struggle, not with arms but with economic resources, with ideas and ideals."[23]

Clay and Murphy both said that British and American representatives met informally after the London conference to decide what they might do next.[24] Though not inaccurate, their accounts seem to emphasize the informality and to minimize the preparatory work that lay behind the meeting in Lewis Douglas's London residence. In September, OMGUS had prepared a study of German governmental structure, describing various alternative approaches the United States might take, depending upon the outcome of the London conference. On September 24, 1947, Clay cabled the Department of the Army saying it was his understanding that OMGUS should proceed to establish a provisional government for Bizonia—or Trizonia if France joined —immediately after the London meeting if the latter failed to unify Germany. Early in November Clay told the American-zone minister-presidents that denazification must be finished before the winter ended, because it should be over before there were national elections. He said the same held true even if a government had to be created for only a portion of Germany.[25] Later, as the London meeting was just beginning, Clay sent instructions that as soon as he could get back from London he (and perhaps Robertson) would meet with the minister-presidents and bizonal officials to discuss "matters of mutual interest" and the minister-presidents' "responsibilities vis-à-vis the bizonal setup." On the day the London meeting ended, the *Frankfurter Rundschau* published a story about plans for such a meeting and reported that a new bizonal constitution would be on the agenda.[26] British and American military governments denied knowledge of such plans, but the meeting held January 7–8, 1948, shows that the story was not without foundation.

*Bizonia Becomes Political.* Two major decisions came out of the informal discussions following the London conference. First, Bevin and Marshall instructed their military governors to develop a political structure for Bizonia, and second, they decided to plan a tripartite government-level conference to discuss long-range German policy with France. To implement the first agreement, Clay and Robertson met the minister-presidents and bizonal officials in Frankfurt on January 7–8, 1948. They assured Germans the meeting was for discussion rather than for presentation of a ready-made plan. They obviously wanted to avoid difficulties and criticisms like those surrounding the previous bizonal reorganization in May 1947. Nevertheless, J. F. J. Gillen's summary of a Clay-Robertson meeting on January 2, 1948, shows that they had in fact agreed on a rather definite plan to reform the Executive Directors into a sort of cabinet, to create a second chamber out of the Executive Committee, to double the size of the Economic Council, to create a bizonal high court and central bank, and to give the Economic Council power to levy customs duties and excise taxes and perhaps to share in income tax collections.[27]

The meeting with the minister-presidents and bizonal officials did produce discussions and agreements, but these all followed the earlier military governors' agreement. Germans asked, for example, if Berlin could be included, and they were told no. They asked about Länder rights, and were told that representatives served their Länder, but also had to consider the general interest. They agreed to double the membership and to create a second chamber. At the end of the meeting the military governors asked Germans to prepare further suggestions and recommendations, but warned them not to get into the area of a German government. Gillen says, however, that Clay assumed a German government would emerge from the new organization.

Two things stood in the way of rapid bizonal reorganization: German apprehension and reluctance, and French objections. In preparing their further suggestions and recommendations, Germans expressed concern that the central taxing powers would threaten the existence of the Länder, that France would never enter into such an arrangement, and that the changes were so fundamental as to prejudice the future government of Germany and thus make unification impossible. They objected particularly to the creation by military government proclamation of a political organization with centralized financial and judicial functions. They were in a quandary whether to go ahead or to try to delay in hopes that unification might still be possible, and they were under serious attack from the Communist party for collaborating with the "dividers of Germany."[28] Again, as it had happened during the Munich minister-presidents' conference in June

1947, French policy and German federalism dovetailed neatly, and in this case it gave rise to considerable dissatisfaction in OMGUS with German-style federalism.*

France registered displeasure with the new bizonal developments as soon as the details became known. Clay discusses at some length the aide-memoir of January 24, 1948, in which France summarized her objections.[29] Clay could hardly have been surprised by the aide-memoir, as he says he was, because he had already had word from Washington that France wanted government-level discussions (as they had on the level-of-industry plan of July 1947) before bizonal reorganization was made final. He protested vigorously on January 16, saying that he was merely implementing government policy, that France had been informed, that French participation would delay the program, and that almost nothing he and Robertson were doing would be wholly acceptable to France. Clay went on to say that the German situation was more desperate than at any time since the surrender. The problem was due not to German inefficiency, but to lack of power in the bizonal administrations. To achieve economic recovery, Germans needed a government, federal in nature, but with sufficient power to solve current economic problems. If that could not be achieved, the military government would have to assume the powers itself and re-assume functions previously delegated to Germans. This move would require a sizable increase in personnel and would be a serious step backward politically.[30]

In this context the United States indicated its readiness to recognize de facto separation of the Saar from Germany and its economic incorporation into France until the peace settlement. It informed France that her objections to bizonal reorganization would be noted, but that the United States and Britain believed they must proceed with reorganization as planned. France persisted, however, and presented her aide-memoir of January 24, 1948. Clay tells us that the United States

* "Vormerkung über eine Besprechung, die ich heute im Auftrage des Herrn Ministerpräsidenten Dr. Ehard mit dem Stellvertreter von General Adcock, Mr. Kenneth Dayton, über den Entwurf einer Proklamation betr. die Wirtschaftsverwaltung des Vereinigten Wirtschaftsgebietes hatte," signed by Dr. Glum, January 25, 1948, Staatskanzlei, Wiesbaden, 1d02. Dayton told Glum that bizonal agencies had failed because the Länder sabotaged them, and he commented that Americans had lost some of their love for federalism.

and Britain held fast and instructed the military governors to go ahead. The governors released their proclamations, effective February 9, 1948.[31] Nevertheless, Clay's speech to the Länderrat on February 3, 1948, indicates that he had modified his position somewhat since early January. At least he no longer implied that a future government would emerge out of the structure, and he frankly admitted that it was an Allied creation. He noted that there had been much talk about the new bizonal organization: some said it was too weak; others that it was too centralized; some did not want a bizonal government; and others objected to the military government's direction. He believed all this proved that one could not please everybody all the time, and some people could never be pleased at all. But he went on to say that the bizonal agencies were transitory and limited to economic and financial matters. They were not intended to prejudice Germany's political future. Clay admitted that Germans had had little to say about the final decision, and added that the military government had assumed the responsibility for creating certain structures that it wanted.[32]

## Six-Power Talks in London

Clay's apparent modification should be seen in the light of the second decision made during the informal talks following the London conference. On January 30, 1948, the Department of Army told Clay that tripartite talks on long-range German policy would commence on February 19. The tentative agenda would include cooperation with the Benelux nations on German affairs, reparations, Germany and the Marshall Plan, control of the Ruhr, security, political and economic organization of the three western zones, provisional territorial arrangements, and Länder boundaries.[33] Although the available records are not complete, Washington had apparently answered the French demands for discussions on Bizonia with an invitation to the tripartite talks Bevin and Marshall had decided to promote after the London conference. To induce a favorable French reply, it appears, the United States recognized France's separation of the Saar from Germany. France then gave Clay a free hand to carry through on the commitments to bizonal reorganization, which would have been extremely difficult to withdraw after the meeting of January 7–8, 1948.

The London six-power conference of 1948 thus served the very practical purpose of avoiding a United States–French showdown on Bizonia, in addition to the purpose of agreeing on long-range policy for Germany.

The records relating to the London six-power conference from February 23 to March 5 and April 20 to June 2, 1948, are not available to the private researcher. We know that the first session achieved preliminary agreement on general principles. We know also that tripartite working parties were set up in Berlin between the two sessions.[34] The working parties consulted with Benelux representatives and received written communications from some British Commonwealth nations. They had been charged with developing preliminary agreements for final decision at the second session. Clay believed, however, that they went into too much detail and gave too little attention to principles. He was particularly disappointed with the progress made by the working party on the future political structure. He has recounted in his book how he went over the heads of the working party to Couve de Murville to achieve an understanding, and then hurriedly dictated a statement that eventually formed the basis for the London decision on a West German government.[35]

Published materials on the London six-power conference show a wide range of agreements, but they do not hide the fact that there were many differences.[36] The conference recommended association of the Benelux countries in German policy determination, and thus gave added weight to the Brussels Pact of March 17, 1948. It recommended security measures, territorial changes, and Länder boundary adjustments. It recommended German participation in the European Recovery Program (ERP), and an international authority for control of the Ruhr. The French government had reservations on the Ruhr proposal, and there was much additional negotiation until a final agreement was reached late in December 1948, and signed in April 1949. In the meantime, British and American military governments in the field had reorganized the Ruhr coal and steel industries in an elaborate program that included the creation of trustee managements.[37] This was done over serious French objections, in part, it seems, to permit more rapid recovery under the ERP; to prevent international management (but not international control); to forestall a possible push for socialization by the new German government or one of its Länder; to forestall possible Soviet demands for a voice in an international management group should the Soviet Union ever agree to German unity; and to assure the continued dominance of the United States in economic and financial affairs (through its superior powers in the Joint Export-Import Agency and the Joint Foreign Exchange Agency), at least so long as the occupation lasted.[38]

The London six-power conference also recommended formation of a West German government by action of the minister-presidents of the three zones. It instructed the military governors to assemble the minister-presidents and to authorize them to convene a constituent assembly that would prepare a constitution for ratification by the German people. The method of ratification was a point of disagreement, especially between France and the United States. France wanted it ratified by the Landtage; the United States by popular referendum. There was, however, a more basic disagreement. Linked closely to the recommendation for a West German government was the decision to draft an occupation statute. The absence of details on such a statute in the official communiqué of the six-power conference is an outward manifestation of the fundamental difference of opinion not only about how the statute should be drawn up but also about whether such a statute should even be drafted at this time. Although the conference records are not available, published materials and records of the discussions between the military governors and Germans charged with drafting the Bonn constitution reveal a great deal.[39] In brief, the Occupation Statute went through countless drafts and was finally referred to government level for decision, because French negotiators wanted more powers reserved to the occupation than Americans and British would accept in Berlin. Clay fought down to the wire against excessive reserved powers, but without success. He argued that the new government would have less power than the Bizonal Economic Council had had. On the day before the Occupation Statute was released as an agreement, he summarized what he considered to be its defects: the Statute permitted any of the military governors to appeal to his government on issues relating to the Occupation Statute itself, to trizonal fusion, to the London agreements, and to agreements on prohibited and restricted industries, the Ruhr, the status of foreign interests in Germany, the Office of European Economic Cooperation, and the IARA. Clay believed that any issue the new German government might take up could somehow be related to one or more of the foregoing issues or agreements, and he showed from past examples what that meant. Past appeals for consultations at the top levels of government had delayed action on the level of industry, equalization of burdens, the lifting of the moratorium on foreign investments, and the patent law; and, he said, there were others. Friedrich's cryptic expression of hope in the provision that the Statute would be reviewed within a year thus achieves a new significance.[40]

## Soviet Protests and the Berlin Blockade

The Soviet Union, which had protested repeatedly and at various levels that the other occupying powers were abandoning Potsdam and going ahead on their own, apparently decided for the first time early in 1948 to match words with action. The Soviet Military Administration had, of course, taken many unilateral steps in its own zone before this. Among other actions, it had supported the SED, promoted land reform and socialization, strengthened labor unions, set up central administrations in its own zone, created a central economic body in 1947, and supported the Volkskongress movement. But Molotov objected to bizonal developments in the foreign ministers' meetings, especially at Moscow and London. Sokolovsky expressed similar views in the Allied Control Council many times. The Soviet government objected to the new level-of-industry plan for Bizonia in August 1947, and there are many more examples of official and semiofficial statements with the same theme.[41] The standard Western response to Soviet protests and objections contained both positive and negative features. On the positive side, it said that the invitation to join in the bizonal experiment was open to all zones and that to make amalgamation easier no political structure had been created. The negative part of the response, especially after the Moscow conference and the Kennan analysis of Soviet conduct, was that the Soviet Union's own policies on reparations, her political support for the SED, her unwillingness to compromise at meetings of the Council of Foreign Ministers, and her policies and practices on other issues had prevented German economic unity in the first place, and that the Soviets were thus the fundamental cause of their own displeasure.[42]

The considerations that prompted the Soviet Union to back its words with action in 1948 are, of course, hidden in Soviet archives unavailable to the researcher. The current interpretation belongs almost exclusively to the "containment school," which sees in Soviet actions and intentions a plan for dominating as great a portion of Europe as possible and for keeping the remainder so weak that it would not be able to withstand the Communist subversion from within and would eventually fall into the Soviet orbit. The Soviet decision to act was, according to this interpretation, designed to bring pressure on the West to stop its rehabilitation of Germany; to discontinue its contribution to social and economic stability in central Europe; and to abandon Berlin, thereby providing a symbolic demonstration of the Soviet Union's dominance in central Europe. Subsequent interpretations of the Berlin airlift, the defense of Berlin, the Marshall Plan, the role of the Bonn government, the place of NATO, the significance of the Berlin Wall, and many other issues and incidents have been influenced by this general view.

There are, however, certain difficulties in the "containment school" interpretation. The most recent summing up of these is by Hans-Peter Schwarz, who has stated that it must be clear by now that the Soviets had no clearly conceived German policy between 1945 and 1949. He cites contradictions in Soviet policy and Russian pragmatic adjustments to existing and changing conditions as evidence.[43] From Schwarz's impressive list, we might note the Soviet shift on reparations from a program of capital goods removals to reparations from current production as a case in point. Another is the change from a demand in March 1946 for a steel production limit of 4.5 million tons annually to a call by Molotov in July for an increase, to a demand at the Moscow conference for a 10- to 12-million-ton limit, and to a reported 12 million tons proposed in October 1947.[44]

In the absence of conclusive documentary evidence on either side of the argument, we might assume Schwarz's point for the moment and apply it to the Soviet decision to blockade Berlin. (To my knowledge, no one has ever considered the origins of the Berlin blockade in the light of counterarguments to the "containment school" interpretation.) If the Soviets were indeed flexible, pragmatic, and undecided about their long-range policy objectives in Germany, they had reason to view American economic priorities and the programs arising from them as manifestations of a plan or a tendency. The halt to dismantling, the original push for interzonal unity by invitation rather than by Allied Control Council agreement, the experiment to promote unity via the minister-presidents' conferences, the drive for bizonal self-sufficiency and its partial justification as an economic magnet for the rest of Germany, the bizonal level-of-industry plan, the Marshall Plan with Germany as a key, and eventual bizonal political reorganization accompanied by political discussions among the six powers in London—all these, when taken together, explain why the Soviet Union suspected that the United States had a long-standing plan to rehabilitate Germany at all costs. It should be made clear at this point that the American actions were in themselves experimental and pragmatic, and that they were designed especially to realize the economic unity promised by Potsdam, which French policy and actions had held in abeyance. Soviet misinterpretations of American intentions can be accounted for at least in part by the way Americans explained their policies and programs to themselves and to the world. We have noted earlier that when Clay asked for government-level pressure on France in November 1945 he got little action, but he did get a discourse on Soviet intentions. After the Moscow conference the tendency to blame the Soviets and leave French policy unremarked became even more obvious. In his Moscow-conference report to the nation, Marshall said the Soviets were responsible for the American decision to go ahead, and he followed the report with the decisions for bizonal reorganization, a new level-of-industry plan, and the Marshall Plan to remove any doubts about his seriousness. Dulles said as much in January 1947, and the Soviet press attacked him repeatedly during the Moscow meeting. The Harriman committee recommended going ahead in West Germany in November 1947, thus implying that the Soviets were the chief obstacle. There are many more examples in the records of the hearings on interim aid and the Marshall Plan, in the chorus of similar views and opinions expressed regularly in the daily press, and last but not least, in the United States government notes answering Soviet protests from time to time.

Given Soviet suspicions of American policy, the Soviet decision to force the issue in the spring of 1948 may be viewed as a response rather than as an initiative, a pragmatic effort rather than the result of a long-range plan. The situation in Germany certainly invited an attempt to fish in muddy waters. Bizonia had all but broken down during the "potato wars" and "meat wars." Germans and Allies were criticizing each other openly on food deliveries and dismantling. The Semler incident suggested high-level German disillusionment with US/UK policies and plans. The disappointment of Germans with plans for bizonal reorganization presented to them on January 7–8 and their fears that going ahead might result in a divided Germany were published widely in the press. French objections to the January 7–8 plans were no secret, and it appeared that there would be a repetition of the level-of-industry dispute that had led to speculations about Clay's resignation, to a Marshall-Clay split, and to various other signs of weakness and disagreement. Furthermore, OMGUS and Washington had been openly criticizing each other on dismantling since October. If the Soviets assumed a deliberate plan or tendency on the part of the West, the time seemed ripe to split the forces necessary to the plan. We know now that their action had the opposite effect, but that effect was in part the result of the Western conviction that Soviet action was itself part of a larger plan, and in part the result of the willingness of the Americans and the British to make major concessions to France and to the Germans because of their own interpretations of Soviet intentions.

Whatever the basis for their decision may have been, the Soviets filed formal protests against the London six-power talks on February 13, 1948, before the talks actually began, and on March 6, at the conclusion of the first session. On March 20 Sokolovsky brought up the recent Prague Declaration on Germany in the Allied Control Council, and asked his colleagues for information on the London discussions. The French representative said he would refer the request to his government, but Clay and Robertson said simply that there was nothing to add to the published communiqué. In the absence of more complete documentation, one can assume that a broadening of the basis of the discussions would have proved disastrous, especially since a package—one that included the Ruhr, German boundaries, German participation in ERP, and a future German government—was at stake. Disagreement on any of the issues was likely to open all the others. Besides, everything was still very tentative, and the fact that the six-power discussions originated partly as an attempt to avoid a United States–French standoff on bizonal reorganization was not out of mind. Failing to get a response from Clay and Robertson, Sokolovsky read a prepared statement that repeated the familiar charges of unilateral action in violation of Potsdam and other agreements, and declared that since no discussions were possible, the meeting was adjourned. He left without requesting the other members' approval, as was customary, and he did not mention future meetings, which was his customary responsibility since he was the chairman at the time. Clay reported that the Soviet delegation was serious and apparently fully aware of the "gravity of their action. . . . I believe we have or are reaching a crisis in our relations."[45]

The story of the way in which the Soviets gradually shut off traffic into Berlin and then finally blockaded it completely has been told often. The significance of the decision to supply the city by air; the heroism of Berliners and Allied personnel who remained in the city; the service of Germans and non-Germans alike, who worked around the clock, day in and day out, to assemble and fly the supplies; and the ultimate success of the airlift—all these are worthy of note, but it is hardly necessary to repeat all this again.[46]

At least two points merit attention, however. Both were slighted at the time because of the tensions of the blockade and the drama of the airlift operations. They have been largely ignored since, apparently because they never came to public attention at the time, and perhaps because the technical aspects of the airlift and the political significance of its success are of greater interest. First, there is evidence in the published State Department "white paper" on Berlin that the Soviets imposed the blockade in retaliation against the London decision to form a new German government. There is also evidence that the State Department accepted this explanation as a basis for further discussion, and its instructions to Ambassador Walter B. Smith for Moscow discussions on Berlin are so clear they bear repeating: "September 1 does not represent the date of formal establishment of such a governmental organization. It is rather the date on

which representatives from the German states will begin the exploratory study of the problems involved in setting up of the common organization. It is certainly not intended that any conclusions that they
reach shall preclude or contravene any agreement arrived at by the
four powers on a government for all Germany."[47]

The second point usually slighted is that the three Western powers
had agreed to a package plan at London in June and that they subsequently made commitments to the Germans that were apparently
much firmer than the State Department's instructions to Ambassador
Smith imply. So far as the Germans were concerned, the plan was to
have the minister-presidents convene a constituent assembly by September 1, 1948. That is a far cry from beginning exploratory study
of problems involved in setting up a common organization. More important still, German agreement to go the route called for at London
had been achieved under such drastic pressures, especially from
OMGUS, that a United States reversal would have been perhaps as
serious *politically* as actual withdrawal from Berlin. Administrative
decisions in the field and the inherent dynamic of previous decisions
had outrun human capacity to keep abreast of all aspects of the situation. The result was that construction of a West German government
continued under the momentum it had achieved. If the Berlin blockade was not to be explained as a Soviet response to a Western initiative that could not—or would not—be reversed, then it had to be
explained in terms of a larger Soviet strategy of containment. The
Soviets' real reasons for imposing the blockade, as well as the ones
they stated publicly, were played down at the time, and they have
apparently been completely forgotten by most of the "containment
school" theorists. The momentum toward a West German government
is thus closely related to the origin of the Berlin blockade; and as the
next chapter will show, it is very revealing of the strict limits imposed
by the Allies on the choices Germans might make regarding their
future as a nation.

# 12 | The July Days

The Department of Army sent detailed instructions to OMGUS on how the London six-power communiqué of June 2, 1948, should be publicized, saying that OMGUS should stress the momentous importance of the agreements, should emphasize the wide range of agreement in contrast to the spectacular disagreements of the Council of Foreign Ministers, and should make clear that previous disagreements had hampered German recovery. The London agreements were limited in scope, the instructions continued, because the USSR did not participate. They could be broadened at any time if the Soviets decided to join. In the meantime, they offered an unprecedented opportunity for Germans to participate in European rehabilitation and to establish a government, limited only by the requirements of the occupation and by international agreements. The instructions said that the new government, which would be organized as a federation, would protect individual rights; and that the relationship between Germans and the occupation powers would be more precisely defined. News media should, however, avoid too much speculation on the nature of the future government. In summary, the instructions concluded, the London agreements represented a profound change of attitude toward Germany.[1]

## German Response to the London Communiqué

Germans who read the document themselves thought otherwise, and they responded in a variety of ways. The minister-presidents of the British and American zones, who met in Düsseldorf on June 5–6, 1948, to discuss ways to increase coal production, expressed their opposition to Ruhr internationalization. However, they said that if the Ruhr must be internationalized, other industrial areas of Europe should be put under similar control bodies and that Germans should have representation on them. Adenauer recalled in his memoirs that Germans shared their general disappointment in the London agreements during a June 9 meeting of the British-zone Zonenbeirat. On June 10, 1948, a CDU party meeting, chaired by Adenauer, passed a resolution calling the London agreements nothing more than a "gilded annexation" of the Ruhr ("die goldene Form einer Annexion"), and charging that the victors wanted economic control without assuming political responsibility. Such annexation, it said, would have grave consequences for the German economy, and would destroy the basis for the Marshall Plan. At the same meeting, Adenauer tells us, the CDU resolved to ask the SPD to help promote uniform statements by all German parties against the published plan. According to Adenauer, the CDU preferred four-power agreement to the London decisions. Furthermore, it wanted to go on record to ensure against criticism in the future, should a new German nationalism arise. Subsequent discussions showed the SPD to be in substantial agreement with the CDU on the undesirability of the Ruhr plan, but it did not favor joint action.[2]

Clay reported the adverse reaction of Germans to the London communiqué, and Washington's reply combined explanation and advice. It said the Ruhr proposal had been released in detail at the request of France, which wanted full discussion during the French parliament's consideration of the agreements. It noted that the communiqué had been kept brief on the subject of a West German government so as not to anticipate in detail the subjects to be discussed at the proposed military governors' meeting with the minister-presidents. Significantly, however, Washington advised Clay to have members of his staff initiate informal discussions with minister-presidents, political leaders, journalists, and others. Americans were to emphasize that Germans would be permitted to make a number of important political decisions. For example, they could decide whether they wanted a government now, and they could determine its form and character.[3] In other words, Americans should give Germans an informal preview of information that was being withheld until the French government had taken an official position on the London agreements. Adenauer implies that the British did likewise. He says that Robertson told the Zonenbeirat on June 29 that the full contents of the London recommendations had not yet been made public.*

## The Frankfurt Documents

*The Presentation.* The three military governors met with the minister-presidents of the three western zones in Frankfurt on July 1, 1948. They presented them with the London decisions on a West German government. The military governors had met on June 30 to plan in minute detail the procedures and methods of presentation. They disagreed on the unanimity principle, which France wanted preserved, especially on financial and economic matters. They also disagreed on the specific Land boundary changes authorized at London; on whether the Germans should be instructed on the method of ratification; and on whether the military governors should tell Germans they had authority from their governments to issue additional instructions on German governmental structure, the role of the executive, emergency powers, police powers, cultural powers, financial powers, and several other matters.[4] The additional instructions were particularly crucial, because Germans had already been told informally that they would have considerable choice in some of these matters. Clay and Robertson argued on June 30 that the list was an

---

* Adenauer, *Erinnerungen*, p. 145. Adenauer says that Robertson's speech induced him to test how far Germany could go under the London agreements. It seems rather strange, however, that Adenauer should have shifted so drastically in nineteen days, unless one assumes the June 10 position to have been basically a Ruhr position and recalls that the CDU had gradually moved toward a West German orientation during the Adenauer-Kaiser dispute over party leadership, national representation, and other issues. There is evidence that the CDU/CSU decided, early in 1948, to turn "rightward and westward," rather than become involved in Jakob Kaiser's troubles with the Soviet Military Administration. Kaiser's ideological tendencies were suspect among certain CDU/CSU circles in the West; Adenauer apparently saw him as a threat to his party leadership; and the eastern zone CDU's socialist tendencies were common knowledge. All of these undoubtedly laid the basis for the orientation toward the West that Adenauer proclaimed when the London agreements opened the possibility in June 1948. Cf. Schwarz, *Vom Reich zur Bundesrepublik*, pp. 467–79.

instruction to the military governors and that Allied liaison officers could transmit the details to Germans as the issues arose. This did not deny the basic limitation on Germans; it simply delayed revelation of the limitation. Clay and Robertson assumed that Germans would work out many of the items to the satisfaction of the Allies and thus make it unnecessary to issue directives.

The assumption reveals considerable disregard for or misunderstanding of the deep political cleavages within the ranks of the minister-presidents and the people they represented. The cleavages had manifested themselves at the Munich conference, in the German Office for Peace Questions (the Friedensbüro), and in the bizonal organizations. But the military government remained aloof from the first two for the most part, and it had deliberately set up the bizonal structures to prevent the full flowering of political controversy in the bizonal agencies. The assumption is important, however, because it explains Clay's bitter disappointment with the results of the Koblenz conference. He was sure the minister-presidents would solve many of the problems on which he could not get French agreement, and when they hesitated at Koblenz, he told them they had placed their destiny in the hands of General Koenig. Particularly noteworthy in this context is the military governors' discussion on June 30 concerning what they might do in the event of German counterproposals. Koenig seemed to think Germans capable of rejecting the offer to form a government, and he apparently expected counterproposals. Clay seemed unwilling to consider the matter and said, "we are all looking at ghosts walking."[5]

Each of the military governors read one document to the minister-presidents. They had determined by lot who would read which and who would chair the meeting. Document I, read by Clay, outlined procedures for calling a constituent assembly by September 1, 1948. It said the Länder could develop their own election procedures, that the government to be created must be federalist so as to protect the Länder and to make German unification easier, that it must guarantee individual rights, and that its constitution would be in force when two-thirds of the Länder had ratified it by referendum. Document II asked the minister-presidents to study Länder boundaries, and outlined procedures for making any changes the minister-presidents might recommend. Document III, read by Koenig, described the relationship of the new German government to the Allied occupation authorities. It said Germans would receive a legislative, administrative, and judicial grant of authority, except in certain reserved areas. The latter included foreign affairs; foreign trade; domestic trade affected by commitments of the occupation authorities; and existing and future controls established by the Allies, such as the Ruhr Authority, reparations, demilitarization, and certain forms of scientific research. Document III said the Allies reserved the right to protect the new constitution and the occupation authorities, and to resume full powers in an emergency. It said that the constitution could be amended only with military government approval, and that all German legislation not in the reserved areas would be effective within 21 days unless acted on by the military governors.[6]

After the three documents had been read, Clay, who chaired the meeting, asked the minister-presidents if they had questions or if they wanted to caucus for an hour or so to prepare a response. The minister-presidents had met informally on June 30, and had agreed in advance not to react during this meeting. They reportedly "showed no emotion," and Reinhold Maier, their spokesman, said a short caucus would not do. He said the issues were so vital that the minister-presidents needed to consult with their governments and their Landtage. They obviously needed time to work out compromises among themselves. They were undoubtedly also induced by the diverse "leaks" that all three military governments had planted to think that delay might result in additional information and/or concessions.[7] Particularly apropos are Maier's words to the Württemberg-Baden Landtag some days later: "The text of the London Agreements was written to be read in France. The decisions were supposed to be made appealing to the French public. The result was an opposite psychological effect in Germany, because we could read only the shadow-side of the decisions. Our job is now to try to translate the communiqué into German. I do not doubt that Germans will be able to use this advantageous occasion to work out a general counterproposal at Koblenz and thus to take a considerable step forward."[8] The July 1 meeting adjourned without discussion; the minister-presidents then met briefly and decided to reconvene in Koblenz a week later.[9]

*The German Reaction.* Despite the minister-presidents' restraint on July 1, German responses to the Frankfurt documents were not slow in coming. Their diversity reflects the variety of political orientations from which they came. Germans commented on the importance of the role assigned to the minister-presidents, and the significance of this to the idea of a national representation was not lost on them. Some expressed hope that Germans would use the new opportunity thrust upon them. Almost universally, however, Germans criticized the proposed Occupation Statute and its implications. Ehard said it was a bitter pill, the "sobering and bitter documentation of the collapse and weakness of Germany. It shows the lot of a conquered nation." Other Bavarians joined in: one said it actually reduced German freedoms and proposed to anchor the reductions in a constitution; another said Germans had learned from experience in the American-zone Länder that constitutions meant little. Maier said Document III was a disappointment; Lüdemann followed suit; various Landtage and political factions expressed similar objections; and the Friedensbüro subjected it to a thorough analysis.[10]

The Friedensbüro asserted that the spirit and tenor of Document III showed that the Allies wanted merely to authorize Germans to participate, but not to determine policy or proclaim objectives of their own that might run counter to those of the Allies. It analyzed the reserved powers to show that even the automatic 21-day period for approval of legislation in the absence of a veto was illusory, because almost every piece of legislation Germans might initiate could be deemed to fall within the reserved powers list.[11] Even in the area of democratization, the Allies had retained an open-ended special responsibility to observe, advise, and assist. In effect, the Friedensbüro analysis concluded, the proposed Occupation Statute would merely legalize the existing situation and allow the Allies to retain the powers they had assumed in the June 5, 1945, declaration of supreme authority. Thus the Germans were being asked not to make a constitution, but to create an administrative apparatus for the convenience of the Allies. Therefore, Germans should ask the military government to issue the Occupation Statute and assume the responsibility for the limitations they imposed. The Friedensbüro said Germans had two alternatives: to refuse to participate on Allied terms or to negotiate. If they decided to negotiate, Germans should strive for a provisional government or for a continuation of a German administration similar to the bizonal administration rather than for a government as such. The limitations specified in the Occupation Statute would make a government meaningless. In any case, they should avoid the forms, names, and symbols of constitution-making. They should not use the terms "constitution" and "state," and they should oppose a popular referendum. In the light of the position the minister-presidents were to take at Koblenz, it is particularly noteworthy that the Friedensbüro analysis declared the July 1, 1948, proposals to be unacceptable without referring to the Berlin crisis or to the question of the East-West division. Nevertheless, the Friedensbüro recognized that one of the objectives of the Allies was to make unification more attractive to the eastern zone Germans, and that the concept of the magnet still prevailed. Given this objective, it said the Frankfurt proposals were all the more unfortunate as a tactic, because they would make West Germany appear to be a "Quisling" government. The Occupation Statute would, in effect, defeat one of the basic purposes of the Allies. A popular referendum would be the occasion for a flood of criticism from the East.[12]

## The Minister-Presidents at Koblenz

The action of the minister-presidents at Koblenz on July 8–10, 1948, becomes clearer if it is viewed in the context of the prior events rather than in the context of subsequent developments.[13] The CDU/CSU caucus in Koblenz on the eve of the full conference reportedly approved the general idea of the Frankfurt documents, but it recommended a delay on boundary redrawing and counterproposals to the Occupation Statute. It rejected unanimously the plan to link the Occupation Statute with a German constitution. The SPD caucus in Rüdesheim differed in tactics, but not in fundamentals. The SPD wanted an administrative apparatus rather than a government with a constitution. It wanted the Allies to proclaim the Occupation Statute before Germans drew up their new "organizational statute" (thus calling for a separation of the two ), and it wanted territorial questions postponed.*

The Koblenz resolutions followed closely the prior arguments, analyses, and recommendations. Regarding Document I, the minister-presidents said they preferred a provisional arrangement. They wanted to postpone a national constitutional convention "until a solution for all of Germany is possible and until German sovereignty has been sufficiently restored." They recommended, instead, election of a representative body (a parliamentary council) to draw up a "basic law," which would be approved by the Landtage and promulgated by the minister-presidents under special authority granted them by the military governors. Regarding Document II, they pleaded for more time, but conceded the desirability of territorial changes in the Länder. As earlier responses had foreshadowed, Document III received the most careful comment and the most thorough recommendations for change. In general, the minister-presidents asked for more German authority and less Allied intervention and supervision. They wanted a clearer definition of the purposes of the occupation, and they asked the Allies to limit supervision and control to achieving those purposes. They wanted directives issued only by top-level military government authorities to top-level German authorities, and they asked that the jurisdiction of Allied courts be limited. And among other things they wanted the international Ruhr authority deleted from the Occupation Statute, and restrictions placed on the military governments' emergency powers.[14]

The minister-presidents' letter of explanation (*Mantelnote*) that accompanied the formal Koblenz resolutions added a new and important dimension to the situation. The letter reflected the appeal of Frau Luise Schröder, the ruling mayor of Berlin, that the minister-presidents do nothing that might be interpreted as an abandonment

---

* "Die CDU-CSU zu den Vorschlägen der Militärgouverneure," Staatskanzlei, Wiesbaden, 1a08/III; OMGUS, CAD, to Clay, Memorandum, Subj: Summary of Current Situation on Minister-Presidents' Meeting, July 9, 1948, WWIIRC 79-1/1; *New York Times*, July 8, 1948, p. 7; July 9, 1948, p. 4; *Süddeutsche Zeitung*, July 10, 1948, p. 1. Cf. Edinger, *Kurt Schumacher*, p. 119, for the undocumented statement that the SPD minister-presidents took their instructions from Hanover, and p. 167, for a similar statement based on Litchfield's account. In an undocumented footnote, Edinger seems to attribute the conclusion to Clay's suspicion, which Edinger believes to be correct.

of that city.[15] The Mantelnote also tried to camouflage the disagreements among the minister-presidents. Specifically, it referred to the inability of the four powers to agree in the past and it welcomed the increased authority the Frankfurt documents proposed to give Germans in a portion of the territory under four-power control; but it stated that the minister-presidents were anxious about the increasing East-West rift. For this reason, it said, the minister-presidents had recommended a provisional arrangement in the three zones, and had opposed the plan for a referendum. "The minister-presidents want to repeat on this occasion that in their opinion a German constitution cannot be created until the whole German people finds it possible to constitute itself [as a nation] through free self-determination; until this time comes only provisional organization measures can be taken." The rest of the letter was a commentary on Länder boundaries and on the Occupation Statute, and a request for an early Allied declaration that the state of war cease.[16]

The differences between the actual Koblenz resolutions and the Mantelnote that accompanied them are thus made clear by internal analysis and by consideration of the nature of the preparations prior to the Koblenz conference. They can be seen most clearly, however, by considering what might have happened if the Western military governors had accepted the Koblenz resolutions carte blanche. Suppose, for a moment, the three governments had granted the limited sovereignty Germans requested in response to Document III, and suppose they had gone ahead to establish a provisional administration with a basic law, and so on. Given previous Soviet and SED charges that Bizonia would divide Germany and the fact that the Soviets were already blockading Berlin, there is absolutely nothing to support the idea that the East-West rift could have been glossed over, ended, or modified. In fact, the opposite is indicated, since such developments would seemingly reveal an even closer collaboration between Allies and Germans than the January 7–8, 1948, Frankfurt proposals had established for Bizonia.

All of these points permit the strong assumption that the minister-presidents disagreed among themselves at Koblenz on policy and on tactics, and that they tried to compromise without much success. The resolutions of the conference show a desire to negotiate for a Western solution. The Mantelnote shows the desire to hold things in abeyance to get larger unification and settlement, possibly to get more concessions, and possibly for other reasons.[17]

## Americans Apply Pressure

Clay, who had predicted German acceptance of the London decisions and who on June 30 still thought discussion of German counterproposals was "looking at ghosts walking," moved with determination to turn the precarious German compromise of Koblenz to his own purposes. Essentially, he and his liaison officers—with the help of Ernst Reuter at Rüdesheim—pointed up the weakness of the argument for delay based on fear of a greater East-West split. In the process they changed the peaceful, economic-magnet concept that Draper had proposed earlier into the hard-line theory that unification required Western strength and determination to resist Communism. Minister-presidents like Wilhelm Kaisen, Max Brauer, Christian Stock, and Reinhold Maier, who had shown some willingness even before Koblenz to gamble on the progress they might achieve by negotiation, gained considerable stature as a result of the American effort. In the end the minister-presidents accepted with only minor modifications the offer to let them create a government. They dropped their legal objections to the Occupation Statute proposed by the Frankfurt Document III. Carlo Schmid and Hinrich Kopf, who continued to argue the legal case against negotiation most effectively, caused Americans to conclude, mistakenly, that Schumacher and the SPD were responsible for the "disastrously irresponsible German move at Coblenz," which "represented catastrophic disregard of the seriousness of the total European situation."[18] In a sense, Clay's quid pro quo for German acceptance was his continued struggle for a more liberal Occupation Statute. He did not achieve as much as he wanted in Berlin, but he continued to try during the government-level discussions until the day the Occupation Statute was announced.

Clay's great pressure on Germans on the one hand, and his desire for a more liberal Occupation Statute on the other is not a paradox. Throughout the occupation and right up to the eve of the July 1, 1948, meeting with the minister-presidents, France had successfully blocked or delayed the policies and programs for a viable economy that he believed were the only basis for effective four-power cooperation. France had held Potsdam in abeyance; France had delayed the bizonal level-of-industry plan, and her insistence on continued coal and Saarland discussions had kept the dismantling list in limbo until Clay and Robertson announced it on their own—only to have the United States Congress intervene. France's encouragement of German federalists had contributed to the collapse of the field-level experiment of promoting unity by minister-presidents' conferences. Her representatives at the London six-power talks, in the Berlin working parties, and elsewhere showed signs of continued French resistance to the policies that Clay believed necessary to solve the German economic problem and, perhaps, to lay the basis for a period of renewed four-power control, during which the United States could (for the first time) operate from a position of economic strength rather than one of economic weakness approaching desperation. Clay's conception was akin to the Länderrat idea writ large, and France was the immediate barrier. His efforts during July 1948 to get the Frankfurt documents accepted by Germans were stimulated in the first instance by his assessment of France's position. His efforts are not to be confused with other actions of his, which arose from the Soviet blockade of Berlin.

Clay met the American-zone minister-presidents in Frankfurt on July 14, 1948, for the first time after Koblenz. His opening remark was: "You have put your fate in General Koenig's hands." Despite initial German protests to the contrary, Clay insisted that the Koblenz resolutions departed significantly from the London agreements in general tone and spirit, though not in each single item. He said he had never dreamed that "the Minister Presidents would submit counterproposals asking for less power than was offered them." Their Koblenz position would require renewed government-level discussions, and Clay predicted possible difficulty with France and certain delay for many, many months. Regarding their concern about East Germany, which they brought up here also, Clay told the minister-presidents they would be charged with splitting Germany no matter what they did. They might as well go ahead and create a strong West Germany to permit "genuine and full economic recovery," and con-

stitute a "real government for the people to rally around." The minister-presidents were not helping him on Berlin at all, he said, because
the greatest hope to prevent war lay in the willingness of anti-Com-
munists to show the courage to face up to the East. He apologized
for setting his judgment of what was best for Germany over the judgments of the minister-presidents themselves. But he said he was convinced that what he had worked for on their behalf in London was
better than the counterproposals the minister-presidents had made.
Kaisen, speaking for his colleagues, said their meeting was one of
the most valuable and momentous conferences they had had with
Clay.[19]

Clay's remarks of July 14 must be seen against the background
of a request by Koenig for an indefinite postponement of a meeting between the military governors and minister-presidents that had
been scheduled for July 15. According to press reports, Koenig
wanted private talks between the military governors first. He suggested a three-man study committee to see how close the military
governors could come to the Koblenz resolutions without going back
to their governments for further discussions. He told reporters that
"the competencies" (the authority to act) of the three generals were
not the same.[20] There is evidence that Koenig wanted to return to
one of the unresolved issues of June 30 and present to Germans the
additional instructions not contained in the Frankfurt documents.
Americans in particular viewed the new French initiative with alarm.
At least one American liaison officer said release of additional terms
at this time would fortify the Germans' suspicion that they had not
been told everything about the London agreements, would negate
some of the things Americans had told Germans informally, and
would strengthen "the position of those who urge rejection of the
London terms (for their own reasons)." He said he was not too hopeful that OMGUS could achieve its objective in any case, but he urged
Clay to insist that the added instructions, which John Ford Golay
calls the "key agreement," were to be a guide for the military governors when they reviewed the German draft constitution and that
they were not intended to be the basis for directives to Germans. Clay
and Robertson had taken a similar position on June 30, and continued
to argue the point in July. We know now that the "key agreement"

was first revealed only in part on October 20, 1948, and released fully to the Parliamentary Council in Bonn on November 22, 1948. The French persistence in this matter suggests that the additional instructions were in fact a French minimum position (a summary of the least they would settle for at London) on the powers of the new German government. In mid-July, however, all Koenig could get was another meeting between military governors and minister-presidents at Frankfurt on July 20, 1948.[21]

## Meetings in Frankfurt and Rüdesheim

On July 20, 1948, Robertson, speaking for the military governors, told the minister-presidents that the Frankfurt documents rested on government-level agreements, that suggestions for fundamental changes would have to be referred back to the governments, and that much difficulty and delay would result from referral. He said the Allied governments wanted Germans to have new power and authority in the areas under the jurisdiction of the three military governors, but that they did not expect Germans to assume responsibility for issues beyond their control (e.g., the East-West split). He said the military governors believed the Koblenz resolutions to be fundamentally different from the Frankfurt documents on the constitution, on ratification, on the timing and the need for boundary changes, and on the timing and details of the Occupation Statute. Robertson suggested the minister-presidents take a few days to consider these differences and plan to meet with the military governors again. Kaisen and Brauer pressed the military governors for details, and after considerable informal discussion the meeting adjourned until later in the day. When it reconvened, Christian Stock reported for the minister-presidents that they would meet and discuss the matter. Both parties agreed to meet again on July 26, and Stock said the minister-presidents would ignore the past (Koblenz) and try to move ahead.[22]

The minister-presidents conferred at Rüdesheim on July 21–22, and some of them met earlier as subcommittees with Allied liaison officers. They discussed the issues raised by the military governors on July 20, but did not take up the Occupation Statute again. Friedrich wrote that the Germans were faced with "the very difficult political issue of how to withdraw from the commitments made at Coblenz." Schwarz went somewhat further, asserting that the minister-presidents decided at Rüdesheim to combine with the Western Allies to win back their own sovereignty and that of the East zone, at the risk of a German division or even eventual war. He attributes the sharp turnabout to the appeal of Ernst Reuter for solidarity and action in the face of the Berlin crisis.[23] Schwarz has logic on his side: Reuter had not been at Koblenz and could thus more easily deviate from its position than the others. Nevertheless, both Friedrich and Schwarz see a much more decisive reversal than actually occurred. They apparently do not regard Koblenz as the compromise it was, and they minimize certain signs of a break appearing before the Rüdesheim meetings. It is clear that Kaisen had been convinced, and his American-zone colleagues strongly influenced, by the meeting with Clay on July 14. Kaisen and Brauer almost certainly helped keep the door open for further discussion on July 20. Stock's remark on July 20 about ignoring the past and trying to go ahead is also noteworthy. There is no question that the facade of unanimity at Koblenz had collapsed under American pressure, and that the Rüdesheim meeting forced a reconsideration. Rüdesheim did not reverse Koblenz completely, however, and Americans still feared that the July 26 meeting might bring a final breakdown in discussion and a suspension of further plans.[24]

Essentially, the minister-presidents' Rüdesheim statement left the door open for further discussion. They said they were ready to assume the responsibilities asked of them in the Frankfurt documents, but they still wanted only a provisional government. They wanted to change "constitution" to "Grundgesetz" (which they translated as "basic constitutional law") so as not to confuse it with a future constitution. They said they wanted Länder boundary changes, and they agreed to make recommendations. They could not meet the September 1, 1948, deadline, however. They objected to ratification by popular referendum, and recommended ratification by the Landtage.[25]

The Rüdesheim debate on the referendum is especially interesting because it shows the dilemma forced upon the minister-presidents by the pressure to establish the constitution accompanied by the American demand that it be ratified by popular referendum. The minister-presidents said a referendum would require a campaign, during which Communists would charge West Germans with dividing Germany permanently. The Communists would be joined by nationalists and other opposition forces on the right in efforts that could defeat the constitution or do it irreparable damage. The referendum therefore "introduced an uncertainty factor into the whole development," and it would be time-consuming. Rejection of the constitution would leave no alternatives, because it would be impossible to return to the London agreements or to the Koblenz resolutions. The minister-presidents preferred ratification by the Landtage as a matter of principle and because they could give reasonable assurance of its acceptance ("wir können ziemlich klar sehen wie die Sache läuft"), while at the same time avoiding the vilification of a campaign that might produce a left-right coalition to defeat it.

At least one minister-president foresaw danger in publishing the German arguments against a referendum. The arguments admitted that there might be a fundamental difference between the popular will and the inclinations of the Landtage, and thus flew in the face of everything the Americans wanted to promote. One German said that if the Americans even suspected such a difference, they would regard the whole operation as useless. The minister-presidents thereupon considered stressing only the idea that a referendum was undesirable because it suggested something permanent. But in the meantime, a report came in that the Allied liaison officers had already been told the real reasons for the German objections and that they had been visibly impressed. The military governors were also sufficiently impressed to delay a decision at first and, in the end, to let the Landtage do it.[26] This is extremely important, because the arguments *against* a popular referendum were also arguments *for* a provisional constitution. Since the latter was only a step toward the real thing, it could be justified even though it was "directed" by the Allies and "managed" through the Landtage without any direct appeal to the popular will.

Hinrich Kopf and Carlo Schmid (both Social Democrats) fought hard against the trend at Rüdesheim. Their influence was great enough to convince American observers that the minister-presidents were not yet as ready to proceed as their official statement implied.

Kopf argued against the decision to draft a "basic constitutional law," and abstained from voting on the final statement. Schmid made a long speech in which he argued that the Americans obviously wanted a West German state that would influence activities beyond its boundaries (the hard-line magnet concept). The Germans at Koblenz had thought they were making recommendations for the internal affairs of the three zones. Now, under pressure, Germans were moving with Americans to establish a state that would represent West Germans by election and East Germans *communis sensus*. Americans and some Germans believed this to be the best possible approach to eventual unity; Schmid and others believed it was not. Neither side could prove its position to be right, but the choice Germans were making was at least clearly stated.[27]

## Frankfurt Again

As agreed earlier, the military governors and minister-presidents met again in Frankfurt on July 26, 1948, to consider the Rüdesheim proposals.[28] After much discussion and several recesses and pauses for consultation among the military governors, the governors agreed to accept a *Grundgesetz*—which was now translated as "Basic Law (provisional constitution)"—and to refer to their governments the minister-presidents' recommendations on the referendum and on the time schedule for suggesting Länder boundary changes. The minister-presidents would in the meantime elect a constituent assembly and continue to study Länder boundaries. The decisions had not been predetermined, however, and the meeting—which appears to have been marked by considerable tension and anxiety—almost ended several times without having reached a decision.

The military governors, after having heard the Rüdesheim report and its rationale from Stock, Arnold, Lüdemann, and Brauer, recessed and then reported back their conclusion that the German position still differed sufficiently from the Frankfurt documents to require referral back to the Allied governments. The meeting could have ended there, and the German minutes record a pause during which no one spoke and the military governors whispered among themselves. Stock, who spoke officially for the Germans at the meeting, then asked if the Germans might know precisely what would be referred back. Koenig listed the referendum, the name of the constitution, and the timing on Länder boundaries as the three items. The meeting seemed about to end again, but Ehard asked to speak. He pleaded that they not break up on this note, and he said it would help matters to know if the military governors had discretion on certain items or if they were firmly bound by the London agreements. Given that knowledge the minister-presidents could consult again on their own position. In any case, Ehard thought the differences on the constitution–basic law issue were not really fundamental and that the timing of Länder boundary changes could be resolved mutually. He saw serious divergences only on the referendum. If the military governors were bound by government decision on the referendum, Ehard said, the minister-presidents would discuss their position further.

Again, the military governors recessed for ten minutes and reported back that they might discuss the constitution–basic law issue, but that they would have to refer the other two items. They emphasized, however, that referral did not constitute refusal. Kaisen then suggested that the minister-presidents be authorized to begin applying the London decisions on the assumption that the German officials were bound by the London positions on the items to be referred. After another brief pause, the final agreement emerged. The stage was set for convening the Parliamentary Council that wrote the Bonn constitution.

One very significant upshot of the July days merits special emphasis. It will be recalled that the initial and fundamental German objections to the Frankfurt documents focused on Document III and the Occupation Statute. Germans thought it depicted the "lot of a conquered nation"; that it reduced the limited freedom Germans already enjoyed under the Länder constitutions and the bizonal administrations; that it linked German participation to the policies and objectives of the Allies; that it legalized the capitulation as defined by the June 5, 1945, declaration of supreme Allied authority; and that Germans were being asked to create an administrative apparatus for the convenience of the Allies. During the July days, especially after the Koblenz meeting, these objections got pushed into the background and were not even debated at Rüdesheim on July 21–22. Stock said on July 26 that "the Ministers-President had not found it necessary to discuss this for the present." The only concession the minister-presidents got in return was a vague promise, on July 20, that the military governors would consider the German recommendations during the drafting of the Occupation Statute, a promise that only Clay seems to have taken seriously. The entire development shows how effectively the political argument of Koblenz (the East-West rift), which loomed large because of the real crisis in Berlin, gradually overshadowed and forced into limbo the legal and constitutional argument which had seemed so basic at first. No one apparently saw this more clearly than Carlo Schmid, who described at Rüdesheim what was happening and stated clearly the choice Germans made on July 26. Germans were, in fact, being asked to accept an expanded version of the earlier OMGUS experiments to establish agent-governments or administrations to build up the areas it controlled so it might better achieve its objectives of economic self-sufficiency and German unity by peaceful aggrandizement of its control area. Document III, which reserved to the Allies specific and elastic powers (existing and future controls established by the Allies), ruled out substantial freedom of choice for Germans within the three zones, except as granted by the military government.

The range of effective choice Germans had in the summer of 1948 was indeed limited. They could stay with the status quo, with its economic frustrations and insecurities, or throw in with the West, which offered them some hope for the future. At the very least it offered an experiment, a pragmatic effort that could hardly be worse than the status quo. Their decision to form the Bonn government was, in this sense, a decision in foreign policy rather than a decision in domestic policy. The Social Democrats, who held fast to their principle of *Einheit und Freiheit,* and who preferred to solve German domestic problems without support from either the East or the West, found it most difficult to make the choice. Therein, perhaps, lies the explanation for the SPD position in the Parliamentary Council and during the early years of the Federal Republic.

Returning to the thoughts expressed at the close of the previous chapter, it may be seen more clearly now that a United States reversal of the decision to convene a constitutional assembly on September 1, 1948, would have been a political disaster of the first order for the United States in Germany. It may be seen, also, that the point of no return had been reached rather quickly because Clay focused on attaining an immediate solution for the continuing frustrations brought about by French intransigence. He asked Germans to support him in a program that would facilitate "genuine and full economic recovery" and produce a magnet for the remainder of Germany, "a real government for the people to rally around."[29] Eventually they accepted; and a United States reversal would have cut the ground out from under them and from under Clay.

# 13 | Democracy or Necessity: The Dilemma Again

The decision to permit Germans to establish the forms, symbols, and rituals of political democracy in West Germany appears to have been the logical outgrowth of the earlier policy to permit local and state elections and to approve Land constitutions. It seems the natural extension of the Länderrat experience to the three western zones, and it bears the marks of a studied grant of political authority to an area that formerly had only administrative competence in certain economic affairs. It appears, further, to have been the result of a natural shift from a policy of punishment to one of rehabilitation; from denazification, demilitarization, dismantling, and the like to reeducation and reorientation (or, as it was called at first, democratization). In the words of the Hessian Land Director of Military Government, it was a transition from the three-year "road back" to a new "road ahead."[1]

But appearances are deceiving. The evidence from administrative practice and policy implementation suggests almost conclusively that American (and Allied) interests on certain key issues assumed priority over democratic ideals. The freedoms Germans enjoyed were simply those not preempted by the Allies because German action satisfactorily reflected the interests of the Allies. The severe limitations placed on the new government have been noted, and we shall turn in a moment to other ways in which Allied interests manifested themselves.

Clay and others have created the impression that the limitations on the Bonn government—many of which Americans accepted reluctantly indeed—were the price Germans had to pay for French participation in the West German experiment. Friedrich, for example, has written that "it would have been very fortunate had the British and American negotiators succeeded in thoroughly convincing the French that a constitution would not be worth the paper it was written on unless it was primarily the work of the Germans themselves. Although this appeared to be the case at the time, unfortunately this proved not to be fully so." John F. Golay and Peter Merkl have reinforced and documented this interpretation, which comes out sharply in studies restricted to the disputes and compromises that led to the adoption and approval of the Basic Law.[2] The weakness of this interpretation is that it bears down so heavily upon French recalcitrance that it makes Americans appear to have been rather completely without interests of their own, seeking only the realization of German democracy and self-rule. But the American position with reference to the work of the Parliamentary Council and American actions in 1948 and 1949 on a variety of issues and problems permit another interpretation.

## American Interests and the Basic Law

During the Bonn deliberations on the Basic Law, France finally forced publication of the limitations on German governmental structure and central powers that had been agreed on at London. France had failed to get the details incorporated into the Frankfurt documents or to get them released immediately after the Koblenz conference, but the military governors released them in part on October 20, 1948, and published them fully in the aide-memoir to the Parliamentary Council on November 22, 1948. Clay had opposed the earlier French attempts to release the limitations. He has published his reaction to the aide-memoir. On November 22, 1948, he cabled Washington, reporting that French actions on Berlin, on the Ruhr, and on certain other matters constituted a serious threat to the American objective of a self-sustaining and unified Germany.[3] There is no doubt that throughout the negotiations on the origins, drafting, and acceptance of the Basic Law and the Occupation Statute, Clay believed the French were unwilling to assign sufficient powers to the new government to provide it with the "adequate central authority" to accomplish the objectives the Allies had intended for it at London. The concept of "adequate central authority" can be challenged from the other pole, however, and Clay was just as positive in his reaction to that as he was in his reaction to French policy.

The crisis in the Parliamentary Council during March and April of 1949 provides an excellent example of Clay's response to the challenge of too much central authority, and it reveals the American interest behind his response. Golay and Merkl have described the issues and maneuvers involved in the crisis. On March 2, 1949, the military governors outlined specific objections to the existing German draft of the Basic Law. The Germans resumed discussions and on March 17 agreed on a revised version, which was a compromise supported by the CDU/CSU coalition and the SPD. The compromise still provided for greater legislative and tax powers in the central government than Americans and French were prepared to accept. The Allied liaison officers made their objections known, and the CDU/CSU withdrew support of the March 17 proposals, which the Bavarian Christian Socialists (CSU) had accepted as a party position only reluctantly in the first place. The SPD saw great political advantage in forcing a vote on the proposals despite the French and American displeasure. A vote would either make the CDU agree to its previous compromise position with the prospect of driving a wedge between the CDU and the CSU, or it would make the CDU abandon its previous position as a result of Allied pressure, with the prospect of handing the SPD an excellent campaign issue later.

American observers, who had analyzed the possible committee and plenary session votes on the issue, predicted success for the SPD tactic and recommended that the military government disapprove the March 17 proposals even before the Germans voted on them. Clay's first decision was to accept the recommendation and to disapprove the March 17 proposals. If the Parliamentary Council passed them anyway "in defiance," he proposed to amend the Basic Law when it came to the military governors for review and to submit the amended version for ratification without returning it to the Parliamentary Council. Three days later—somewhat calmed—Clay analyzed the situation in detail. He said the SPD opposed financial decentralization because it would deny the federal government access to suffi-

cient revenue to pay compensations for the SPD program of nationalization. He also warned that, if Germans voted the March 17 proposals, the French military governor would certainly veto the Basic
Law and ask for government-level talks. The result would be discussions and long delays reminiscent of the London conference, the level-
of-industry talks, the coal talks, and other matters.[4]

It is not clear whether Clay was more concerned with the prospect
of further French discussion and delays or that of socialism. The
SPD accused him at the time of deliberately promoting federalism
in order to frustrate nationalization. Golay has tried to counter this
accusation, but he is not very convincing.[5] Clay's opposition to nationalization is a matter of record. His official position was to permit
Germans to decide the issue whenever they were in a position to exercise a free choice at the national level. His internal correspondence
shows that he hoped free enterprise would become so firmly established in the meantime that Germans would never exercise that
choice. His insistence on federalism was undoubtedly related to his
position on socialism, but his concurrent concern about further
French discussions and delays shows that the issue in March 1949
was more complex than the SPD thought. As a matter of fact, if the
SPD had been correct, the easiest thing for Clay to do at this point
would have been to sit back and enjoy it while Koenig carried the
ball. His concern that the French would wreck prospects for economic
stability prevented that, however.

The three foreign ministers, who met in Washington early in April
1949, took up the matter and issued a statement on April 5 to encourage the Parliamentary Council to continue its discussions and negotiations. They also instructed the military governors to make concessions to centralization if the Germans could not agree. The release
date of such concessions was left to the discretion of the military
governors. Clay delayed its release, though he was pressured hard to
let it out. He said that it would be undignified to do so while the SPD
was still discussing tactics in Hanover, that release would be an open
capitulation to the SPD, and that concessions to the SPD would violate his commitment to political neutrality. He did not say that his
action took the CDU/CSU off the hook, but he did say the SPD could
not hold to its extreme position much longer. He also became angry

because he thought British liaison officers were "back-dooring" him.*
He finally agreed to release the list of concessions, but only after
Germans had resumed discussions in the Parliamentary Council. This
condition removed the stigma of capitulation to the SPD that earlier
release would have implied.[6]

The implementation of the London agreement to form a West German government thus shows that Allied interests encroached upon
democratic ideals; that the Allies insisted on certain conditions, structures, and power relationships that Germans might or might not have
accepted on their own accord. This insistence is significant because
it suggests that the Allied decision to establish the Bonn government
was not a major departure from previous policies and practices during the occupation. The events of 1948–49 are therefore a continuation, not a break. They are in a sense simply another experiment,
another pragmatic attempt to achieve basic Allied objectives with
the help of a German agent-government. The decision to build a West
German government was not accompanied by abandonment of interests. In fact, the evidence reveals intensified efforts to ensure the per-
petuation of certain Allied policies and practices in the future.

In summary, we have seen how Americans encouraged and promoted minister-presidents' conferences; how they recoiled when the
minister-presidents seemed intent upon promoting their own bizonal
politics; how they kept "hands off" at Munich in 1947; and how they
resisted the minister-presidents' recommendations on dismantling
and peace questions, only to return to the minister-presidents again
in July 1948, when they seemed useful and necessary. We have seen
how American denazification policy and practice remained stringent
to meet the OMGUS conception of Washington's requirements, and
how Washington's requirements changed so rapidly that it embarrassed even OMGUS. We have seen how the same thing happened on
dismantling, and the story on decartelization is so similar that it need
not be told in this context. We have seen how bizonal merger grew
out of an American experiment to force economic unity and central
administrations at the field level; how the bizonal structures and

* Clay did not elaborate on what he meant by this expression, but he was probably indicating his belief that the British were telling SPD leaders further concessions would be made if the SPD held firm to its position.

functions were kept minimal in anticipation of the Moscow conference; how they were changed to meet the requirements of bizonal self-sufficiency and to preclude nationalization; and how they were changed again in the face of the Frankfurt-Länder disputes and the failure of the London foreign ministers' conference. We have seen how Americans built the Länderrat; how they strengthened it for their own purposes and over German objections; and how they reduced its power to make room for the bizonal experiment in self-sufficiency. We shall now turn to a consideration of the complete abandonment of the Länderrat in 1948. After that we shall take up certain other ways in which Allied interests manifested themselves on the eve of the creation of the Bonn government.

## American Interests in the Field

*The Länderrat.* It has been shown earlier that the Länderrat lost its economic function to the Bizonal Economic Council in June 1947, and that Erich Rossmann proposed a new political role for it in August. Not much came of the proposal for at least three reasons: the British-zone Germans suspected that the Länderrat would lead to a federal type of government; serious political differences existed between Schumacher and Rossmann; and OMGUS never used the Länderrat as a political sounding board the way Rossmann had hoped. The Länderrat's inability to convene a minister-presidents' conference in November 1947 is evidence of its political impotence. Nevertheless, the Länderrat continued to play an important role in those areas not within the competence of the Bizonal Economic Council. It remained active in dealing with problems concerning labor, refugees, land reform and resettlement, education, civil service, and other matters. Clay, in fact, recognized the importance of its noneconomic functions in July 1947, when he said he had been "too tough" on the Länderrat.[7]

An economic committee of the Länderrat, charged with coordinating American-zone positions on Economic Council actions, was kept going even after June 1947. In January 1948, when the two powers determined to strengthen the Economic Council again, Clay wanted all economic decisions centralized in Frankfurt. He instructed his staff to get the Länderrat "out of the economic field without delay." On February 3 he asked the minister-presidents to transfer their functions to the new bizonal second chamber (also called "the Länderrat") at Frankfurt. He said the military governors wanted the Länderrat and the Zonenbeirat (British zone) dissolved, and there is internal evidence that Clay hoped to induce Robertson to close the British-zone central agencies for coal, steel, and other industries. The British moved slowly, however, and American-zone Germans protested that they would be caught short if they moved too fast.[8]

The matter seemed still to be in flux when, on about April 19, 1948, Carl Friedrich unexpectedly asked Werner Hilpert, the deputy minister-president of Hesse, why Germans were so anxious to dissolve the Länderrat. Hilpert's report of the conversation reveals his puzzlement, but clarification came shortly. Four days later, the Zonenbeirat resolved to continue its functions and those of the central agencies in the British zone, despite the new Frankfurt administration. Rossmann reported that the resolution had had the prior sanction of the British military government. The Länderrat thereupon petitioned OMGUS to allow it to continue also. Clay gave his approval on May 7, 1948.[9]

Ten days after he approved its continuation, Clay wrote: "The Länderrat *must* go. Next meeting must be the last on a zonal basis." On June 1, 1948, in his regular speech at Stuttgart, Clay told the Länderrat that he would not return to Stuttgart for further Länderrat meetings. He said that in the future he and Robertson would meet the minister-presidents of the combined zones in Frankfurt and he encouraged the minister-presidents to transfer the spirit of the Länderrat into the bizonal administration. Noting that "the Länderrat has been an institution of democracy," he thanked the minister-presidents and all concerned for their great service to the German people. At no time, however, did he reveal what had prompted his sudden decision on May 17.[10]

Germans thought Clay had spoken to be heard in the British zone. They continued to argue for delay in moving to Frankfurt until the British made similar moves.[11] Apparently unaware of Clay's firm intentions, the Hessian delegate tried to arrange a meeting of the Länderrat for July, but Reinhold Maier (who often sensed or heard about

American plans before his colleagues) stalled. Maier said Clay told the minister-presidents in June that a meeting in July "would be a mistake." An inquiry at the Regional Government Coordinating Office showed Maier to be correct. Württemberg-Baden would not agree to a meeting without prior military approval, and Maier warned that OMGUS might publicly prohibit an unapproved meeting. The future of the Länderrat was soon made quite clear. Although it was to remain active in certain matters until September 30, 1949, when it was dissolved and the final phasing out of its activities was begun,[12] the withdrawal of the RGCO from Stuttgart on July 19, 1948, robbed the Länderrat of its direct channel of communication with OMGUS in Berlin, and thus drastically reduced its effectiveness.[13]

*Labor-Management Codetermination.* The issue that prompted Clay to abandon the Länderrat on May 17, 1948, was labor-management codetermination. His memorandum that the Länderrat must go appears on a staff report describing the Länderrat Labor Committee's plan to continue zonal coordination of labor policies because it believed several pieces of legislation in preparation should not be delayed until a bizonal department of labor could be set up. Among the pieces of legislation was a works-council bill that had been pending in the Hessian Landtag for nine months and was on the verge of enactment. The bill gave works councils codetermination rights with management in personnel matters, social and welfare matters, and major economic decisions. It provided that works-council representatives would sit on the boards of directors and have access to company records. They would have a voice in decisions to change the purpose of the enterprise, to buy or sell the enterprise, and to introduce new work methods and production plans.[14] In the normal procedure, Hessian enactment would have been followed by referral to the Länderrat to secure zonal coordination, and possibly, zonal uniformity. Bremen had already provided for such legislation in its constitution, and the prospects for zonal action were good—or ominous.

Clay was on record against labor codetermination by a single Land. In his letter of September 5, 1947, approving the Bremen constitution, he said OMGUS would not approve Land legislation that changed industrial management methods. He believed such change affected all of Germany and could therefore be decided upon only by the German people as a whole. Clay had crystallized a similar position on nationalization at the same time. It might be observed that both positions were stated in such a way that zonal action would be embarrassing and difficult to block.[15] His decision on May 17, 1948, to abandon the Länderrat simply prevented consideration of codetermination on a zonal basis. It kept the issue at Land level where he had already prohibited its enactment. It is also important to note that bizonal consideration of the issue was precluded by lack of administrative machinery.

OMGUS, urged by the War Department, had prevented creation of a bizonal manpower or labor department from the outset. Germans and certain OMGUS officials had pushed for such a department, but without success. In December 1946, while Clay was in Washington, OMGUS reported that it had not considered a bizonal manpower agency because labor relations and trade unions were political in nature. Upon his return, Clay said he did not want a bizonal labor department because it had not been named at Potsdam as one of the central agencies to be established. He was aware that Potsdam had not provided for a central food and agriculture department, but he justified it as a bizonal agency because Byrnes had mentioned it at Stuttgart.[16] Late in 1947, the labor committee of the Frankfurt Economic Council drafted a law creating a bizonal labor department. Clay continued to delay. He reported to Washington in January 1948 that such an agency would be the first bizonal one not contemplated at Potsdam. He justified food and agriculture as an exception again, now arguing that that department had been approved at Moscow.* In any case, he wanted to hold off on labor at least until the new bizonal organization had had time to function for a while. In February OMGUS finally agreed to go ahead. Nevertheless, it predicted a preparation period of several months, a time span that should be compared with the one month required to reorganize the entire bizonal administration in January 1948. The department was not estab-

---

* CINCEUR to Dept. of the Army, Jan. 20, 1948, WWIIRC 110-3/1. It might be recalled here that Clay mentioned food and agriculture as an agency Americans would add to the Potsdam list of five as early as October 17, 1945. The occasion was the American-zone minister-presidents' meeting to organize the Länderrat. ("Sitzung des Ministerpräsidentenrats Bayern, Württemberg-Baden, Hessen, Bremen mit der U.S.-Militärregierung am 17. Oktober 1945," Staatskanzlei, Wiesbaden, 1g06/01.)

lished until September 1948, when plans for a West German government were under way. Clay fought a holding action to the end.[17]

On May 26, 1948, the Hessian Landtag passed its works-council
law by a 70–14 margin and sent it to the military government for
review as required.[18] (The SPD, CDU, and the KPD voted for the
law; the LPD against.) In mid-June James Newman, the Director of
the Office of Military Government for Hesse, informed Minister-
President Stock that the usual fourteen-day OMGUS review period
for such legislation was being extended. He advised Stock to postpone publication or implementation of the law until further notice.
Newman said higher headquarters was pressed with other business
and that the extension was not to be interpreted as a veto or suspension. Clay was, in fact, busy with negotiations to implement the London decisions, with currency reform, and with the Berlin crisis. He
was also having difficulty because disagreements and lack of coordination in Washington had resulted in instructions to Murphy to approve the law and instructions to Clay to disapprove it. Clay finally
proposed to approve the law as it applied to personnel and welfare
matters and to suspend its economic codetermination provisions.[19]
He said economic codetermination would "affect commerce between
the States" and should therefore be a matter for a future central government to decide. The Hessian law, he continued, would encourage
the Ruhr miners to demand similar privileges to the detriment of coal
production and economic recovery. Codetermination would strength-
en trade unions against management already weakened by denazification and decartelization. It would give Communists in the works
councils a voice in economic affairs out of proportion to their political strength in West Germany.* Clay argued for suspension rather
than disapproval, to take some of the sting out of Communist and
trade union criticism, which he predicted would come.

The matter was finally settled in Clay's favor during William Dra-

* Note that Clay used the argument of the adverse effect of denazification on
management here, whereas he had used evidence to the contrary to try to stop Washington from changing his denazification policy in 1947. Clay used similar techniques
on other occasions, and this explains why he often enjoyed such an advantage in
policy determination when the departments in Washington used OMGUS information on which to decide policy. Occasionally, however, he failed to convince, as the
examples of denazification, reparations and dismantling, and decartelization show.

per's and Frank Wisner's personal visits to the theater.[20] Stopping the Hessian momentum without a serious crisis or irreparable damage to the delicate negotiations on the proposals for a West German government proved difficult, however. Clay apparently promised Minister-President Stock not to make a final decision without first talking with him. There is evidence that the military government tried to get Stock to take executive action to amend the law and delete the features objectionable to OMGUS. Such action was doomed to failure by the popularity of the law in Hesse, illustrated by the fact that the Hessian government had already sent out 20,000 brochures on the law and was preparing to fill additional orders for some 40,000 more. Stock told Clay that advice from his cabinet, from labor officials in the Hessian government, and from trade union leaders was unanimous that the law could not be amended without resubmission to the Landtag, which had passed it so decisively. On September 3, 1948, Clay made his decision, which had already been drafted on August 3, only to be held up while less drastic action was tried in order to achieve the same purpose. He wrote Stock that OMGUS would not approve economic codetermination on a state basis, because it was a matter for Germans under their new constitution to decide. He said he was not vetoing the law, but suspending it until the new government could consider the matter.[21] Stock reported his negotiations with Clay to the Landtag on September 22, 1948. He said he had argued that OMGUS had not reserved the appropriate powers to itself when the constitution was accepted in 1946, and that he had threatened to resign if OMGUS decided to use such powers now. Clay had, however, based his decision upon Allied Control Council Law #22, saying that Hesse had gone beyond its provisions permitting codetermination in certain areas. Stock read Clay's September 3 letter into the record, and the Landtag resolved to accept the situation, noting however that the military government had interfered in a "purely German matter" ("rein deutsche Angelegenheit") which had the support of an overwhelming majority. The resolution said much damage had been done to the democratic institutions the military government had been so concerned to set up.[22]

The sequel to the Hessian episode shows even more clearly the priority of interests over ideals. It also reinforces the conclusion that

Clay's federalism was essentially pragmatic, a concept he invoked when certain issues arose, rather than a matter of principle. In December 1948, the French-zone military governor approved a South Baden works-council law. Although there is no evidence that he had done so on his own decision in Hesse, Clay asked for trizonal consultation prior to French approval, only to discover that Koenig had already acted. Clay then protested France's unilateral action as a violation of an agreement at London to consult. Koenig said he could not oppose the law, because it applied to one of the social fields that France wanted kept under Länder authority when the Basic Law came into effect. Clay thereupon asked Washington to use its power to get French suspension. His arguments were the familiar ones, but they included the idea that a federal government in Germany could not survive with some states socialist, some free enterprise, and some mixed. Whether he was right or wrong may be academic, but the limits of Clay's desire to foster federalism are made rather clear by his action on this issue.[23]

The way in which Americans promoted their many other interests varied from the preventive and limiting measures they followed on codetermination to very positive measures designed to establish certain policies and practices as a guarantee for the future. Especially in 1948 and 1949, as the promulgation of the Occupation Statute and the adoption of the West German constitution drew nearer, Americans moved with determination on a number of issues to assure a carry-over of American interests into the new government or to make rejection of those interests subject to specific action on the part of the new government. The detailed backgrounds of the various issues and the American approach to each of them are interesting and significant, but they are beyond the scope of this study. Nevertheless, the general pattern of the American initiative and the variety of approaches may be illustrated by focusing in this chapter on a few of the more prominent issues, such as trade licensing, civil service reform, general claims, and school reform. Reorientation, a special case, will be taken up in the next chapter.

*Trade Licensing: Gewerbefreiheit.* On the issue of trade licensing, OMGUS asserted power to achieve its objective, but ended up promoting the sort of Länder diversity that Clay had found so unacceptable in the matter of codetermination. An OMGUS study done in June 1948 showed that German nongovernmental business and vocational groups took an active part in the review of applications for new business licenses and that some 35 per cent of all applications were being denied. OMGUS officials believed this guild type of regulation to be harmful, and issued a directive calling upon the Länder to present within 90 days proposals that would eliminate nongovernmental agency influence and either eliminate the licensing requirement or at least make licenses easier to obtain. In November 1948, when neither the Länder nor the Bizonal Economic Council had agreed on satisfactory remedial action, OMGUS issued a directive abrogating all German licensing laws in the American zone. Bizonal Economic Council representatives pleaded for repeal of the directive in order to preserve bizonal uniformity and for other reasons, but Clay insisted that the U.S. zone action stand. In December he told Germans there was no point in discussing the issue with OMGUS any further.[24] In brief, the action was unilateral. It had been taken without consultation between the military governors and, since neither the British nor the French zones followed suit, it created as much diversity in trade licensing practices among the Länder as codetermination would have.*

*Civil Service Reform.* OMGUS had long tried to achieve basic and significant civil service reform in the American zone. Essentially it had attempted to break the two-track system of officials (*Beamte*)

---

* The diversity did not materialize, however, because Germans objected violently to the regulation. They procrastinated at first and then devised methods to circumvent application of the policy. Instructive, in this respect, is a speech Reinhold Maier made to an audience of handicraft organization representatives in December 1948. He said Americans had prejudiced the future with their policies on dismantling, denazification, destruction of war industries, decartelization, and now on trade licensing. His words on trade licensing bear quotation: "Cease your paternalism! We understand something about this too. We certainly know more about German handicrafts than you. Don't consider us to be more stupid than we are, and you yourselves to be brighter and more rational than you are. We have the order. We will deal with it reasonably and intelligently, at the same time that we keep our abiding faith in our handicrafts!" (Hört auf mit der Bevormundung. Wir verstehen von diesen Dingen auch etwas. Vom deutschen Handwerk verstehen wir bestimmt mehr als ihr. Haltet uns nicht für dümmer, als wir sind, und euch selbst nicht für gescheiter und überlegener, als ihr seid. Die Anweisung is da. Wir wollen ihr mit warmem Herzen für unser Handwerk, gleichzeitig aber mit Verstand und Klugheit begegnen.") *Frankfurter Rundschau*, Dec. 15, 1948, p. 1.

and employees (*Angestellte*) and to make entry and advancement more competitive. Failing to achieve its objectives fully, OMGUS took action to ensure some carry-over of its program into the new government. Since the British agreed on the need for civil service reform, bilateral action was possible in this case, and the power was centralized in Bizonia rather than in each of the Länder. After many threats, much pleading, and endless negotiations, the American and British military governors issued their own identical civil service laws for the bizonal administrations, effective March 15, 1949. The American military government tried, albeit without full success, to transfer the new bizonal civil service regulations to the new government in Bonn, because "the obvious intent of the law [U.S. MG Law #15] was to establish a new Federal Civil Service system, and it was so understood both by Germans and Military Government."[25] The major opposition came from the Länder, where there was little sympathy for the new Allied civil service system. The military government sought its objectives by reducing states' rights and establishing uniformity first at the bizonal and then at the federal level.

*General Claims.* The general claims law (Law Concerning Redress of National Socialist Wrongs) provides an example of an issue on which Americans wanted action badly enough to reverse a former position completely, and to take unilateral action over the objections of their allies. The American-zone Länderrat had drafted a general claims law in September 1948, only to have OMGUS return it on March 16, 1949, because it did not provide adequately for displaced persons' claims. The Länderrat revised the law to meet the objections of OMGUS and resubmitted it on April 26, 1949. On June 29, 1949, OMGUS returned the draft without action, saying the law's legal and financial provisions affected all of Germany. In accord with its views on nationalization and codetermination, OMGUS said the law should be a matter for the new government rather than for any one Land or group of Länder.[26]

Under severe pressure from Washington and from several special interest groups, and despite a British request that the Americans not promulgate the law unilaterally, OMGUS turned about completely between June and August of 1949. On August 4, 1949, OMGUS sent its approval of the law to the American-zone Länderrat. It said that because the general claims law resembled a bizonal immediate-aid law, OMGUS had reconsidered its original position. Essentially, however, the change had occurred because of the pressures and because Americans believed the chances that such a law would be passed by the new government were almost zero unless the three powers exerted pressure that might go well beyond even what was legal under the Occupation Statute. The arguments against the law were formidable: it neither provided dependable cost estimates, nor defined the sources of revenue for payment of claims; it would establish a unique law in the American-zone Länder; it would affect German foreign exchange (and thus all of Germany), because many claimants lived outside Germany; and so on. These arguments notwithstanding, the political significance of the law was apparently great enough to cause its promulgation on the eve of the inauguration of the West German government.[27] The arguments against it were not ignored, however, for the Germans were told that approval of the law did not constitute approval of a specific method of financing payment of claims.

*School Reform.* School reform may serve as a last illustration of the numerous actions with which Americans tried to bind the future. Holding to the American tradition that education is a local matter and best decentralized in the states, OMGUS always worked at Land level to achieve its educational reform objectives. It tried to do so by persuasion rather than by military government order. The result, for the historian, is that the events of 1948–1949, as well as their extensive and significant background, present a diversity of activity, accomplishment, and failure that defies brief summary. Nevertheless, certain policies and objectives were general and consistent. The basis for German school reforms was the list of recommendations made in September 1946 by a U.S. Education Mission, headed by George F. Zook, the president of the American Council on Education. Zook's ten-member commission recommended a comprehensive school system below the university, a common six-year elementary school, increased emphasis on social studies and cultural subjects, improved teaching aids and library facilities, educational exchanges, and other things.[28]

In January 1947, OMGUS translated the Zook mission's recommendations into directives. Land military government officers were to instruct Germans in their Länder to prepare statements of aims and objectives in education and to submit them to the military government for evaluation.* The Länder statements were to be based on fifteen principles that OMGUS had prepared. They called for equal educational opportunity for all, free tuition, free textbooks and materials, compulsory school attendance from the ages of 6 to 15 and compulsory part-time education from 15 to 18. OMGUS wanted elementary and secondary schools to be two consecutive levels of education, rather than a double or triple track after the fourth or fifth year that would separate students bound for the professions from those seemingly headed toward jobs requiring low skills. Schools were to emphasize civic responsibility and a democratic way of life, to promote international good will, and to provide vocational guidance, and health education. Universities were to offer professional teacher education. School administrations were to be sensitive to the wishes of the people.[29]

German Land governments worked up proposals throughout 1947, but in a review at the end of 1947 American officials reported great disappointment. Bremen's plan was most satisfactory, because it adhered closely to the OMGUS fifteen principles. Hesse was next in line, but OMGUS still objected to Hesse's tuition requirement for higher-income families, to the continued foreign language requirement, and to tax-supported private schools. Württemberg-Baden had not completed its plan, and had asked for more time. Bavaria's proposals were deemed to be totally unsatisfactory because they retained the dual-track system, continued to charge tuition, continued both public and private schools, held fast to the foreign language requirement, and generally ignored all but four of the fifteen principles.

Americans had, in fact, kept close liaison with developments in the Länder. They sponsored much discussion, exchange, and other activity, and Clay spoke to the Länderrat about education on May 6, 1947. His remarks were extremely critical of Bavaria.[30] The Land military government detachments continued to try persuasion on into 1948, but in the face of continued German procrastination and de-

---

* The U.S. caution about centralism in education is clear in the word "evaluation." In other matters, such German proposals were to be submitted for "approval" and "review."

lay—some of which was due to lack of buildings, facilities, equipment, supplies, teachers, and the like—persuasion turned to pressure. Then, in anticipation of increased German freedom under the new government, pressure was replaced by direct orders.

In Hesse, for example, the military government submitted its December 1947 critique of the Hessian plan and asked for a new set of proposals by April 1, 1948, and a plan for implementation by the opening of school in September. In August 1948, the Hessian military governor summarized the history of the attempts at reform and issued an order which, in effect, created a six-year elementary school and required implementation of the January 1947 OMGUS principles. The order was to be effective "in the first school year beginning after the date of this directive," or in September 1948. The Hessian ministry took the edge off the order simply by declaring April 1, 1949, to be the beginning of the next school year, a return to pre-occupation practice. In February 1949, the military government agreed to postpone the order until 1950. It was later postponed again until 1951, and it apparently died quietly thereafter.[31]

Compared with what happened in Bavaria, the Hessian situation was mild indeed. OMGUS had always been most critical of the Bavarian educational plans and proposals, and the attitude of the Bavarian Minister of Culture, Alois Hundhammer, did not help matters. He went his own way and failed to attend Länderrat education committee meetings or to send adequate representatives, a fact that prompted Clay to "particularly urge the Education Minister of Bavaria to attend the educational meetings of the Länderrat because I believe he would have much to learn from his associates in Hesse and Württemberg-Baden."[32]

In December 1947, OMGUS rejected the Bavarian proposals and detailed the reasons for the rejection. The Office of Military Government for Bavaria ordered a revision by February 1, 1948.[33] Dissatisfied with Bavarian progress on April 1, 1948, Murray van Wagoner, the Land Director of Military Government for Bavaria, gave Minister-President Ehard a September 1 deadline to provide free tuition and free textbooks, and to show progress on plans to establish a six-year common elementary school by 1949. Nevertheless, the Bavarian Landtag adjourned on July 31, 1948, without having passed an education law. On August 4, 1948, the military government ordered the Bavarian government to establish free tuition and free textbooks, and confiscated all school books to prevent their sale except as directed by the military government.[34]

When Minister-President Ehard received the order, he reacted so strongly that some OMGUS observers believed he would interfere with the orderly completion of the negotiations for a West German government. He reportedly said the order was "my reward for my attitude at Koblenz and Frankfurt." He wondered how Americans expected Germans to develop a constitution if they went about slapping democratic-minded men in the face. One report said Ehard was "angry, very irritated, really burned up." Clay eventually asked van Wagoner to have Ehard come to Berlin. Ehard came almost three weeks later, and the two agreed on a gradual program to establish free tuition and textbooks by 1951. By that time Americans would no longer be issuing orders on education.[35]

The juxtaposition of interests and democratic ideals was never so clear in reality as it appears to be in description. The two often coincided, as when German local elections and German administrations provided personnel to replace the Allied manpower that rapidly melted away through demobilization, or when bizonal agencies were backed by a representative economic council to reduce conflict between the agencies and the field. In any event, Americans explained and rationalized in highly idealistic terms the policies and practices obviously designed to achieve basic American objectives. When Germans disagreed, Americans justified their resort to restriction, control, and pressure as necessary to correct past German "deviations" (denazification and dismantling), to ensure future German "uniformity" (civil service and education), or to counteract German actions that were contrary to their own best interests (nationalization and codetermination). Thus, carrying out American ideals was still thought to be the main goal. Germans explained and rationalized their interests and actions in the same way. Bavarians, during the so-called potato and meat wars for example, were in effect arguing from a position governed by provincial Bavarian economic interest when they asserted that a federal political structure would provide guarantees against the rise of another Hitler. Established political leaders in the Länder argued against encroachment on their prerogatives by bizonal administrations in the name of federalism, constitutional responsibility, and electoral accountability. Germans argued against dismantling and reparations in the name of European recovery, European stability, and insurance against Communism with such conviction that—had they not been Germans—they might have testified with great success before the United States congressional committees in favor of the Marshall Plan.

Americans had one other interest—reorientation or reeducation— which merits separate treatment, in part because it received such persistent restatement, and in part because Americans regarded it as the avenue through which interests and ideals would be reconciled.

# 14 | Looking Backward and Forward

American policy plans, directives, and pronouncements left no doubt that the military government intended to reorient German public life through an extensive reeducation, or democratization effort.* The two major policy directives to the military governor envisioned a peaceful, democratic German society. JCS 1067, issued in April 1945, directed the military governor to prepare "for an eventual reconstruction of German political life on a democratic basis." It emphasized nonfraternization and other restrictive measures for the immediate post-surrender period, however, and did not outline specific actions that might prepare for eventual democratic reconstruction. JCS 1779, issued in July 1947, was much more specific on democratic political reconstruction, but it denied any wish to impose American forms of democracy and social organization on Germans. It also said no other external forms should be imposed. It directed the military governor not to discriminate between authorized parties but to seek uniform treatment for all parties. In effect, it envisioned a tranquil political arena marked by parties as voluntary associations, equal in privilege, competing regularly for the electorate's preferment. It nevertheless said that "the re-education of the German

* This program was referred to variously as one of "reorientation," "democratization," and "reeducation." Although differences could be detected among the three terms, their meanings were never clearly fixed. Generally speaking, "democratization" referred to efforts at institutional change, and "reeducation" referred to ideological programs. "Reorientation," although frequently used as a synonym for "reeducation" (especially toward the end of the occupation), was also at times taken as synonymous with "democratization" or used as an umbrella term for all the various efforts at changing German society. The discussion of the programs in this chapter necessarily reflects the vagaries of OMGUS usage.

people is an integral part of policies intended to help develop a democratic form of government and restore a stable and peaceful economy."

## Reorientation

Despite the Americans' belief that the connection between reorientation and sociopolitical democracy was obvious, OMGUS never brought its ideological reorientation and its political programs together organizationally. Political programs were developed by the Civil Administration Division, the Governmental Structures Branch, the Regional Government Coordinating Office, and by the military governor himself. Reorientation in the sense of reeducation rested mainly with the Education and Religious Affairs Branch (later Education and Cultural Affairs Division), the Internal Affairs and Communications Division, and the Information Control Division. Only in July 1948 did OMGUS try to coordinate the activities of all divisions engaged in reorientation.[1] By that time, however, Americans had already decided on a West German government. There is evidence that coordination was prompted by the realization that the political program had moved far ahead of OMGUS hopes for reorientation and democratization. Litchfield wrote later on that 1948 "was at least three years too late to be developing agreed policies for the reform of the police system, for the democratization of the civil service, for the creation of new roles for the citizen, for the introduction of public hearings into the legislative process, or for the planning of a new and effective pattern of local and state government." He might have added school reform to the list. He said it was too late "because German minds were closed or closing, . . . because vested interests had been created, and . . . because the influence of the occupation forces was already largely dissipated."[2]

Americans had not neglected reorientation before 1948. They had a most active information program of their own. They licensed only those German newspapers and publishers whom they had determined to be in sympathy with American objectives and principles. They kept licencees under surveillance and sometimes reprimanded them, occasionally changed them, and even removed some.[3] Americans also worked for school reform and curriculum changes; they tried to convince Germans that they were guilty of past political and moral errors; they promoted exchanges of persons; they established America Houses and information centers; they formed German-American clubs; and they carried out a host of similar projects. Military government officials held press conferences regularly and hoped Germans would adopt the habit. Individuals, groups, and some field officers promoted public discussion of issues and problems; they sponsored citizens' forums and public interest groups; and they laid the groundwork for the full-scale reorientation program that mushroomed after 1948.[4]

Despite the plethora of activity, the military government's own contemporary interpretations and analyses show clearly the basis for the pessimism Litchfield expressed later. An OMGUS study of November 1947 concluded that little was being done in a systematic way regarding democratization. At least one OMGUS agency used the study's findings to recommend a drastic cut in field personnel. Another study, done in February 1948, said democratization plans had been haphazard, that "previous attempts by Military Government to persuade or coerce German *Land* governments to adopt democratic policies in such fields as education, civil service, and public administration have often been a failure."[5] The Office of Military Government for Hesse concluded that the democratization program was inadequate. Democratic structures had been organized, and each major military government section had developed, willy-nilly, a program to reorient the German people in its own particular sphere. The press division had taught democratic journalism; education officers had tried to influence political leaders; all divisions had negotiated exchanges of persons; some had established film programs; the America Houses had provided libraries, sponsored lectures, organized discussion groups, and stimulated other activities; and the Army had instituted youth activities programs. But, it said, the programs were diverse and were directed mainly toward the German counterparts of military government officials. Military government officials in Hesse believed a more coordinated program was needed in the "long uphill educational battle against the forces of tradition, of political and social apathy, and postwar cynicism."[6]

*Two Interpretations.* It might be suggested that the failure of Americans to connect their reorientation and political programs more closely rested on an article of faith. Americans seem to have assumed that once the enemies of peace and democracy had been purged, once the socioeconomic chaos of total war and defeat had been erased, and once Germans had been started off with a few institutions within which their new freedoms could be exercised, they would continue to develop social, economic, and political policies that reflected the universal principles of free men everywhere. In other words, Americans assumed that Germans, once freed from the *Gleichschaltung* of totalitarian Nazism ("particular will"), would translate—or help Americans to translate—the "general will" into concrete social, economic, and political action.

It can be argued—and it has been with good effect—that the American political program and the reorientation effort were inherently related, and thus needed no formal connection. According to this view, denazification, demilitarization, decartelization, industrial deconcentration, and dismantling each had its own internal causes and objectives, but all had in common the effect of removing from positions of power the Establishment of the Nazi era or the "older" Germany. Paralleling the negative programs, Americans promoted institutional changes in education, the civil service, land tenure, political parties, electoral procedures, and the like. As with the negative programs, the reforms had multiple and diverse motives and purposes, but in common they revealed the desire to create a social, economic, and political environment conducive to a new democratic leadership. John D. Montgomery and Lewis J. Edinger both seem to have used such a model as the unifying theme of their studies.[7]

Montgomery and Edinger each concluded that achievement fell short of promise. Montgomery, in his analysis of the artificial revolution on behalf of democracy, said the experiment lacked a clear theoretical foundation. He also believed that the program was insufficiently understood in the United States and abroad, and that the institutional changes did not attract new leaders in Germany and Japan. Edinger, who was more interested in the result than the process, suggested that the post-totalitarian elites are not fundamentally different from the earlier ones.

The two interpretations above—the first of which I put forward in a community study I did earlier—do not take into account adequately the tremendous significance of the high priorities Americans assigned to economic unity, to cost reduction, to French cooperation, to free enterprise, to anti-Communism, and to containment of the Soviet Union. This study has shown that the politics of the American occupation were governed largely by a range of interests rather than by the attempt to democratize Germany. Of course, Americans hoped to have it both ways in the end; they wanted their interests protected and they wanted German democracy. But when the two clashed, Americans applied power where their highest priorities were. Even reorientation, which was supposed to close the gap between the two, was in some ways just another way of using power to advance American interests.

*Reorientation as American Interest.* As early as 1947, when the new Länder constitutions in the American zone became effective, a disagreement developed within OMGUS regarding the future of the reeducation and reorientation objectives of the military government. At the time, the Civil Administration Division assumed the position that the September 30, 1946, OMGUS directive defining the relationship between the military government and the constitutional Land governments precluded further active and functional military government intervention in education at Land level. According to this view, OMGUS could only advise and suggest. The Education and Religious Affairs Branch insisted on a positive and functional approach, however. It based its position on a draft of a revised policy directive being prepared in Washington. The directive was finally issued in July 1947 as JCS 1779. The appropriate section reads: "You will require the German Länder authorities to adopt and execute education programs designed to develop a healthy, democratic educational system which will offer equal opportunity to all according to their qualifications."[8] In February, however, the disagreement was passed up to the military governor to solve, and Clay decided that "Education or Re-education is the one constructive field in which we have a *positive* mission—in which we must have *efficiency* as well as democracy. Therefore for this phase as well as for *ICD* matters, I deviate 'tho to a minimum' from the desire to turn full responsibility over to the Germans. I side with Education."[9] Thus, as in other matters previously discussed, OMGUS assigned its own objectives a higher priority than it did those that Germans might have developed. The incident is interesting also because it foreshadowed the arguments and rationale for the full-scale reorientation effort in 1948 and following.

The London agreements to form a West German government led to another reassessment of the future of reorientation, and this produced disagreement in Berlin and in Washington. One group, including at first Clay, the Department of the Army, and the State Department, believed the London agreements required a reduction in reorientation activities. Some believed they would have to be cut drastically. A second group, consisting of field-level spokesmen in Germany and the Civil Administration Division of OMGUS, argued that the program needed to be enlivened, coordinated, and expanded rather than cut.[10] This second group had formed beginning late in 1947, when various studies of the democratization effort produced severe criticism of the program and its lack of success. It has been noted that one conclusion from the studies was that field personnel be cut, but there was also another conclusion: that a greater effort be initiated. The Civil Administration Division of OMGUS went on record in February 1948 in favor of giving democratization top priority. Some of the Länder, particularly Württemberg-Baden, had an active program under way early in 1948. Some detachments in other areas had experimented with reorientation activities late in 1947. On March 1, 1948, OMGUS advanced the Education and Religious Affairs Branch to division status and defined one of its objectives as a democratic-reorientation mission.[11] Thus, by the time the London agreements were announced in June 1948, a group interested in reorientation, with considerable following and an organizational base, had already formed within OMGUS.

Throughout July and August of 1948, the future of reorientation seemed in doubt. The program, which had been financed largely from income derived from American-controlled newspapers and magazines, was in financial difficulty because of the currency reform. Washington seemed convinced that tripartite agreements prohibited further direct activity. Furthermore, Clay favored a drastic cut in

field-level personnel. Clay finally yielded to his advisers and to dele-
gations of field representatives who pleaded their case with him. He
agreed to continue the program, not so much on principle as because
France and Britain had similar programs. OMGUS created an inter-
divisional reorientation committee on July 26, 1948, and Litchfield
provided the leadership in bringing Washington around.[12]

Litchfield admitted that the London agreements had changed
things, that what had formerly been done by direction of the military
government must now be done by "influence, encouragement, . . .
advice and . . . leadership." But he also argued that the Allied governments had reserved to themselves the power necessary to ensure fulfillment of the basic purpose of the occupation. Specifically, he noted,
they reserved power to "ensure the observance of the Constitutions
which they have approved." Since the constitutions contained guarantees of civil liberties, independent judiciaries, free political parties,
free press, free speech, and the like, Litchfield was certain that reorientation was in fact a reserved power. He said OMGUS planned to
expand its reorientation program, and concluded with this summary:
"Whereas on the one hand it has been our policy to divest Military
Government of direct responsibility in the interest of turning it over
to German agencies, it has, on the other hand, been our parallel plan
to guide, assist and influence the German people in the direction of
that democratization and reorientation which constitutes the basic
purpose of the occupation. Thus, as we are reducing our controls on
the one hand, we are expanding our budget and staff and our efforts
in the direction of a more effective reorientation effort. The London
Agreements assist in both processes."[13]

By the fall of 1948 the case for reorientation had been won. In
September 1948, OMGUS got authority to recruit "a modest" number of officers to work in a "program which goes variously under the
name of democratization, reorientation, or cultural affairs." These
were to be the first people OMGUS had recruited for such purposes,
and the fact that it was done only after plans for the West German
government were under way seems highly suggestive. In October the
Department of the Army agreed to make available $2,400,000 from
GARIO funds (Government Aid and Relief in Occupied Territories)
to carry the reeducation and reorientation program for the next two

years. It also suggested that GARIO and ECA counterpart funds might be used. OMGUS worked out a financial support plan that used these counterpart funds rather than the GARIO dollars.[14]

Once Washington and Clay agreed to the program, it mushroomed rapidly in Germany. Alonzo Grace, the director of the OMGUS Education and Cultural Relations Division, outlined some of its purposes to a five-day conference of reorientation officers in Berchtesgaden in October. He said the program aimed to instill in Germans the desire to maintain and protect a society based on the natural rights of man. "Those who would trade the natural rights of man for material security, in the end lose both," he said, ignoring the essence of the German acceptance of bizonal developments and the Occupational Statute. "A distressed but redeemed people may sell jewels and Meissen for bread," he continued, "but an unredeemed people will sell freedom and the rights of man as easily as they did some fifteen years ago."[15] A month later Murray van Wagoner told a field officers' seminar that "we are now engaged in changing the course of history and tradition. . . . The hope of our mission lies with the people. . . . It is difficult to change the thought processes of the bureaucrat, the old-guard politician, and the moss-backed professors." He compared the reorientation officers' tasks with the work of Christian missionaries: both were engaged in spreading a religion based on human dignity, and both got "pleasure in seeing the growth of a new religion." He went on to outline a program for public forums, town hall meetings, and the like, which I have described in my Marburg study.[16]

## The West German Government as Agent-Government

*Implications of the Reorientation Program.* The rationale and the content of the reorientation program developed during the summer and fall of 1948 suggest a number of conclusions. First, the argument used by Litchfield to define reorientation as a reserved power could be used for any issue that arose. It thus serves to point up again the fact that the new Bonn government was conceived as an agent-government that would exist at the sufferance of the Allies. Second, it is clear that the people who promoted and sold the program were motivated at least partly by selfish interests: the desire to protect their assignments and to build empires in Germany. Third, if Americans believed they had to go to the people in 1948 to promote democratic ideals against bureaucrats, old-guard politicians, and moss-backed professors, they were in fact revealing their basic distrust of the officials who had risen to power under the occupation, the people with whom the Allies were negotiating for a new West German government. Fourth, if reorientation at the grass-roots level was such a necessity after 1948, it was an admission that denazification, decartelization, industrial dismantling, demilitarization, and the other punitive programs that had been justified in part as programs to change elites in Germany were in fact failures. Fifth, if, therefore, the arguments of reorientation's promoters were true—that democratization had been a failure previously and that an enlivened, coordinated, well-staffed, and well-financed effort was necessary—it follows that the Bonn government had not really arisen out of the democratization interest of Americans, and thus was not really a stage in the development of German political democracy. It follows also that Bonn's predecessor organizations (the Länderrat, the Economic Council, and so on) had not been examples of democratization either.

The findings of this study point to the conclusion that the West German government, when established in 1949, had more in common with the earlier pragmatic experiments in which Americans sought cooperation from a German agent-government than with a government in the traditional sense. The German minister-presidents had realized this at Koblenz and Rüdesheim. They drew the consequences by insisting on a Basic Law rather than a constitution; on ratification by Landtage rather than by popular referendum. The Parliamentary Council realized it and "enacted this Basic Law ... to give a new order to political life for a transitional period." It provided, further, that "this Basic Law shall become invalid on the day when a constitution adopted in a free decision by the German people comes into force."

*Summary of Events Leading to the West German Government.* The interpretation just presented is based on an analysis of the connections between the events that led to the formation of the Bonn government. The inability of the 1947 bizonal administration to solve the economic problems of the area, to reduce the British and American subsidies to Germany, or to develop adequately so it might contribute to the economic recovery of Europe, led to the decision to strengthen Bizonia in January 1948. The decision was made only after the London conference of 1947 had failed to agree on a four-power German settlement. When Britain and the United States announced their bizonal reorganization plans early in January 1948, France protested at government level. It seemed that Bizonia was in for another period of talks, discussions, and delays reminiscent of the struggle from July to December in 1947 to get a new level-of-industry and reparations list promulgated.

Instead of repeating the discussions of 1947, the three powers agreed to do among themselves, and in cooperation with the Benelux powers, what the foreign ministers had failed to do in London: confer on the full range of German problems and arrive at a six-power agreement and a trizonal German working arrangement. Once the London talks of 1948 were under way, the Soviet Union stepped up its critique of and opposition to bizonal and West German developments. Soviet officials eventually walked out of the Allied Control Council in March, stating that it had become superfluous in the light of the London talks. The Soviets also appear to have decided to gamble on the chance that they could explode the London talks or make the results of the talks unacceptable to West Germans. They succeeded in neither, but their gamble was not without effect. When the London talks reconvened and continued, the Soviets gradually put economic pressures on Berlin, perhaps still gambling on inducing a negative German response to the London talks. In June, when the three powers announced a new currency, the Soviets blockaded the city completely. Although the records of the London talks are not available, there appears to be enough evidence to suggest that the London agreements went much further toward development of a West German government than the original plan to improve Bizonia and to seek French support for it or a possible trizonal organization had intended. This seems to have occurred because of the Soviet action in Berlin and because of the Communist coup in Czechoslovakia. The negotiations in Germany for acceptance of the London agreements, described previously, suggest rather strongly that events in the field also forced a more rapid development toward a West German government than was originally intended.

When the Germans saw the results of the London agreements in June and July, they objected. They focused essentially on the concessions made to France at London to get three-power unity. They singled out the provisions regarding the Ruhr and the powers that would be reserved to the Allies in the proposed Occupation Statute as their specific targets. The minister-presidents prepared counterproposals at Koblenz. But they responded to the Soviet gamble and tried to justify the counterproposals by pleading their unwillingness to divide Germany permanently. Judging from the content of the July documents and the unreleased portions of the London agreements, the German counterproposals would have made further French participation doubtful and further government-level discussion certain. Clay, it will be recalled, told the American-zone minister-presidents after Koblenz that they had put their fate in France's hands. Americans, therefore, focused on the rationale for the German counterproposals rather than on their essence. They argued that the Berlin crisis showed Germany to be divided already, an argument strengthened by the timing of the Soviet blockade of Berlin and by the decision of Americans to supply the city by air. They argued that West Germans could hardly make things worse, but they could perhaps make them better. They could accept the Allied experiment (thus keeping France to its agreements and away from the conference table) and develop an economically prosperous West Germany that would be an irresistible magnet to draw the eastern zones into a unified Germany. Thus, economic rehabilitation and the promise of eventual unity by attraction of the East were neatly tied into one package. At the same time, Germans could atone for their past aggression by contributing positively to the rehabilitation of Europe, and they could become a working partner in the Western program for the containment of Communism.

According to one close observer of the situation at the time, Germans got a Basic Law or constitution that was "made primarily for international purposes." The Western Allies wanted it "in order to provide a partner for the western European integration, a better-equipped situation for Marshall aid, and primarily in order to strengthen a friction point which could not be left soft any longer."[17] If this is true, Germans did what Carlo Schmid said they were doing at Rüdesheim; they accepted Allied (especially American) priorities as their own for the time being and found it unnecessary to discuss the Occupation Statute until later.

This conclusion is neither an intentional nor an unintentional attempt to becloud or belittle the fact that Germans in the Parliamentary Council used the opportunity presented them to write into the Basic Law much that was traditionally German, to draw upon the German experience as a source of their work, and to construct with deliberation a government (within the framework of Allied limitations and the transitional character it was to assume) that would meet the needs of the situation as they interpreted it. Golay and Merkl have demonstrated that beyond question, and Hans-Peter Schwarz has filled in much of the detail on the ideological and theoretical backgrounds. Neither is this an attempt to ignore the fact that, once in operation, the Bonn government under Chancellor Konrad Adenauer gradually, but decisively, regained much of the sovereignty that the occupation powers had reserved to themselves in 1949. The story of how that occurred is beyond the scope of this study. It did not have to go the way it did, however. The Allies had not relinquished their power and abandoned their interests in 1949. It is therefore to the credit of the Bonn government that it exploited (in the best sense) the common ground of Allied and German interests in European recovery and containment of the Soviet Union to achieve concession after concession. The creation of the Bonn government gave Germans for the first time a forum from which they could proclaim their interests, and it gave them an administrative machinery through which they could further them.

In this situation, the American reorientation program, which continued into the fifties, remained essentially what it had always been under the occupation: a manifestation of an American interest. It was an interest fostered in part by empire-builders and in part by idealists who hoped it might have some long-range impact. Before 1949, democratization was mainly a political program that emphasized institutional changes, applied by a military governor committed by conviction and by policy directive to maintain an impartial attitude toward party differences. For the most part the promoters of broader reorientation functioned on the fringes of the structure in which real power existed and was applied. Their marginal status explains the fact that their occasional successes in getting Germans to assert themselves as democratic spokesmen often annoyed and occasionally embarrassed those who wielded power. After 1949, reorientation had to contend with the gradually increasing authority of Germans, many of whom saw reorientation as pure Americanization or, in the words of its most severe critic, "character-washing."[18]

# A Note on Sources

The published materials I used directly in preparing this study are identified in the Notes. The unpublished materials I used are, on the American side, the OMGUS and War/Army Department records of the occupation. The OMGUS records include, among other things, the files of the OMGUS headquarters in Berlin; the American-zone headquarters in Frankfurt; the Regional Government Coordinating Office in Stuttgart; the Offices of Military Government for Bavaria in Munich, for Hesse in Wiesbaden, for Württemberg-Baden in Stuttgart, and for Bremen. They contain much material left by the American staffs of the Allied Control Council and of the bizonal agencies. The War/Army Department records include the papers of the Civil Affairs Division, the Plans and Operations Division, the Assistant Secretaries of the Army, the Under Secretaries of the Army, and the Secretaries of the Army during the period of the occupation.

The American sources were opened to me freely. When I began my research, the OMGUS records were in Kansas City, Missouri. They were subsequently moved to the World War II Records Center in Alexandria, Virginia, and they are currently being transferred to a permanent center in Suitland, Maryland. There is as yet no complete catalog or index to the materials. There is a card index that locates certain subjects, names, and issues by box and shipment number. There are also rather extensive shipping inventory lists that identify file-folder headings or decimal-file folders and locate them by box and shipment numbers. Particular documents cited in this study may be located by the box and shipment numbers. For example, number 235/15 identifies footlocker number 235 of shipment number 15 as they were stored in Kansas City. In Alexandria the contents of each footlocker were transferred to three or fewer boxes for storage. Thus, the same record might be found in 235-1/15; 235-2/15; or 235-3/15 in Alexandria. The boxes are now being broken down again, but I do not know what symbols will be used to identify the sections.

The records are most interesting to use. They remain in essentially the same condition and order they were in during military government operations in Germany. Most of them are still in the original file folders, apparently in the order they were kept in the filing cabinets of the various offices and divisions in Berlin, Frankfurt, Stuttgart, and elsewhere. The only exceptions are certain materials gathered by the OMGUS historical office in 1949 (which are in separate boxes), and certain materials retained for use by the Office of the United States High Commissioner for Germany after 1949. Some of the HICOG materials came to the center in separate shipments. The rest are in the custody of the Department of State and have not been made available to me. The files contain much duplicate material and they contain working papers, first and later drafts, interoffice memoranda, buck slips, and numerous other raw materials that might long since have disappeared in a records-screening program.

The War/Army Department papers are stored separately in Alexandria by originating office and division. They are filed according to the Army decimal filing system, and materials dealing with Germany and German policy are usually—though not always—separated from the other things. There are separate collections of incoming and outgoing cables.

Research in the American records of the occupation is hardly feasible without security clearance. Some materials are still classified, and much of the unclassified material is in file folders containing classified documents that cannot easily be sorted for the researcher without clearance. Most classified documents can be declassified by the archivists in whose custody the records are kept. Certain documents require Army and State Department decisions. In either case, declassification is by individual letter, cable, or document. Where Army or State Department decisions are necessary, declassification decisions are made on the actual note the researcher takes from the classified document. Thus, the researcher must have clearance to see, identify, and take notes from the materials he wishes declassified. The procedure is time-consuming, but most of my requests for declassification were granted.

German governments and agencies made their records of the occupation period available to me on a generous basis. The most extensive materials I used are in the Hessian Staatskanzlei and Staatsarchiv in Wiesbaden. The office of the German minister-presidents' conference was in Wiesbaden, and the records of that office remain in the Staatskanzlei. They include the usual correspondence and record materials of such an office. There are also minutes of the various conferences of the minister-presidents, except for the one held in Koblenz in July 1948 and the one held in Wiesbaden in October 1947. The Staatskanzlei has an extensive collection of Länderrat materials. Included in this are the minutes and records of the Länderrat and the Länderrat Direktorium meetings; of the executive sessions of the American-zone minister-presidents; and of the "internal discussions" between Clay (and sometimes other Americans) and the minister-presidents. The latter were kept by the executive secretary of the Länderrat, and I have found no comparable records of these meetings in the OMGUS materials. There are also materials in Wiesbaden relating to bizonal agencies and to the occupation of Land Hesse.

The Staatsarchiv, Hessen, has the papers of the first Hessian minister-president, Karl Geiler. These contain minutes and records of the early minister-presidents' meetings and material on the formation of the Länderrat and on some of Geiler's activities after he left office. The Staatsarchiv also has papers left by Hermann Brill, the State Secretary in the Chancellery, who was on the Board of Directors of the Institut für Zeitgeschichte and the Deutsches Büro für Friedensfragen. Brill's papers contain the most complete file of materials on these organizations that I have found. They also contain materials relating to the minister-presidents' conferences and the occupation period in general.

The Federal Archives in Koblenz have materials on the Länderrat, the minister-presidents' conferences, the Institut für Zeitgeschichte, and the Deutsches Büro für Friedensfragen. It received many of the records from the Württemberg-Baden government, which had formally been designated as the agency to phase out the work of the Länderrat and its agencies. The Baden-Württemberg Staatsarchiv in Ludwigsburg has retained certain personnel records of the Länderrat and its own Länderrat liaison records. The liaison records tend to duplicate the more extensive collection I found in Hesse. The Federal Archives in Koblenz have a considerable collection of papers from bizonal agencies, particularly the German offices. The Bundestag library in Bonn has a collection of minutes and summaries of discussions between the Bipartite Board (Clay and Robertson) and German officials in bizonal agencies. It has records of the American-zone Länderrat meetings, of the British-zone Zonenbeirat meetings, and of the Bizonal Economic Council and Länderrat (Frankfurt) meetings.

# Notes

# Notes

The following list includes abbreviations used in the text as well as those used in the Notes. Abbreviations that appear only as parts of file numbers are not listed.

| | |
|---|---|
| AGWAR | Adjutant General, War Department |
| BICO | Bipartite Control Office |
| CAD | Civil Affairs Division |
| CDU | Christian Democratic Union (Christlich-Demokratische Union) |
| CG | Commanding General |
| CNO | Chief of Naval Operations |
| CINCEUR | Commander in Chief, Europe |
| CSCAD | Chief of Staff, Civil Affairs Division |
| CSU | Christian Social Union (Christlich-Soziale Union) |
| DMG | Deputy Military Governor |
| DPB | Denazification Policy Board |
| ECA | Economic Cooperation Administration |
| ERP | European Recovery Program |
| FDP | Free Democratic Party (Freie Demokratische Partei) |
| FEA | Foreign Economic Administration |
| HICOG | Office of the U.S. High Commissioner for Germany |
| IARA | Inter-Allied Reparations Authority |
| JCS | Joint Chiefs of Staff |
| KPD | German Communist Party (Kommunistische Partei Deutschlands) |
| LDP | Liberal Democratic Party (Liberal-Demokratische Partei) |

OMGUS    Office of Military Government for Germany, United
        States
PIO    Public Information Office
PRO    Public Relations Office
RFC    Reconstruction Finance Corporation
RGCO    Regional Government Coordinating Office
SED    Socialist Unity Party (Sozialistische Einheits-
        partei Deutschlands)
SPD    Social Democratic Party (Sozialdemokratische Partei
        Deutschlands)
SWNCC    State-War-Navy Coordinating Committee
USFET    United States Forces, European Theater
US Group CC    United States Group, Control Council
WARCAD    War Department, Civil Affairs Division
WARSEC    Secretary of War
WWIIRC    World War II Records Center

## NOTES

### Chapter 1

1. Lucius D. Clay, *Decision in Germany* (Garden City, 1950), pp. 16–18.

2. Robert Murphy, *Diplomat Among Warriors* (Garden City, 1964), p. 251.

3. See Hans-Peter Schwarz, *Vom Reich zur Bundesrepublik. Deutschland im Widerstreit der aussenpolitischen Konzeptionen in den Jahren der Besatzungsherrschaft 1945–1949* (Neuwied, 1966), p. 110, for a recent statement of the prevailing view. See also Nicholas Balabkins, *Germany Under Direct Controls: Economic Aspects of Industrial Disarmament, 1945–1948* (New Brunswick, 1964), pp. 207–8, and Hubertus Prinz zu Löwenstein, *Deutschlands Schicksal, 1945–1957* (Bonn, 1957), p. 19.

4. USFET, Subj: Administration of Military Government in the U.S. Zone in Germany, July 7, 1945, WWIIRC, box 361–2, shipment 5 (hereafter cited as WWIIRC 361–2/5.)

5. OMGUS, Chief of Staff, Memorandum to All Divisions and Offices, Subj: Revision of Existing Directives for Military Government in Germany, Dec. 2, 1945, *ibid.*, 367–2/5. (The memo repeats the cables.)

6. See Lutz Niethammer, "Die amerikanische Besatzungsmacht zwischen Verwaltungstradition und politischen Parteien in Bayern 1945," *Vierteljahrshefte für Zeitgeschichte* (Heft 2, 1967), 153–210; Caspar Schrenck-Notzing, *Charakterwäsche: Die amerikanische Besatzung in Deutschland und ihre Folgen* (Stuttgart, 1965), pp. 176–78.

7. See Paul Y. Hammond, "Directives for the Occupation of Germany: The Washington Controversy," in Harold Stein, ed., *American Civil-Military Decisions: A Book of Case Studies*, a Twentieth Century Fund Study (University of Alabama Press, 1963), pp. 438–39, for a reference to the pressure Morgenthau applied.

8. Clay to John J. McCloy, April 26, 1945, WWIIRC, ASW 370.8; Clay to McCloy, June 29, 1945, *ibid.*, 410/3.

9. McCloy to Clay, Nov. 23, 1945, *ibid.* Cf. Hammond, "Directives for the Occupation of Germany," p. 439, who has quoted the passage with a slight error.

10. AGWAR to OMGUS, Jan. 3, 1946, WWIIRC 362–2/5.

11. U.S. Congress, 80th Cong., 1st Sess., House Committee on Appropriations. Hearings . . . on First Deficiency Appropriation Bill for 1947 (Washington, 1947), Feb. 25, 1947, pp. 700, 740.

12. U.S. Dept. of State, *Department of State Bulletin*, XIII, 960–64; XV, 496–501. See also Hajo Holborn, *American Military Government, Its Organization and Policies* (Washington, 1947), pp. 215–22.

13. Raymond Dennet and Robert K. Turner, eds., *Documents on American Foreign Relations*, VIII, 208–9.

14. Elfte Tagung des Länderrats . . . 6 Aug. 1946, Staatskanzlei, Wiesbaden, 1g06/01, contains a translation of Clay's speech to the Länderrat. Cf. *Frankfurter Rundschau*, Aug. 9, 1946, p. 1; Nov. 7, 1946, p. 2.

15. Clay to McCloy, April 26, 1945, WWIIRC, ASW 370.8.

16. Harry S. Truman, *Year of Decisions* (Garden City, 1955), p. 341.

17. Quoted in J. F. J. Gillen, *State and Local Government in West Germany, 1945–1953* (Mehlem, 1953), p. 3.

18. Russell Hill, *Struggle for Germany* (New York, 1947), p. 30. Millis was an editorial writer and Barnes the foreign editor for the *New York Herald Tribune*.

19. Clay to McCloy, April 26, 1945, WWIIRC, ASW 370.8.

20. US Group CC, Chief of Staff, to DMG, Subj: Policy Agreements within US Group CC, May 1, 1945; US Group CC, Director, Political Div., to General Milburn, Chief of Staff, Subj: Basic Preliminary Plan, April 24, 1945, *ibid.*, 3–1/1.

21. Murphy, *Diplomat Among Warriors*, p. 251.

22. USFET, Clay, to WARCAD, Hilldring, May 7, 1945, WWIIRC 177–1/3.

23. US Group CC, Memorandum, Subj: Factual Reports on Conditions in Germany, June 15, 1945; O. P. Echols, Director, Internal Affairs and Communications Div., to Lewis W. Douglas, Adviser, Office of the CG, US Group CC, June 20, 1945, *ibid.*, 5–1/1; Robert R. Bowie, Memorandum for General Clay, Subj: Report of Field Survey of Regional Government in Bavaria, June 5, 1945, *ibid.*, 10–3/1.

24. Calvin B. Hoover, Economic Intelligence Branch, Economic Div., US Group CC, to Director, Economic Div., Subj: Report of Economic Situation in Germany, July 2, 1945, *ibid.*, SAOUS 091.3.

25. Robert R. Bowie, Memorandum for General Clay, Subj: Report of Field Survey of Regional Government in Bavaria, June 5, 1945, *ibid.*, 10–3/1.

26. Hammond, "Directives for the Occupation of Germany," p. 425; Clay, *Decision in Germany*, pp. 16–17.

27. Hilldring to Clay, May 21, 1945, WWIIRC 177–1/3.

28. Clay to McCloy, June 16, 1945, *ibid.*, ASW 370.8.

29. McCloy to Clay, June 21, 1945, WWIIRC, ASW 370.8.

30. U.S. Dept. of State, *Foreign Relations of the United States, Diplomatic Papers. The Conference of Berlin (The Potsdam Conference) 1945*, 2 vols. (Washington, 1960), Docs. 420, 421 (hereafter cited as *Potsdam Papers*); Harold Ickes to Truman, June 14, 1945; Truman to Stimson, June 15, 1945; Stimson to Truman, July 4, 1945; Hilldring, Memorandum, Subj: Coal Situation in Europe, June 21, 1945; Hilldring, Memorandum for Asst. Secretary of War, Subj: Coal Production and Exports in Germany, Oct. 6, 1945, WWIIRC, OSW 463.3. See also, Balabkins, *Germany Under Direct Controls*, pp. 113, 122, and Truman, *Year of Decisions*, pp. 496–97.

31. Henry L. Stimson and McGeorge Bundy, *On Active Service in Peace and War* (New York, 1947), p. 583.

32. Stimson to Truman, July 4, 1945, WWIIRC, OSW 463.3; *Potsdam Papers*, I, Doc. 849, pp. 754–57.

33. William L. Clayton to McCloy, June 18, 1945, WWIIRC, WDSCA 014; *Potsdam Papers*, I, Doc. 336, pp. 468–70; II, Doc. 865, pp. 800–801.

34. Secretary of War to Secretary of State, July 4, 1945, WWIIRC, WDSCA 014; *Potsdam Papers*, I, Doc. 342, pp. 479–82.

35. *Ibid.*, II, Doc. 884, pp. 821–23.

36. *Ibid.*, Doc. 865, pp. 800–801.

37. The section is Part iii, par. 49(b), which followed President Roose-

velt's memorandum of March 23, 1945, regarding German policy. Cf. Hammond, "Directives for the Occupation of Germany," p. 420.

38. Clayton to McCloy, June 18, 1945, WWIIRC, WDSCA 014.

39. McCloy to Clay, June 21, 1945, *ibid.*, ASW 370.8.

40. Clay to McCloy, June 29, 1945, *ibid.*, 410/3.

41. Herbert Feis, *Between War and Peace: The Potsdam Conference* (Princeton, 1960), p. 223; *Potsdam Papers*, I, Docs. 429, 510.

42. *Ibid.*, Docs. 429, 430, 433; SHAEF to War Dept., July 9, 1945; War Dept. to USFET, July 10, 1945; SHAEF to War Dept., July 11, 1945, WWIIRC, WDSCA 014.

43. Clay, *Decision in Germany*, p. 38.

44. Walter Millis, ed., with the collaboration of E. S. Duffield, *The Forrestal Diaries* (New York, 1951), pp. 79–80.

45. See Holborn, *American Military Government*, p. 60.

46. Clay, *Decision in Germany*, pp. 41–42; OMGUS, CAD, Local Government Branch, to Director, CAD, Subj: Berlin Agreement, Aug. 7, 1945, WWIIRC 165-3/3.

47. See Feis, *Between War and Peace*; John L. Snell, *Wartime Origins of the East-West Dilemma Over Germany* (New Orleans, 1959); James F. Byrnes, *Speaking Frankly* (New York, 1947); Truman, *Year of Decisions*; Wilhelm Cornides, *Die Weltmächte und Deutschland: Geschichte der jüngsten Vergangenheit 1945–1955* (Tübingen, 1957); Ernst Deuerlein, *Die Einheit Deutschlands: Ihre Erörterung und Behandlung auf den Kriegs- und Nachkriegskonferenzen 1941–1949. Darstellung und Dokumentation* (Frankfurt, 1957); Rudolf Fiedler, *Würfelspiel um Deutschland, 1944–1956: Eine kritische Untersuchung der Zerstückelungs- und Wiedervereinigungspolitik* (Düsseldorf, 1957); Elmar Krautkrämer, *Deutsche Geschichte nach dem zweiten Weltkrieg: Eine Darstellung der Entwicklung von 1945 bis 1949 mit Dokumenten* (Hildesheim, 1962); Wolfgang Marienfeld, *Konferenzen über Deutschland. Die alliierte Deutschlandplanung und -politik 1941–1949* (Hannover, 1963); Hubertus Prinz zu Löwenstein, *Deutschlands Schicksal, 1945–1957* (Bonn, 1957); Boris Meissner, *Russland, Die Westmächte und Deutschland: Die Sowjetische Deutschlandpolitik 1943–1953* (Hamburg, 1953); Richard Thelenius, *Die Teilung Deutschlands: Eine zeitgeschichtliche Analyse* (Hamburg, 1957); Emil Shäfer, *Von Potsdam bis Bonn: Fünf Jahre deutsche Nachkriegsgeschichte* (Lahr, 1950); Schwarz, *Vom Reich zur Bundesrepublik*.

48. The notes are printed in *Europa-Archiv*, 9. J. (July 20, 1954), pp. 6745–46.

49. *Ibid.*, p. 6747.

50. *Ibid.*, p. 6748. See also F. Roy Willis, *The French in Germany, 1945–1949* (Stanford, 1962), p. 27.

*Chapter 2*

1. Clay, *Decision in Germany*, pp. 72–73; Murphy, *Diplomat Among Warriors*, p. 285.

2. Hammond, "Directives for the Occupation of Germany," p. 438.

3. Copy of memorandum from Byrnes to Truman, Subj: Termination of the Informal Policy Committee on Germany, Aug. 30, 1945, WWIIRC, WDSCA 014 Germany.

4. B. U. Ratchford and William D. Ross, *Berlin Reparations Assignment: Round One of the German Peace Settlement* (Chapel Hill, 1947), p. 82; Draft of a Preliminary Report to the German Standard of Living Board by the Working Staff of the Board, *A Minimum German Standard of Living in Relation to Industrial Disarmament and Reparations* (stamped date, Sept. 10, 1945), WWIIRC 199–2/3.

5. Byron Price, Memorandum to the President, Nov. 9, 1945, *ibid.*, 177–3/3.

6. Clay to McCloy, Sept. 3, 1945, *ibid.*, ASW 370.8.

7. Ratchford and Ross, *Berlin Reparations Assignment*, pp. 78–79.

8. Draft of a Preliminary Report of the German Standard of Living Board, p. 1, WWIIRC 199–2/3.

9. *Ibid.*, p. 5. Cf. Ratchford and Ross, *Berlin Reparations Assignment*, pp. 82–83.

10. *New York Times*, Oct. 8, 1945, p. 1.

11. See, for example, Senator Wheeler's remarks in *Congressional Record*, 79th Cong., 1st Sess., Senate, Nov. 27, 1945, pp. 11015, 11033. For a general presentation see H. Bradford Westerfield, *Foreign Policy and Party Politics: Pearl Harbor to Korea* (New Haven, 1957), particularly chaps. 9 and 10.

12. J. H. Hilldring, CAD, Memorandum for the Secretary of War, Subj: Comments on Preliminary Report by the Working Staff of the German Standard of Living Board, Oct. 9, 1945, WWIIRC, ASW 370.8; Hammond, "Directives for the Occupation of Germany," pp. 438–39.

13. US Group CC to War Dept., Sept. 26, 1945, WWIIRC, WDSCA 014 Germany; Clay to McCloy, Oct. 3, 1945, *ibid.*, ASW 370.8.

14. Frederick Winant, Memorandum, Sept. 14, 1945 (on the tentative

report of the Calvin Hoover Working Staff of the German Standard of Living Board), *ibid.*, 149–2/3.

15. Byron Price, Memorandum to the President, Nov. 9, 1945, *ibid.*, 177–3/3.

16. McCloy to Clay, Nov. 23, 1945, *ibid.*, 410/3.

17. *Ibid.* Cf. Hammond, "Directives for the Occupation of Germany," p. 439.

18. OMGUS, Chief of Staff, Memorandum to All Divisions and Offices, Subj: Revision of Existing Directives for Military Government in Germany, Dec. 2, 1945, WWIIRC 367–2/5.

19. Hilldring, Memorandum for the Secretary of War, Dec. 3, 1945, Subj: Recommendations of Byron Price Report on Germany, WWIIRC, OSW 091 Germany; AGWAR to OMGUS, Dec. 8, 1945; Chronology, prepared by OMGUS, Control Office, draft, *ibid.*, 362–2/5; Hilldring, CAD, Memorandum for the Asst. Secretary of War, Subj: Statement of U.S. Political Policies in Germany, Feb. 13, 1946, *ibid.*, WDSCA, 014 Germany.

20. Clay, *Decision in Germany*, pp. 35–36; 109–10; 131.

21. *Ibid.*; Clay to McCloy, Oct. 5, 1945, WWIIRC, ASW 370.8.

22. *Ibid.*

23. *Ibid.*

24. Based on drafts and working papers of OMGUS staff, in WWIIRC 99–2/5.

25. *Ibid.*

26. Bruce G. Leighton, Ad Hoc Interdepartmental Committee to Handle FEA Projects, to Committee, Subj: Industrial Disarmament of Germany—Ad Hoc Committee Studies. Report on Mission to Germany, Oct. 18, 1945, WWIIRC, WDSCA 014 Germany.

27. *Ibid.* See Ratchford and Ross, *Berlin Reparations Assignment*, p. 89, for a comment on Soviet representatives' assumptions.

28. US Group CC, Office of the Assistant Deputy for Resources, "Reparations Directive to the Industry Division with Respect to Removals of Industrial Capital Equipment," Aug. 8, 1945, WWIIRC 177–2/3. Italics are in the original.

29. US Group CC, Industry Div., to DMG, Subj: Industrial Disarmament of Germany (draft), n.d. (cover letter is dated Sept. 24, 1945), WWIIRC 145–3/15.

30. Ratchford and Ross, *Berlin Reparations Assignment*, p. 89.

31. Bruce G. Leighton, Member, and A.M. Hartman, Secretary, Memo-

randum to Office of CNO, Navy Dept., Subj: Ad Hoc Committee Reports on FEA Projects Nos. 1, 2, and 3: Report on Consultation with US Gp CC, Sept. 5, 1945, WWIIRC 10–3/1. A similar report may also be found in *ibid.*, WDSCA 014 Germany.

32. US Group CC, Industry Div., to DMG, Subj: Industrial Disarmament of Germany (draft), n.d. (cover letter is dated Sept. 24, 1945), WWIIRC 145–3/15.

33. Hilldring, CAD, to Assistant Secretary of War, Memorandum, Subj: Subjects Discussed with General Clay in Washington (1 Nov. to 5 Nov. 1945), Nov. 7, 1945; "Resumé of Meeting at State Department 3 November 1945," Subj: Current Questions in the Military Government of Germany, attached to foregoing memorandum, WWIIRC, ASW 370.8 Germany.

34. See Hilldring, Memorandum for the Asst. Secretary of War, Subj: Coal Production and Exports in Germany, Oct. 6, 1945, *ibid.*, OSW 463.3, which uses OMGUS figures to show that the coal directive goals could not be met.

35. See particularly, James S. Martin, *All Honorable Men* (Boston, 1950); George S. Wheeler, *Die amerikanische Politik in Deutschland (1945–1950)* (Berlin, 1958), and *Who Split Germany? Wall Street and the West German Trade Union Leaders* (Berlin, 1962); Cedric Belfrage, *Seeds of Destruction: The Truth about the U.S. Occupation of Germany* (New York, 1954).

36. See Manuel Gottlieb, *The German Peace Settlement and the Berlin Crisis* (New York, 1960), pp. 15–16, 38–39, 97, 102–3, 128–29, 164–65, and Schwarz, *Vom Reich zur Bundesrepublik*, pp. 76ff and 105, for discussions of the policy of "ambivalence," and "postponement."

37. See particularly, L. L. Matthias, "Wie kam es zur Teilung Deutschlands?" *Neuer Vorwärts* (Dec. 3, 1954), pp. 9–10, which has been quoted and cited widely in the literature. See also, Stefan Doernberg, *Die Geburt eines neuen Deutschland 1945–1949: Die antifaschistisch-demokratische Umwälzung und die Entstehung der DDR* (Berlin, 1959); Wheeler, *Die amerikanische Politik in Deutschland*; and Gerhard Baumann, "Wer brach das Potsdamer Abkommen? Optik und Realität der Wiederaufrüstung," *Die politische Meinung, Monatshefte für Fragen der Zeit*, 3. J. Heft 31 (Dec. 1958), pp. 57–62.

38. John Foster Dulles, *War or Peace* (New York, 1950), p. 3; James F. Byrnes, *All In One Lifetime* (New York, 1958), p. 317; Truman, *Year of Decisions*, p. 552.

39. Hilldring, Memorandum for the Secretary of War, Dec. 3, 1945, Subj: Recommendations of Byron Price Report on Germany, WWIIRC, OSW 091 Germany.

40. Robert R. Patterson, Secretary of War, to Dean Acheson, Acting Secretary of State, Dec. 28, 1945, *ibid.*, WDSCA 014 Germany; McCloy to Clay, Nov. 23, 1945, *ibid.*, ASW 370.8.

41. Hammond, "Directives for the Occupation of Germany," pp. 438–39.

42. *Ibid.*; AGWAR to OMGUS, Dec. 8, 1945, WWIIRC 365–2/5.

43. Patterson to Acheson, Dec. 28, 1945, *ibid.*, WDSCA 014 Germany.

44. Acheson to Secretary of War, Jan. 12, 1946, *ibid.*

45. AGWAR from WARCAD to OMGUS, Dec. 8, 1945, WWIIRC 365–2/5; "The Reparation Settlement and the Peacetime Economy of Germany," *Department of State Bulletin*, XIII (Dec. 16, 1945), 960–64.

46. Ratchford and Ross, *Berlin Reparations Assignment*, p. 102.

47. Hilldring, CAD, Memorandum for the Asst. Secretary of War, Subj: Statement of U.S. Political Policies in Germany, Feb. 13, 1946, WWIIRC, WDSCA 014 Germany.


*Chapter 3*

1. Clay to McCloy, April 26, 1945; July 15, 1945; June 29, 1945; Sept. 16, 1945, WWIIRC, ASW 370.8; US Group CC, Economics Div., to CG, US Group CC, June 11, 1945, Subj: Brief on Supply, *ibid.*, 14–2/1(AG 337); Bruce G. Leighton, USNR, and others, Memorandum to Office of CNO, Navy Dept., Subj: Ad Hoc Committee Reports on FEA Projects Nos. 1, 2, and 3: Report on Consultation with US Group CC, Sept. 5, 1945, *ibid.*, 10–3/1; Murphy, *Diplomat Among Warriors*, p. 270.

2. Calvin B. Hoover, Economic Intelligence Branch, Economic Div., US Group CC, to Director, Economic Div., Subj: Report of Economic Situation in Germany, July 2, 1945, copy in WWIIRC, SAOUS 091.3.

3. Robert R. Bowie, Memorandum for General Clay, Subj: Report of Field Survey of Regional Government in Bavaria, June 5, 1945, WWIIRC 10–3/1; Hqs, US Group CC, Memorandum, Subj: Factual Reports on Conditions in Germany, June 15, 1945, *ibid.*, 5–1/1.

4. Bruce G. Leighton, Ad Hoc Interdepartmental Committee to Handle FEA Projects, to Committee, Subj: Industrial Disarmament of Germany —Ad Hoc Committee Studies, Report on Mission to Germany, Oct. 18, 1945, WWIIRC, WDSCA 014 Germany.

5. Clay to McCloy, Oct. 5, 1945, WWIIRC, ASW 370.0, Communications for Clay. See also a chronology prepared by OMGUS, Control Office (entry for Sept. 24, 1945) in WWIIRC 362–2/5.

6. Extract from Minutes of the Divisional Staff Meeting, OMGUS, Sept. 29, 1945, WWIIRC 3–1/1.

7. USFET to CG, Eastern and Western Military Districts, Oct. 1, 1945, copy in Bundesarchiv, Koblenz, Z1/14; USFET, Subj: Coordination of German Länder Governments and Special Administrative Services (Sonderverwaltungen) in the American Zone, Oct. 5, 1945, WWIIRC 34–2/11.

8. "Report on Conference of Representatives of German Economic Control Agencies at Höchst, 10, 11, 12 October 1945"; "Ausschuss: Ständiges Sekretariat der drei Länder," Oct. 11, 1945, Geiler Papers, Staatsarchiv Wiesbaden; OMGUS, Hugh B. Hester to Deputy Chief, Economics Branch, Subj: Conference of German Economic Officials, Nov. 7, 1945, WWIIRC 119–1/1.

9. Reinhold Maier, *Ein Grundstein Wird Gelegt: Die Jahre 1945–1947* (Tübingen, 1964), p. 149.

10. "Sitzung des Ministerpräsidentenrats Bayern, Württemberg-Baden, Hessen, Bremen mit der U.S.-Militärregierung am 17.Oktober 1945...," in Anton Pfeiffer, "Der Länderrat der amerikanischen Zone: Seine Geschichte und staatsrechtliche Würdigung," Ph.D. dissertation, Munich, 1948, appendix 1. Also in Staatskanzlei, Wiesbaden, 1g06/1.

11. *Ibid.*; Maier, *Ein Grundstein Wird Gelegt*, p. 149.

12. Hqs., Seventh Army, Western Military District, "Fifth Meeting of the Deputy Military Governor with Army Commanders, Minutes," Oct. 18, 1945, WWIIRC 364–2/5.

13. OMG, US Zone, Hayden N. Smith to Walter Dorn, Oct. 24, 1945; Dorn to Adcock, Subj: Suggestions for a U.S. Staff at the Stuttgart Secretariat, Oct. 24, 1945, WWIIRC 34–2/11; "Besprechung über das Sekretariat in Stuttgart am 1.11.45, Olgastrasse 11," in Staatskanzlei, Wiesbaden, 1g08; Hqs. MG. E–1 Co. A 2nd MG Regt., 1 Nov. 1945—Agenda, in Bundesarchiv, Koblenz, Z1/14. See also "Notes on Interview with Mr. F. S. Hannaman, Special Assistant for Policy and Coordination, Economics Adviser, [by] D. G. White ["& J. F. Gillen" in pencil], 7 July 1949," copy in WWIIRC 362–2/5. This document shows that when the OMGUS Historical Division began to write its histories in 1949 it was generally assumed that the OMGUS Economics Division had originated the idea of the Länderrat in the first place.

14. "Beschlüsse und Ergebnisse der Tagung des Länderrats... 6.Nov. 1945," copy in Staatskanzlei, Wiesbaden, 1g06/01; USFET to RGCO,

Subj: Establishment of German Transportation Agencies for Control of the Transportation System in the U.S. Zone of Germany, Dec. 7, 1945, WWIIRC 376–2/5.

15. RGCO to Clay, Dec. 21, 1945, *ibid.*, 42–3/11.

16. "Beschlüsse und Ergebnisse der Tagung des Länderrats ... 6.Nov. 1945," copy in Staatskanzlei, Wiesbaden, 1g06/01.

17. USFET to CG, Eastern and Western Military Districts, Subj: Regional Government Coordinating Office, Nov. 2, 1945, WWIIRC 98–3/15.

18. I have been unable to locate the plan itself. However, the criticisms and later reports refer to it in sufficient detail to reveal its main features.

19. Anton Pfeiffer, Bavaria, to General Secretary des Länderrats, Jan. 7, 1946; "Auszug aus dem Protokoll der Kabinettsitzung [Hessen] vom 24.Januar 1946," in Geiler Papers, Staatsarchiv, Wiesbaden.

20. RGCO, Subj: Meeting of the Liaison Officers held in Stuttgart, 10 Jan. 1946 (dated Jan. 11, 1946), WWIIRC 39–2/11.

21. OMGUS, to Distribution, Subj: Regional Government Coordinating Office, Dec. 20, 1945, WWIIRC 98–3/15; OMGUS, Legal Div. to Charles Fahy, Chairman, DPB, Subj: Denazification Policy, Jan. 3, 1946, *ibid.*, 177–1/3; German Draft of Proposed Denazification Law prepared by Ministers of Justice, Dec. 22, 1945, mimeo, *ibid.*, 107–1/15; Erich Rossmann, "Denkschrift über die Entwicklung des Länderrats," March 29, 1946, Länderrat Papers, Staatsarchiv, Wiesbaden, folder 61; Länderrat, U'Ausschuss für Aussenhandel beim Länderrat, Sitzung am 14.1.1946, *ibid.*, folder 165; RGCO to Rossmann, 30.1.1946, *ibid.*, folder 63; RGCO to Rossmann, Feb. 12, 1946, Bundesarchiv, Koblenz.

22. Erich Rossmann, "Denkschrift über die Entwicklung des Länderrats," March 29, 1946, Länderrat Papers, Staatsarchiv, Wiesbaden, folder 61.

23. "Niederschrift über die Besprechung der Ministerpräsidenten im Anschluss an die ausserordentliche Länderratstagung betr. Ernährungsfragen am 29.3.1946," Staatskanzlei, Wiesbaden, 1g06/01.

24. "Interne Sitzung des Länderrates am 2.4.1946," Staatskanzlei, Wiesbaden, lg06/01.

25. *Ibid.* "Von der einen Seite werde gebremst, die andere Seite— nämlich die amerikanische—verlange volle Verantwortung." The indirect discourse is quoted from the *Protokoll.*

26. "Zweite interne Länderratstagung ... 7.Mai 1946," Staatskanzlei, Wiesbaden, lg06/01.

27. Graf v. Wedel to Herrn v. Fries, Bericht über die Tagung in Birkenstein b./Schliersee vom 15.–17.5.46, dated May 18, 1946; Wedel to

Geiler, May 20, 1946, Länderrat Papers, Staatsarchiv, Wiesbaden, folder 63; RGCO, Pollock, to Rossmann, May 16, 1946, Staatskanzlei, Wiesbaden, 1d04/06.

28. Pollock to Clay, May 20, 1946, WWIIRC 39–3/11; Der Gross-Hessische Länderratsbevollmächtigte, Stuttgart, to Geiler, May 20, 1946, Staatskanzlei, Wiesbaden, 1d04/06.

29. "Dritte interne Länderratssitzung ... 27.Mai 1946," Staatskanzlei, Wiesbaden, 1g06/01. Maier's words, in German, were: "Wir spüren hier in Stuttgart den Druck, der von der Militärregierung ausgeht, am deutlichsten. Ich beschwöre Sie, tun Sie in der Sache einen entscheidenden Schritt."

30. *Ibid.*, with attached new statute.

31. "Vierte interne Länderratssitzung ... 4.Juni 1946," Staatskanzlei, Wiesbaden, 1g06/01; Direktorium des Länderrates, "Protokoll über die erste Sitzung ... 21.Juni 1946," *ibid.*, 1g10; *Die Neue Zeitung*, June 21, 1946, p. 1.

32. See especially, Lia Härtel, *Der Länderrat des amerikanischen Besatzungsgebietes*, herausgegeben im Auftrag der Ministerpräsidenten von Bayern, Hessen, Württemberg-Baden und des Präsidenten des Senats der Freien Hansestadt Bremen vom Direktorium des Länderrats (Stuttgart, 1951); Heinz Guradze, "The Laenderrat: Landmark of German Reconstruction," *The Western Political Quarterly*, III (June 1950), 190–213; Anton Pfeiffer, "Der Länderrat der amerikanischen Zone: Seine Geschichte und staatsrechtliche Würdigung," Ph.D. dissertation, Munich, 1948; Reinhold Maier, *Ende und Wende: Das schwäbische Schicksal 1944–1946, Briefe und Tagebuchaufzeichnungen* (Stuttgart, 1948), and *Ein Grundstein Wird Gelegt: Die Jahre 1945–1947* (Tübingen, 1964). See particularly Maier's speech commemorating the twentieth anniversary of the Länderrat's founding, "Vorbereitung auf Deutschland: Erinnerungen an die Bildung des Länderrats der US Zone—Wiederherstellung der staatlichen Ordnung," *Südwest Merkur*, Nov. 12, 1965, pp. 3ff.

33. Clay, *Decision in Germany*, p. 102. Cf. J. F. J. Gillen, "U.S. Military Government in Germany: American Influence on the Development of Political Institutions," (Karlsruhe, 1950), manuscript in WWIIRC, p. 143, for the statement that the Länderrat "declined increasingly in importance as its economic powers were assumed by the bizonal agencies."

34. Carl J. Friedrich *et al.*, *American Experiences in Military Government in World War II: American Government in Action* (New York, 1948), p. 206.

35. Chief, Local Government Branch, OMGUS, to Director, Civil Ad-

ministration Div., Subj: Reports on Formation of Central Administration in Russian Zone, Aug. 15, 1945, WWIIRC 165–3/3.

36. Annelies Dorendorf, *Der Zonenbeirat der britisch besetzten Zone: Ein Rückblick auf seine Tätigkeit*, auf Beschluss des Zonenbeirats herausgegeben und eingeleitet von seinem ehemaligen Generalsekretär Dr. Gerhard Weisser ... mit einem Geleitwort von Bundesminister ... Robert Lehr (Göttingen, 1953). Cf. Hans Schlange-Schöningen, *Im Schatten des Hungers: Dokumentarisches zur Ernährungspolitik und Ernährungswirtschaft in den Jahren 1945–1949* (Hamburg, 1955), esp. pp. 33ff.

37. See especially, Harold Zink, *American Military Government in Germany* (New York, 1947) and *The United States in Germany* (Princeton, 1957); Drew Middleton, *The Struggle for Germany* (Indianapolis, 1949); Julian Bach, *America's Germany: An Account of the Occupation* (New York, 1946); Oliver J. Frederiksen, *The American Military Occupation of Germany, 1949–1953* (Darmstadt, 1953); Eugene Davidson, *The Death and Life of Germany: An Account of the American Occupation* (New York, 1959); Joseph R. Starr, "U.S. Military Government in Germany: Operations from Late March to Mid-July 1945," (Karlsruhe, 1950), manuscript in WWIIRC; Carl Dreher, "Close-Up of Democracy," *The Virginia Quarterly Review*, XXIII (Winter 1947), 89–107; and Leonard Krieger, "The Inter-Regnum in Germany: March–August 1945," *Political Science Quarterly*, LXIV (December 1949), 507–32.

38. For details see my *A German Community under American Occupation: Marburg, 1945–1952* (Stanford, 1961) and Wiebke Fesefeldt, *Der Wiederbeginn des kommunalen Lebens in Göttingen: Die Stadt in den Jahren 1945 bis 1948* (Göttingen, 1962).

39. Schwarz, *Vom Reich zur Bundesrepublik*, p. 122.

40. Clay to McCloy, Sept. 16, 1945, WWIIRC, ASW 370.8. The letter is partially quoted in J. F. J. Gillen, *State and Local Government in West Germany, 1945–1953* (Mehlem, 1953), p. 8.

41. Hilldring to Petersen, July 29, 1946, comments on Hilldring's concern and his arguments with Clay while Hilldring was still head of the War Department, Civil Affairs Division. For statistics on the rapid decrease of military government personnel in Germany see Frederiksen, *The American Military Occupation of Germany*, p. 33.

42. Clay, *Decision in Germany*, p. 88. See also, US Group CC, Civil Administration Division, Subj: Memorandum dealing with the implementation of those portions of the Berlin agreement which deal with "the intention of the Allies that the German people be given the opportunity to prepare for the eventual reconstruction of their life on a democratic and

peaceful basis," Aug. 4, 1945, in James K. Pollock, James H. Meisel, and Henry L. Bretton, *Germany Under Occupation: Illustrative Materials and Documents*, revised edition (Ann Arbor, 1949), pp. 112–14.

43. Maier, *Ein Grundstein Wird Gelegt*, pp. 210–11, wrote: "Dieses Programm begrüssten wir von ganzem Herzen."

44. "Niederschrift über die Kabinettsitzung am 30.11.1945."; Geiler to Walther Fisch, Nov. 29, 1945 and Nov. 30, 1945; KPD, Frankfurt to Gross-Hessische Staatsregierung, Nov. 28, 1945, Geiler Papers, Staatsarchiv, Wiesbaden; Der Länderrat, Kurzbericht über die Sitzung vom 4.12.45, Staatskanzlei, Wiesbaden, 1g06/01; "Beschlussprotokoll über die Sitzung des Kabinetts am 18.Dezember 1945," *ibid.*; Pollock *et al.*, *Germany Under Occupation*, p. 119.

45. Clay to McCloy, Sept. 16, 1945, WWIIRC, ASW 370.8; Gillen, *State and Local Government*, p. 42. Bremen, the fourth Land of the American zone, was not created until January 21, 1947 (OMGUS to War Dept., Subj: Establishment of Land Bremen, Jan. 28, 1947, WWIIRC, WDSCA 014 Germany).

46. USFET, Subj: Organization of Military Government, Sept. 26, 1945, *ibid.*, 367–2/5.

47. USFET, Subj: Reorganization of Military Government Channels in Order to Develop German Responsibility for Self-government, Oct. 5, 1945, *ibid.*, 3–1/1; OMG, Hesse, Organizational Direction No. 12, Dec. 28, 1945, Kansas City Records Center, Box 7, Shipment 5; OMG, Bavaria, to Wilhelm Högner, Dec. 26, 1945, Staatskanzlei, Wiesbaden, AZ/3a02; Pollock *et al.*, *Germany Under Occupation*, pp. 143–46, contains an undated USFET letter directive Subj: Action to Strengthen German Civil Administration in the U.S. Zone, which Gillen, *State and Local Government*, p. 67, note 205, dates as Nov. 21, 1945.

48. Pollock *et al.*, *Germany Under Occupation*, p. 144.

49. OMG, Hesse, Organizational Direction No. 12, Dec. 28, 1945, Kansas City Records Center, Box 7, Shipment 5.

50. OMG, Bavaria, to Wilhelm Högner, Dec. 26, 1945, Staatskanzlei, Wiesbaden, AZ/3a02; Pollock *et al.*, *Germany Under Occupation*, p. 145.

51. Zink, *The United States in Germany*, p. 179.

*Chapter 4*

1. Clay, *Decision in Germany*, p. 72.

2. Acheson to Patterson, Jan. 12, 1946, WWIIRC, WDSCA 014 Germany.

3. *Die Neue Zeitung*, Feb. 18, 1946, p. 3; April 8, 1946, p. 1.

4. AGWAR to OMGUS, April 26, 1946, WWIIRC 358–2/5; O. P. Echols to Clay, April 6, 1946, *ibid.*, 177–1/3, states that the State Department–French discussions were being held at lower levels and that there was little hope for success.

5. McCloy to Clay, Nov. 23, 1945, WWIIRC, ASW 370.8.

6. OMGUS, PRO, press release, Coordinating Committee Statement, Dec. 21, 1945, WWIIRC 1–1/4.

7. Pollock to Clay and Murphy, Memorandum, Subj: French Approaches to Dr. Maier, Minister-President of Württemberg-Baden, to Move to Baden Baden, April 8, 1946, WWIIRC 39–3/11.

8. Beschlussprotokoll über die Sitzung des Kabinetts am 31.Januar 1946, Staatskanzlei, Wiesbaden; OMG, Hesse, to OMGUS, Feb. 4, 1946; OMGUS to OMG, Hesse, Feb. 5, 1946, WWIIRC 5–1/1.

9. Bericht Nr. 1 der Vertretung Berlin des Hessischen Staatsministeriums: Der Minister für Wirtschaft und Verkehr, (24.1–5.2.46), Geiler Papers, Staatsarchiv, Wiesbaden.

10. OMGUS, Monthly Report of the Military Governor, #8, March 20, 1946, Food and Agriculture, p. 7; #12, July 20, 1946, Food and Agriculture, p. 6. Cf. Balabkins, *Germany Under Direct Controls*, p. 100, who says that from June 1, 1945, to June 30, 1946, the British military government imported 1,245,000 tons of food into the British zone and the United States 461,000 tons into the U.S. zone.

11. Speech by Clay to Länderrat, March 29, 1946, WWIIRC 22–1/1; OMGUS, PRO, press release, March 29, 1946, *ibid.*, 1–1/4.

12. Clay, *Decision in Germany*, p. 266.

13. Davidson, *The Death and Life of Germany*, pp. 135–38; "Protokoll, Zusammenkunft mit Präsident a.D. Hoover, 13.4.46," Geiler Papers, Staatsarchiv, Wiesbaden.

14. Echols to Clay, March 26, 1946, WWIIRC 177–1/3.

15. Echols to Clay, April 6, 1946, *ibid.*

16. Echols to Clay, April 19, 1946, with enclosed "Address by Major General O. P. Echols, Director, Civil Affairs Division, War Department, Before Writers' Board . . . 17 April 1946"; Draft of hearings before Special Committee Investigating the National Defense Program, U.S. Senate, Executive Session, *Military Government in Germany*, April 5, 1946; Clay to Echols, May 2, 1946, WWIIRC 177–1/3.

17. Staatsministerium Gross-Hessen, Der Minister für Wirtschaft und Verkehr, Vertretung Berlin, Economics Div., OMGUS, "Bericht Nr. 2 vom 6.2–10.3," [1946], Geiler Papers, Staatsarchiv, Wiesbaden.

18. OMGUS, PRO, press release, May 4, 1946, WWIIRC 1–1/4.

19. OMGUS to Dept. of Army, Dec. 6, 1947, *ibid.*, 39–1/1.

20. Clay, *Decision in Germany*, pp. 120–22, esp., "Our first break with Soviet policy in Germany came over reparations," p. 120. Cf. Wilhelm Cornides, *Die Weltmächte und Deutschland*, p. 153, who sees the dismantling halt as a "suspension of reparations deliveries to the Soviet Union." For similar views see Michael Balfour and John Mair, *Four Power Control in Germany and Austria 1945–1946* (London, 1956), pp. 135–36; Krautkrämer, *Deutsche Geschichte nach dem zweiten Weltkrieg*, pp. 107–8; Hill, *Struggle for Germany*, pp. 156–62; and Manuel Gottlieb, *The German Peace Settlement and the Berlin Crisis* (New York, 1960), pp. 126–27.

21. See *Potsdam Papers*, esp., Vol. II, documents 896, 929, 940.

22. Clay to Sokolovsky, April 20, 1946, WWIIRC 263–2/7.

23. Clay, *Decision in Germany*, pp. 120–22.

24. OMGUS, PRO, Transcript of Clay Press Conference, May 27, 1946, WWIIRC 1–1/4.

25. OMGUS, Special Report of the Military Governor, Economic Data on Potsdam Germany, Sept. 1947, p. 13.

26. Maier, *Ein Grundstein Wird Gelegt*, p. 154; Walter Strauss, "Die gesamtdeutsche Aufgabe der Ministerpräsidenten während des Interregnums 1945–1949," in Hans Seidel (hrsg.), *Festschrift zum 70. Geburtstag von Dr. Hans Ehard* (Munich, 1957), p. 88; "Abschiedsrede des Generalsekretärs des Länderrats Erich Rossmann . . . 28.September 1948," Staatskanzlei, Wiesbaden, 1g02/06.

27. Pollock to Murphy, Dec. 12, 1945, with enclosure "The Länderrat during its First Two Months," dated Dec. 10, 1945, WWIIRC 34–2/11.

28. Von Fries, "Aktenvermerk: Anruf Graf Wedel aus Stuttgart," Jan. 22, 1946; Wedel to von Fries, Jan. 23, 1946; Beschlussprotokoll über die Sitzung des Kabinetts am 24.Januar 1946, Geiler Papers, Staatsarchiv, Wiesbaden; Kaisen to Rossmann, Jan. 19, 1946; Rossmann to Pollock, Jan. 22, 1946; Pollock to Rossmann, Jan. 28, 1946; Länderrat Papers, Bundesarchiv, Koblenz, Z1/235.

29. Geiler to addressees, Jan. 30, 1946, *ibid.*, wrote, in part: "Da die amerikanische Militär-Regierung möchte, dass der Wunsch nach einem solchen Treffen von den drei Ministerpräsidenten an sie herangetragen wird, sollte ein solcher gemeinsamer Antrag der drei Ministerpräsidenten in Stuttgart vorbereitet werden. . . ."

30. Rossmann to Kaisen, Feb. 11, 1946, *ibid.*; Pollock to Rossmann, Feb. 1, 1946, WWIIRC 39–3/11.

31. Pollock to Rossmann, Jan. 28, 1946, Länderrat Papers, Bundesarchiv, Koblenz, Z1/235; OMGUS, Economics Div., to RGCO, Subj: Meeting between the Ministerpräsidenten of the U.S. Zone and German Officials of the British Zone, Feb. 4, 1946, WWIIRC 39–3/11.

32. Pollock, [untitled report of meeting on Feb. 6], Feb. 8, 1946; Oberpräsident, North Rhine Province [Robert Lehr], Aide-Memoir, Feb. 15, 1946 [in English], WWIIRC 39–3/11; F. Bartsch (Pressereferent), "Bericht über eine Sitzung, an der leitende Beamte aus der englischen Zone und die Ministerpräsidenten der Länder der amerikanischen Zone teilnahmen," 6.2.1946, Staatskanzlei, Wiesbaden, AZ/1a08; "Besprechung mit Regierungsvertretern aus der britischen Zone vom 6.Februar 1946," [by Erich Rossmann], Geiler Papers, Staatsarchiv, Wiesbaden.

33. Based on the Bartsch report, which is the most complete.

34. According to the Bartsch report, Högner said: "Man wird uns entschieden zurückweisen."

35. From Rossmann's report: "Man müsse versuchen hier zu Zwischenlösungen zu kommen, um Schritt für Schritt Neuland zu gewinnen." Indirect discourse is from the record.

36. Pollock to Rossmann, Feb. 4, 1946, Länderrat Papers, Bundesarchiv, Koblenz.

37. Based on Pollock's report.

38. *Frankfurter Rundschau*, March 1, 1946, p. 1; *Die Neue Zeitung*, March 4, 1946, p. 4.

39. *Frankfurter Rundschau*, March 1, 1946, p. 1.

40. RGCO, Highlights of Food and Agriculture and Economics Conferences of German Officials from the British and the U.S. Zones in Frankfurt/Main on Feb. 27–28, 1946, WWIIRC 39–3/11; Gross-Hessisches Staatsministerium, Der Minister für Wirtschaft und Verkehr, to Staatskanzlei, March 4, 1946 [Resolutions attached], Staatskanzlei, Wiesbaden, ld18.

41. Rossmann to Pollock, March 2, 1946, Länderrat Papers, Bundesarchiv, Koblenz; "Sechste Tagung des Länderrates in München . . . 5. März 1946," Staatskanzlei, Wiesbaden, 1g06/01.

42. At this point, the available record of the meeting notes that the British General Rassier said to his interpreter: "Die Leute träumen ja!" "Konferenz der süddeutschen Ministerpräsidenten mit den Oberpräsidenten und Chefs der Länderregierungen in der britischen Zone am 28.2. 1946," Bundesarchiv, Koblenz, Z1/230. No author is indicated, but other evidence suggests it was Rossmann. See Rossmann to Preller, April 18, 1946, *ibid.*

43. "Sechste Tagung des Länderrates in München . . . 5.März 1946," Staatskanzlei, Wiesbaden, 1g06/01; Pollock to OMGUS, CAD, March 11, 1946, WWIIRC 39–3/11.

44. See Hans Georg Wieck, *Christliche und Freie Demokraten in Hessen, Rheinland-Pfalz, Baden und Württemberg 1945/46* (Düsseldorf, 1958), pp. 190–91, for a description of a CDU/CSU meeting on April 3, 1946, during which certain decisions were made regarding Jakob Kaiser's work for the CDU. See also Ernst Deuerlein, *CDU/CSU 1945–1947: Beiträge zur Zeitgeschichte* (Cologne, 1957), p. 79.

45. A. F. Pabsch, Memorandum, Subj: Highlights as Noted by This Observer at the Meeting between German Officials from the US and British Zone, April 6, 1946; RGCO, "Report of the Joint Meeting Between German Officials from American and British Zones Held in Stuttgart . . . April 3, 1946," WWIIRC 39–3/11; RGCO to OMGUS, April 9, 1946, *ibid.*, 2–2/1; Länderrat, Besprechung mit Vertretern aus der britischen Zone am 3.4.1946 in Stuttgart. . . , Bundesarchiv, Koblenz, Z1/1221; *Die Neue Zeitung*, April 8, 1946, p. 6.

46. Pollock to Clay, April 9, 1946, WWIIRC 2–2/1.

47. "Vierte interne Länderratssitzung . . . 4.Juni 1946," Staatskanzlei, Wiesbaden, 1g06/01; *Frankfurter Rundschau*, April 30, 1946, p. 2.

48. RGCO, Meeting with Liaison Officials, June 20, 1946, WWIIRC 39–2/11; "Niederschrift über die 10. Tagung des Länderrats . . . 2.Juli 1946," Staatskanzlei, Wiesbaden, 1g06/01. Cf. Schlange-Schöningen, *Im Schatten des Hungers*, pp. 75, 100, who has the dates confused.

49. See my "American Military Government and the Education of a New German Leadership," *Political Science Quarterly*, LXXXIII (June 1968), 248–67.

50. Pollock to Clay, July 22, 1946; Lippmann to Pollock, July 29, 1946, WWIIRC 34–2/11.


*Chapter 5*

1. Willis, *The French in Germany*, pp. 34–35.

2. Arthur H. Vandenberg, *The Private Papers of Senator Vandenberg*, ed. by Arthur H. Vandenberg, Jr., with the collaboration of Joe Alex Morris (Boston, 1952), p. 281.

3. Fleming, *The Cold War and Its Origins*, Vol. I, esp., p. 358.

4. Clay, *Decision in Germany*, p. 123.

5. See above, pp. 56–57.

6. Clay, *Decision in Germany*, pp. 73–78.

7. Clay's account is confusing at this point. He says he first sent a letter that "apparently did not reach the heads of departments" and then followed it up with the cable. The available records contain no such letter, but there is one dated July 19, 1946. Since the May 26 cable was in response to a request of the War Department on May 23, which Clay also does not mention, and since he doesn't refer to the July 19 letter elsewhere, it appears likely that he did not recall the exact sequence of messages at this point.

8. AGWAR to OMGUS, June 14, 1946, WWIIRC 211–3/5.

9. *Europa Archiv*, Sept. 1946, pp. 105–6; Beate Ruhm von Oppen, ed., *Documents on Germany Under Occupation 1945–1954*, issued under the auspices of the Royal Institute of International Affairs (London, 1955), pp. 144–47.

10. Byrnes, *Speaking Frankly*, pp. 179–87; Clay, *Decision in Germany*, pp. 127–30. See also Deuerlein, *Die Einheit Deutschlands;* Cornides, *Die Weltmächte und Deutschland;* and Marienfeld, *Konferenzen über Deutschland.*

11. Byrnes, *Speaking Frankly*, p. 187.

12. Clay to Echols, July 19, 1946, WWIIRC 177–1/3.

13. Clay, *Decision in Germany*, pp. 129–30.

14. *Ibid.*, p. 77.

15. Clay to Echols, July 19, 1946, WWIIRC 177–1/3, in which he wrote: "While occupied Germany is busily discussing the Molotov statement, our own Military Government people have no ready up-to-date summarized version of our policy or objectives which they could use in discussions with our German people."

16. Pollock to Rossmann, Jan. 30, 1946, Länderrat Papers, Staatsarchiv, Wiesbaden, folder 63.

17. RGCO to OMGUS, Feb. 11, 1946, with enclosed "Proposals of the Ministerpresident for Greater Hesse, Prof. Dr. Geiler, on the Establishment of Main Central Administrations in Accordance with the Resolutions of the Potsdam Conference," WWIIRC 255–2/17.

18. Draper to Clay, Feb. 28, 1946, WWIIRC 148/3; OMGUS, Internal Affairs and Communications Div., to Chief of Staff, Subj: Proposal of Dr. Geiler March 9, 1946, with Clay's March 15 handwritten comment thereon, *ibid.*, 14–1/1.

19. OMGUS, Memorandum, Subj: Interdivisional Committee on German Governmental Structure, March 15, 1946, WWIIRC 14–1/1; OMG-

US, Special Report of the Military Governor, Central German Agencies, May 1, 1946, *ibid.*, 211–3/5.

20. OMGUS, CAD, to Chief of Staff, Subj: U.S. Plan for Over-all German Government, May 3, 1946, WWIIRC 14–1/1; OMGUS, Special Report of the Military Governor, Central German Government, June 1, 1946, *ibid.*, 99–2/15.

21. Clay to Echols, July 19, 1946, WWIIRC 177–1/3.

22. Howard C. Petersen to Clay, Aug. 5, 1946, WWIIRC, ASW 091 Germany; Robert P. Patterson to Clay, Aug. 6, *ibid.*, 177–1/3.

23. AGWAR to OMGUS for Clay, Aug. 12, 1946, WWIIRC 177–3/3.

24. Clay to Echols, July 19, 1946, WWIIRC 177–1/3; Clay to AGWAR for CAD, Aug. 13, 1946, *ibid.*, 5–2/1; Clay to Patterson, Aug. 16, 1946, *ibid.*, 177–3/3.

25. Clay to Patterson, Aug. 16, 1946, WWIIRC 177–3/3.

26. Clay, *Decision in Germany*, pp. 165–68, quotes his instructions.

27. Clay to Robertson, July 21, 1946, WWIIRC 166–2/3; Pollock to Clay, July 22, 1946, *ibid.*, 34–2/11.

28. Lippmann to Pollock, July 29, 1946, WWIIRC 34–2/11.

29. See, for example, *Congressional Record*, 79th Cong., Senate, Jan. 18, 1946, p. 121; Feb. 5, 1946, p. 895; Feb. 27, 1946, p. 1699; March 29, 1946, pp. 2799–2811.

30. Wolfgang Friedmann, *The Allied Military Government of Germany* (London, 1947), p. 88.

31. Clay's note was handwritten to Henry Parkman, Civil Administration Div., on a concurrence paper dated Aug. 5, 1946, in WWIIRC 166–2/3.

32. OMGUS, CAD, to Office of Staff Secretary, Subj: Achievement of Objectives of Potsdam Agreement with Respect to Central German Agencies, Oct. 25, 1946, WWIIRC 55–3/1; Draper to Chief of Staff, Subj: Staff Study, "Bizonal Agencies," Oct. 25, 1946, *ibid.*, 148/3; RGCO to Rossmann, Subj: Resolutions Adopted at the Bremen Conference, Oct. 16, 1946, Bundesarchiv, Koblenz, Z1/237; *Frankfurter Rundschau*, Nov. 7, 1946, p. 2.

33. "Rede von Generalleutnant Lucius D. Clay bei der 13. Sitzung des Länderrats. . . 8.10.1946," Staatskanzlei, Wiesbaden, 1g06/01.

34. OMGUS, PRO, Speech by Brigadier General William H. Draper, Jr., . . . at Meeting of the Executive Committee for Economics at Minden (press release), Oct. 11, 1946, WWIIRC 1–1/4.

35. RGCO, Speech of Lt. General Lucius D. Clay . . . Länderrat, 6 Aug. 1946, Geiler Papers, Staatsarchiv, Wiesbaden; RGCO, Speech of Major

General Adcock... Länderrat Directorate on 12 Aug. 1946; RGCO, Address by General Draper, 12 Aug. 1946, WWIIRC 34–2/11.

36. OMGUS to Directors, OMG, Bavaria, Hesse, Württemberg-Baden, Subj: Elections in the U.S. Zone, Feb. 4, 1946, Staatskanzlei, Wiesbaden, AZ/3a02.

37. A copy of the agreement is in the Staatskanzlei, Wiesbaden, 1d02, and there is one printed in *Die Neue Zeitung*, Sept. 16, 1946, p. 8. See also Walter Vogel, *Westdeutschland 1945–1950: Der Aufbau von Verfassungs- und Verwaltungseinrichtungen über den Ländern der drei westlichen Besatzungszonen*, Teil II (Boppard am Rhein, 1964), p. 123, note 2, for a description of the contract's origin and approval as well as a commentary on the agency's proper title.

38. Köhler was referring to a January 10, 1947, resolution of the justice ministers of the American zone to the effect that the interzonal agencies had no authority to legislate. The resolution is in General Sekretariat, Länderrat, to RGCO, Jan. 20, 1947, with enclosed translation of resolution, 10.1.47, WWIIRC 37–2/1.

39. Interne Länderratssitzung am 22.1.47, Staatskanzlei, Wiesbaden, 1g06/01.

40. RGCO to OMGUS, Aug. 17, 1946, with enclosure: "Decision of the Württemberg-Baden Cabinet of 14 Aug. 1946: Directives for the Württemberg-Baden Representatives relating to the Establishment of Bi-Zonal Institutions," WWIIRC 34–2/11.

41. RGCO to Adcock, Aug. 14, 1946, WWIIRC 2–2/1; Adcock to RGCO, Aug. 19, 1946, *ibid.*, 34–2/11.

42. RGCO to OMGUS, Sept. 27, 1946, [a report on a special Länderrat meeting at Marktheidenfeld, Bavaria, Sept. 26, 1946], WWIIRC 22–1/11.

43. See AGWAR to OMGUS, Sept. 19, 1964, WWIIRC 256–2/17.

44. Byrnes, *Speaking Frankly*, pp. 187–92; Clay, *Decision in Germany*, pp. 78–79; Murphy, *Diplomat Among Warriors*, pp. 302–3; James P. Warburg, "Byrnes and the German Economic Problem," CBS Network Broadcast, Sept. 12, 1946, copy in WWIIRC, SAOUS 091.3 Germany; Deuerlein, *Die Einheit Deutschlands*, p. 173; Friedmann, *The Allied Military Government of Germany*, pp. 20, 31, 188; Balfour and Mair, *Four Power Control*, p. 141; Hill, *Struggle for Germany*, pp. 133–35; Schwarz, *Vom Reich zur Bundesrepublik*, pp. 115–19.

45. When I asked Clay in December 1966 if he wrote Byrnes's speech, he said anyone who knew Byrnes also knew that no one wrote his speeches for him.

46. Clay, *Decision in Germany*, p. 8. Italics are mine.

47. Ratchford and Ross, *Berlin Reparations Assignment,* p. 195.

48. "Erklärung der Ministerpräsidenten von Bayern, Württemberg-Baden und Gross-Hessen, abgegeben auf der Länderratstagung vom 10.9.1946," Staatskanzlei, Wiesbaden, 1g06/01.

49. "Ansprache des Herrn Generalleutnant Clay anlässlich der achten Länderratstagung in Stuttgart am 7.Mai 1946," Staatskanzlei, Wiesbaden, 1g02/06; "Vierte interne Länderratssitzung . . . 4.Juni 1946," *ibid.,* 1g06/01.

50. Thilo Vogelsang, *Hinrich Wilhelm Kopf und Niedersachsen* (Hanover, 1963), p. 81; OMGUS, PRO, press release, Aug. 16, 1946, WWIIRC 1–1/4; *Die Neue Zeitung,* Aug. 19, 1946, p. 2; *Frankfurter Rundschau,* Aug. 20, 1946, p. 1; Beschluss-Protokoll über die Sitzung des [hessischen] Kabinetts . . . 14.Aug. 1946, Staatskanzlei, Wiesbaden.

51. "Interne Sitzung des Länderrats vom 6.9.1946," *ibid.,* 1g06/01.

52. "Niederschrift über die Besprechung mit General Adcock und Oberst Dawson am 10.Sept. 1946"; "Niederschrift über die interne Sitzung der Ministerpräsidenten am 10.9.1946 in Stuttgart," Staatskanzlei, Wiesbaden, 1g06/01.

53. Vogelsang, *Hinrich Wilhelm Kopf,* p. 81.

54. Kaisen to Rossmann, Sept. 17, 1946, Bundesarchiv, Koblenz, Zl/230; Kaisen to Geiler, Sept. 17, 1946, Geiler Papers, Staatsarchiv, Wiesbaden.

55. Kaisen to Geiler, Sept. 17, 1946, *ibid.;* OMGUS, CAD, Daily Journal, Sept. 24, 1946, WWIIRC 9–2/1. I do not know if the delegates availed themselves of the offer of air transport.

56. "Notiz für Herrn Ministerpräsident," Oct. 2, 1946, Geiler Papers, Staatsarchiv, Wiesbaden; *Süddeutsche Zeitung,* Oct. 8, 1946, p. 1.

57. Sources for the Bremen conference are: Erste Interzonenkonferenz der Länderchefs am 4. und 5. Oktober 1946, [minutes]; Kurzprotokoll der ersten Interzonenkonferenz der Chefs der Länder und Freien Städte vom 4./5. Oktober 1946, Geiler Papers, Staatsarchiv, Wiesbaden; "Ansätze einer deutschen Repräsentation," *Europa-Archiv,* 3. J. (Feb. 1948), pp. 1143ff.; *Süddeutsche Zeitung,* Oct. 8, 1946, p. 1.

58. Walter Strauss, "Die gesamtdeutsche Aufgabe der Ministerpräsidenten während des Interregnums 1945–1949," in Hans Seidel (hrsg.), *Festschrift zum 70. Geburtstag von Dr. Hans Ehard* (Munich, 1957), pp. 85–96.

59. Erste Interzonenkonferenz der Länderchefs am 4. und 5. Oktober 1946 [minutes], p. 17, Geiler Papers, Staatsarchiv, Wiesbaden.

60. See above, p. 82.

*Chapter 6*

1. For results and commentary see Office of the High Commissioner for Germany (HICOG), *Elections and Political Parties in Germany 1945–1952* (Bad Godesberg, 1952).

2. AGWAR to OMGUS, Oct. 13, 1946; OMGUS to AGWAR, Oct. 15, 1946; OMGUS, from Petersen to AGWAR for WARSEC, Oct. 14, 1946, WWIIRC 177–1/3.

3. Litchfield *et al.*, *Governing Postwar Germany*, App. A and B.

4. OMGUS, Subj: Bizonal Unification and Existing Länder and Länderrat Organizations, Oct. 21, 1946, WWIIRC 147–2/5; OMGUS, Subj: Revision of Military Government Plans and Operations Necessitated by Adoption of German Land Constitutions and Bi-Zonal Agreement with British Military Government, Oct. 25, 1946, *ibid.*, 29–3/11.

5. Litchfield, "Emergence of German Governments," in Litchfield *et al.*, *Governing Postwar Germany*, p. 27; RGCO, "Rede von Lt. General L. D. Clay . . . 16. Tagung des Länderrats . . . 8.Januar 1947," Staatskanzlei, Wiesbaden, 1g06/01. The RGCO had tried to define the relationship on Dec. 23, 1946. Clay answered on Jan. 11, saying he had delayed his reply in order to discuss the matter at the Länderrat meeting. Dawson to Clay, Dec. 23, 1946; Clay to Dawson, Jan. 11, 1947, WWIIRC 34–1/1.

6. *New York Times*, Jan. 10, 1947, p. 8L; "Interne Länderratssitzung am . . . 8.Jan. 1947," Staatskanzlei, Wiesbaden, 1g06/01.

7. "Interne Länderratssitzung am 22.1.1947"; Interne Länderratssitzung in Stuttgart . . . 4.2.1947"; "Interne Länderratssitzung am 11.2.-1947," Staatskanzlei, Wiesbaden, 1g06/01; "Interne Direktoriumssitzung am 13.2.1947," *ibid.*, 1g10; OMGUS, Legal Div., Memorandum, Subj: Resolution of Ministers of Justice of the Three States of the U.S. Zone of Occupation that Interzonal Agencies have no Authority to Enact Legislation, Feb. 10, 1947; OMGUS, Legal Div., to Deputy Military Governor, Subj: Resolution of Ministers of Justice Concerning Authority of Bizonal Agencies, Feb. 12, 1947, WWIIRC 166–2/3; Clay, handwritten memo to Col. Whipple and Mr. Rockwell, dated Feb. 19, 1947, attached to a Brief on Ministers of Justice Opinion Regarding Authority of Bizonal Agencies, dated Feb. 12, 1947, *ibid.*, 37–2/1.

8. "Interne Länderratssitzung am . . . 8.Jan. 1947," Staatskanzlei, Wiesbaden, 1g06/01.

9. RGCO, "Report of the Meeting of the Minister Presidents, the Ministers of Economics, & the Ministers of Labor of the U.S. & British Zones

in Düsseldorf, Essen & Minden on 23, 24 and 25 January 1947," Jan. 29, 1947, WWIIRC 34–2/11; OMGUS, Industry Branch, Memorandum, Field Trip to Minden to attend Textile Conference with British and German Representatives, Jan. 30, 1947, *ibid.*, 263/17; *Frankfurter Rundschau*, Jan. 25, 1947, p. 1; *Süddeutsche Zeitung*, Jan. 30, 1947, p. 1; *Die Neue Zeitung*, Jan. 31, 1947, p. 5.

10. RGCO, Liaison Meeting, Feb. 27, 1947, WWIIRC 39–2/11; Beschluss-Protokoll über die Sitzung des Kabinetts, 26.Februar 1947, Geiler Papers, Staatsarchiv, Wiesbaden; Niederschrift über die Besprechung der Ministerpräsidenten der amerikanischen und britischen Besatzungszonen über die Einrichtung einer Leitstelle zur Vorbereitung der Friedensverhandlungen, Jan. 25, 1947, Länderrat Papers, Staatsarchiv, Wiesbaden, folder 61.

11. There was a meeting scheduled for February 22, but see Dorendorf, *Der Zonenbeirat*, p. 37, for a discussion of problems and delays.

12. *Frankfurter Rundschau*, Feb. 18, 1947, p. 1.

13. In WWIIRC 34–2/11.

14. Conference of Clay and Minister-Presidents, 23 Feb. 1947, WWIIRC 99–1/15.

15. The official record of the meeting and Reinhold Maier's description of it in Maier, *Ein Grundstein Wird Gelegt*, pp. 364–65, do not correspond at all. Maier's book should, in fact, be read with considerable caution throughout.

16. RGCO, Liaison Meeting, Feb. 27, 1947, WWIIRC 39–2/11; Beschluss-Protokoll über die Sitzung des Kabinetts, 26.Februar 1947, Geiler Papers, Staatsarchiv, Wiesbaden; RGCO to Rossmann, Subj: Meeting Scheduled for 28 Feb. 1947, Feb. 24, 1947, Bundesarchiv, Koblenz, Z1/230. Lutz Niethammer, who has had access to Bavarian records, verified in a letter to me on April 21, 1967, that Minister-President Ehard also grasped the full significance of Clay's remarks.

17. See letter in Walter Vogel, *Westdeutschland, 1945–1950*, Teil, II, p. 379.

18. RGCO to Rossmann, Subj: Meeting Scheduled for 28 Feb. 1947, Feb. 24, 1947, Bundesarchiv, Koblenz, Z1/230; "Besprechung mit General Clay am 4.2.1947," Staatskanzlei, Wiesbaden, 1g06/01.

19. Except where otherwise cited, the sources used to describe the denazification program are C. J. Friedrich, "Denazification, 1944–1946," in Friedrich *et al.*, *American Experiences in Military Government*, pp. 253–75; William E. Griffith, "The Denazification Program in the United States Zone of Germany," Ph.D. dissertation, Harvard University, 1950; John H. Herz, "The Fiasco of Denazification in Germany," *Political Sci-*

*ence Quarterly*, LXIII (Dec. 1948), 569–94; John G. Kormann, "U.S. Denazification Policy in Germany, 1944–1950" (Mehlem: Office of U.S. High Commissioner for Germany, 1952, mimeographed); Pollock *et al.*, *Germany Under Occupation*; Harold Zink, "The American Denazification Program in Germany," *Journal of Central European Affairs*, VI (Oct. 1946), 227–40; OMGUS, Monthly Report of the Military Governor, #34, April 1948, Denazification (Cumulative Review), 1 April 1947–30 April 1948; and U.S. Dept. of State, *Germany, 1947–1949*.

20. Hilldring to Assistant Secretary of War, Memorandum, March 4, 1946, WWIIRC, ASW 091 Germany; Edward F. Witsell, Acting Adjutant General, to Miriam Stuart, Society for the Prevention of World War III, Jan. 24, 1946, *ibid.*

21. For evidence of activity in the Länder, see Sitzungsprotokoll der Kabinettssitzung vom 24.10.45, Staatskanzlei, Wiesbaden; Niederschrift, Kabinett-Sitzung vom 6.12.45, Geiler Papers, Staatsarchiv, Wiesbaden; German Draft of Proposed Denazification Law prepared by Land Ministers of Justice, Dec. 22, 1945, WWIIRC 107–1/15; and "Ausserordentliche Sitzung des Länderrats ... 5.März 1946," Staatskanzlei, Wiesbaden, 1g06/01.

22. Charles Fahy to Clay, Nov. 9, 1945; Milburn to Bowie, Nov. 27, 1945, WWIIRC 14–1/1.

23. OMGUS, Special Orders 228, Nov. 30, 1945, par. 17, WWIIRC 367–2/5.

24. Preliminary Report by Working Committee to DPB, Dec. 20, 1945, WWIIRC 124–3/15; Report of the DPB to Deputy Military Governor, Jan. 15, 1946, *ibid.*, 13–3/1.

25. See my articles "The Artificial Revolution in Germany," *Political Science Quarterly*, LXXVI (March 1961), 88–104, and "Die Bedeutung der Besatzungszeit 1945–1949," *Aus Politik und Zeitgeschichte*, B 18/65 (May 5, 1965), 47–53, where I have suggested that American assumptions about the nature of man and his political instincts and about the historical evolution of American democracy influenced OMGUS to expect German cooperation in the endeavor.

26. Pollock to Rossmann, Jan. 30, 1946, Geiler Papers, Staatsarchiv, Wiesbaden.

27. "Mr. Fahy's Remarks—February 11," copy in WWIIRC 35–2/11; Mr. Fahy (Erklärung vom 11.Februar 1946), copy in Geiler Papers, Staatsarchiv, Wiesbaden.

28. "Erklärung von Bowie, 12.2.1946"; "Erklärung von Bowie, 13.2.-46," Geiler Papers, Staatsarchiv, Wiesbaden.

29. Beschluss-Protokoll über die Sitzung des Kabinetts am 21.Februar

1946; Beschluss-Protokoll, 25.Februar 1946, Geiler Papers, Staatsarchiv, Wiesbaden.

30. Walter L. Dorn, "The Future of the Law for Liberation," n.d. [April 1947], WWIIRC 148–1/5. For Geiler's views, see Memorandum, "Conversation between Dr. Pollock, Col. Oppenheimer, and Dr. Geiler," Feb. 22, 1946, *ibid.*, 23–2/11, and Geiler, "Erklärung des Ministerpräsidenten von Gross-Hessen ... zu dem Gesetz zur Befreiung von Nationalsozialismus und Militarismus," March 4, 1946, Staatskanzlei, Wiesbaden, 1g06/01. For Maier's, see *Ein Grundstein Wird Gelegt*, p. 182, 264–65.

31. "Ausserordentliche Sitzung des Länderrats ... 5.März 1946," Staatskanzlei, Wiesbaden, 1g06/01, contains a summary of four points that Germans got into the law.

32. Dorn, "The Future of the Law for Liberation," n.d. [April 1947], WWIIRC 148–1/5. See my "American Denazification and German Local Politics, 1945–1949: A Case Study in Marburg," *The American Political Science Review*, LIV (March 1960), 83–105, for denazification's impact at the level of application.

33. RGCO, Speech of ... Clay, Delivered at the Fourteenth Meeting of the Länderrat, Stuttgart, 5 Nov. 1946, Bundesarchiv, Koblenz, Z1/65.

34. Wheeler, *Die amerikanische Politik in Deutschland*, pp. 163–64.

35. Maier, *Ein Grundstein Wird Gelegt*, pp. 320–22.

36. "Interne Besprechung der Herren Ministerpräsidenten mit General Clay am 5.August 1947," Staatskanzlei, Wiesbaden, 1a08/01.

37. "Rede von ... Clay bei der 13. Sitzung des Länderrats ... 8.10.-1946," Staatskanzlei, Wiesbaden, 1g06/01.

38. "Niederschrift über die 1. Sitzung des Denazifizierungsausschusses des Länderrats mit Vertretern der britischen Zone am 24.10.1946," WWIIRC 125–2/15. A second meeting, scheduled for November 7, 1946, in Bad Homburg, was apparently canceled.

39. OMGUS, Internal Affairs and Communications Div., to Chief of Staff, Subj: Discrepancies in Implementing Law for Liberation from National Socialism and Militarism, Nov. 1, 1946, WWIIRC 120–2/15.

40. U.S. Congress, Senate, Special Committee Investigating the National Defense Program, "Confidential Report to the Special Committee Investigating the National Defense Program on the Preliminary Investigation of Military Government in the Occupied Areas of Europe, November 22, 1946," George Meader, Chief Counsel, esp. Exhibit VI, pp. 6ff and 49–51 (mimeographed).

41. *Frankfurter Rundschau*, Nov. 5, 1946, p. 1.

42. *Die Neue Zeitung*, Dec. 16, 1946, p. 1.

## Chapter 7

1. Conference of ... Clay and Minister-Presidents, 23 Feb. 1947, WW-IIRC 99–1/15; RGCO to Rossmann, Feb. 7, 1947, Bundesarchiv, Koblenz, Z1/76; RGCO to Rossmann, Feb. 24, 1947, *ibid.*; "Besprechung mit General Clay am 4.2.1947," Staatskanzlei, Wiesbaden, 1g06/01.

2. Schwarz, *Vom Reich zur Bundesrepublik*, p. 551, shows that Kurt Schumacher made a speech on the idea on March 31, 1947. Although he fails to establish the connection with Schumacher's speech, Schwarz credits three people with publicizing the idea widely: Erik Reger, the publisher of the Berlin newspaper *Der Tagesspiegel*, who in turn drew ideas from Wilhelm Röpke, the Swiss professor and publicist. Ernst Friedländer wrote in a similar vein in *Die Zeit*. Significantly, however, all three seem to have hit on the idea only after the Moscow conference. Schwarz, pp. 402–5, says Reger's first article appeared April 29, 1947.

3. *Die Neue Zeitung*, March 4, 1946, p. 4.

4. See, for examples, *Frankfurter Rundschau*, May 3, 1947, p. 1; *Die Neue Zeitung*, May 9, 1947, p. 1; OMGUS, PRO, "Speech by ... Draper ... at Meeting of the Executive Committee for Economics at Minden" (press release), Oct. 11, 1946, WWIIRC 1–1/4.

5. Patterson to Palmer Hoyt, *Denver Post*, Dec. 27, 1946, WWIIRC, OSW 091 Germany.

6. U.S. Congress, House Committee on Appropriations, Hearings on the 1st Deficiency Appropriations Bill, 1947, p. 768 (Feb. 25, 1947).

7. *Die Neue Zeitung*, Nov. 25, 1946, p. 1.

8. *Die Neue Zeitung*, Jan. 20, 1947, p. 1; Jan. 24, 1947, p. 2; *New York Times*, Jan. 3, 1947, p. 12L. The *Times* quoted Don D. Humphrey, Draper's deputy, and Lawrence Wilkinson, the chief of the OMGUS Industry Branch.

9. *New York Times*, Jan. 1, 1947, p. 1; *Die Neue Zeitung*, Jan. 24, 1947, p. 2; March 3, 1947, p. 2; "Bericht über die 10. Sitzung des Verwaltungsrats für Wirtschaft in Minden am 21.2.1947," Staatskanzlei, Wiesbaden, 1d06–01; OMGUS to AGWAR, Feb. 28, 1947, WWIIRC 32–1/1.

10. OMGUS, CAD, Subj: Plan to Create a Political Organization for the Combined U.S./British Zones (draft), April 26, 1947, WWIIRC 166–2/3.

11. Henry Parkman, Civil Administration Div., Personal Notes on "General Clay's Meeting," Feb. 15, 1947, WWIIRC 166–2/3. Cf. Con-

ference of Clay and Minister-Presidents, 23 Feb. 1947, *ibid.*, 99–1/15, for Ehard's remark to Clay that a man who was not allowed to become a mail carrier in the American zone could be a ministerial director in the British zone.

12. OMGUS, Legal Div. Opinion, Subj: Enforcement of Food and Agriculture Collection Program, Jan. 2, 1947, WWIIRC 132–3/1; OMG, Bavaria, Food and Agriculture Branch, to Director, Feb. 25, 1947, *ibid.*, 126–1/1; "Interne Länderratssitzung am 10. und 11.3.1947," Staatskanzlei, Wiesbaden, 1g06/01; "Bericht über die Sondersitzung des Verwaltungsrats für Wirtschaft in Minden am 21.Januar 1947," *ibid.*, 1d06–01; *New York Times*, Jan. 1, 1947, p. 1; April 3, 1947, p. 15; *Süddeutsche Zeitung*, Feb. 22, 1947, p. 1.

13. Friedmann, *The Allied Military Government of Germany*, pp. 145–46.

14. Zink, *The United States in Germany*, p. 181; Gillen, *U.S. Military Government in Germany*, pp. 40–41; OMG, Hesse, to Minister President, Subj: Socialization of Property, December 2, 1948, WWIIRC 217–1/8; OMGUS to Chief of Staff/US Army, Jan. 17, 1949, *ibid.*, SAOUS 004 Germany.

15. Excerpts from Minutes of General Clay's Staff Meeting of Saturday, Oct. 12, 1946, copy in Ferguson Committee Papers, WWIIRC. Cf. James Martin, *All Honorable Men* (Boston, 1950), pp. 197–99, who reported Clay's sympathy for a strict U.S. decartelization law, but did not seem to know what Clay's reasons were.

16. Garland S. Ferguson, Samuel S. Isseks, and A. T. Kearney, "Report of the Committee Appointed to Review the Decartelization Program in Germany," April 15, 1949, 126 pp. and about 2 linear feet of testimony and exhibits. See especially the testimony of Draper, p. 69, and Martin, pp. 17–19. WDSCA to OMGUS, Nov. 29, 1946, WWIIRC, WDSCA 014 Germany; Copy of Draper's prepared Statement for Senate Appropriations Committee on Decartelization, dated July 21, 1947, WWIIRC, WDSCA 014 Germany.

17. OMGUS to War Dept. Dec. 7, 1946, WWIIRC, WDSCA 014 Germany.

18. *New York Times*, Jan. 17, 1947, p. 8L.

19. "Bericht über die 7. Sitzung des Verwaltungsrats für Wirtschaft in Minden am 16./17.Januar 1947," Staatskanzlei, Wiesbaden, 1d06–01. All members voted for Agartz, except the Bavarian, who abstained.

20. The *New York Times* story, January 17, 1947, p. 8L, reported that Rudolph Müller, the ousted chairman, said the vote of no confidence had

been "handtailored in Hanover," the SPD headquarters. Cf. Lewis J. Edinger, *Kurt Schumacher: A Study in Personality and Political Behavior* (Stanford, 1965), pp. 118–19.

21. "Gemeinsame Sitzung mit Vertretern der MR am 13.1.1947"; "Bericht über die 8. Sitzung des Verwaltungsrats für Wirtschaft in Minden am 31.1.47," Staatskanzlei, Wiesbaden, 1d06–01.

22. "Speech of . . . Clay, Delivered at the Seventeenth Meeting of the Länderrat . . . 4 February 1947," WWIIRC 28–1/11; RGCO to Rossmann, Feb. 8, 1947; March 24, 1947, Bundesarchiv, Koblenz, Z1/237; "Interne Direktoriumssitzung am 27.2.1947," Staatskanzlei, Wiesbaden, 1g10.

23. Clay to Col. Whipple and Mr. Rockwell, Memorandum, Feb. 19, 1947, WWIIRC 166–2/3.

24. Vogel, *Westdeutschland 1945–1950,* Teil II, p. 379. The similarity of the March 12 letter and Clay's memorandum is noteworthy.

25. U.S. Dept. of State, *Germany, 1947–1949,* pp. 57–63.

26. *New York Times,* March 21, 1947, p. 1; April 2, 1947, p. 10. See also, Clay, *Decision in Germany,* pp. 149–50.

27. John Foster Dulles, "Europe Must Federate or Perish," *Vital Speeches,* XIII (Feb. 1, 1947), 234–36.

28. John Foster Dulles, *War or Peace* (New York, 1950), p. 102.

29. U.S. Dept. of State, *Germany, 1947–1949,* p. 59.

30. *New York Times,* April 25, 1947, p. 4.

31. "Protokoll über die interne Besprechung mit General Clay aus Anlass der Länderratstagung am 15.4.1947," Staatskanzlei, Wiesbaden, 1a08/01; Litchfield to Parkman, Memorandum, April 17, 1947; Parkman to Litchfield, Subj: Bizonal Political Unification, April 17, 1947, WWIIRC 166–3/3; *New York Times,* April 16, 1947, p. 12.

32. Clay, *Decision in Germany,* p. 174; *Die Neue Zeitung,* April 28, 1947, p. 1.

33. OMGUS, CAD, Subj: Plan to Create a Political Organization for the Combined U.S./British Zones (draft), April 26, 1947, with marginal notes dated May 4, May 11, and May 20, WWIIRC 166–3/3.

34. "Interne Besprechung mit General Clay am 6.5.47," Staatskanzlei, Wiesbaden, 1a08/01; *Die Neue Zeitung,* May 9, 1947, p. 1.

35. OMGUS, Governmental Affairs Advisor, C. J. Friedrich, Memorandum, Subj: Interviews at Minden, May 21, 1947; OMGUS, CAD, to Military Governor, Subj: Discussions with Ministers-President Regarding Bizonal Reorganization, May 28, 1947, WWIIRC 166–3/3. See "Konferenz der Ministerpräsidenten der britischen und amerikanischen Besat-

zungzonen ... Vorkonferenz am Sonntag den 15.Juni 1947," Staatskanzlei, Wiesbaden, 1a08/II, for Walter Strauss's remark, "Wir sehen
uns jetzt einem von den Besatzungsmächten gesetztem Recht gegenüber,
auf dessen Einzelausgestaltung Deutsche und deutsche Stellen keinen
Einfluss genommen haben."

36. Proclamation #5 is published in Pollock *et al.*, *Germany Under
Occupation*, pp. 229–34.

37. "Interne Besprechung mit General Clay am 3.6.1947," Staatskanzlei, Wiesbaden, 1a08/01.

38. Bericht der Vorkonferenz der Sachverständigen an die Konferenz
der Ministerpräsidenten über die Anwendung der Vorschriften der Proklamation Nr. 5 und des dazu gehörigen Agreement, May 15, 1947, Länderrat Papers, Staatsarchiv, Wiesbaden, folder 24; "Konferenz der Ministerpräsidenten der US-Zone und der britischen Zone in Wiesbaden
am 15. und 16. Juni 1947"; "Kurzprotokoll der Ministerpräsidenten-
konferenz am 16. Juni 1947," Staatskanzlei, Wiesbaden, 1a08/II.

39. "Konferenz der Ministerpräsidenten der US-Zone und der britischen Zone in Wiesbaden am 15. und 16. Juni 1947," Staatskanzlei,
Wiesbaden, 1a08/II. The German reads: "Es ist auch sehr zweifelhaft,
ob der Experte, der heute hier erschienen ist, die letzte authentische
Erklärung abgeben konnte."

40. WDSCA to Clay, May 7, 1947, WWIIRC, WDSCA 014 Germany.

41. OMGUS to AGWAR, May 8, 1947, WWIIRC 37–2/1; Schlange-
Schöningen, *Im Schatten des Hungers*, pp. 114–17.

42. See, for example, *New York Times*, March 31, 1947, p. 6; April
3, 1947, p. 13.

43. *Ibid.*, May 25, 1947, p. 8; OMGUS to AGWAR, May 8, 1947,
WWIIRC 37–2/1.

44. "Interne Besprechung mit General Clay am 3.6.1947," Staatskanzlei, Wiesbaden, 1a08/01; "Konferenz der Ministerpräsidenten der
US-Zone und der britischen Zone in Wiesbaden am 15. und 16. Juni
1947," *ibid.*, 1a08/II.

45. OMGUS, CAD, to Military Governor, Subj: Discussions with
Ministers-President Regarding Bizonal Reorganization, May 28, 1947,
WWIIRC 166–3/3.

46. *New York Times*, May 18, 1947, p. 42.

47. "Interne Besprechung mit Oberstleutnant Winning am 4.Juni
1947," Staatskanzlei, Wiesbaden, 1a08/01.

48. Clay to Parkman, Memorandum, July 28, 1947, WWIIRC 166–3/3.

49. The speech was sent to Clay on August 16. RGCO to Clay, Subj:

Secretary General Rossmann's Address on the Future of the Länderrat, Aug. 16, 1947, WWIIRC 34–1/1.

## Chapter 8

1. See my article, "The Origins of the *Institut für Zeitgeschichte: Scholarship, Politics, and the American Occupation, 1945–1949*," *American Historical Review*, LXX (April 1965), 714–31.

2. Schwarz, *Vom Reich zur Bundesrepublik*, esp. pp. 631–38.

3. Wilhelm Högner, *Der Schwierige Aussenseiter: Erinnerungen eines Abgeordneten, Emigranten und Ministerpräsidenten* (Munich, 1959), pp. 290–91; Wieck, *Christliche und Freie Demokraten*, pp. 192–93; Bayerische Staatskanzlei, "Die Deutsche Ministerpräsidenten-Konferenz in München vom 6. bis 8. Juni 1947," Staatskanzlei, Wiesbaden, 1a08/I, reprinted by Bayerische Landeszentrale für Politische Bildungsarbeit (Munich, 1965), 128 pp.; Hans Ehard, "Vom ersten Versuch die Einheit wiederzugewinnen," *Bayerische Staatszeitung*, Nr. 23 (June 8, 1962), p. 1.

4. *Süddeutsche Zeitung*, May 13, 1947, p. 1; May 17, 1947, p. 3; Ehard, interview, March 9, 1967.

5. "Interne Besprechung mit General Clay am 6.5.47," Staatskanzlei, Wiesbaden, 1a08/01. I have put this into English from: "Was Sie brauchen, ist eine Regierung, und ich weiss ebenso genau wie Sie, was das Fehlen einer solchen Regierung bedeutet." This was not so new, however, for he had said on January 8, 1947, that everybody knew Germany needed a government, but that the most that could be done now was to set up a model in the American zone that might take hold in the other zones. "Interne Besprechung mit General CLAY am 8.1.1947," *ibid.*

6. "Interne Länderratssitzung am 5./6.5.1947," Staatskanzlei, Wiesbaden, 1g06/01; Rossmann to RGCO, May 5, 1947, with enclosed copy of Robertson's speech to the Zonenbeirat meeting on April 30, 1947, Bundesarchiv, Koblenz, Z1/230. Note the correspondence in time between the British action on February 21 and Clay's February 23 meeting with the American-zone minister-presidents. Dorendorf, *Der Zonenbeirat*, p. 37, attributes the British-zone order to hold everything in abeyance to Robertson's deputy, General Bishop.

7. *Süddeutsche Zeitung*, May 10, 1947, p. 1.

8. *Ibid.*

9. *Süddeutsche Zeitung*, May 12, 1947, p. 1; May 13, 1947, p. 1.

10. Krautkrämer, *Deutsche Geschichte nach dem zweiten Weltkrieg*, p. 276; *Süddeutsche Zeitung*, May 20, 1947, p. 1.

11. Bayerischer Landtag, Verhandlungen, 16. Sitzung, May 28, 1947, pp. 457–58.

12. Bayerische Staatskanzlei, "Die Deutsche Ministerpräsidenten-Konferenz . . . 6. bis 8. Juni 1947," Staatskanzlei, Wiesbaden, 1a08/I. Cf. *Frankfurter Rundschau*, Dec. 30, 1947, p. 2, for an interview with Rudolf Paul after he fled Thuringia to the West, in which he said that the Soviet-zone minister-presidents' May 28 telegram was designed to "explode the conference," and that Ehard's answer required additional discussion in the Soviet zone on what to do to make it fail.

13. Bayerische Staatskanzlei, "Die Deutsche Ministerpräsidenten-Konferenz . . . 6. bis 8. Juni 1947," Staatskanzlei, Wiesbaden, 1a08/I.

14. Vogelsang, *Hinrich Wilhelm Kopf*, pp. 96–97; *Süddeutsche Zeitung*, June 3, 1947, p. 1.

15. *Süddeutsche Zeitung*, May 31, 1947, p. 1; June 3, 1947, p. 1; *Die Neue Zeitung*, June 2, 1947, p. 1. The Bavarian list of topics that could not be discussed reads, in German: "Staatsrechtliche Fragen hinsichtlich des zukünftigen staatlichen Aufbaues Deutschlands, Fragen des Finanzausgleichs, die bei der Behandlung des Steuerproblems leicht aufgeworfen werden könnten, Grenzfragen und Reparationen."

16. Deuerlein, *Die Einheit Deutschlands*, p. 191; Krautkrämer, *Deutsche Geschichte nach dem zweiten Weltkrieg*, p. 121, wrote "Ehard durfte die Einladung erst ergehen lassen, nachdem die Tagesordnung von Clay gebilligt war." Thilo Vogelsang, *Das geteilte Deutschland* (Munich, 1966), p. 64, said "Nachdem Ehard die Gestaltung der Tagesordung eingehend auf die ursprünglichen Einwände General Clays abgestimmt hatte, ergingen am 7. Mai die Einladungen. . . ." Cf., also, Schwarz, *Vom Reich zur Bundesrepublik*, p. 633, who at least keeps it in most general terms.

17. OMGUS, CAD, to Military Governor, Subj: Agenda of Ministers-President Conference, 6–7 June 1947, dated June 4, 1947, WWIIRC 177–2/3.

18. Hessischer Landtag, Stenographischer Bericht, 14. Sitzung, June 17, 1947, pp. 311–12; especially, p. 325. Cf. Ehard's May 14, 1947, radio address in Bayerische Staatskanzlei, "Die Deutsche Ministerpräsidenten-Konferenz . . . 6. bis 8. Juni 1947," Staatskanzlei, Wiesbaden, 1a08/I.

19. Württemberg-Hohenzollern, Landtag, Verhandlungen, 2. Sitzung, June 12, 1947, pp. 5ff; Schleswig-Holstein, Landtag, Wortprotokoll, 2. Sitzung, June 13, 1947, pp. 6–9. Cf. Anton Pfeiffer, "Zerbrochenes Porzellan," *Süddeutsche Zeitung*, June 7, 1947, p. 1; Rossmann to RGCO, June 9, 1947, WWIIRC 42–3/11; Württemberg-Baden, Landtag, Ver-

handlungen, 25. Sitzung, June 11, 1947, pp. 577–80; RGCO to OMGUS, June 14, 1947, Subj: Munich Conference of Minister Presidents, WWIIRC 256–2/17.

20. Bayerische Staatskanzlei, "Die Deutsche Ministerpräsidenten-Konferenz . . . 6. bis 8. Juni 1947," Staatskanzlei, Wiesbaden, 1a08/I.

21. *Frankfurter Rundschau*, June 10, 1947, p. 2; *Süddeutsche Zeitung*, June 7, 1947, p. 1. Two of the Soviet-zone minister-presidents left Munich at 7:15 A.M.; the other three at 10:00 A.M.

22. RGCO to OMGUS, Subj: Munich Conference of Minister Presidents, June 14, 1947, with copy of Rossmann's report, WWIIRC 256–2/17.

23. See especially Reinhold Maier's report in Württemberg-Baden, Landtag, Verhandlungen, 25. Sitzung, June 11, 1947, pp. 577–80.

24. OMGUS, CAD, to Military Governor, Subj: Agenda of Ministers-President Conference, 6–7 June 1947, dated June 4, 1947, WWIIRC 177–2/3.

25. Niederschrift über eine Besprechung der Ministerpräsidenten der amerikanischen und britischen Besatzungszonen über die Einrichtung einer Leitstelle zur Vorbereitung der Friedensverhandlungen, 25.Januar 1947, Länderrat Papers, Staatsarchiv, Wiesbaden, folder 61; Rossmann to Winning, Feb. 19, 1947, with enclosed resolutions of the Wiesbaden minister-presidents' conference, dated February 17, 1947, WWIIRC 34–2/11.

26. *New York Times*, January 6, 1947, p. L3; Abteilung II (Hans Mayer) to Hermann Brill, Subj: Besprechung mit Herrn Dr. Vogel am 14.1.1947, with attachment "Was bedeutet der Rücktritt von Byrnes für Deutschland?" Staatskanzlei, Wiesbaden, 1h-i; Georg Vogel to Hermann Brill, Jan. 23, 1947, *ibid*.

27. The Hanover agency had, in fact, scheduled interzonal meetings and prepared a number of tentative reports on the areas under Polish administration, some of which apparently found their way into the office of Ambassador Murphy. See Anlage 5 zum Protokoll der internen Länderratssitzung vom 10.9.1946, Betr., "Forschungsgemeinschaft für ernährungswirtschaftliche Fragen," Staatskanzlei, Wiesbaden, 1g06/01; "Niederschrift über die Sitzung in Frankfurt a.M. am 19.12.1946 betreffend Forschungsgemeinschaft für ernährungswirtschaftliche Fragen"; Schumacher to Dietrich, Dec. 24, 1946; Schumacher to Geiler, Dec. 24, 1946; Geiler to Schumacher, Jan. 6, 1947; Geiler to Dietrich, Jan. 6 and Feb. 4, 1947, Geiler Papers, Staatsarchiv, Wiesbaden.

28. *New York Times*, Jan. 10, 1947, p. 8L; "6. interne Direktoriums-

sitzung . . . 7.1.47," Staatskanzlei, Wiesbaden, 1g10; "Interne Länder-ratssitzung am . . . 8.Jan. 1947," *ibid.*, 1g06/01; "Interne Besprechung mit General CLAY am 8.1.1947," *ibid.*, 1a08/01.

29. "Interne Länderratssitzung am 10. und 11.3.1947," Staatskanzlei, Wiesbaden, 1g06/01; "Interne Besprechung mit General Clay am 11.3. 1947," *ibid.*, 1a08/01; R. H. Wells, CAD, Memorandum, Subj: Bureau for Peace Questions, March 12, 1947, WWIIRC 147–2/5.

30. A copy of the agreement, signed by Christian Stock, Reinhold Maier, and Hans Ehard, dated April 15, 1947, is in WWIIRC 33–1/11.

31. Dr. Pünder to addressees, March 24, 1947; Hermann Brill, "Bericht von einer Besprechung über Verfassungsfragen," March 14, 1947; Fritz Eberhard to Stock, April 1, 1947; Besprechung über Ver-fassungsfragen auf Einladung des Leiters des Deutschen Büros für Friedensfragen, 14.April 1947; Brill to Walter Strauss, April 25, 1947; Kopf to Minister Presidents of the American zone, March 25 and March 26, 1947, Länderrat Papers, Staatsarchiv, Wiesbaden; Gebhard Seelos, "Soll der Friedensvertrag unterschrieben werden?" March 20, 1947, Staatskanzlei, Wiesbaden, ih-i; Friedrich to Parkman, Subj: The Future of Constitutional Government in Germany and the Peace Settlement, March 14, 1947, WWIIRC 162/3.

32. Eberhard to Brill, May 17, 1947, with enclosed "Liste der zunächst geplanten Untersuchungen," May 16, 1947; Eberhard, "Richt-linien für die Arbeit des Friedensbüros," May 21, 1947, Friedensbüro Papers, Staatsarchiv, Wiesbaden.

33. Deutsches Büro für Friedensfragen, Entwurf eines Vertrages über die Bildung eines Verbands Deutscher Länder," May 20, 1947, Friedens-büro Papers, Staatsarchiv, Wiesbaden.

34. RGCO to OMGUS, Governmental Affairs Adviser, May 19, 1947; Friedrich to Winning, May 23, 1947, WWIIRC 33–1/11.

35. Eberhard to Hessian Staatskanzlei, July 1, 1947; Staatskanzlei to Eberhard, July 5, 1947, Friedensbüro Papers, Staatsarchiv, Wiesbaden; "Beschluss, Celle, den 4.7.1947," as Anlage 3 to Kurzprotokoll, Achtund-dreissigste Tagung des Direktoriums des Länderrats am 24.Juli 1947, Staatskanzlei, Wiesbaden, 1g10.

36. Protokoll über die erste Vollsitzung der Sachverständigen-Be-sprechung am 10.Juli 1947, Friedensbüro Papers, Staatsarchiv, Wies-baden.

37. Protokoll über die Vollsitzung (Sachverständigen-Besprechung in Friedensfragen) am 11.Juli 1947, Friedensbüro Papers, Staatsarchiv, Wiesbaden.

38. Karl Arnold to Stock, July (no day), 1947; Stock to Arnold, Aug. 12, 1947, Friedensbüro Papers, Staatsarchiv, Wiesbaden; "Interne Länderratssitzung ... 4.8.1947," Staatskanzlei, Wiesbaden, 1g06/01; Protokoll der Sitzung des Verwaltungsausschusses des Deutschen Büros für Friedensfragen am 17.Oktober 1947, Munich, Friedensbüro Papers, Staatsarchiv, Wiesbaden. At the October meeting the Bavarian representative said Bavaria would refuse to participate if political party representatives were admitted to the Friedensbüro.

39. Deutsches Büro für Friedensfragen "Vorschläge für eine deutsche Stellungnahme zur Londoner Konferenz," Nov. 4, 1947, WWIIRC 33–1/11; "Empfehlungen des Verwaltungsrates des Deutschen Büros für Friedensfragen zur aussenpolitischen Lage" (draft), Nov. 6, 1947, Friedensbüro Papers, Staatsarchiv, Wiesbaden.

40. Eberhard and Forster, "Aktenvermerk über eine Besprechung von Staatssekretär Dr. Eberhard und Dr. Forster mit Minister de Charmasse, dem politischen Berater des französischen Oberbefehlshabers in Baden-Baden am Freitag, den 7.November 1947"; Hermann Brill to Stock, Subj: Besprechung mit dem Ministerpräsidenten von Rheinland-Pfalz, Herrn Dr. Altmaier, Nov. 10, 1947; Rossmann, memorandum, Anruf von Ministerpräsident Kopf, Hannover, bei Generalsekretär Rossmann, Nov. 10, 1947, Friedensbüro Papers, Staatsarchiv, Wiesbaden.

41. Rossmann, "Die staatsrechtliche Entwicklung in Deutschland seit der bedingungslosen Kapitulation," speech before Parliamentary Advisory Committee of Länderrat, Nov. 18, 1947; Rossmann to SPD, Bezirk Württemberg-Baden, Feb. 28, 1948, Staatskanzlei, Wiesbaden, 1g02–06.

*Chapter 9*

1. *New York Times,* Jan. 2, 1947, p. 3L; p. 26L; Jan. 3, 1947, p. 11L; March 10, 1947, p. 4; March 12, 1947, p. 6.

2. *New York Times,* Feb. 4, 1947, p. 10L; Feb. 6, 1947, p. 10L; March 7, 1947, p. 11L.

3. This is brought out most clearly in International Chamber of Commerce, Paris, 39th Meeting of the Executive Committee, April 1–2, 1947, copy attached to letter of Philip D. Reed, Chairman, U.S. Associates, to Draper, May 7, 1947, WWIIRC 263-3/17.

4. Clay to Marshall, May 2, 1947, WWIIRC, ASW 091 Germany.

5. *Ibid.*

6. Dulles, *War or Peace,* p. 105. Cf. Murphy, *Diplomat Among War-*

*riors,* p. 308, for the statement that the Moscow conference has been called the "birthplace of the Marshall Plan."

7. Max Beloff, *The United States and the Unity of Europe* (London, 1963), p. 14; *New York Times,* April 25, 1947, p. 4.

8. Beloff, *The United States and the Unity of Europe,* pp. 14–21, says all three of these were the basis for the Harvard speech. Cf. Joseph M. Jones, *The Fifteen Weeks (February 21–June 5, 1947)* (New York, 1955), pp. 199ff, and *passim.* Harry B. Price, *The Marshall Plan and Its Meaning* (Ithaca, N.Y., 1955), pp. 22–23, quotes excerpts from the Kennan Policy Planning Staff memorandum of May 23, 1947. He indicates that the memorandum was secret at the time, but that it has been declassified. He cites an interview with Kennan at that point, but he does not identify the location of the Kennan staff memorandum. I was unable to locate it in the materials to which I had access.

9. OMGUS to AGWAR, June 26, 1947, WWIIRC, ASW 091 Germany.

10. Clay to AGWAR for Petersen, July 6, 1947, WWIIRC, WDSCA 014 Germany.

11. Memorandum, R. M. Cheseldine, Planning Branch, to General Noce, CAD, July 14, 1947, WWIIRC, WDSCA 387.6, is the earliest evidence I have found that Washington was working on a policy statement to answer Clay. There was obviously much disagreement in Washington, the details of which are not open to the private researcher.

12. OMGUS, Monthly Report of the Military Governor, #27, Reparations and Restitution, Aug.–Sept. 1947, pp. 17–21; Clay to AGWAR, July 12, 1947, WWIIRC, WDSCA 014 Germany.

13. AGWAR to Clay, July 15, 1947, WWIIRC, ASW 091 Germany. An interesting sidelight reveals something of Clay's anger at the order not to publish. The U.S. representative to the IARA, a Mr. Dorr, was to get a preview copy of the plan from OMGUS on July 16. After Clay got the order, he refused to give Dorr a copy and the latter appealed to the State Department. Thereupon the War Department ordered Clay to release a copy to Dorr on July 24, but Clay refused and appealed the order back to the War Department. Before anything else happened, Clay cabled again saying to ignore the appeal, because Murphy had given Dorr a copy he had received from the American Embassy in Paris, which in turn had received it from the British Embassy.

14. Petersen to Hilldring, July 15, 1947, WWIIRC, ASW 091 Germany.

15. U.S. Dept. of State, *Germany, 1947–1949,* pp. 356–62. Cf. *New York Times,* July 19, 1947, p. 1; July 20, 1947, pp. 1, 28; July 21, 1947, p. 16 (editorial) ; July 27, 1947, p. E3.

16. Royall to Clay, July 28, 1947, WWIIRC, WDSCA 014 Germany. The coal conferees had to be consulted because, as part of the planning on self-sufficiency, Berlin had agreed to raise the price of German export coal from $10 to $15 per ton, and Washington had ordered a delay in making the increase. See WARCAD to OMGUS, July 16, 1947, *ibid.*, ASW 091 Germany. For Kenneth Royall's Dec. 10, 1947, testimony on the new level-of-industry plan and its delay, see U.S. Congress, 80th Cong., 1st Sess., 1947, Senate Committee on Appropriations, Hearings on European Interim Aid and Government and Relief in Occupied Areas (Washington, 1947). For a discussion of the coal-price problem, see Balabkins, *Germany Under Direct Controls*, p. 124.

17. Petersen to Clay, July 23, 1947, WWIIRC 9-35/16; Royall to Clay, Aug. 9, 1947, *ibid.*, 10-35/16. Clay was not mollified, however, and when he was advised that the plan might be released he told Washington to go ahead.

18. *New York Times*, July 20, 1947, p. 1.

19. U.S. Dept. of State, *Germany, 1947–1949*, pp. 356–57.

20. Petersen to Secretary of War, June 12, 1947, WWIIRC, ASW 091 Germany. For exact figures and a breakdown, see OMGUS, Monthly Report of the Military Governor, #44, Feb. 1949, Statistical Annex, p. 137.

21. *New York Times*, June 20, 1947, p. 10.

22. Clay to Petersen, June 24, 1947, WWIIRC, ASW 091 Germany.

23. This conforms with the tentative policy statement transmitted to Clay by Washington on May 1, 1947. See AGWAR to Clay, May 1, 1947, WWIIRC 9-35/16.

24. Clay to Petersen, June 24, 1947, WWIIRC, ASW 091 Germany.

25. Clay to Petersen, June 28, 1947, WWIIRC, ASW 091 Germany.

26. Petersen to Secretary of War, June 12, 1947, WWIIRC, ASW 091 Germany.

27. Petersen to Clay, June 25, 1947, WWIIRC, ASW 091 Germany.

28. Petersen to Clay, July 1, 1947; July 8, 1947, WWIIRC, ASW 091 Germany.

29. "Speech of . . . Clay . . . seventeenth meeting of the Länderrat . . . 4 Feb. 1947," Staatskanzlei, Wiesbaden, 1g06/01; OMGUS to Land Offices, Feb. 13, 1947, WWIIRC 121-1/15.

30. OMG, Hesse, Minutes of a Conference, 9 April 1947, dated April 10, 1947, WWIIRC 33-1/1; Beschluss-Protokoll über die Sitzung des Kabinetts am 11.April 1947, Staatskanzlei, Wiesbaden.

31. Walter L. Dorn, "The Future of the Law for Liberation," n.d., WWIIRC 148-1/5. Dorn's paper is undated, but it is in a file of papers that permits dating it early in April. He says in his unpublished manu-

script, "The Unfinished Purge," that he wrote it in the spring and gave it to Clay on May 15. He also says there is no copy of the manuscript anywhere in the OMGUS records, but I found it in two places.

32. OMGUS, Internal Affairs and Communications Div., Subj: Desirable Changes in the Law for Liberation from National Socialism and Militarism in Denazification Procedures in the U.S. Zone, April 1, 1947; OMGUS, Political Affairs, Memorandum, Subj: The Crisis in Denazification and Need for Change, May 2, 1947, WWIIRC 148-1/5.

33. Württemberg-Baden, Der Minister für politische Befreiung, "Denkschrift über die gegenwärtigen Probleme der Entnazifizierung," Jan. 11, 1947, WWIIRC 31-3/11; Hessischer Landtag, Stenographischer Bericht, 18. Sitzung, July 4, 1947, pp. 447–90; President Keil, Württemberg-Baden Landtag, to Clay, Aug. 12, 1947, Staatskanzlei, Wiesbaden, lg06/01; "Interne Besprechung mit General Clay am 6.5.47," ibid., la08/01; Württemberg-Baden, Landtag, Verhandlungen, 38. Sitzung, July 25, 1947, p. 927; 39. Sitzung, Aug. 1, 1947, pp. 943–79; Frankfurter Rundschau, July 5, 1947, p. 1; July 10, 1947, p. 1. Dorn, "The Unfinished Purge," contains summaries of German views and arguments.

34. U.S. Congress, 80th Cong., 1st Sess., 1947, Senate Committee on Appropriations, Hearings on European Interim Aid and Government and Relief in Occupied Areas (Washington, 1947), p. 737. See also Daniel Noce, CAD, to Royall, Memorandum, Oct. 8, 1947, WWIIRC, WDSCA 014 Germany.

35. Clay later asked the RGCO director to write out the instructions in the form of a memorandum from typewritten notes he had used. The memorandum is "Proposal submitted by General Clay as outline of his position on 9 Sept. 1947," WWIIRC 35-2/11.

36. "Protokoll, Interne Länderratssitzung . . . 23.9.1947," Staatskanzlei, Wiesbaden, lg06/01; "Gemeinsame interne Sitzung des Länderrats und des Parlamentarischen Rats des Länderrats . . . 23.9.1947"; "Ausserordentliche Tagung des Parlamentarischen Rates beim Länderrat am 30.September 1947," ibid., lg10; RGCO, Special Meeting of Parliamentary Advisory Committee and Länderrat in Presence of Denazification Ministers, Sept. 30, 1947, WWIIRC 35-2/11.

37. Daniel Noce, CAD, to Royall, Memorandum, Oct. 8, 1947, WWIIRC, WDSCA 014 Germany; OMGUS, Monthly Report of the Military Governor, #27, Denazification and Public Safety, Aug.-Sept. 1947, pp. 1–2; Delbert Clark, Again the Goose Step: The Lost Fruits of Victory (Indianapolis, 1949), pp. 97–98.

38. "Gemeinsame interne Sitzung des Länderrats und des Parlamen-

tarischen Rats des Länderrats . . . 23.9.1947," Staatskanzlei, Wiesbaden, lg10. Indirect discourse is from the Protokoll.

*Chapter 10*

1. See U.S. Congress, 80th Cong., 1st Sess., 1947, Senate Committee on Foreign Relations, Hearings on Interim Aid for Europe (Washington, 1947), Nov. 10, 1947, p. 2, for letter from Truman to Vandenberg, Sept. 30, 1947; pp. 2–10, for Marshall's statement; Nov. 14, 1947, pp. 237–42, for Dulles's statement. Cf. Dulles, *War or Peace*, pp. 106–7.

2. U.S. Congress, 80th Cong., 2nd Sess., 1948, Senate Committee on Foreign Relations, Hearings on United States Assistance to European Economic Recovery, Jan. 8–Feb. 5, 1948 (Washington, 1948), pp. 1–10, 32, 465, 586–591; *ibid.*, 1st Sess., 1947, Senate Committee on Foreign Relations, Hearings on Interim Aid for Europe (Washington, 1947), pp. 99–101, 237–42; President's Committee on Foreign Aid, *European Recovery and American Aid: A Report by the President's Committee on Foreign Aid* (Washington, 1947), p. 120.

3. AGWAR to CINCEUR, June 20, 1947; CINCEUR to AGWAR, June 28, 1947, WWIIRC 166-1/3.

4. Asst. Secretary of War to OMGUS, July 10, 1947, WWIIRC, ASW 091 Germany.

5. Allen W. Dulles, "Alternatives for Germany," in Hoyt Price and Carl E. Schorske, *The Problem of Germany*, with an introduction by Allen W. Dulles (New York, 1947), pp. xi–xxv; U.S. Congress, 80th Cong., 1st Sess., House Committee on Appropriations, Hearings on First Deficiency Appropriation Bill for 1947 (Washington, 1947), p. 838; M. S. Szymczak, Memorandum to the President, May 14, 1947, WWIIRC, SAOUS 091.3 Germany; Waldo G. Bowman to Robert Patterson, July 21, 1947, *ibid.*, 177-1/3; Robert Moses, Report to Secretary of War, July 12, 1947, *ibid.*; Richard H. Whitehead to Clay, Sept. 25, 1947, *ibid.*, 147/3; Charles H. Murray and George T. Fonda, "Report on Inspection and Investigation of Factors Deterring Industrial Production as Related to Public and Industrial Relations," Sept. 27, 1947, *ibid.*, 177-3/3; *New York Times*, June 16, 1947, p. 2; Hoover to John Taber, in *ibid.*, May 27, 1947, p. 6; CINCEUR to AGWAR, Aug. 30, 1947, WWIIRC, WDSCA 014 Germany; Clay, *Decision in Germany*, pp. 236–37; RGCO, "Meeting of Selected German Officials with Congressional Group," Stuttgart, Sept. 9, 1947, WWIIRC 31-2/11; U.S. Congress, 80th Cong., 2nd Sess., House Select Committee on Foreign Aid, *Final Report on Foreign Aid* (Washington, 1948), esp. pp.

113–31; President's Committee on Foreign Aid, *European Recovery and American Aid*, p. 120.

6. Committee on Foreign Relations, Hearings . . . , Jan. 8, 1948, pp. 11–12.

7. U.S. Dept. of State, *Germany, 1947–1949*, p. 59; Dulles, "Europe Must Federate or Perish," *Vital Speeches*, XIII (Feb. 1, 1947), 234–36; Mr. X [George Kennan], "The Sources of Soviet Conduct," *Foreign Affairs*, XXV (July 1947), 566–82.

8. Jones, *The Fifteen Weeks*, pp. 138–40, 150–51, 175–76.

9. Lewis Herold Brown, *A Report on Germany* (New York, 1947); Gustav Stolper, *German Realities* (New York, 1948); Freda Utley, *The High Cost of Vengeance* (Chicago, 1949).

10. Brown, *A Report on Germany*, p. ix.

11. Maier, *Ein Grundstein Wird Gelegt*, p. 363.

12. Gottlieb, *The German Peace Settlement*, pp. 15–16, 38–39, and *passim*; Schwarz, *Vom Reich zur Bundesrepublik*, pp. 76ff.

13. Clay to Draper, Oct. 20, 1947; Draper to Royall, Oct. 22, 1947; Royall to Forrestal, Oct. 27, 1947, WWIIRC, OSA 004 Germany.

14. RGCO, "Speech of . . . Clay . . . Twenty-fourth Meeting of the Länderrat . . . 9 September 1947," Staatskanzlei, Wiesbaden, 1g06/01. The source for Clay's definition appears to have been Matthew Woll, "What Next for Europe?" *International Free Trade Union News*, II (Sept. 1947), p. 1, which crossed Clay's desk and received his initials; it contains a section reading very similarly marked in pencil.

15. OMGUS, Economics Div., to OMG, Hesse, Nov. 1, 1947, WWIIRC 33-2/1.

16. OMG, Hesse, to Minister President, Subj: Socialization of Property, Dec. 2, 1948, WWIIRC 217-1/8.

17. RGCO, "Meeting of Selected German Officials with Congressional Group," Stuttgart, Sept. 9, 1947, WWIIRC 31-2/11.

18. U.S. Congress, 80th Cong., 2nd Sess., House Select Committee on Foreign Aid, *Final Report on Foreign Aid*, pp. 127–29.

19. OMGUS, Governmental Affairs Adviser, C. J. Friedrich, to Clay, Subj: Impending Problems Connected with Denazification, April 28, 1948, WWIIRC 110-3/1. Italics are Friedrich's.

20. OMGUS, Internal Affairs and Communications Div., to Deputy Military Governor, Subj: Report on Effect of Denazification upon Industry in U.S. Zone of Occupation, Oct. 9, 1947, WWIIRC 125-1/15; Clay, *Decision in Germany*, pp. 259–62.

21. Draft letter, CAD to MG, March 15, 1948, Subj: Denazification

Program, WWIIRC 255-3/17. The letter was apparently not sent, and the details were worked out in another way. See OMGUS, Political Affairs, Memorandum: Further Information with Reference to Secretary of Army Department's Telephone Conversation on Denazification with General Clay, March 17, 1948, *ibid.*, 148-1/15.

22. Protokoll über die ausserordentliche Sitzung des Entnazifizierungsausschusses beim Länderrat am 19.März 1948, Länderrat Papers, Staatsarchiv, Wiesbaden, folder 93; Beschluss-Protokoll über die Sitzung des [hessischen] Kabinetts, 19.März 1948, Staatskanzlei, Wiesbaden.

23. OMGUS to Distribution, Subj: Expediting Completion of Denazification Trials in the US Zone, March 28, 1948, WWIIRC 110-3/1; RGCO to Rossmann, April 2, 1948, Subj: Delay in Notifying Länder of Military Government Action, *ibid.*, 34-1/11.

24. OMGUS, CAD, to Chief of Staff, Subj: Future Denazification Program, May 1, 1948; OMGUS, CAD, to Chief of Staff, Subj: Status of Denazification, Aug. 31, 1948, WWIIRC 110-3/1; OMGUS, CAD, to Chief of Staff, Subj: Proposed Amendments to the Law for Liberation from National Socialism and Militarism, Aug. 1, 1949, *ibid.*, 222-3/5.

25. *Potsdam Papers*, II, Doc. 940, pp. 888–92; Doc. 929, pp. 873–76; Clay to Sokolovsky, April 20, 1946, WWIIRC 263-2/17; OMGUS to WDSCA, Jan. 22, 1947, *ibid.*, WDSCA 387.6; OMGUS to CAD, Oct. 2, 1947, *ibid.*; OMGUS to AGWAR, Oct. 20, 1946, *ibid.*, 4-2/1; *New York Times*, Feb. 21, 1947, p. 27L. There are apparently no reliable figures on the actual reparations Germany paid. See *Europa-Archiv*, 9. J. (April 5, 1954), pp. 6481–82, for a discussion of the problem and for references to various estimates. Balabkins, *Germany Under Direct Controls*, refers to the problem. Other publications I have found helpful are G. W. Harmssen, "Reparations, Social Product, Standard of Life: Essay on the Balance of Economics," (Bremen, 1948), mimeographed, copy in WWIIRC, SAOUS 387.6 Germany; and Gustav von Schmoller, "Die Besatzungskosten in den drei westlichen Besatzungszonen," put out by Deutsches Büro für Friedensfragen, Nov. 15, 1948, in Staatsarchiv, Wiesbaden.

26. Deputy Director, OMGUS, Economics Div., to William H. Draper, Subj: A Possible Program for Reparations out of Current Production, Nov. 2, 1946, WWIIRC 177-3/3; Draper to Don D. Humphrey, Nov. 18, 1946, *ibid.*, WDSCA 387.6; Russell Hill, *Struggle for Germany*, pp. 123–24.

27. CINCEUR to AGWAR, July 12, 1947, WWIIRC, WDSCA 014 Germany.

28. U.S. Dept. of State, *Germany, 1947–1949*, p. 356–57.

29. Draper to Clay, Nov. 22, 1947; Hays to Draper, Nov. 24, 1947; Hays to Draper, Dec. 6, 1947, WWIIRC, SAOUS 463.3; Economics Branch, CAD, to Chief, CAD, Dec. 10, 1947, *ibid.*, CSCAD 014 Germany; OMGUS to Draper, Feb. 20, 1948, *ibid.*, SAOUS 463.3; CSCAD to CINCEUR, Jan. 18, 1948, *ibid.*, 85-1/1.

30. *New York Times*, Feb. 6, 1947, p. 8L; Marshall to Vandenberg, Feb. 4, 1948, with enclosed memorandum, "The German Reparation Program," printed in U.S. Congress, 80th Cong., 2nd Sess., Senate Committee on Foreign Relations, Hearings on United States Assistance to European Economic Recovery, pp. 497–503.

31. See U.S. Congress, 79th Cong., 2nd Sess., Senate, *Congressional Record*, Feb. 5, 1946, p. 895, and *New York Times*, April 25, 1947, p. 3, for early congressional attempts to interfere piecemeal.

32. The full list is printed in *Frankfurter Rundschau*, Oct. 18, 1947, p. 4.

33. Control Commission for Germany, British Element, Public Relations Branch, "Deputy Military Governor's Press Conference on 16th October 1947," copy in WWIIRC 263-3/17. The published figures on how many plants would have been dismantled under the 1946 plan vary considerably—no central list was ever published, and announcements came at various times. Also, some calculations are made according to "declaration of availability," some according to allocations, and some according to the actual beginning of dismantling operations. See Karl Brandt, *Germany: Key to Peace in Europe* (Claremont, Calif., 1949), p. 48, for a low figure of 742 plants; OMGUS, Monthly Report of the Military Governor, #48, Reparations (Cumulative Review) Sept. 1945–June 1949, p. 4, for a figure of "about 1500"; and Cornides, *Die Weltmächte und Deutschland*, p. 97, for an IARA estimate of 1,800 plants.

34. Control Commission for Germany, British Element, Public Relations Branch, "Deputy Military Governor's Press Conference of 16th October 1947," copy in WWIIRC 263-3/17.

35. *Die Neue Zeitung*, Oct. 6, 1947, p. 1; Oct. 13, 1947, p. 1.

36. See, for example, Beschluss-Protokoll über die ausserordentliche Sitzung des Kabinetts, 17.Oktober 1947; "Erklärung der Regierung zur Liste der Demontagen in der amerikanischen und britischen Zone," Oct. 17, 1947, Staatskanzlei, Wiesbaden, Ia08/II; Württemberg-Baden, Landtag, Verhandlungen, 49. Sitzung, Oct. 17, 1947, p. 1192; 50. Sitzung, Oct. 31, 1947, pp. 1224ff; Nordrhein-Westfalen, Landtag, Stenographischer Bericht, 17. Sitzung, Oct. 29, 1947, pp. 1–54; Bayerischer Landtag, Verhandlungen, 32. Sitzung, Oct. 30, 1947, pp. 92–129; 33. Sitzung,

Oct. 31, 1947, pp. 133–39; *Die Neue Zeitung*, Oct. 20, 1947, p. 1; German Mines Supplies Organization, Essen-Heisingen, to Regional Economic Officer, Subj: Dismantling List and Mining Industry, Oct. 28, 1947, copy in WWIIRC 103-3/11.

37. Württemberg-Baden, Landtag, Verhandlungen, 49. Sitzung, Oct. 17, 1947, p. 1192.

38. Bipartite Board to BICO, July [17], 1947, Subj: Discussion of the Subject of Reparations by the German Economic Council, WWIIRC 37-2/1. (Exact date determined from another source.)

39. *Frankfurter Rundschau*, Oct. 23, 1947, p. 1; "Kurzprotokoll, Sechsundzwanzigste Tagung des Länderrats am 4.Nov. 1947," Staatskanzlei, Wiesbaden, lg06/01. Cf. Erich Köhler, *Ohne Illusionen: Politik der Realitäten* (Wiesbaden, 1949), pp. 27–29, whose speech to the Hessian Municipal League on Oct. 18, 1947, reflects the moderate position taken at Wiesbaden.

40. "Erklärung der Vorsitzenden des Zweimächte-Kontrollamtes hinsichtlich der Frage der Reparationen aus der Bizone, 28.Okt. 1947," Bundestag Library, Bonn; *Frankfurter Rundschau*, Oct. 30, 1947, p. 1.

41. CSCAD to OMGUS, Dec. 4, 1947, WWIIRC 371-3/5; R. M. Cheseldine, Memorandum for the Record, Dec. 17, 1947, *ibid.*, WDSCA 387.6; OMGUS to Department of Army, Dec. 6, 1947, *ibid.*, 39-1/1; U.S. Congress, 80th Cong., 1st Sess., Senate Committee on Appropriations, Hearings on European Interim Aid and Government and Relief in Occupied Areas, pp. 669–85.

42. Draper to Harriman, Dec. 17, 1947, WWIIRC, SAOUS 387.6 Germany (Reparations); T. N. Dupuy, Assistant to Under Secretary of the Army, Memorandum for the Record, Subj: Meeting Between Secretary Marshall and Secretary Royall on 19 Jan. 1948, *ibid.*, 014.1 Germany/ State; Memorandum, Draper to Royall, Jan. 19, 1948, *ibid.*; CSCAD to CINCEUR, Feb. 19, 1948, *ibid.*, CSCAD 387.6. The cabinet technical committee consisted of the Secretaries of Interior, Commerce, and Agriculture, who were to work closely with State and Army.

43. CSCAD to OMGUS, Aug. 7, 1948, WWIIRC, SAOUS 387.6 Germany.

44. CINCEUR to Dept. of the Army, Aug. 28, 1948, WWIIRC, SAOUS 387.6 Germany.

45. ECA Industrial Advisory Committee, "Report on Plants Scheduled for Removal as Reparations from the Three Western Zones of Germany," Jan. 1949, copy in WWIIRC 376-3/5; Draper to Clay, Nov. 16, 1948; Clay to CAD, Nov. 18, 1948; Draper to Clay, Nov. 23, 1948; Dept. of

the Army to OMGUS, Jan. 25, 1949, WWIIRC, SAOUS 387.6 Germany/ Advisory Committee. Cf. Zink, *The United States in Germany*, pp. 257ff.

46. *Die Neue Zeitung*, May 27, 1948, p. 1; Aug. 28, 1948, p. 1; "Wortprotokoll der Ministerpräsidenten-Konferenz am 31.Aug. 1948 . . . Rüdesheim," Staatskanzlei, Wiesbaden, 1a08/III.

47. *Die Neue Zeitung*, Sept. 28, 1948, p. 1; Clay to Koenig, Sept. 14, 1948, WWIIRC 85-1/1; Büro der Ministerpräsidenten, "Report on the Effect of Envisaged Dismantling on Germany's Economic Situation and her Role in European Reconstruction," Frankfurt, 1948; Verwaltung für Wirtschaft, "Neuster Stand der Demontagen," Sept. 30, 1948; Büro der Ministerpräsidenten, "Besprechung mit Herrn W. B. Lochleng," Sept. 29, 1948, Staatskanzlei, Wiesbaden.

48. "Konferenz der Ministerpräsidenten der drei Westzonen am 1.10.1948," Staatskanzlei, Wiesbaden, 1a08/III; "Notes on Meeting Held between Military Governors and Ministers President on 29th October, 1948," WWIIRC 106-2/11. Cf. Schwarz, *Vom Reich zur Bundesrepublik*, p. 141.

49. "Notes on Meeting Held between Military Governors and Ministers President on 29th October, 1948," WWIIRC 106-2/11.


*Chapter 11*

1. Kathleen McLaughlin in *New York Times*, June 26, 1947, p. 8. Cf. "Speech of the Minister President of Land Hesse, Mr. Stock, at Frankfurt/ Main on 25 June 1947," Staatskanzlei, Wiesbaden, 2e08/27.

2. *Süddeutsche Zeitung*, July 26, 1947, p. 1; *Frankfurter Rundschau*, July 26, 1947, p. 1. See also, Vogelsang, *Hinrich Wilhelm Kopf*, pp. 107–8; Högner, *Der Schwierige Aussenseiter*, pp. 293–301; Deuerlein, *CDU/ CSU 1945–1957*, pp. 87–88; Robert H. Slover, "The Bizonal Economic Administration of Western Germany," Ph.D. Dissertation, Harvard University, 1950, pp. 134–35; "Akten Notiz über die Besprechung mit Brigadegeneral Cowley, Mr. Dayton und den übrigen Herren des Stabes," Aug. 6, 1947; "Besprechung bei dem Zweizonenkontrollamt," Aug. 15, 1947, in V.W.G. Besprechungen—Militär-Regierung, Bundestag Library, Bonn.

3. BICO to OMGUS, Sept. 17, 1947, WWIIRC 37-2/1; *Frankfurter Rundschau*, Sept. 25, 1947, p. 1.

4. "Akten-Vermerk über die Besprechung bei der Militärregierung im Anschluss an die Ueberreichung der Bekanntmachung über die Errichtung einer deutschen Kohlenbergbauleitung, 19.11.1947," V.W.G. Besprechungen—Militär-Regierung, Bundestag Library, Bonn; OMGUS,

CAD, to Litchfield, Subj: Notes on the CAD Meeting held on 28 Oct., WWIIRC 256-2/17; Draper to Clay, Oct. 30, 1947; Clay to Draper, Oct. 30, 1947, *ibid.*, 9-35/16; *Frankfurter Rundschau,* Oct. 30, 1947, p. 1; Nov. 1, 1947, p. 2.

5. Schlange-Schöningen, *Im Schatten des Hungers,* p. 168.

6. Adcock to OMGUS, Oct. 22, 1947, WWIIRC 37-2/1.

7. Remarks by C. L. Adcock before the Land Ministers of Food and Agriculture, Frankfurt a/M, Oct. 13, 1947; OMG, Bavaria, to OMGUS, Nov. 6, 1947, WWIIRC 119-2/1; OMGUS to Addressees, Oct. 29, 1947, *ibid.*, 37-2/1; Schlange-Schöningen, *Im Schatten des Hungers,* pp. 166–71; Vogelsang, *Hinrich Wilhelm Kopf,* p. 111; Balabkins, *Germany Under Direct Controls,* pp. 86–87.

8. OMGUS, Proclamation No. 6, Amending Proclamation No. 5, Economic Council, WWIIRC 359-1/1.

9. Schwarz, *Vom Reich zur Bundesrepublik,* pp. 257–60, 331–44; *Frankfurter Rundschau,* Nov. 13, 1947, p. 1; Dayton to Clay, Dec. 4, 1947, WWIIRC 79-1/1; "Protokoll, Interne Länderratssitzung am 1.12. 1947," Staatskanzlei, Wiesbaden, 1g06/01.

10. Litchfield to Pollock, July 2, 1947, WWIIRC 254-1/17; Robertson to Clay, July 21, 1947; Clay to Robertson, July 22, 1947; C. L. Adcock, Memorandum to General George P. Hays, Oct. 15, 1947, *ibid.*, 37-2/1.

11. Adcock to Hays, Oct. 28, 1947, WWIIRC 37-2/1.

12. "Akten-Vermerk über die Besprechung bei der Militärregierung im Anschluss an die Ueberreichung der Bekanntmachung über die Errichtung einer deutschen Kohlenbergbauleitung, 19.11.1947," V.W.G. Besprechungen—Militär-Regierung, Bundestag Library, Bonn; "Vormerkung über eine Besprechung, die ich heute im Auftrage des Herrn Ministerpräsidenten Dr. Ehard mit dem Stellvertreter von General Adcock, Mr. Kenneth Dayton, über den Entwurf einer Proklamation betr. die Wirtschaftsverwaltung des Vereinigten Wirtschaftsgebietes hatte," by Dr. Glum, Jan. 25, 1948, Staatskanzlei, Wiesbaden, 1d02.

13. Semler to Clay, Jan. 9, 1948; Jan. 14, 1948, WWIIRC 107-2/1. A copy of Semler's speech, "Speech by Dr. Semler, Executive Director of the Economics Department of the Bizonal Organization, Held on 4 January 1948 at Erlangen," is in the same file. His postmortem defense, "Kommentar zu meiner Erlanger Rede," Feb. 1948, may be found in Staatskanzlei, Wiesbaden, 1d02 as well as in WWIIRC 102-2/15.

14. Clay to Marshall, May 2, 1947, WWIIRC, ASW 091 Germany.

15. BICO, Commerce & Industry Group (US) to BICO, Subj: Speech by Dr. Semler, Jan. 20, 1948, WWIIRC 405-1/3; Memorandum, OMGUS,

CAD to Chief of Staff, Subj: Speech made by Dr. Semmler [*sic*] at Erlangen, Jan. 16, 1948, *ibid.*, 107-2/1.

16. OMGUS to Dept. of the Army, Jan. 28, 1948, WWIIRC 107-2/1.

17. Bayerischer Landtag, Verhandlungen, 54. Sitzung, Feb. 18, 1948, pp. 864, 884; OMG, Bavaria, CAD, to Governor van Wagoner, Subj: Report of Meeting with Minister President on the Semler Matter, Feb. 18, 1948, WWIIRC 102-2/15.

18. Royall to Lovett, Sept. 3, 1947, with enclosures, WWIIRC 146-2/15; Draper to Clay, Jan. 27, 1948, *ibid.*, SAOUS 014.1 Germany; OMGUS, PIO, press release, Jan. 28, 1948, *ibid.*, 1-2/4; CSCAD, Noce to Draper, March 23, 1948, *ibid.*, SAOUS 014.1 Germany.

19. CSCAD to CINCEUR, Sept. 19, 1947; CINCEUR to AGWAR, Sept. 28, 1947, WWIIRC, WDSCA 014 Germany.

20. Draper to Clay, with enclosed policy statement, Dec. 5, 1947, WWIIRC, SAOUS 000.1 Germany/Politics.

21. Petersen to Royall, Memorandum of topics and subjects for discussion with Clay in Theater, July 29, 1947, WWIIRC, ASW 091 Germany; CSCAD to OMGUS, Oct. 14, 1947, *ibid.*, WDSCA 014 Germany; *Frankfurter Rundschau*, Oct. 30, 1947, p. 1; U.S. Congress, 80th Cong., 1st Sess., Senate Hearings on European Interim Aid and Government and Relief in Occupied Areas, Dec. 11, 1947, pp. 733–34. Cf. Schwarz, *Vom Reich zur Bundesrepublik*, p. 122, who seems to think the Allied decision to delay bizonal reorganization until after the London foreign ministers conference was made with German public opinion in mind.

22. U.S. Dept. of State, *Germany, 1947–1949*, p. 66.

23. Clay, *Decision in Germany*, pp. 346–48. CSCAD to OMGUS, Dec. 18, 1947, WWIIRC 39-2/1, is a Department of the Army cable advising OMGUS, Information Control Division, to emphasize similar views in its German programs.

24. Clay, *Decision in Germany*, p. 176; Murphy, *Diplomat Among Warriors*, p. 312.

25. OMGUS, CAD, to Military Governor, Subj: Planning in the Field of German Civil Government, Sept. 24, 1947, WWIIRC 254-3/17; OMGUS to AGWAR, Sept. 24, 1947, *ibid.*, 9-25/16; Interne Besprechung mit General Clay am 4.Nov. 1947, Bundesarchiv, Koblenz, Z1/26.

26. Adcock to Clay, Memorandum, Nov. 20, 1947; Hays to Adcock, Nov. 28, 1947, WWIIRC 37-2/1; *Frankfurter Rundschau*, Dec. 16, 1947, p. 2.

27. BICO, "Meeting of US and British Military Governors, Chairmen of the Bipartite Control Office, Land Directors, and Regional Commis-

sioners with the Minister Presidents and Bizonal Officials ... 7 January 1948," Staatskanzlei, Wiesbaden, 1d02/11; "Konferenz der Generäle Clay und Robertson mit den Ministerpräsidenten am 7.Januar 1948," *ibid.*, 1a08/01; Gillen, *U.S. Military Government in Germany*, pp. 166–72.

28. Werner Hilpert to Stock, Jan. 26, 1948, Staatskanzlei, Wiesbaden, 1d02; Nordrhein-Westfalen, Landtag, Stenographischer Bericht, 28. Sitzung, Feb. 5, 1948, pp. 2–39; Hessischer Landtag, Stenographischer Bericht, 31. Sitzung, Jan. 15, 1948, pp. 986–89; "Erklärung, die von Senatspräsident Kaisen am 27.1.48 gegenüber den Besatzungsmächten abgegeben werden soll," Staatskanzlei, Wiesbaden, 1d02; "Rahmenentwurf für eine Erklärung der Ministerpräsidenten der Bizone zu dem Entwurf einer Proklamation betr. die Wirtschaftsverwaltung des Vereinigten Wirtschaftsgebietes," n.d., transmitted to Stock on Jan. 31, 1948, *ibid.*; *Süddeutsche Zeitung*, Jan. 31, 1948, p. 1; Feb. 7, 1948, p. 1; "Conference Between the Director of Bremen Military Government and the President of the Senate of Land Bremen," Feb. 21, 1948, WWIIRC 108-1/1; Litchfield to Clay, Carrier Sheet, Subj: Reorganization Attitudes of Bizonal Leadership, Jan. 20, 1948, *ibid.*, 255-2/17.

29. Clay, *Decision in Germany*, pp. 178–79.

30. Clay to Draper, Jan. 16, 1948, WWIIRC 255-3/17.

31. Dept. of the Army to CINCEUR, Jan. 17, 1948, WWIIRC 255-3/17; Clay, *Decision in Germany*, pp. 176–80; U.S. Dept. of State, *Germany, 1947–1949*, pp. 466–81.

32. "Rede von General Lucius D. Clay ... 29. Tagung des Länderrats am 3.Februar 1948," Staatskanzlei, Wiesbaden, 1g06/01.

33. Draper to Clay, Jan. 30, 1948, WWIIRC 108-1/1. Cf. Gillen, *U.S. Military Government in Germany*, pp. 184–91.

34. Gillen, *U.S. Military Government in Germany*, p. 190, says there were six working parties, but a seventh did work for a time.

35. Clay to Draper, April 13, 1948, WWIIRC 108-2/1; Clay, *Decision in Germany*, pp. 397–400.

36. U.S. Dept. of State, *Germany, 1947–1949*, pp. 75–84. Cf. Clay, *Decision in Germany*, pp. 335–42, 394–409; Litchfield, "Emergence of German Governments," in Litchfield *et al.*, *Governing Postwar Germany*, pp. 38–48; and Friedrich, "Rebuilding the German Constitution, I," *The American Political Science Review*, XLIII (June 1949), p. 468 .

37. U.S. Dept. of State, *Germany, 1947–1949*, pp. 332–44, 348–56.

38. U.S. Dept. of State, *Germany, 1947–1949*, pp. 450–60; CINCEUR to CSCAD, Nov. 17, 1948; Nov. 22, 1948, WWIIRC 108-2/1.

39. Friedrich, "Rebuilding the German Constitution, I," pp. 471–74; Litchfield, "Emergence of German Governments," in Litchfield et al., Governing Postwar Germany, pp. 43–46. Both Friedrich and Litchfield were in close touch with developments at the time. They helped draft various versions of the Occupation Statute, and they analyzed other drafts.

40. CINCEUR to Dept. of Army, April 7, 1949, WWIIRC 11-35/16; Friedrich, "Rebuilding the German Constitution, I," p. 474.

41. U.S. Dept. of State, Germany, 1947–1949, p. 362; New York Times, Jan. 1, 1947, p. 1; Feb. 28, 1947, p. 8L; March 16, 1947, p. 1; Die Neue Zeitung, March 3, 1947, p. 2; OMGUS to AGWAR, June 20, 1947, WWIIRC 37-2/1.

42. See, for examples, U.S. Dept. of State, Germany, 1947–1949, pp. 59, 66, 84, 362–63.

43. Schwarz, Vom Reich zur Bundesrepublik, pp. 261–69, esp., p. 266: "Soviel dürfte deutlich geworden sein: von einer zielbewussten, klaren Deutschlandpolitik der Sowjetunion während der Jahre 1945 bis 1949 kann keine Rede sein. Zu offenkundig sind die Widersprüche, zu deutlich die pragmatische Ausrichtung der Ziele nach den jeweiligen Gegebenheiten."

44. Don D. Humphrey to Draper, Subj: A Possible Program for Reparations Out of Current Production, Nov. 2, 1946, WWIIRC 177-3/3; New York Times, March 20, 1947, p. 1; March 23, 1947, p. 12; Hill, Struggle for Germany, pp. 123–24.

45. CINCEUR to Dept. of the Army, March 20, 1948, WWIIRC, CSCAD 014 Germany.

46. See Jean Edward Smith, The Defense of Berlin (Baltimore, 1963); W. Phillips Davison, The Berlin Blockade: A Study in Cold War Politics (Princeton, 1958); O. M. von der Gablentz, Documents on the Status of Berlin, 1944–1959 (Munich, 1959); Frank Howley, Berlin Command (New York, 1950); Walther Kiaulehn, Berlin: Schicksal einer Weltstadt (Munich, 1958); Curt Riess, Berlin–Berlin 1945–1953 (Berlin, 1954); Robert Rodrigo, Berlin Airlift (London, 1960); Hans Speier, Divided Berlin (New York, 1961); and Franklin M. Davis, Jr., Come as a Conqueror: The United States Army's Occupation of Germany, 1945–1949 (New York, 1967).

47. U.S. Dept. of State, The Berlin Crisis: A Report on the Moscow Discussions, Dept. of State Publication 3298 (Washington, 1948), esp., pp. 19, 21–22; Drew Middleton, "He Holds the Berlin Bridge," New York Times Magazine (July 4, 1948), pp. 6ff; C. J. Friedrich, "Memorandum

Concerning Governmental Developments in Germany Leading up to the Convening of the Constitutional Convention," Oct. 11, 1948, WWIIRC, WDSCA 014 Germany.

## Chapter 12

1. Dept. of the Army to OMGUS, June 5, 1948, WWIIRC 268-2/5; CSCAD to OMGUS, June 6, 1948; OMGUS, PIO, press release, June 7, 1948, *ibid.*, 108-1/1.

2. "Bericht über das Ergebnis der Ministerpräsidentenkonferenz in Düsseldorf am 5.–6.Juni 1948," Staatskanzlei, Wiesbaden, 1a08/II; Konrad Adenauer, *Erinnerungen, 1945–1953* (Stuttgart, 1965), pp. 140–43; *Frankfurter Rundschau*, June 8, 1948, p. 1; June 12, 1948, p. 1; C. J. Friedrich, "Memorandum Concerning Governmental Developments in Germany Leading up to the Convening of the Constitutional Convention," Oct. 11, 1948, WWIIRC, WDSCA 014 Germany.

3. Dept. of the Army to CINCEUR, June 11, 1948, WWIIRC 108-1/1; Dept. of the Army to CINCEUR, June 15, 1948, *ibid.*, 10-35/16.

4. CINCEUR to Dept. of the Army, July 5, 1948, WWIIRC 147-1/15; Gillen, *U.S. Military Government in Germany*, pp. 200–202; John Ford Golay, *The Founding of the Federal Republic of Germany* (Chicago, 1958), p. 12 and Appendix B.

5. Draft Verbatim Minutes, Meeting of the U.S., U.K., and French Military Governors, 30 June 1948, WWIIRC 110-2/11.

6. "Konferenz der 3 Militärgouverneure mit den Ministerpräsidenten der 3 Zonen am 1.Juli 1948," Staatskanzlei, Wiesbaden, 1a08/III; *New York Times*, July 2, 1948, p. 2 (for copies of Documents I, II, and III).

7. *New York Times*, July 2, 1948, p. 2; Friedrich, "Memorandum Concerning Governmental Developments in Germany Leading up to the Convening of the Constitutional Convention," Oct. 11, 1948, WWIIRC, WDSCA 014 Germany.

8. Württemberg-Baden, Landtag, Verhandlungen, 77. Sitzung, July 7, 1948, pp. 1855–58. The quotation from Maier is freely translated from: "Der Text der Londoner Protokolle ist für die Augen der französischen Oeffentlichkeit geschrieben. Ihr sollten die Beschlüsse schmackhaft gemacht werden. Die umgekehrte psychologische Wirkung trat damit in Deutschland ein. Auf diese Weise konnten wir nur die Schattenseiten lesen. Wir müssen jetzt darangehen, die Protokolle ins Deutsche zu übersetzen. Ich zweifle nicht daran, dass morgen and übermorgen in

Koblenz ein deutscher Generalgegenvorschlag zur Ausarbeitung gelangt, welcher die nicht ungünstige Stunde in voller Einigkeit nützt und uns ein entscheidendes Stück vorwärts bringt."

9. "Konferenz der 3 Militärgouverneure mit den Ministerpräsidenten der 3 Zonen am 1.Juli 1948," Staatskanzlei, Wiesbaden, 1a08/III.

10. Vogelsang, *Hinrich Wilhelm Kopf*, p. 122; *New York Times*, July 6, 1948, p. 4., *Süddeutsche Zeitung*, July 3, 1948, p. 1; July 6, 1948, p. 1; July 10, 1948, p. 2; *Frankfurter Rundschau*, July 6, 1948, p. 2; Württemberg-Baden, Landtag, Verhandlungen, 77. Sitzung, July 7, 1948, pp. 1855–58; Schleswig-Holstein, Landtag, Wortprotokoll, 13. Tagung, July 6, 1948, pp. 5–9.

11. Cf. CINCEUR to Dept. of Army, April 7, 1949, WWIIRC 11-35/16.

12. Protokoll der Sitzung des Rechtsausschusses beim Deutschen Büro für Friedensfragen, Stutt., 2.Juli 1948, (with attachment) "Zu Dokument 3 ... Gutachten zu den Erklärungen der Militärgouverneure über die Grundsetze für ein Besatzungsstatut vom 1.Juli 1948 (Dokument Nr. 3) erstattet von dem durch den Rechtsausschuss beim Friedensbüro in Stuttgart eingesetzten Sachverständigenausschuss für Besatzungsfragen"; Deutsches Büro für Friedensfragen, Versuch einer Stellungnahme zu den drei Frankfurter Dokumenten (Stuttgart, 5.Juli 1948), Friedensbüro Papers, Staatsarchiv, Wiesbaden.

13. Cf. Merkl, *The Origin of the West German Republic*, pp. 50–54; Golay, *The Founding of the Federal Republic of Germany*, pp. 13–17; Litchfield, "Emergence of German Governments," in Litchfield *et al.*, *Governing Postwar Germany*, pp. 39–40; C. J. Friedrich, "Rebuilding the German Constitution, I," *The American Political Science Review*, XLIII (June 1949), pp. 468–69; Vogelsang, *Hinrich Wilhelm Kopf*, pp. 122–25; and Schwarz, *Vom Reich zur Bundesrepublik*, pp. 606–18. It is, of course, easy to read backwards from the known to the unknown, and this natural inclination is evident in the studies just cited; but the current interpretations are affected by other factors as well. The minutes of the full discussions at Koblenz are not available, but some of the later materials are. The Koblenz Protokoll is not among the records of the minister-presidents' conferences that I have used, and I have been unable to find anyone who has it or knows of its existence. Schwarz has relied on interviews with Carlo Schmid and on the minutes of the later meetings. Vogelsang has used notes left by Hinrich Wilhelm Kopf, and he has also used minutes of the later meetings. Though both leave the im-

pression that they saw the Koblenz Protokoll, neither reveals any of its specific contents.

14. Litchfield *et al.*, *Governing Postwar Germany*, Appendix D, pp. 548–551.

15. Schwarz, *Vom Reich zur Bundesrepublik*, p. 611. Cf. Nordrhein-Westfalen, Landtag, Stenographischer Bericht, 49. und 50. Sitzungen, July 14–15, 1948, p. 632, for a similar statement by Minister President Karl Arnold.

16. Litchfield *et al.*, *Governing Postwar Germany*, Appendix D, pp. 545–48.

17. Cf. Schwarz, *Vom Reich zur Bundesrepublik*, pp. 613–14, who identifies three groups in the subsequent meeting at Rüdesheim. The differences at Koblenz may be seen reflected in the various minister-presidents' reports to their Landtage. Hessischer Landtag, Stenographischer Bericht, 43. Sitzung, July 13, 1948, pp. 1476–81; Niedersächsischer Landtag, Stenographischer Bericht, 39. Sitzung, July 13, 1948, pp. 1985–94; Nordrhein-Westfalen, Landtag, Stenographischer Bericht, 49. und 50. Sitzungen, July 14–15, 1948, pp. 629–707; Bremen Bürgerschaft, Verhandlungen, #16, Aug. 12, 1948, pp. 319ff; Bürgerschaft zu Hamburg, Stenographischer Bericht, 16. Sitzung, July 28, 1948, pp. 449–51; Bayerischer Landtag, Verhandlungen, 83. Sitzung, July 30, 1948, pp. 1828–34; Rheinland-Pfalz, Landtag, Stenographisches Protokoll, 35. Sitzung, July 29, 1948, pp. 861ff; Württemberg-Hohenzollern, Landtag, Verhandlungen, 30. Sitzung, July 13, 1948, pp. 408ff; Die Ergebnisse der Koblenzer Ministerpräsidenten-Konferenz, Rundfunkansprache von Bürgermeister Brauer, gehalten im Nordwestdeutschen Rundfunk am 14. Juli 1948, copy in WWIIRC 255-3/17.

18. Litchfield, "Emergence of German Governments," in Litchfield *et al.*, *Governing Postwar Germany*, pp. 38, 40.

19. Robert H. Lochner, OMG, Hesse, "Summary of General Clay's meeting with the Minister-Presidents of the American zone (14 July 1948)," dated July 23, 1948, WWIIRC 177-2/3; Beschluss-Protokoll über die Sitzung des Kabinetts, 14.Juli 1948, Staatskanzlei, Wiesbaden; Friedrich, "Memorandum Concerning Governmental Developments in Germany Leading up to the Convening of the Constitutional Convention," Oct. 11, 1948, WWIIRC, WDSCA 014 Germany; Litchfield to Clay, Subj: Analyses of Deviations of Coblenz from London, July 19, 1948; Litchfield to Pollock, July 20, 1948, *ibid.*, 254-1/17. Cf. *Frankfurter Rundschau*, July 23, 1948, p. 1, for a letter from Wilhelm Kaisen in which

he said, among other things, that "the French resistance in London also cast its shadow over Koblenz." ("Frankreichs Widerstand in London warf seine Schatten auch auf Koblenz.")

20. *New York Times*, July 15, 1948, p. 17; July 16, 1948, p. 6.

21. Golay, *The Founding of the Federal Republic of Germany*, pp. 12, 85, and Appendix B; Friedrich to Clay, Memorandum, July 18, 1948, WWIIRC 79-1/1.

22. "Gemeinsame Konferenz der Militärgouverneure General Clay (US-Zone), General Robertson (brit.Zone) und General Koenig (franz.-Zone) mit den elf Ministerpräsidenten der drei Westzonen," dated in Frankfurt July 20, 1948, Staatskanzlei, Wiesbaden, 1a08/01; Clay, *Decision in Germany*, pp. 410–11.

23. Friedrich, "Rebuilding the German Constitution, I," *The American Political Science Review*, XLIII (June 1949), p. 471; Schwarz, *Vom Reich zur Bundesrepublik*, pp. 613–15.

24. OMGUS, CAD, to Military Governor, Subj: Ministers-President Action Since Last Meeting with Military Governors, July 25, 1948, with attached copy of Rüdesheim resolutions, WWIIRC 177-3/3.

25. "Aide Memoire der Ministerpräsidenten-Konferenz vom 22. Juli 1948 im Jagdschloss Niederwald zu den Erklärungen der Militärgouverneure vom 19.Juli 1948, den Beauftragten der Militärgouverneure am 22.Juli 1948 übergeben," Staatskanzlei, Wiesbaden, 1a08.

26. "Konferenz der Ministerpräsidenten auf dem Jagdschloss Niederwald ... 21. und 22. Juli 1948"; "Sitzung der Militärgouverneure und der Ministerpräsidenten am 26.Juli 1948," Staatskanzlei, Wiesbaden, 1a08/III; 1a08/01; OMGUS, CAD, to Military Governor, Subj: Ministers-President Action Since Last Meeting with Military Governors, July 25, 1948, with attached copy of Rüdesheim resolutions, WWIIRC 177-3/3.

27. "Konferenz der Ministerpräsidenten auf dem Jagdschloss Niederwald ... 21. und 22. Juli 1948," Staatskanzlei, Wiesbaden, 1a08/III; Schwarz, *Vom Reich zur Bundesrepublik*, pp. 615–16.

28. Litchfield *et al.*, *Governing Postwar Germany*, Appendix E, pp. 552–61, is the only known published source of minutes for this meeting, and it is the only published record of the July meetings I have seen. I have also used "Sitzung der Militärgouverneure und der Ministerpräsidenten am 26.Juli 1948," Staatskanzlei, Wiesbaden, 1a08/01.

29. Robert H. Lochner, OMG, Hesse, "Summary of General Clay's meeting with the Minister-Presidents of the American zone (14 July 1948)," dated July 23, 1948, WWIIRC 177-2/3.

*Chapter 13*

1. OMG, Hesse, 1948 Historical Report, Vol. 1, Narrative, pp. 158–59.

2. C. J. Friedrich, "Rebuilding the German Constitution, I," *The American Political Science Review,* XLIII (June 1949), p. 468. Cf. Clay, *Decision in Germany,* pp. 412–40; Golay, *The Founding of the Federal Republic of Germany,* esp. pp. 92–112; Merkl, *The Origin of the West German Republic,* esp. pp. 114–27.

3. Golay, *The Founding of the Federal Republic of Germany,* pp. 85, 93; Clay, *Decision in Germany,* pp. 414–16.

4. CINCEUR to Dept. of the Army, April 4, 1949, WWIIRC 118-2/1; CINCEUR to Dept. of the Army, April 7, 1949, *ibid.,* 209–2/5.

5. Golay, *The Founding of the Federal Republic of Germany,* pp. 99–100.

6. Dept. of the Army to CINCEUR, April 19, 1949; CINCEUR to Dept. of the Army, April 19, 1949; CINCEUR to Dept. of the Army, April 21, 1949, WWIIRC 209-2/5; Clay, *Decision in Germany,* p. 432.

7. OMGUS, Memorandum from Clay to Mr. Parkman, July 28, 1947, WWIIRC 116-3/3.

8. "Interne Besprechung mit General Clay . . . 3.2.1948," Staatskanzlei, Wiesbaden, 1a08/01; "Protokoll, Interne Länderratssitzung am 2.2.1948," *ibid.,* 1g06/01; Länderrat des amerikanischen Besatzungsgebietes, "Denkschrift über das Problem des Länderrats," March 1, 1948, *ibid.,* 1g02/06; Länderrat, Memorandum on the Länderrat Problem, March 1, 1948, Bundesarchiv, Koblenz, Z1/17; OMGUS, CAD, to Clay, Subj: Länderrat Request for Liaison Officer, March 13, 1948, WWIIRC 82-2/1; "Protokoll, Interne Länderratssitzung . . . 7./8. April 1948," Staatskanzlei, Wiesbaden, 1g06/01.

9. Werner Hilpert to Minister-Presidents Ehard, Maier, and Stock, betr., Zukunft des Länderrats der US-Zone, April 20, 1948, Staatskanzlei, Wiesbaden, 1g02/06; Rossmann to Minister-Presidents, April 26, 1948, with enclosed "Beschluss des Zonenbeirats vom 24.4.1948 über die Zukunft des Zonenbeirats und der zonalen Dienststellen," *ibid.,* 1d02/11; Länderrat to Clay, April 28, 1948, Bundesarchiv, Koblenz, Z1/17; OMGUS, CAD, to Clay, May 7, 1948, Subj: Continuation of the Functions of the Länderrat (bearing Clay's handwritten memorandum of approval), WWIIRC 108-2/1.

10. OMGUS, Manpower Div., to Military Governor, Subj: Zonal Coordination in Manpower Field, April 26, 1948 (bearing Clay's handwrit-

ten note of May 17 that "The Länderrat *must* go . . ."), WWIIRC 82-2/1; RGCO, Speech of General Lucius D. Clay, . . . Länderrat, June 1, 1948, Bundesarchiv, Koblenz, Z1/65.

11. Graf v. Wedel to Hermann Brill, betr., Die Weiterarbeit des Länderrats, June 7, 1948, Staatskanzlei, Wiesbaden, 1g02/06; Wedel to Brill, Subj: Länderrat, June 12, 1948, Staatsarchiv, Wiesbaden.

12. See Länderrat des amerikanischen Besatzungsgebietes to Members of Parlamentarischen Rats des Länderrats, Subj: Schlussbericht . . . , Sept. 1949, Staatskanzlei, Wiesbaden, 1g02/06; Notes on Speech by Wedel to Interne Länderrat Tagung, Oct. 22, 1949, in Bundesarchiv, Koblenz, Z1/16; Württemberg-Baden, Staatsministerium to Bavaria, Hesse, and Bremen, Oct. 29, 1949. Cf. Hartel, *Der Länderrat des amerikanischen Besatzungsgebietes*, and Heinz Guradze, "The Laenderrat: Landmark of German Reconstruction," *The Western Political Quarterly*, III (June 1950), 190–213.

13. Der hessische Länderratsbevollmächtigte to Rossmann, July 7, 1948; Konrad Wittwer to Wedel, July 8, 1948, Bundesarchiv, Koblenz; Winning to Rossmann, July 19, 1948, Staatskanzlei, Wiesbaden, 1g02/06.

14. *Frankfurter Rundschau*, May 27, 1948, p. 1; CINCEUR to Dept. of the Army, June 19, 1948, WWIIRC 82-1/1.

15. OMGUS to August Hagedorn, President of the Bürgerschaft, Sept. 5, 1947, WWIIRC 209-3/5; RGCO, Speech of General Lucius D. Clay . . . Länderrat, 9 Sept. 1947, Staatskanzlei, Wiesbaden, 1g06/01.

16. OMGUS to AGWAR, Dec. 4, 1946, WWIIRC, WDSCA 014 Germany; OMGUS to AGWAR, Jan. 5, 1947, *ibid.*, 43-1/7.

17. OMGUS to Dept. of the Army, March 18, 1948, WWIIRC 361-2/5. Cf. Vogel, *Westdeutschland, 1945–1950*, I, 32.

18. Hessischer Landtag, Stenographischer Bericht, 40. Sitzung, May 26, 1948, pp. 1327–46, 1348–56.

19. OMG, Hesse, to Minister-President, Subj: Works Council Law for Hesse, June 16, 1948, WWIIRC 217-1/8; CINCEUR to Dept. of the Army, June 19, 1948, *ibid.*, 82-1/1.

20. Draft cable from Draper to Clay, June 23, 1948, WWIIRC, SAOUS 004.6 Germany. A note on the draft says that it was not sent because Draper and Wisner took up the matter personally on their trip to Europe.

21. *Frankfurter Rundschau*, Aug. 2, 1948, p. 2; Aug. 31, 1948, p. 1; Sept. 3, 1948, p. 2; Sept. 13, 1948, p. 2; Clay to Stock, Sept. 3, 1948, WWIIRC 82-1/1.

22. Hessischer Landtag, Stenographischer Bericht, 46. Sitzung, Sept. 22, 1948, pp. 1636–47; *Frankfurter Rundschau*, Sept. 23, 1948, p. 1. Cf.

OMGUS to OMG, Hesse, Aug. 24, 1949, WWIIRC 209-3/5, and Taylor Cole, "Labor Relations," in Litchfield et al., Governing Postwar Germany, p. 374.

23. Koenig to Clay, Jan. 6, 1949; CINCEUR to Dept. of the Army, Jan. 10, 1949; Dept. of the Army to CINCEUR, Jan. 13, 1949, WWIIRC 209-3/5; Draper to Clay, Jan. 17, 1949; Clay to Draper, Jan. 18, 1949, ibid., SAOUS 014.1 Germany; Draper to Clay, Feb. 11, 1949, ibid., 10-35/16.

24. OMGUS to Dept. of the Army, June 22, 1948, WWIIRC, WDSCA 014 Germany; OMGUS, Licensing of Businesses (press release), July 30, 1949; OMGUS, Subj: Licensing of New Businesses, June 15, 1948; Nov. 29, 1948; March 28, 1949, in Ferguson, Isseks, and Kearney, "Report of the Committee Appointed to Review the Decartelization Program in Germany," and attached papers, WWIIRC 335; Protokoll über die Besprechung mit den Generälen am 10.Dezember 1948; Protokoll über die Besprechung mit den Militärgouverneuren bei BICO am 15.Dezember 1948, Bundestag Library, Bonn; OMGUS, Report of the Military Governor, #43, Jan. 1949, p. 81; Frankfurter Rundschau, Dec. 21, 1948, p. 1; Dec. 22, 1948, p. 2 (editorial).

25. OMGUS, Subj: Military Government Law No. 15, "Bizonal Public Servants," to Land Directors, Feb. 23, 1949, with Law #15 attached, WWIIRC 145-1/5; OMGUS, Report of the Military Governor, #44, Legal and Judicial Affairs (cumulative review), p. 1; Francomb Frankfurt to OMGUS and Bercomb for Bipartite Board Secretariat, Aug. 25, 1949, ibid., 209-3/5.

26. Länderrat Request, L 36-6, Subj: Draft Law Concerning Redress of National Socialist Wrongs (General Claims Law), April 26, 1949; OMGUS to Dr. Philip Auerbach, General Attorney for Racial, Religious, and Political Persecutees of Bavaria, July 14, 1949; OMGUS, CAD, to DMG, memorandum, Subj: General Claims Law, July 8, 1949; OMGUS to Secretary General, U.S. Zone Länderrat, Aug. 4, 1949, WWIIRC 209-3/5. Cf. Härtel, Der Länderrat des amerikanischen Besatzungsgebietes, pp. 104–11.

27. Joint Letter, World Jewish Congress, American Jewish Committee, Jewish Agency for Palestine, and American Jewish Joint Distribution Committee, to McCloy, June 30, 1949; President, American Assoc. of Former European Jurists, to McCloy, July 15, 1949; McCloy to Dept. of the Army, July 20, 1949; OMGUS to Secretary General, U.S. Zone Länderrat, Aug. 4, 1949; Dept. of the Army to OMGUS, July 29, 1949, WWIIRC 209-3/5.

28. George F. Zook to Clay, Sept. 20, 1946, WWIIRC 4-3/1; OMGUS, Report of the Military Governor, #16, Education and Religious Affairs, Nov. 20, 1946, pp. 1–2.

29. OMGUS, Report of the Military Governor, #20, Education and Religious Affairs, Jan.-Feb., 1947, pp. 6–7.

30. RGCO, Speech of General Lucius D. Clay . . . Länderrat, 6 May 1947, Staatskanzlei, Wiesbaden, 1g06/01. See also *New York Times,* March 27, 1947, p. 14; OMGUS, Governmental Structures Branch, to OMGUS, CAD, Subj: Länder Plans for School Reform, Dec. 11, 1947, WWIIRC 255-1/17; Sitzung des Sonderausschusses für Kulturpolitik am 23. 24. und 25.4.1947 in Stuttgart, Staatsarchiv, Wiesbaden; Högner, *Der Schwierige Aussenseiter,* p. 239; OMGUS, Education and Religious Affairs Branch, to Director, OMG, Bavaria, Subj: Educational Reform in Bavaria, Dec. 1, 1947; Clay to Ehard, Nov. 18, 1947, WWIIRC 102-2/15.

31. OMG, Hesse, to Minister-President, Subj: The Six-Year Elementary School, Aug. 22, 1948, Kansas City Records Center 49/8; OMG, Hesse, 1948 Historical Report, I, Narrative, pp. 184–85; OMGUS, Report of the Military Governor, #44, Feb. 1949, p. 45; R. A. Irving, comp., "Chronology, M. G. Det. E1A2 (E-5), Office of Military Government for Hesse and Office of the Land Commissioner for Hesse, 1944–1950" (Wiesbaden, OLCH, n.d.), p. 103.

32. Sitzung des Sonderausschusses für Kulturpolitik am 23. 24. und 25.4.1947 in Stuttgart, Staatsarchiv, Wiesbaden; RGCO, Speech of General Lucius D. Clay . . . Länderrat, 6 May 1947, Staatskanzlei, Wiesbaden, 1g06/01.

33. OMGUS, Education and Religious Affairs Branch, to Director, OMG, Bavaria, Subj: Educational Reform in Bavaria, Dec. 1, 1947; OMG, Bavaria, to Minister-President, Subj: Rejection of School Reform Plan for Bavaria, Dec. 23, 1947, WWIIRC 102-2/15. Cf. *Süddeutsche Zeitung,* Jan. 13, 1948, p. 1, for an interview with Murray van Wagoner, the Military Governor of Bavaria, who said he hoped he would not have to dictate educational reform in Bavaria.

34. OMG, Bavaria, to Hans Ehard, April 1, 1948; OMG, Bavaria, to Minister-President, Subj: Orders of Military Government Requiring Free Textbooks and Other Learning Aids and Free Tuition, Aug. 4, 1948, WWIIRC 102-2/15.

35. OMG, Bavaria, CAD, to Mr. Al D. Sims, Subj: School Reform, Aug. 4, 1948; Typewritten note of telephone conversation, Aug. 7, 1948, between Murray van Wagoner and Clay, WWIIRC 102-2/15; Memoran-

dum, John Elliott to Litchfield, Subj: School Reform Decree Reaction in Bavaria, Aug. 14, 1948, *ibid.*, 254-1/17; Memorandum, OMG, Bavaria, CAD, to Dr. Albert Schweizer, CAD, Aug. 30, 1948, *ibid.*, 102-2/15.

*Chapter 14*

1. OMGUS, General Orders, No. 29, July 26, 1948, Subj: Establishment of Inter-Divisional Reorientation Committee, WWIIRC 160-1/3.

2. Edward Litchfield, "Political Objectives and Legal Bases of Occupation Government," in Litchfield *et al.*, *Governing Postwar Germany*, p. 6.

3. B. B. McMahon to *Süddeutsche Zeitung*, printed in *Süddeutsche Zeitung*, June 25, 1946, p. 1; OMGUS, PRO, press release, Oct. 14, 1946, WWIIRC 1-1/4; OMGUS, Information Control, Subj: Political Complexion of the German Licensed Press (U.S. Zone), Jan. 17, 1947, *ibid.*, 32-2/1; *Frankfurter Rundschau*, Aug. 21, 1947, p. 1; Aug. 23, 1947, p. 1. Cf. Harold J. Hurwitz, "U.S. Military Government in Germany: Press Reorientation," 2 vols. (Karlsruhe, Historical Div., European Command, 1950), manuscript in WWIIRC; Edward C. Breitenkamp, *The U.S. Information Control Division and Its Effects on German Publishers and Writers, 1945 to 1949* (Grand Forks, N. Dak., 1953); and Marshall Knappen, *And Call It Peace* (Chicago, 1947).

4. See my case study, *A German Community under American Occupation: Marburg, 1945–1952* (Stanford, 1961).

5. Kenneth Dayton, CAD, to Control Office, OMGUS, Subj: Program for Improving MG Operation at Local Level, Nov. 1947; OMGUS, Control Office and CAD, to Chief of Staff, Subj: Reduction of Liaison and Security Detachments, Nov. 29, 1947; OMGUS, Control Office, Subj: Report on Field Trip, Dec. 1–5, 1947, Dec. 9, 1947; OMGUS, CAD, Subj: Functions of L & S Detachments, Feb. 16, 1948; OMGUS, Control Office, to Chief of Staff, Subj: Functions of L & S Detachments, Feb. 20, 1948, Kansas City Records Center, 356/5.

6. OMG, Hesse, Historical Report, 1948, I, Narrative, pp. 266–98.

7. John D. Montgomery, *Forced to be Free: The Artificial Revolution in Germany and Japan* (Chicago, 1957); Lewis J. Edinger, "Post-Totalitarian Leadership," *The American Political Science Review*, LIX (March, 1960), 58–82.

8. U.S. Dept. of State, *Germany, 1947–1949*, pp. 40–41, quoting JCS 1779, part VI, par. 23a.

9. OMGUS, CAD, to Chief of Staff, Subj: Military Government Regu-

lations for Education, Feb. 3, 1947, with Clay's personal note of Feb. 10, 1947, thereon, WWIIRC 256-3/17.

10. Buck slip, OMGUS, CAD, to Chief of Staff, Subj: Letter dated 16 June 1948 from General Noce to General Gailey, July 10, 1948, WWIIRC 84-3/1; Dept. of the Army to OMGUS for Litchfield, June 24, 1948; OMGUS to Dept. of the Army, July 1, 1948, *ibid.*, 108-1/1.

11. OMGUS, Control Office, to Chief of Staff, Subj: Functions of L & S Detachments, Feb. 20, 1948, Kansas City Records Center, 356/5; OMGUS, Report of the Military Governor, #34, Education and Cultural Affairs (cumulative review), May 1947–April 1948, p. 2. Cf. *A German Community under American Occupation*, pp. 185–88.

12. OMGUS to OMG, Bavaria, July 4, 1948; Buck slip, OMGUS, CAD, to Chief of Staff, Subj: Letter dated 16 June from General Noce to General Gailey, July 10, 1948, WWIIRC 84-3/1; Dept. of the Army to OMGUS for Litchfield, June 24, 1948; OMGUS to Dept. of the Army, July 1, 1948, *ibid.*, 108-1/1; James L. Sundquist to Mr. Freese, Subj: L & S Offices, Aug. 18, 1948, *ibid.*, 367-1/5.

13. OMGUS, CAD, to Deputy Asst. Secretary of State for Occupied Areas, July 31, 1948, WWIIRC 84-3/1.

14. OMGUS, Control Office, to Personnel Office, Subj: Recruitment of Liaison and Security Officers, Sept. 20, 1948, WWIIRC 367-1/5; CINCEUR to Dept. of the Army, Oct. 9, 1948; CSCAD to CINCEUR, Oct. 12, 1948; CINCEUR to Dept. of the Army, Oct. 14, 1948, *ibid.*, SAOUS 350 Germany.

15. Alonzo Grace to Clay, Oct. 26, 1948, with enclosed copy of Grace's speech: "Out of the Rubble: An Address on the Reorientation of the German People. The Berchtesgaden Conference," dated Oct. 8, 1948, WWIIRC 108-2/1.

16. Murray van Wagoner, Opening Address to Field Operations Division Seminar, Nov. 17, 1948, WWIIRC 108-2/1.

17. Hans Simons, "The Bonn Constitution and its Government," in Hans J. Morgenthau, ed., *Germany and the Future of Europe* (Chicago, 1951), p. 114. Cf. "Aufzeichnung über die Besprechung in Königstein ... am 29.Mai 1949," in V.W.G., Besprechungen, Militärregierung, Bundestag Library, Bonn.

18. Schrenck-Notzing, *Charakterwäsche.*

# Index

# Index

Aachen, 3, 46

Acheson, Dean, 31–32, 52, 168

Adcock, Clarence, 36, 82–88 passim, 180–81, 190

Adenauer, Konrad, 66, 208f, 209n, 256

Agartz, Victor, 118

Allied Control Council xiv, 18–36 passim, 50, 74–77 passim, 88–93 passim, 139, 143, 191; U.S. member in, 10–14 passim, 22–23, 52f, 56–61 passim, 74, 88, 170–74 passim, 203; reserved powers of, 93, 99, 236; and denazification, 104, 104n; Soviet protest in, 114, 201–5 passim, 254

Allied Reparations Commission, 27–28

America Houses, 247

American Council on Education, 240

American zone, 7–8, 11ff, 38, 49–51, 140–44 passim, 238–40 passim; and interzonal union, 5, 32, 67–71 passim, 74, 80, 86f, 111; imports and exports, 10–13 passim, 52, 54, 79, 175; food rations in, 22, 35, 54f, 96, 110, 127, 152–57 passim; Länder governments in, 37, 47–51, 56, 63, 80–85 passim, 92–103 passim, 193, 240–43 passim, 249; denazification in, 40, 101–10, 115, 158–62, 171–74, 195; interzonal trade, 53–54, 65, 68, 82, 175; industrial recovery in, 58–61 passim, 158, 202–3; political reconstruction in, 67–73 passim, 110f, 118, 129f, 212, 243–49 passim, 253; and Bizonia, 83, 86, 94, 97, 118, 125–26, 188–89; school reform, 110, 151, 240–

43, 246–47. See also Congress; Länderrat; Office of Military Government for Germany; Regional Government Coordinating Office; State Department; United States; War/Army Department; Washington

Anti-fascist Committees, 46

Antwerp, 149

Army Department, see War/Army Department

Arnold, Karl, 156, 156n, 179, 184, 222

Association for a Democratic Germany, 147

Atlantic Community, 193–94

Balabkins, Nicholas, 188

Barnes, Joseph, 6

Basic Law, 200, 209f, 213ff, 219–23 passim, 226–31, 236f, 240, 253–56 passim. See also Bonn government; West Germany

Bavaria, 49, 65, 92, 131–44 passim, 193; and Länderrat, 37, 39–43 passim, 51, 190; and Bizonia, 99, 115, 189–93 passim, 243; and denazification, 105, 105n, 108–9, 171–72; school reform in, 241, 242–43

Belgium, 9

Benelux nations, 198f, 254

Berlin, 4, 6, 12ff, 18, 123, 196, 227; blockade of, 47, 107, 201–6, 213–20 passim, 224, 235, 254f; socialization law in, 117–18; and Minister-presidents' conferences, 132, 139, 214–15, 220